HUGH DU PUISET

HUGH DU PUISET
BISHOP OF DURHAM

BY

G. V. SCAMMELL

Sometime Fellow of Emmanuel College, Cambridge
and Lecturer in Diplomatic in the
University of Durham

CAMBRIDGE
AT THE UNIVERSITY PRESS
1956

PUBLISHED BY

THE SYNDICS OF THE CAMBRIDGE UNIVERSITY PRESS

London Office: Bentley House, N.W.1
American Branch: New York

Agents for Canada, India, and Pakistan: Macmillan

Printed in Great Britain at the University Press, Cambridge
(Brooke Crutchley, University Printer)

CONTENTS

v

PREFACE

THIS essay was awarded the Prince Consort Prize of the University of Cambridge in 1952, and is now printed with a number of revisions and some amplification. I have not, through the exigencies of time and space, attempted to fulfil the *dictum* of Stubbs that the biography of Hugh du Puiset 'would be a diplomatic or political history of at least fifty eventful years of English national life' (*Historical Introductions to the Rolls Series*, ed. Hassall, p. 213 n.), but have tried to examine certain less familiar aspects of his career.

The considerable charter evidence for the episcopate will shortly be published in a volume of *acta*, and I have only printed below such documents as were not easily available and which are essential to the elucidation of the text. For the place-names of the counties of Durham and Northumberland I have used the forms accepted by the Ordnance Survey, and not those of A. Mawer, in *Place-Names of Northumberland and Durham* (Cambridge, 1920), which, in some instances, are unsatisfactory.

My thanks are due to those whose criticisms and advice have helped me at various stages, especially to Professor M. D. Knowles and Professor Walther Holtzmann. I must also record my gratitude to Dr J. Conway Davies, the Rev. J. C. Dickinson, Mr C. N. L. Brooke, and Dr Eleanor Rathbone, who have answered a number of queries, and to the Rev. G. E. Culkin and Mrs W. Levison for the loan of books not easily accessible.

I am grateful to the Deans and Chapters of Canterbury, York, Durham and Chichester, and the President and fathers of Ushaw College for allowing me access to their muniments, and to the Durham Colleges Research Committee for financial assistance in the early stages of this work. I wish especially to record my gratitude to the Master and Fellows of Emmanuel College, without whose encouragement this research might not

vii

have been undertaken, and who have made a generous financial contribution to the cost of publication of the book. Above all I owe a great debt to my wife, who has read and criticized the whole of my text, and who, indeed, has made this volume possible.

G. V. S.

DURHAM

17 June 1954

LIST OF ABBREVIATIONS

The following abbreviations are used throughout:

Arch. Ael.	*Archaeologia Aeliana*
BB	*Boldon Book*
BF	*Book of Fees*
BM	British Museum
Bouquet	*Rerum Gallicarum et Francicarum Scriptores*, ed. Bouquet, re-ed. Delisle
Brand	J. Brand, *History and Antiquities of Newcastle upon Tyne*
Cal. Doc. France	*A Calendar of Documents preserved in France, 918–1206*, ed. Round
Cart. Ant.	PRO, Cartae Antiquae Rolls
CChR	*Calendar of the Charter Rolls*
CClR	*Calendar of the Close Rolls*
Chronicles	*Chronicles of the Reigns of Stephen, Henry II and Richard I*, ed. Howlett
CPR	*Calendar of the Patent Rolls*
DB	*Recueil des Actes de Henri II, Roi d'Angleterre et Duc de Normandie Concernant les Provinces Françaises*, ed. Delisle and Berger
DC	Dean and Chapter
Devizes	Richard of Devizes, *De Rebus Gestis Ricardi Primi*, in *Chronicles*, III
Diceto	Ralph of Diceto, *Opera Historica*, ed. Stubbs
Early Oxford Charters	*Facsimiles of Early Charters in Oxford Muniment Rooms*, ed. Salter
Early Sources	Anderson, *Early Sources of Scottish History*
EHR	*English Historical Review*
EYC	*Early Yorkshire Charters*
Fantosme	Jordan Fantosme, *Chronique*, in *Chronicles*, III
FPD	*Feodarium Prioratus Dunelmensis*
Gerald of Wales	Gerald of Wales, *Opera*, ed. Brewer, Dimock and Warner
Gervase of Canterbury	Gervase of Canterbury, *Opera*, ed. Stubbs
Gesta	Benedict of Peterborough, *Chronicle of the Reigns of Henry II and Richard I*, ed. Stubbs
HMC	Historical Manuscripts Commission

Hoveden	Roger of Hoveden, *Chronica*, ed. Stubbs
Hutchinson	W. Hutchinson, *The History and Antiquities of the County Palatine of Durham*
JL	*Regesta pontificum romanorum ad annum 1198*, ed. Jaffé, re-ed. Loewenfeld
JTS	*Journal of Theological Studies*
LR	*Liber Rubeus de Scaccario*
Mansi	J. D. Mansi, *Sacrorum Conciliorum nova et amplissima collectio*
Materials	*Materials for the History of Thomas Becket*, ed. Robertson and Sheppard
Mon. Ang.	*Monasticon Anglicanum*, re-ed. Caley
NCH	*A History of Northumberland*, ed. Northumberland County History Committee
Newburgh	William of Newburgh, *Historia Rerum Anglicarum*, in *Chronicles*, I and II
North Durham	J. Raine, *The History and Antiquities of North Durham*
PL	*Patrologia Latina*, ed. Migne
PR	*Pipe Roll*
Priory of Finchale	*The Charters of endowment, Inventories and Account Rolls of the Priory of Finchale*, ed. Raine
PRO	Public Record Office
PU	*Papsturkunden in England*, ed. Holtzmann
Reg. Ant. Linc.	*The Registrum Antiquissimum of Lincoln*
Reg. Pal. Dun.	*Registrum Palatinum Dunelmense*
R.H.C. Occ.	*Recueil des Historiens des Croisades (Occidentaux)*
RS	Rolls Series
Scriptores Tres	*Historiae Dunelmensis Scriptores Tres*, ed. Raine
SS	Surtees Society
Stubbs	W. Stubbs, *Historical Introductions to the Rolls Series*, ed. Hassall
Surtees	R. Surtees, *The History and Antiquities of the County Palatine of Durham*
Symeon	Symeon of Durham, *Opera*, ed. Arnold
Torigni	Robert of Torigni, *Chronica*, in *Chronicles*, IV
TRHS	*Transactions of the Royal Historical Society*
VCH	*Victoria County History*
YAJ	*Yorkshire Archaeological Journal*

For the abbreviations used in referring to the Durham capitular records, see below, pp. 316–7.

CHAPTER I

EARLY CAREER AND ELECTION
TO DURHAM

I. ANTECEDENTS

HUGH DU PUISET was descended from a savagely able family born of the wreckage of the Carolingian empire, when a well-placed castle guaranteed life and wealth, and office was hereditary title to plunder.[1] Based on the castle of Le Puiset (near Chartres),[2] controlling the Paris-Orleans road, and the rich indefensible 'lands of the saints', Hugh's ancestors robbed their way to success with a violence remarkable even in the France of the period. By the end of the eleventh century they had become castellans of Le Puiset and *vicomtes* of Chartres, thereby titular vassals, occasional allies, and eventual relatives of the great house of Blois-Chartres.

Their genealogy is obscure.[3] The line appears to derive from one Harduin, *miles et provisor*, or *miles Carnotensis civitatis*, who occurs in the household of Odo of Blois in 985.[4] From him there descended Gilduin (*c.* 1019–48), who witnessed a charter of Odo II of Blois as *vicomte* of Chartres *c.* 1028,[5] and who seems

[1] Marc Bloch, *La Société Féodale; Les Classes et le Gouvernement des Hommes*, 16–45.

[2] The date of the appearance of a castle at Le Puiset is uncertain, its first definite mention being in 1031 (Bouquet, XII, 32 and 795). According to Suger of St Denis (*Vie de Louis VI le Gros*, ed. H. Waquet, 132), it was built by Queen Constance to protect some of the many possessions of the abbey of St Denis, though it seems, in fact, to have been part of her schemes against her son, Henry I (cf. Charles Pfister, *Études sur le Règne de Robert le Pieux, 996–1031*, 82–3). Its strategic position is indicated by the successive attempts of strong kings to bring it under control.

[3] Cf. Charles Cuissard, 'Les Seigneurs du Puiset', 313–98; A. de Dion, 'Le Puiset aux XIe et XIIe siècles'. Much of this information is recapitulated in Stubbs, 211, n. 1, and by J. L. La Monte, 'The Lords of Le Puiset on the Crusades', 100–18. A genealogy is attempted below, App. v.

[4] *Un Manuscrit Chartrain du XIe siècle*, ed. R. Merlet and J. A. Clerval, 115; *Obituaires de la Province de Sens*, ed. A. Longnon, M. A. Molinier, A. Vidier and L. Mirot, II, 18.

[5] *Cartulaire de l'abbaye de S. Jean-en-Vallée de Chartres*, ed. R. Merlet, no. 1; *Cartulaire de Marmoutier pour le Dunois*, ed. E. Mabille, no. XCIX.

to have succeeded a certain Geoffrey in that office. About the same time there appears a Hugo, *vicedominus de Puteolo*,[1] possibly one of Gilduin's many children. Gilduin, *ex vicecomite monachus*, was followed at Chartres by his sons, Harduin (*c.* 1048–50), and Evrard I (*c.* 1050–70).[2]

Evrard II, who had succeeded his father and namesake *c.* 1070, became a monk at Marmoutier some five years later, and his titles then passed to his brother, Hugh, lord of Le Puiset (*c.* 1075–94),[3] whose remarkable deeds formed a fitting prologue to the style of his successors. He was one of those petty tyrants whose lives were passed in war or such violent recreations as might fill the short interludes between campaigns. Like his fellows and relatives of Beaumont, Roucy, Rochefort and Montlhéry, with lands straddling the routes from Paris to Orleans, Mantes, Dreux and Chartres, and rich at the expense of the neighbouring religious, he would have limited Capetian authority to the immediate environs of Paris.[4] He repulsed Philip I from Le Puiset in 1079 with a vigour sufficient to convince the indolent monarch of the virtues of friendship.[5] Recovered from illness, with its attendant spasm of piety,[6] and reconciled with his nominal suzerain, he aided Philip to the desired bed of Bertha de Montfort (wife of Fulk of Anjou), by the simple expedient of imprisoning (1092) the distinguished ecclesiast and canonist, Ivo of Chartres, who unwisely spoke unwholesome truth on such illicit passions.[7]

---

[1] *Cart. Marmoutier*, no. xxxv; H. d'Arbois de Jubainville, *Histoire des Ducs et des Comtes de Champagne*, I, 316; Bouquet, IX, 723.

[2] *Un Manuscrit Chartrain*, 154, 163; *Cart. Marmoutier*, nos. CX and CXVII.

[3] Evrard, *militis*, and Hugh, his brother, *de Puteolo*, witnessed a charter of Philip I at Orleans in 1066 (*Recueil des Actes de Philippe Ier, Roi de France (1059–1108)*, ed. M. Prou, no. XXXVII, and cf. *Recueil des chartes de l'abbaye de S. Benoît-sur-Loire*, ed. M. Prou, no. LXXVI). Hugh occurs in the royal presence near Senlis in 1070 (*Recueil de chartes et documents de S. Martin-des-Champs*, ed. J. Depoin, no. 15, and cf. *Recueil...Philippe Ier*, no. LIII), and was much with the king in the period *c.* 1070–7.

[4] For the ramifications of the family, see La Monte, *art. cit.* 100. For their significance, see Auguste Fliche, *Le Règne de Philippe Ier Roi de France*, 313–26. Their manners may be studied in two letters of Ivo of Chartres (Bouquet, XV, 152–3, nos. 127 and 129).

[5] Suger, *op. cit.* 132; Fliche, *op. cit.* 313–15.

[6] *Cart. Marmoutier*, no. CXLIV.

[7] Suger, *op. cit.* 134; Bouquet, XIV, 702; XV, 77.

Hugh was succeeded (*c.* 1094) by his son, Evrard III, who, *mire superbie*, joined the First Crusade,[1] thus marking to his successors what was to prove a convenient and profitable road to a new land. Before his departure Evrard surrendered his titles to his brother, Hugh II, who as regent (*c.* 1097–1106) for his nephew Hugh III (Evrard's son), continued the traditional exploitation of the church of Chartres[2] before wisely departing for Palestine, there to gain the handsome principality of Jaffa. In this he was eventually succeeded by his son and namesake, whose manifold charms so influenced Queen Melisende of Jerusalem as to move her husband to rightful jealousy, and set in motion the intricate mechanism of Oriental intrigue.[3]

At Le Puiset and Chartres Hugh had meanwhile been replaced (*c.* 1106–8) by his brother, Guy de Méréville, one-time canon of Chartres, who, abundantly endowed with the natural aptitudes of his house, was shortly excommunicated *propter intolerabiles exactiones quas exercet in possessionibus ecclesie Carnotensis.*[4] After Guy came his nephew, the remarkable Hugh III (*c.* 1108–28), father of the future bishop of Durham. He was a man of almost proverbial greed and energy, a great oppressor of the pious and the innocent, and one whose wickedness far surpassed the meagre range of contemporary monastic simile.[5] Lord of Le Puiset and Chartres, a vassal of the king,[6] the bishop of Paris, and the counts of Mellent[7] and Blois,[8] Hugh was

[1] *Cartulaire de l'abbaye Cardinale de la Trinité de Vendôme*, ed. C. Metais, no. CCXC; Bouquet, XII, 68 and 218B; Suger, *op. cit.* 130; Ordericus Vitalis, III, 481.

[2] Ivo of Chartres, Letters nos. LXIX, LXX, in Bouquet, XV, 119; Achille Luchaire, *Louis VI le Gros, Annales de sa vie et de son Règne*, no. 24.

[3] Ordericus Vitalis, IV, 239; William of Tyre (*R.H.C. Occ.* I), 629–33; La Monte, *art. cit.* 105–6; S. Runciman, *The Kingdom of Jerusalem and the Frankish East, 1100–87*, 190–3, where there is some confusion in the Puiset ancestry.

[4] *Cartulaire de l'Église de Notre Dame de Paris*, ed. M. Guérard, I, 41; Bouquet, XV, 136, note f; Ivo of Chartres, Letter no. cxix, in Bouquet, XV, 148.

[5] His deeds are told by Suger of St Denis in chapter XIX of his *Vie de Louis VI*; see also the *Fragmentum* in Bouquet, XII, 64, and the *Continuatio Historiae Aimonii* (Bouquet, XII, 123). The wars against Le Puiset are traced in detail by Achille Luchaire (*Louis VI, sub annis*).

[6] Le Puiset was on the royal demesne, see *Libellus Hugonis Floriacensis Monachi* (Bouquet, XII, 795); Suger, *op. cit.* 140–2; Pfister, *op. cit.* 121; W. M. Newman, *Le Domaine Royal sous les premiers Capétiens*, 157).

[7] *Recueil...S. Martin*, I, no. 124.

[8] Gilduin of Chartres had referred to Odo of Blois as his lord as early as 1040 (*Cart. Marmoutier*, nos. XXI and C). The tenure is also mentioned in *Recueil...*

strengthened by succession to the county of Corbeil, and a profitable marriage with Agnes of Blois, sister of Count Theobald and of his brother, Stephen, the future king of England.[1] He fought in alliance with Theobald and his uncle, Henry I of England, against Louis VI, in accordance with his own inherited distaste for Capetian authority, and the Anglo-Norman practice of using Blois and its satellites as a lever under the Capetians, whilst they in turn encouraged Angevin intrigue in Normandy.[2] His rule opened with a series of savage encroachments on the possessions of the widowed countess of Blois, whose son, Theobald, was as yet a minor. These activities, combined with a similar handling of the property of the sees of Sens, Orleans, Paris and Chartres, and of the abbeys of Fleury and St Denis, together with his oppression of a variety of lesser houses and individuals, brought an army under Louis VI against him and led to the fall of Le Puiset in 1111. The castle was destroyed, Hugh imprisoned, and his victims theoretically recompensed. But he soon bought his freedom at the price of his recent title to the valuable castle of Corbeil, rebuilt Le Puiset, and fell on his former prey *instar canis diu catenati*. Together with the lords of Montlhéry, Rochefort and Château-fort, he joined the alliance which Theobald of Blois had raised against Louis VI at the instigation of Henry of England. Once again Le Puiset was taken (1112)—this time betrayed by Theobald—the walls thrown down, the moats filled, the ground levelled, and once again Hugh escaped. He returned to his old calling with such brazen vigour that once more the harassed Louis marched against him. The castle was razed, and Hugh

S. Martin, I, no. 128 and *Cart. Marmoutier*, no. xxxv. Together with his wife, Agnes, and his sons, Evrard and Burchard, Hugh appears among the *barones* of Theobald of Blois, *c.* 1125–8 (*Cartulaire de l'abbaye de S. Père de Chartres*, ed. M. Guérard, II, 412; *Cartulaire de Notre Dame de Chartres*, ed. E. de Lépinois and L. Merlet, I, 108).

[1] Hugh acquired Corbeil through his mother, Alice, daughter of Count Burchard II (Bouquet, xv, 96 and 104). For the Blois marriage, see *Cart. Marmoutier*, no. clx; Dion, *art cit.* 20–9. Stephen, when king of England, refers to Hugh of Durham as his nephew (DC Durham, I. 1. Reg. no. 1, printed in *Scriptores Tres*, App. no. xxvii).

[2] Bouquet, xii, 71; Ordericus Vitalis, iv, 304. The early rivalry of Blois and Anjou is examined by Pfister, *op. cit.* 47–82 and 224–5. For the relationship of Normandy and Blois, see Luchaire, *Louis VI*, lxxxvi–xciii and ciii–cvi; A. L. Poole, *From Domesday Book to Magna Carta*, 123.

stripped of his possessions (1118).[1] Such, however, was his native persistence, and such the ineffectiveness of the royal authority that, despite having murdered the king's personal friend, Hugh, once more reconciled with the count of Blois, was able to retain his lands and titles till *c.* 1129, when he wisely trod the ancestral road to Jerusalem as the persistent Louis prepared for yet another attack on the anarchical baronage of the Beauvaisis.[2]

Meanwhile, the Norman alliance returned good interest to the house of Blois. Henry I heaped favours on his nephew, Stephen, whom he had brought up with his own children, granting him the three great Honors of Eye, Boulogne and Lancaster, creating him count of Mortain, and securing him the golden hand of the heiress of the county of Boulogne.[3] Stephen's younger brother, the Cluniac monk Henry of Blois, was appointed abbot of the great house of Glastonbury by an act of royal power in 1126, when still under thirty, and three years later the same grace gave him the rich see of Winchester in plurality.

After the death of Henry I the harvest of favour was brought in. Stephen secured the crown of England by one of his characteristically rare acts of vigour, whilst Henry of Winchester rapidly emerged as one of the most considerable personalities of the century. His generosity, personal splendour, and dignities in plurality, suggest at once the magnificence of Wolsey and the tastes of the *Curia* of Leo X. Brother of the king, son of a count of one of the greatest houses in Europe, bishop and legate, his birth, opportunities and ambitions made him a decisive influence in the politics of Stephen's reign.[4] Rich,

---

[1] Ordericus Vitalis, IV, 288; Suger, *op. cit.* 159–69, and see above, p. 3, n. 5.

[2] Hugh issued a charter in favour of Tiron in 1129, which concludes with the phrase *tota curia Puteacensis que tunc erat plenaria, ipse enim vicecomes tunc volebat ire Jerusalem* (*Cartulaire de l'abbaye de la Sainte Trinité de Tiron*, ed. L. Merlet, I, 127–8); about this time he appears together with Theobald and Stephen of Blois (*Cart. Notre Dame de Chartres*, I, 108, n. 6; *Cart. Marmoutier*, no. CLXXIX; *Cartulaire de Notre Dame de Josaphat*, ed. Charles Métais, no. XLVI).

[3] *Gesta Stephani Regis Anglorum* (in *Chronicles*, III), 5; Newburgh, I, 31; *EYC*, III, 119; James Tait, *Medieval Manchester and the Beginnings of Lancashire*, 4, 163–4; *Early Sources*, II, 54.

[4] Knowles, *The Episcopal Colleagues of Archbishop Thomas Becket*, 34–7.

active and versatile, he tempered an individual variant of the Gregorian concept of the Church with an undying sense of his own needs and interests.[1]

In a world where the great family made politics he controlled a circle wider, if on the whole less able, than that which under bishop Roger, *in regno a rege secundus*, held Salisbury, Lincoln and Ely with such profit and skill. A Cluniac obtained Bath in 1136, and another, a royal relative, was given Winchcombe in 1138. In 1140 an election at Malmesbury was quashed, and Winchester put in his own candidate. Master Hilary, a learned clerk of his household, celebrated as a lawyer at the papal *Curia*, was appointed dean of Twineham, and eventually bishop of Chichester. Jocelin de Bohun, one of Winchester's archdeacons, became bishop of Salisbury in 1142. An episcopal nephew received Exeter in 1138. A royal relative appeared at St Benet's of Holme (1141–6), and later (1149)—after his removal had reputedly been engineered by that indelicate stratagem subsequently employed against Archbishop Sandys—at Chertsey.[2] Meanwhile, one of Stephen's own illegitimate children, *Gervase, dictus de Blois*, had become an unworthy abbot of Westminster (1138), whose possessions he allegedly plundered in the interests of his mother.[3] Another relative, Henry de Sully, was a candidate for Salisbury in 1140, York in 1141, and Lincoln in 1148 before he finally acquired Bermondsey.[4] Yet another nephew, William fitzHerbert, treasurer of York, eventually secured the archbishopric in 1153,[5] after much tribulation, his troubled history culminating in canonization in the thirteenth century.[6]

---

[1] Lena Voss, *Heinrich von Blois*, 14; Knowles, *The Monastic Order in England*, 284, 287–93.

[2] This Hugh is obviously not Hugh du Puiset, as H. E. Malden thought (*TRHS*, 3, v, 142), but an illegitimate son of Theobald IV of Blois, who later became abbot of Lagny (Torigni, 218–19), cf. *Register of the Abbey of St Benet of Holme*, ed. J. R. West, 194–5. His promotion to Chertsey is contained in a remarkable charter of Stephen, where he is described as *nepos meus*, in the Chertsey cartulary, BM, Cotton MS., Vit. A XIII, fo. 57 (cf. *Mon. Ang.* I, 423, note a).

[3] John of Worcester, *Chronica*, ed. J. R. H. Weaver, 53; John Flete, *History of Westminster Abbey*, ed. J. A. Robinson, 88–9, 142.

[4] He was later abbot of Glastonbury and bishop of Worcester (*Mon. Ang.* I, 573).

[5] Most of these interventions are noted in Voss, *op. cit.* 42–4.

[6] *The Register of William Wickwane*, ed. W. Brown, no. 723; R. K. Richardson in *Arch. Ael.* 3, IX, 105.

It was this wave of purposeful favour which brought Hugh du Puiset to office. Apparently the younger son of Hugh III,[1] he appears to have come to England *c.* 1130, when his father departed to Palestine, leaving the possessions and violent traditions of the house to his eldest son, Evrard IV (*c.* 1129–90).[2] Hugh first appears as archdeacon of Winchester in 1139[3]— which preferment he doubtless owed to his uncle—and is probably to be identified with that *Hugo de Pusat* who held land in the city of Winchester in 1148.[4]

His early career was largely concerned with the Blois attempt to strengthen its position in the north. It seems that he was probably dispatched to York to reinforce the family interest at a critical moment, and there acquired (*c.* 1143), through the influence of William fitzHerbert, archbishop-elect and nephew and chaplain of the king, the valuable office of treasurer and archdeacon of the East Riding, which fitzHerbert himself had previously held.[5] His activities in this preferment were of the more spectacular variety, and his *acta* accordingly rare. Sometime between 1143 and 1153 he issued a florid writ for the nuns of St Mary of Swine, in which he styles himself, with characteristic bravura, 'by the grace of God treasurer and archdeacon'.[6] As Hugh the treasurer he witnessed a notification by

---

[1] *Cart. Josaphat*, no. xxx; cf. Stubbs, 211, n. 1; La Monte, *art. cit.* 101.

[2] For Evrard's depredations see Achille Luchaire, *Études sur les Actes de Louis VII*, nos. 73, 115, 116; Bouquet, xvi, 8; *Archives de la Maison Dieu de Châteaudun*, ed. M. L. Merlet and A. de Belfort, no. xvii.

[3] *Winchester Cathedral Cartulary*, ed. A. W. Goodman, 4, no. 5; Hugh is also described by Gervase of Canterbury as *Wintoniae archidiaconus* (Gervase of Canterbury, I, 157).

[4] *Liber Wintoniensis*, in *Domesday Book*, III, 552, col. I. The family of Puiset was already represented in England by Ebrard, bishop of Norwich, son of Adelaide II du Puiset and Roger of Montgomery (Ordericus Vitalis, II, 412). He was a clerk of the chapel royal under Henry I, and archdeacon of Salisbury (J. H. Round, *Ancient Charters prior to 1200*, no. 4; Ordericus Vitalis, III, 425–6; *Cartulary of Colne Priory*, ed. J. L. Fisher, no. 1). Ebrard had a brother, Arthur (*Registrum Primum of Norwich*, ed. H. W. Saunders, 62). Ebrard's *familia*, which included the episcopal *nepotes*, Richard, William, Ebrard, Herbert, Simon, Reginald, Adam and Peter (BM, Cotton Charter, II, 1; Cotton Roll, II, 21; Campbell Charter, XII, 1), appears to have had no connexion with the Puiset-Blois alliance.

[5] Symeon, II, 320. It seems probable that Puiset succeeded fitzHerbert as treasurer in 1143, since William appears to have retained the office after his election to the archbishopric in 1141 (*EYC*, II, no. 1153; C. T. Clay, 'Early Treasurers of York', 11).   [6] *EYC*, III, no. 1360.

the dean and chapter of York in favour of the church of Hexham,[1] an agreement between Byland and Richard Cruer,[2] and a charter of Archbishop Murdac for Fountains.[3]

The struggle for the north was renewed in 1140, after the death of Archbishop Thurstan of York. The Blois family had two major, but only momentarily linked, groups of opponents. On the one hand there was David of Scotland, a man of the calibre of Henry I, and by far the ablest Scottish ruler of the twelfth century. He was an uncle of the Empress Matilda, willing to assist his niece's attempts to secure the crown at what seemed a particularly propitious moment, and at the same time a vigorous warrior in his own designs on the northern counties. Almost since Stephen's accession there had been steady Scottish pressure south, only momentarily checked by the Battle of the Standard. Northumberland was lost in 1139, and after a vain attempt to win over Bishop Geoffrey of Durham in 1138,[4] David was involved in an endeavour (which came near to success), to intrude his own chancellor William Cumin into the vacant see.[5]

On the other hand there was a body of ecclesiastical reformers, governed by the growing influence of Archbishop Theobald of Canterbury and the moderation of William of St Barbara, dean of York, and later bishop of Durham. But above all, and initially swamping all other influences, was the rapturous zeal of the newly founded Cistercian and Augustinian houses of Yorkshire, whipped into action first by William of Rievaulx, then by Henry Murdac, abbot of Fountains, and ever urged on by the impatient virtue of Bernard of Clairvaux, who would have staffed the church with angels of his own definition.[6]

For secular control of the north it was important to have amenable political candidates at York and Durham, a fact realized by David and Stephen alike. So it was that the former supported Cumin for Durham, whilst the latter vetoed the candidature of Waltheof of Kirkham, the future saint and a

---

[1] *EYC*, I, no. 450 (1143–53).   [2] *EYC*, IX, no. 76.
[3] *EYC*, I, no. 71 (1151–3).
[4] Richard of Hexham, *De Gestis Regis Stephani* (*Chronicles*, III), 157.
[5] For a summary of the power and influence of David of Scotland, see Poole, *From Domesday to Magna Carta*, 274–5. See also below, p. 129.
[6] Knowles. 'The Case of St William of York'.

member of the reforming party, for the archbishopric on the grounds of his relationship to the Scottish royal house.[1] But for Stephen to secure York, or later Durham, meant an automatic affront to the views, aspirations and power of the reformers, who objected to the unsatisfactory methods and candidates of the royal party.

The Blois interest in Yorkshire, guided by Henry of Winchester, was an incongruous medley, any element of which was alone well calculated to offend the austerity of St Bernard or Murdac. It was generally supported by the conservative local baronage, and members of the blood, such as William fitz-Herbert and the typically acquisitive William of Aumâle. FitzHerbert, some of whose preferments have already been noticed, was a son of Emma, half-sister of Stephen, and that Herbert of Winchester, chamberlain and treasurer of Henry I, who occurs in Domesday as a tenant-in-chief of two manors in Hampshire.[2] The family was enfeoffed in Yorkshire at three fees by Archbishop Thomas II, c. 1108, and also at Lissington in Lincolnshire,[3] whilst in 1133 William received from Henry I the churches of Wallop (Hants) and Market Weighton (Yorks), and the chapel of Grateley (Hants).[4] William of Aumâle, *sub Stephano rex verior*, as a Yorkshire writer observed,[5] was the grandson of Odo of Champagne, and thereby head of the senior line of the house of Blois. He succeeded his father, Stephen III, in the honour c. 1127, and subsequently distinguished himself at the Battle of the Standard, being thereafter created earl of York by Stephen. He had extensive holdings and connexions in the north; in Scotland, Yorkshire and the counties of the north-west,[6] and having acquired Howden from the church of Durham, was not above suggesting that he might advocate the

---

[1] *Vita Sancti Waltheni Abbatis* (in *Acta Sanctorum*, Die Tertia Augusti, 256, col.1).
[2] R. L. Poole, 'The Appointment and Deprivation of St William of York'; Clay, *art. cit.* 7. See also J. Bilson, 'Weaverthorpe Church and its Builder', 59.
[3] *EYC*, I, no. 25. The land lay at Londesborough, Towthorpe, Weaverthorpe, Helperthorpe, Lutton, Thirkleby, Sherburn, Birdsall, Mowthorpe and elsewhere in the East Riding. The church of Weaverthorpe was granted to Nostell by Herbert fitzHerbert and his brother, William, c. 1121–7 (*EYC*, I, no. 26; III, no. 1428).   [4] *EYC*, I, no. 132.   [5] Newburgh, I, 103.
[6] *EYC*, III, 26–7; *Early Sources*, II, 150 and notes; G. H. White, 'Stephen's Earldoms', esp. 52.

claims of Waltheof to York in return for a lease on some of the estates of the see—a proposal the future saint is said to have rejected *in spiritu vehementi*.[1]

To this unstable faction there was added the indignation of such old Benedictine houses as York, Whitby and Selby, indelicately handled by zealous reformers, and the loyalties of Hugh Puiset and Robert de Gant, St Barbara's successor in the deanery of York, and later Stephen's chancellor.[2] Beyond these lay a number of lesser families, whose origins and relationship remain somewhat obscure. From that of Nuvel (holding in Durham and Yorkshire) there came Ralph, bishop of the Orkneys, an active suffragan in the northern province, as also, in all probability, that Master Paulinus who lived to refuse the see of Carlisle.[3] More remote was a commercial element in York city itself, which eventually came to contain both Puisets and Nuvels.

In 1141 Stephen attempted to give York to his nephew, Henry de Sully, a maladroit move which foundered, with typical fatuity, on Henry's own greed—or pessimism—in wishing to retain the abbey of Caen in plurality. The next candidate, the wealthy, indolent and immoral William fitz-Herbert, was equally unsatisfactory. Opposed by the abbots of Rievaulx and Fountains, and the Augustinian priors of Kirkham and Guisborough, fitzHerbert leisurely, or cautiously,[4] manœuvred for his see, during which time neither he nor Henry of Winchester was free from the suspicion of making certain adjustments in the form of papal mandates authorizing inquiries into the manner of his election. Eventually, under the

---

[1] *Vita...Waltheni*, 256, cols. 1-2.   [2] *EYC*, II, 432-6.

[3] For Ralph, bishop of the Orkneys, see John of Worcester, ed. Weaver, 26; Symeon, II, 293; *Early Sources*, II, 227, n. 12. For Master Paulinus, see *EYC*, I, 244-5, and VI, nos. 82, 83; Thoresby Soc. *Miscellanea*, IV, 209 ff. It has been suggested (*EYC*, I, 244-5) that Master Paulinus may have been a son of Bishop Ralph. This seems certain, for *c.* 1133-40, Bishop Geoffrey of Durham granted to Paulinus, son of Ralph, bishop of the Orkneys, and his brothers, Garmondsway, in the county of Durham (below, App. II, no. 13). In 1184 Puiset, as bishop of Durham, settled a dispute concerning a third part of the vill of Garmondsway, between Radulf, son of Paulinus of York, and Ilger of Ketton and others ('A Second Calendar of the Greenwell Deeds', ed. J. Walton, no. 30). For the possessions of the family in Yorkshire, see *EYC*, I, nos. 230, 298, 308.

[4] C. N. L. Brooke and A. Morey, 'The Cerne Letters of Gilbert Foliot and the Legation of Imar of Tusculum in 1145'.

guidance of Bernard and Henry Murdac, and with the favour of the Cistercian pope, Eugenius III (commonly regarded as Bernard's puppet), fitzHerbert was driven from his see despite powerful support in Rome. 'A barren tree must fall, it matters not how', commented Bernard.[1] Such proceedings, and especially the role of Henry Murdac therein, did not pass unopposed in Yorkshire. Certain of William's supporters and relatives, amongst whom, in view of future events, it would not be fanciful to number Hugh Puiset, made an armed raid on a grange of Fountains, Murdac's own abbey.[2]

Worse was to come. At Richmond, in July 1147, Murdac was himself elected to the archbishopric, despite William of Aumâle's exclusion of St Barbara, and the efforts of Henry of Winchester, Robert de Gant and Hugh Puiset to secure the see for Master Hilary.[3] Thereupon there arose great disturbances. Stephen sequestrated the archbishop's revenues, whilst Murdac, having returned from his consecration at Trèves, fled (1148) to the safety of Ripon, from whence he excommunicated Puiset, who was presumably mainly responsible for much of the opposition and violence in York. Hugh, supreme in the archiepiscopal city, maintained service in the minster in defiance of his sentence—to which, in a spirit worthy of his ancestors, he replied in like style. Murdac sought safety in the remoter corners of his diocese, whilst in 1149–50 Puiset, now clearly Winchester's lieutenant, withdrew to protect the temporalities of his uncle's see during the latter's absence in Rome.[4] His removal from the northern scene brought an immediate weakening in the Blois opposition. His own archdeaconry was pillaged and his clerks imprisoned,[5] whilst Murdac's sentence

---

[1] The election has been described in detail by Knowles, 'The Case of St William of York'.

[2] Symeon, ii, 319; *A Continuation of the Lives of the Archbishops of York* (*Historians of the Church of York*, ed. J. Raine, ii, 224–5); *Memorials of the Abbey of St Mary of Fountains*, ed. J. S. Walbran, 103; *PU*, iii, no. 62.

[3] Symeon, ii, 320–1; *A Continuation of the Lives*, *loc. cit.*; Gervase of Canterbury, i, 135. For Master Hilary, see above, p. 6.

[4] Symeon, ii, 322–4; *A Continuation of the Lives*, 225; *Memorials of Fountains*, *loc. cit.*; Newburgh, i, 56–7.

[5] The writ of Stephen to his ministers in Yorkshire, that the canons of St Peter's and the clerks of the archdeaconry of Hugh Puiset shall have his peace,

was now respected, for it was necessary for Prince Eustace, Stephen's son, to constrain the clerks of York to perform the divine office when he visited the city in 1149.[1] Early in 1150 a superficial calm was restored. Through the efforts of Henry of Winchester Eugenius III requested the archbishop to moderate his wrath, and Puiset was consequently absolved at Yarm, Eustace and Murdac being likewise reconciled after a conversation, *solus cum solo*.[2]

II. ELECTION TO DURHAM

The quarrel broke out afresh in a new setting when William of St Barbara, bishop of Durham, who had gained and held his see with such difficulty, died on 13 November 1152.[3] Here Prior Laurence and Archdeacon Wazo, rivals, it would seem, since at least 1147, each anxious to snatch this excellent windfall from the other, each wishing *alter ab altero eligi*, renewed their struggle for precedence.[4] Whilst their intrigues dragged through the inevitable tedium—and from Reginald of Durham we hear of the frequent consultations between clergy and people—the young Roger Conyers, hereditary constable, and by royal appointment keeper of the vacant see, took the convenient opportunity to plunder his trust.[5]

At length, on 22 January 1153—perhaps after Archdeacon Wazo, possibly a Blois protégé, had been sent, or had departed

with their goods, anything unjustly taken to be restored (*EYC*, I, no. 138), there dated 1138–53, would seem to refer to Puiset's absence, and probably passed in 1149, when the king was at York (Symeon, II, 323; *A Continuation of the Lives*, 225; Gervase of Canterbury, I, 141).

[1] Symeon, II, 324.

[2] Symeon, II, 325; *A Continuation of the Lives*, *loc. cit.*; R. L. Poole, 'John of Salisbury at the Papal Court' (*Studies in Chronology and History*, ed. A. L. Poole, 254–5). [3] Symeon, II, 328. See also above, p. 8 and below, p. 129.

[4] *Scriptores Tres*, 4. The prior and archdeacon of Durham had the main voices in the election of a bishop (Symeon, *loc. cit.*; *PU*, II, no. 29), which would identify the competitor as Wazo, archdeacon of Durham, and not his colleague, Rannulf, archdeacon of Northumberland. Laurence had been subprior and Wazo archdeacon in 1147 when the offices of prior and subprior had been adjudged superior to that of archdeacon of Durham (below, pp. 140–1).

[5] *Scriptores Tres*, *loc. cit.*; Symeon, *loc. cit.*; *Libellus de Vita et Miraculis Sancti Godrici*, ed. J. Stevenson, 232; *Libellus de admirandis Beati Cuthberti Virtutibus Reginaldi monachi Dunelmensis*, ed. J. Raine, 104. For the family of Conyers, see below, pp. 42, 43 n. 2, 192.

to consult Henry of Winchester—an election by acclamation was made.[1] The clergy and people, faced with the prospect of civil anarchy, the jealousies of the elders of their church, and the authoritarian zeal of Archbishop Murdac, bestowed the see unanimously (*uno animo, una voce*) upon Hugh Puiset.[2] The reasons are not far to seek. He may have come to the attention of the Durham notabilities in 1144, when fitzHerbert had arranged a truce between St Barbara and the intruder, William Cumin.[3] He may have been recommended by Henry of Winchester or even by the disappointed Archdeacon Wazo. But on his own recent showing he was clearly the strong man of good connexions the situation demanded, especially when memories of Cumin's activities were so fresh. At the time of his election, according to the Durham chronicler, he was about twenty-five—in fact probably nearer thirty—a pluralist archdeacon who knew much of the world and something of the routine of ecclesiastical life.[4] His character had been formed in the violence of faction, and moulded by the indolent opulence of William fitzHerbert, and the grand, but practical style of Henry of Winchester, whose flair for organization, distinguished tastes, and enviable financial competence were with him to the end. He was a man of proved ability and obvious consequence, commended to his electors as one well fitted to serve the interests of their church.[5]

If not a direct royal nominee—though he was to receive such encouragement short of active support as the declining family interest could still muster—Puiset was so clearly of the cause

[1] A notification by Henry of Winchester, possibly of this date, is addressed to Hugh (Puiset), archdeacon of Winchester, and witnessed, amongst others, by Wacius, archdeacon of Durham (PRO, Exchequer, Treasury of Receipt, Ancient Deed, E 40/A 6112). Archdeacon Wazo was also with Henry of Winchester in 1148 (*Cal. Doc. France*, no. 1395). A Master Wazo was in the service of Henry of Blois in 1139–41 (Voss, *Heinrich von Blois*, 173).

[2] *In die Sancti Vincentii*, DC Durham, B II, 35, fo. 277; Symeon, *loc. cit.*; Gervase of Canterbury, I, 157–8; *Undecimo Kal. Februarii, Scriptores Tres, loc. cit.*; Symeon, I, 167, 169; *In die Sancte Agnetis, A Continuation of the Lives*, 226.

[3] Symeon, I, 155; II, 316.

[4] *Scriptores Tres, loc. cit.*; according to Newburgh, II, 436–7, Puiset died (1195) at the age of seventy, which would make him twenty-seven or twenty-eight at the time of his election, and put the year of his birth *c.* 1125.

[5] *Scriptores Tres, loc. cit.*; Newburgh, I, 79–80; II, 437.

as to make Stephen's assent to the election a foregone conclusion. But such grace was not universally forthcoming. The
recent demonstration of his abilities by the new bishop-elect
was no recommendation to the austerity of Bernard of Clairvaux, or his disciple, Henry Murdac, the *de facto* arbiters of such
matters in the north. They knew Puiset as a vigorous warrior
in an unrighteous cause, and one whose acts of love were neither
little nor unremembered.[1] For some five years Hugh had been
Murdac's chief opponent in York; a man who destroyed his
property and ignored his strictures. In all save determination
there was complete antithesis. The archbishop's greedy definition of his metropolitan authority, his officious piety, and his
hopes for Durham, were equally jarred. He held the election
uncanonical, as made without his consent, and the elect
notoriously unsuitable, not only by reason of his youth, but by
his total inexperience in matters spiritual, and his well-known
addiction to the ways of the flesh. In the choice of a bishop, he
pointed out, less worldly criteria were required than a certain
distinction of bearing and birth.[2]

News of the election had been immediately conveyed to
Murdac. His reaction was swift, and the leaders of the chapter
were summoned to answer for contempt and disobedience.
They vainly sought to appease a man who knew not moderation. He ignored their explanations, and before the end of
February had excommunicated the principal electors, declaring
the election null, and forbidding his own chapter to give any
support to Durham's projected appeal to Rome. The convent
prepared an elegantly phrased letter to Eugenius III, explaining
the unanimity and complete propriety of the election, and the
entirely commendable character of the bishop-elect. Further,
remembering that excellent precept *nam tua res agitur paries cum
proximus ardet*, they explained their wrongs more generally to
all lovers of peace, detailing the canonical form of the election,

---

[1] Newburgh, II, 440–1. He perhaps underestimates Hugh's fidelity when he
writes, *paulo ante episcopatum diversis ex matribus tres spurios fuderat*. For these
children, see below, App. v.

[2] *Scriptores Tres, loc. cit.*; *A Continuation of the Lives*, 226; Symeon, II, 329;
Gervase of Canterbury, I, 157–8; Newburgh, I, 78–9. For Murdac, see Knowles,
Monastic Order, 239.

the suitability of their candidate, and those harsh measures whereby the archbishop had turned their rejoicing to woe.[1]

On 4 March, the prior and archdeacons, together with Nicholas, prior of Brinkburn, one of the religious of the diocese who had participated in the election, vainly sought absolution from Murdac at York.[2] The archbishop, running before the storm of a popular rising, sought the shelter of Beverley, where he ignored the attempts of Stephen and Eustace to intercede for Durham. In the meanwhile the bishop-elect appears to have retired to the south, doubtless to Winchester, already a centre for the distressed or disinherited of the Blois faction. His supporters in the north, discouraged by the tight circle of Cistercian influence, were perhaps somewhat distressed by this disdain, but their burden was lightened when, at the request of the papal legate, Theobald of Canterbury, Murdac lifted his sentences. Puiset returned to York in August, possibly after having submitted to a penitential scourging at Beverley, but still unconsecrated, failed to gain any support from the metropolitan chapter, chilled by the ways of their archbishop.[3]

With Canterbury's support, and armed with a brief but pessimistic commendatory letter from Henry of Winchester, the leaders of the chapter—the prior, Archdeacon Wazo and a number of clerks—together with their elect, departed for the *Curia* sometime in August.[4] According to Reginald of Durham one of these clerks, Master Laurence (not to be confused with the prior of that name), inspired with a fitting reverence for the weighty words of the hermit Godric that two Laurences would never return, ensured the future safety of his soul and the good name of the saint by turning monk at St Albans en route.[5] The

---

[1] Below, App. 1; *PU*, III, no. 92; Symeon, *loc. cit.*; *A Continuation of the Lives, loc. cit.*; *Scriptores Tres*, 4–5; Symeon, I, 167.

[2] *A Continuation of the Lives, loc. cit.*; Symeon, II, 329.

[3] Symeon, I, 169; II, 329; *Scriptores Tres*, 5. The intervention of Theobald is ignored by the York historian (*loc. cit.*).

[4] Symeon, I, 168; II, 330; *A Continuation of the Lives, loc. cit.*; Newburgh, I, 79; Gervase of Canterbury, I, 157–8; Voss, *Heinrich von Blois*, 68, n. 64.

[5] *Libellus...Godrici*, 232–3; Symeon, *loc. cit.* Laurence was a former pupil of Hugh of St Victor, and celebrated in his day for his sermons (Flete, *History of Westminster*, 91). He was well connected in Cistercian circles, being something of

bearing and dignity of the remainder of the party on their travels were, as the patriotism of the Durham chronicler has it, a source of honour to their church and edification to the inhabitants of those countries through which they passed.[1]

They were fortified for their crossing of the Alps by the glad news of the death of Eugenius III, *cui tota partis adversae spes incumbebat*, and thus encouraged appear to have reached Rome early in December.[2] The new pope, Anastasius IV, listened sympathetically to the sighs of the widowed church, but it appears that Murdac had representatives in Rome, who again raised the question of Puiset's tender years.[3] Such objections were, however, quashed by suitably flattering precedents from Holy Writ quoted by the Durham chapter, whence it appeared that Joash had reigned when but seven, and David, though youthful in years, had been as an ancient in council. Convinced, so it was said, by this timely if somewhat inapposite erudition, Anastasius consecrated Puiset on 21 December.[4]

Whilst in Rome, Hugh is reputed to have given able support to the pleas of William fitzHerbert, who arrived there late in December. From this, together with that natural sympathy inspired by William's appearance and the sure support of Cardinal Gregory, a man *profundissime astutie atque animi vere Romani*, it resulted that following the death of Murdac the future saint was restored to his see, and granted the pallium *quod nunquam eatenus impetrare poterat*.[5]

The return from the *Curia*, not apparently commenced till

a protégé of St Bernard, a friend of Maurice of Rievaulx and a relative of Ailred. He later became abbot of Westminster, and as such his obit was recorded at Durham (DC Durham, B IV, 24, fo. 20). There is mention of another member of the family in the Westminster Register, BM, Cotton MS., Faust. A III, fo. 329. Most of this information has been collected by F. E. Croydon in *Medieval and Renaissance Studies*, II (1950), 169–71. See also below, p. 20.

[1] *Scriptores Tres, loc. cit.*

[2] *Scriptores Tres*, 6; cf. an indulgence of Anastasius IV, 15 December 1153, (DC Durham, Cart. I, fo. 40ᵛ; *Scriptores Tres*, App. no. XXVIII; *JL*, no. 9779).

[3] *Scriptores Tres*, 6; Newburgh, I, 79–80.

[4] The date of consecration is given as *XIII kal. Jan.* in DC Durham, B II, 35, fo. 277ᵛ; *Scriptores Tres, loc. cit.*, gives *in festivitate sancti Thome Apostoli*. Cf. Gervase of Canterbury, I, 157–8; Symeon, I, 168, 169.

[5] Newburgh, *loc. cit.*; Gervase of Canterbury, *loc. cit.*, says that fitzHerbert arrived in Rome on 24 December, but cf. Torigni, 178 and Knowles, 'The Case of St William of York', 162–77.

sometime in February, was accomplished in what was to become characteristic style. Prior Laurence fell ill in France, but Puiset, untroubled, 'impatient of such delays', left him to die attended by a few followers, and made haste for England where, rejoiced by news of the death of Murdac, he was enthroned at Durham on 2 May 1154.[1] Shortly afterwards he received fitzHerbert in his see, and when, in June, the archbishop died in somewhat mysterious circumstances it was Hugh who was responsible for his burial. Thereafter he appears to have joined Stephen, who, now reconciled with the future Henry II, was engaged in an attempt to pacify the north. He was with him at the siege of Drax in July, at York in August, and at Lincoln in early October as the king made his final way to London.[2]

The election to Durham had been of the general pattern of those at York in 1141 and 1147, the chapter encouraged by timely messages from Henry of Winchester, the family interest supported by Stephen and Eustace.[3] By extremist standards it was irregular from the age and character of the elect. In other respects it showed something of that comparative canonical regularity which emerged with other things less desirable from the weakness of the crown. It was a free choice made by the clergy, people and religious of the diocese,[4] indeed probably the second and last of such pattern in the reformed see before monastic interest and papal policy limited the electoral body to the cathedral chapter. Murdac's criticisms were directed less against the process of election, than the failure of the church of Durham to treat his views of his archiepiscopal authority with that submissive deference he demanded.

As the royal power waned that of Rome waxed with a vigour which, in large measure, determined the character of the next fifty years of English ecclesiastical history. Durham's appeals in 1153 are examples of that contact with the papal *Curia* which has been particularly associated with the legation of Henry of

---

[1] *PU*, II, no. 82; *Scriptores Tres*, 6; Symeon, I, 169.

[2] *Libellus...Cuthberti*, 198; Hoveden, I, 213. William fitzHerbert returned to England in April 1154, was at York in May and died 8 June (Newburgh, I, 80). For Puiset's itinerary, see below, App. III.

[3] *Scriptores Tres*, 5.

[4] Above, p. 13, n. 2; *PU*, III, no. 92; see below, App. I.

Winchester, but which relates more closely to the removal of
the strong hand of the Anglo-Norman kings, the short episode
of Cistercian power, and the influx into the English hierarchy
of men trained at continental centres of the new canonist
learning.[1] It is remarkable that the chapter appealed to a
Cistercian pope. The Yorkshire appeals to Eugenius III against
fitzHerbert were to a guaranteed justice, but it is hard to believe
that Durham could have expected as much from the same source,
despite the initial presence in its delegation of the well-con-
nected Master Laurence. Certainly Henry of Winchester felt
there was little cause for optimism.[2] Yet neither the appeals of
1153, nor that of fitzHerbert to the man who had authorized
his deposition, were acts of despair. That Murdac found it
worth his while to forbid any York support for the Durham
appeal, and that Archbishop Theobald appears to have supported the second attempt, suggest what might be expected of
Eugenius in a charitable mood. It would seem that the papal
interventions in the Durham election of 1143, as in those at
York in the same period, together with the presence in the
diocese of clerks who had some experience of the *Curia*, had
made their impression. Once allowance has been made for the
obsequiousness customary in such documents, the draft appeal
of 1153 reveals a belief, explicit in the journey *ad limina*, that the
church of Durham, *licet in extremis terrarum posita*, might find at
Rome an authority to hear its griefs with justice. The history
of the northern elections from 1141 to 1153 is a striking example
of the way in which royal weakness and the experience of
Roman vigour could foster that spirit which Henry II was to
find so distasteful.

The election has other points of interest. As an episode in
the rivalry of the two metropolitans it marked a victory for
Canterbury. In family history it was the end of the most
spectacular part of the career of Henry of Winchester. His role
in 1153 was insignificant as against his earlier interventions at
York, or at Durham, when in 1141–3 the electors had refused

---

[1] M. Cheney, 'The Compromise of Avranches of 1172, and the spread of
Canon Law in England'; Raymonde Foreville, *L'Église et la Royauté en Angleterre.
sous Henri II*, 55.   [2] Voss, *Heinrich von Blois*, 68, n. 64.

to proceed without his advice, and eventually, under his guidance, had made a canonical choice in almost impossible circumstances.[1] His prominence had now been forfeited with his legation to Archbishop Theobald, whose frequent acta, scattered through cartularies and registers, are testimony of active authority. The new legate's growing influence, an addition to the prestige of Canterbury, was effective in the elections to Hereford in 1148, Coventry in 1149, and Worcester in 1150. The trouble created by Murdac and his disciples in the north gave him further opportunities. So, shortly after Murdac's death, he intervened at Selby to settle the claims of the rival abbots, and it was he who secured the absolution of the Durham electors, and favoured their journey to Rome.[2]

The Blois triumph in 1154 was primarily due to the deaths of Eugenius, Bernard and Murdac, but the family position was, on the whole, stronger than it had been at York. Puiset was an abler and less notorious character than fitzHerbert. Stephen's interventions, if as ineffectual as ever, were of necessity more discreet than his similar efforts in 1141. Moreover, Puiset had the advantage of local nomination and fairly enthusiastic support in an area where the Cistercians had but slight foothold, and, in face of the convent of Durham, little chance of increasing it. The family cause had the added benefit of the interested heroism of the electoral body, high Gregorians, as in 1143, in the defence of their rights, if now more opportunist in their exercise. The chapter and its adherents were determined to keep a candidate of such promise, whose virtues were much enhanced by blocking that promotion the prior and archdeacon were equally loth to see the other enjoy. Above all, the great wave of Cistercian power had already spent its strength. The furious zeal and ferocious piety of Murdac had their inevitable result, and the lesson of his régime in Yorkshire was well marked. If Puiset was only consecrated after the death of Eugenius III, the fact that one of the most active supporters of

---

[1] Symeon, I, 144, 163; II, 313–17.
[2] *The Coucher Book of Selby Abbey*, ed. J. T. Fowler, I, 44–5. For the activities of Archbishop Theobald, see Foreville, *op. cit.* 11–12.

2-2

his election was Nicholas, prior of Brinkburn,[1] is perhaps a sign that the Austin-Cistercian alliance which had broken fitzHerbert was itself cracking. Moreover, given the character and beliefs of the archbishop, and his unfortunate experience of Puiset, Durham's nomination reads as a deliberate move to hold discomforting Cistercian virtue at a safe distance. Murdac's ways were not those that inspire love, nor his ideals those of most mortals, least of all of a wealthy Benedictine chapter.

St Bernard had his candidate for the see in 1143 in that Master Laurence whose career has already been noticed.[2] But Durham, more moderate than the metropolitan chapter, for the electoral body was comparatively free from powerful Cistercian influences, took, in William of St Barbara, a milder member of the reforming party. The new bishop, however, encouraged by Eugenius III, granted the Cistercians of Newminster—then ruled by the future St Robert, a close friend of Bernard—and the canons of Guisborough, land at Wolsingham and Trimdon, within the modern County Durham. Jealous fears of a penetration of the patrimony of St Cuthbert were speedily awakened, as is suggested by the fact that the charter for Newminster has been tampered with, and as it stands contains the phrase *ita ut non faciant ibi Abbatiam*.[3] Murdac presumably had his own plans for 1153—possibly Master Laurence was to have stood again, and his withdrawal to St Albans marked their abandonment. But the archbishop's own disruptive activities, the inclinations and comparative failure of St Barbara as a bishop,

---

[1] It was Nicholas who, together with Archdeacon Wazo, had announced the news of Puiset's election to Murdac (Symeon, II, 329). Brinkburn was a house of Austin canons in Northumberland founded, probably in the time of Henry I, by William Bertram. For what little is known of it, see *Cartulary of Brinkburn*, ed. W. Page, and J. C. Dickinson, *The Origins of the Austin Canons*, 125.

[2] There exists a copy of a letter, dating February–March 1143, from Bernard and William of Rievaulx, commending Master Laurence to Prior Roger and the convent of Durham as a suitable candidate for the see (DC Durham, B IV, 24, fo. 96; Thomas Rud, *Codicum MSS Ecclesiae Cathedralis Dunelmensis Catalogus Classicus*, 208 f.; F. E. Croydon, *art. cit.*). For Master Laurence see above, p. 15, n. 5.

[3] *Vita Sancti Roberti Novi Monasterii*, ed. P. Grosjean, 352. The gift exists in two versions (DC Durham, 1. 2. Pont. nos. 3 and 3*, printed in *FPD*, lxiii–lxiv). The intervention of Eugenius is recalled in a charter of Prior Absalon of Durham (1154–8) (DC Durham, Reg. 1, § II, fo. 1, printed in *Newminster Cartulary*, ed. J. T. Fowler, 47). Puiset replaced Wolsingham by Chopwell (see below, p. 209).

and the unhappy situation in the diocese, clearly indicated to the electors the need for a man of practical competence. The Cistercians made no important settlement in the heart of the diocese, and Durham was spared the humiliations and tribulations which York had suffered.

The year 1154 closed an epoch. The deaths of Eugenius III, Murdac and Bernard ended that direct Cistercian intervention in the ecclesiastical politics of the northern province which had reached a climax in 1147–53. Thenceforward the Cistercian role was less vigorous and less prominent, and the Order tended to concentrate on its domestic affairs, and, with occasionally unfortunate enthusiasm, on the exploitation of its many acres. The deaths of Stephen, Eustace and fitzHerbert, together with the eclipse of Henry of Winchester, marked the end of the effective power of the house of Blois in England. The two parties thus dissolved, the north enjoyed a comparative ecclesiastical peace until Geoffrey Plantagenet arrived at York.

The wave of family power which had carried Puiset to office seeped away to leave him an almost isolated example of a dated style; high birth untouched by learning, monasticism or the royal bureaucracy—a fashion outmoded in the world of Henry II and Becket, Foliot or Hugh of Avalon. But if the events of 1153–4 deprived him of that active role in national politics for which he had been chosen, at least he found in his new diocese a fitting and profitable field for his energies and ambitions.

CHAPTER II

THE BISHOP IN POLITICS
1154–95

DESPITE the waning of the family fortunes Hugh Puiset was in a position of considerable strength in 1154. He had no notable record of opposition to the new dynasty. He was a young man popularly established in what was potentially a wealthy see. Distance from the main centres of political life, however distressing to ambition, brought at least the consolation of a certain independence, for there were few neighbours able or willing to stay the episcopal will.[1] He was, moreover, more fortunate in his new sovereign than he might have been willing to admit. It was not the royal policy to destroy the immunist, and even before the experiences of his later years Henry II showed himself a man of political moderation.[2] In any case the agglomeration of lands which had come to the Angevin was well calculated to absorb a good part of his furious energies, and since he was in addition both ambitious and legalistic he was much occupied with the tenacious prosecution of distant frontier claims.[3] All this, combined with the reactions of the unpredictable royal children to their fond but masterful parent, meant that England was not, except in a financial sense, the centre of the Angevin 'empire', and was so spared the concentrated vigour of Henry's attentions.

Puiset's independence was further strengthened by his connexion with the family of Blois, which for the next half-century was to be the *de facto* authority in the ill-constituted Capetian monarchy. Their vast possessions encircled the royal lands of the Île-de-France in a horseshoe which swept out from Chartres, Tours and Blois in the west, past Bourges, Dijon and Langres, almost to Verdun and St Quentin in the east.[4] After the death of Theobald IV in 1152, the Blois principalities,

---

[1] Below, pp. 183–4.　　　　　　　　　　　　　[2] Stubbs, 116.
[3] Cf. A. L. Poole, *From Domesday to Magna Carta*, 330–2.
[4] A. Longnon, *Documents Relatifs au comté de Champagne et de Brie, 1172–1361*, I, pl. I.

united since 1125, were divided among his able descendants. Sancerre went to another Stephen, who, in 1170, was considered as a potential ruler of the Holy Land.[1] Champagne passed to Henry the Liberal, a man of taste who corresponded with John of Salisbury on literary matters, and whose wife, Marie de France, inspired some of the poetry of Chrétien de Troyes.[2] As count palatine of Troyes Henry received the homage of the counts of Sancerre and Blois, and was increasingly regarded as the head of the family. Related through his mother to the imperialist anti-pope, Victor IV, he was the leader of that party in France which supported the Emperor Frederick against Alexander III in 1162, and in general his interests lay towards the empire.[3] Champagne's political connexions with England were of the slightest, and it is therefore interesting to find that in 1172 a charter of Henry, given at Troyes, in favour of the church of St Jean-en-Châtel, was witnessed, amongst others, by Burchard Puiset, archdeacon of Durham,[4] and that the count's literary circle included a certain *Willelmus Anglicus*.[5]

Blois-Chartres passed to Theobald V, a man whom the author of the *Gesta* described as one *qui semper regi Anglie speciem dilectionis sub velamento iniquitatis et perfidie pretendebat*.[6] He had something of his father's notorious aversion to the Capetians shortly moderated by marriage into the royal house,[7] a handsome share in the direction of national affairs and an increasing distaste for the dangerous growth of Angevin power in Normandy.[8] The family of Puiset, lords of Le Puiset, *vicomtes* of Chartres, and possessors of a variety of ecclesiastical preferments at

---

[1] Torigni, 164.

[2] Torigni, 164. For Henry the Liberal, see H. d'Arbois de Jubainville, *Histoire des Ducs et des Comtes de Champagne*, III, bk. VI, chs. 2 and 5.

[3] D'Arbois de Jubainville, *op. cit.* III, 63–70; Ch. Petit-Dutaillis, *Histoire du Moyen Âge* (vol. IV, pt. II of the *Histoire Générale*, ed. Glotz), 221–2.

[4] *Cartulaire de Montiéramey*, in the *Collection des Principaux Cartulaires du Diocèse de Troyes*, ed. C. Lalore, VII, no. 60; d'Arbois de Jubainville, *op. cit.* III, *acta* no. 204. The Burchard archdeacon, *cognatus meus*, who appears with Archbishop William of Sens in a charter of Henry the Liberal in 1175, may well be the archdeacon of Durham (J. Carnandet, *Le Trésor des pièces rares…de la Champagne et de Brie*, I, 311).

[5] D'Arbois de Jubainville, *op. cit.* III, 190, n. 3.   [6] *Gesta*, I, 53.

[7] A. Fliche, *L'Europe Occidentale de 888–1125*, 529–30.

[8] For the influence of Angevin Normandy on the Blois possessions, see d'Arbois de Jubainville, *op. cit.* II, 420–1.

Orleans[1] and Chartres,[2] had their closest ties with the counts of Blois-Chartres, to whose *acta* they are frequent witnesses.[3]

One of the most distinguished members of the Blois interest was William of the White Hands, brother of Henry and Theobald. He rose to high office with a speed and facility which are good testimony to the influence of his relatives. When scarcely thirty he was bishop of Chartres (1165), in which capacity he was able to restrain the destructive tendencies of his brethren of Le Puiset.[4] In 1168 he added to this dignity the archbishopric of Sens—a combination of wealth and power which brings to mind the earlier fortunes of his uncle, Henry of Winchester. In 1176 William surrendered Sens and Chartres for the archbishopric of Rheims and, legate since 1169, he became ten years later cardinal priest of Sancta Sabina. Patron of a number of famous scholars, and eventually the leading politician of his house, he had considerable influence at Rome and almost supreme power in France—*regis et regni quasi dominus*, as Gervase of Canterbury put it.[5]

Louis VII, *paulo autem simplicior quam deceret principem*,[6] was easy prey for the ambitions of such magnates. The astute Adela of Champagne, sister of Henry the Liberal, was married to the

[1] A Burchard du Puiset, at first archdeacon of Orleans, succeeded Robert as chancellor of Chartres. He was probably a son of Hugh III and accordingly brother of Hugh of Durham, see below, App. v. He may be that Burchard, nephew of the subdean of Orleans, who witnessed *c.* 1133–45 a charter of Bishop Geoffrey of Chartres (*Cartulaire de l'abbaye de la Madelaine de Châteaudun*, ed. L. Merlet, no. IX). As Burchard the chancellor he occurs in 1176 (*Archives de la Maison Dieu de Châteaudun*, no. XXIII), 1178 (*Cart. Marmoutier*, I, no. CLXXXIX), 1179 (*Cart. Notre Dame de Chartres*, I, no. XCIII), and 1176–86 (*Cart. S. Jean-en-Vallée*, no. 99). The obit of Burchard Puiset, archdeacon, is entered under 5 December in the Orleans necrology (*Obituaires de la Province de Sens*, III, 129). It is uncertain to whom this refers; it may well be Burchard Puiset of Durham who died on 6 December (*Scriptores Tres*, 18).

[2] Three relatives, Geoffrey de Lèves (d. 1149), Goselin de Mussy (d. 1155) and Reginald of Bar were bishops of Chartres. For the relationship, see *Cart. de S. Jean-en-Vallée*, 272; *Cart. de la Léproserie du Grand Beaulieu*, ed. R. Merlet and M. Jusselin, no. 97.

[3] See below, App. v.   [4] *Cart. Notre Dame de Chartres*, III, 169–70.

[5] Gervase of Canterbury, I, 260; Torigni, 225; Diceto, I, 412–13. In general see J. Mathorez, *Guillaume aux Blanches Mains, Évêque de Chartres*, 1–24; A. Cartellieri, *Philipp II August, König von Frankreich*, *passim*; J. R. Williams, 'William of the White Hands and Men of Letters', in *Haskins Anniversary Essays in Medieval History*, ed. C. H. Taylor and J. L. La Monte, 365–87.

[6] Newburgh, I, 223.

king. Henry and his brother, Theobald, in turn married Marie and Alix, daughters of Louis by his first wife, just as earlier the ill-fated Eustace, son of Stephen of England, had married one of the royal sisters. Later in the century Hugh du Puiset, a son of the bishop of Durham, was for a short time chancellor of France,[1] and William of the White Hands became principal adviser to the crown. During the madness of Louis VII the family survived, though not without difficulty, the attempts of the count of Flanders to dislodge it, and from 1182 until his death, Archbishop William remained chief councillor, governing the kingdom with his sister, Adela, when Philip Augustus was in Palestine.[2]

This same interest flourished in England, though with less splendour and consequence. It seems highly probable that Henry of Winchester exercised some influence on Puiset during the early years of the reign of Henry II. There is evidence of contact between the two sees. An entry in Boldon Book suggests that Arco, the steward, who had land at Langley (Co. Durham), was an old family servant there rewarded for long service in Winchester and Durham alike.[3] If Wazo, an archdeacon of Durham, seems to have known Winchester, it is equally important to note that the chronicler Jordan Fantosme, a Winchester clerk, was so well informed on northern affairs in 1173-4. Moreover, Henry of Winchester and Hugh of Durham took a similar stand during the papal schism of 1159, and perhaps the general discretion of Durham's earlier years as a bishop is to be attributed (as Stubbs suggested) to the experienced caution of the doyen of the episcopal bench.

Puiset maintained some connexion with his former fellows of the patronage of Winchester, Henry de Sully, Hilary of

---

[1] *Gesta*, I, 241; Hoveden, II, 193. He is the *Hugo Secundus* who appears as chancellor *c*. August 1179 to the end of October 1180. (L. Delisle, *Recueil des Actes de Philippe Auguste*, lxxxvi; H. F. Delaborde, E. Berger, Ch. Petit-Dutaillis, C. Brunel, J. Monicat, *Recueil des Actes de Philippe Auguste*, I, nos. 1 and 15; A. Luchaire, *Études sur les Actes de Louis VII*, 59, 61.) Stubbs makes his dates 1180-5 (Hoveden, II, 193). During his period of office Hugh was responsible for at least thirteen royal charters. His premature death is reputed to have caused his father great sorrow (Newburgh, II, 441). See also below, App. v.

[2] Ch. Petit-Dutaillis, *La Monarchie Féodale en France et en Angleterre*, 201-2; and in Glotz, IV, ii, 221-2.   [3] *BB*, 32; see below, p. 228.

Chichester and Jocelin of Salisbury, but this was slight and of no political significance. He witnessed (1189–91) a number of charters concerning or issued by Sully as abbot of Glastonbury, and the two cousins were jointly responsible for some timely assistance to Master Peter of Blois.[1] Together with Hilary of Chichester Hugh attempted to mediate between the abbot of St Albans and the bishop of Lincoln in 1159.[2] His ring was subsequently used by Henry II to invest Hilary with the chapel of Pevensey,[3] and in 1174 he was commissioned by Alexander III to join Jocelin of Salisbury in the investigation of certain disputes between York and Canterbury.[4]

In an equally unobtrusive way he replaced the aged Henry of Winchester as guardian of the claims of kinship. His patronage ranged from one of Stephen's illegitimate sons and his offspring to an obscure *Stephanus, cognatus meus.*[5] His own amatory ventures brought, through Alice de Percy, contact with a mildly distinguished Anglo-Norman house.[6] Politically this was of little moment, for despite the extent of their possessions the Percies took no decisive role in the twelfth century. But at least it gave Puiset Jocelin of Louvain, or Jocelin the Castellan, an important servant of the Angevin, as a brother-in-law and guaranteed the bishop's son a fair stake in the north of England.[7]

Such family connexions may have been scant recommendation for the favour of Henry II, whose parents had been much exercised to displace Blois influence in England and Normandy, and whose every trouble was exploited by the same faction.

---

[1] *Two Chartularies of the Priory of St Peter at Bath*, ed. W. Hunt, II, 33; Adam of Domerham, *Historia de Rebus Gestis Glastoniensibus*, ed. T. Hearne, I, 232–4; *Report of the Historical Manuscripts Commission, DC Wells*, I, 24, 47. Henry de Sully became abbot of Glastonbury 16 September 1189. The mention, in the charters, of Bishop Reginald of Bath limits their dates to 16 September 1189 to 26 December 1191. See also below, p. 104.

[2] Below, p. 86.

[3] Below, App. II, no. 11; in an inquest taken in the fourteenth century there is reference to 'a charter of Henry II bearing his waxen seal and a certain golden ring provided for the purpose by Hugh, bishop of Durham, fixed to it' (*Cartulary of the High Church of Chichester*, ed. W. Peckham, no. 887).

[4] *PU*, II, no. 141. [5] See below, pp. 228–9.

[6] See below, App. V. In view of the eminence of the house of Blois as compared with that of Percy, there seems no reason to attach anything beyond the obvious significance to this liaison.

[7] See below, pp. 223–4.

But the king was a man of moderation, and Puiset was of the blood royal, untainted by such a record of partisanship as Winchester and, until Winchester's death, tactfully submissive to the Angevin will. He was, moreover, the representative of a family the king sought to use, and backed by the weight of an interest well worthy of respect, even if we discount the imposing strategies suggested to modern eyes by the stud book ramifications of pedigree, but in practice generally obscured by local and personal issues.

Puiset probably withdrew to his diocese in 1154[1] when Henry II commenced what he described as the restoration of the customs of his grandfather. Henry of Winchester sought the shelter of his parent house of Cluny and there characteristically employed himself in reforming its finances, whilst in England the sheriff of Hampshire was engaged in the demolition of six of his castles.[2] It seems unlikely that Hugh was in the royal presence in the south before 1160, though he generally joined the king in his northern peregrinations. Thus he was at Lincoln and York in 1155, and Newcastle, Durham and York in 1158, on which occasion there was complaint from the borough of Scarborough as to the exactions of archdeacons and rural deans and ominous dissidence in the royal entourage as to how the matter was to be handled.[3]

From 1160 to 1162 Durham appears to have been with the king in Normandy, and had evidently gained some considerable measure of royal favour. He was the only bishop holding an English see to witness the important treaty between Louis VII and Henry II in May 1160 (when those present included his cousin, Henry of Champagne),[4] and when the king made a grant to Hilary of Chichester, he borrowed Hugh's ring to authenticate it.[5] Perhaps the causes of this friendship are not far to seek. Henry was attempting to round off Normandy by the re-acquisition of that vital barrier, the Norman Vexin, the

---

[1] But cf. Torigni, 182, where a variant reading gives his presence at Henry's coronation.

[2] Torigni, 186; Diceto, i, 301; PR 2 Henry II, 54; Voss, *Heinrich von Blois*, 115; Knowles, *Monastic Order*, 290.

[3] *Materials*, iii, 44–5; below, App. iii, *sub annis*.

[4] Below, App. iii, *sub anno*.   [5] Above, p. 26, n. 3.

price originally paid for Louis VII's recognition of the Angevin title to the duchy (September 1149).[1] An agreement had been made in August 1158 between Louis and Henry, that the former's daughter, Margaret, was to have the whole of the Norman Vexin as her marriage portion.[2] This *entente* was short-lived. Henry tried to enforce a claim on Toulouse, failed, and set Theobald of Blois to attack the Beauvaisis.[3] A truce was arranged in December 1159, followed by a peace in May 1160, finally ratified the following October. Louis granted the Vexin to Henry II as the marriage portion of his daughter on her projected marriage to Henry's son and namesake. The elder Henry was to be put in possession on the day of the Assumption three years after the conclusion of peace, provided a contract of marriage should have been made between the two infants with the consent of the church within the period. Were Louis's daughter to die within this time, the whole was to revert to the French crown. It was further arranged that during the interim years the castles of the Vexin should be in the custody of the Templars.[4] In November, as a result of Louis's marriage to Adela of Blois, Henry broke his terms. He ignored the stipulated three years, secured papal approval for the union of the two children and seized the dowry, which was eventually confirmed in his possession in 1169.[5]

The Angevin policy was of considerable efficacy, if questionable morality. It was shaped by an appreciation of the simplicity of Louis VII and a careful use of the opportunities offered by the papal schism of 1159. In this the Blois family were affected as relatives of the imperialist anti-popes, as neighbours circumscribed by Henry's holdings in Anjou and Normandy, and as opponents to the resultant danger to their own will to control the throne of France. The old alliance of Blois and Normandy had become irrelevant in 1135. It was some time before a new policy replaced it, and from 1152 to 1160 the

[1] Ralph of Coggeshall, *Chronicon Anglicanum*, 12; Bouquet, XII, 127.
[2] Torigni, 196; *Continuatio Beccensis* (in *Chronicles*, IV), 318.
[3] Torigni, 203; *Continuatio Beccensis*, 324.
[4] Bouquet, XVI, 21–3; *DB*, I, 251; Newburgh, I, 159.
[5] Newburgh, I, 159; Diceto, I, 303–4; Torigni, 208; Gervase of Canterbury, I, 167–8.

counts, in danger of being crushed between Capetian and Angevin, swung ineffectively from side to side. As late as 1159–60 Theobald V was foolish enough to support Henry until the unpleasant prospect of Angevin control of the Vexin (with the consequent domination of the north-east of the county) was too rapidly realized. There is no doubt that this eventuality had some bearing on the move to subject Louis to matrimonial direction. At the same time Henry presumably saw in the marriage of Louis and Adela, Blois's untimely embrace of an authority his own children might yet claim, and an unwelcome omen of a revival of Capetian power.[1]

By judicious hesitations and a short flirtation with the Blois family Henry gained an important concession from the embarrassment of Alexander III, then anxious for the weight of Angevin recognition. Blois was notoriously hostile to the pope; the anti-popes, Victor IV and Paschal III, were both of their faction;[2] Henry the Liberal sought to gain his own political independence by committing Louis to Barbarossa in 1162;[3] in the summer of 1160 it was suspected that Henry of Winchester and his nephew of Durham would have declared for the imperialist had they only dared.[4] In view of the Angevin's

[1] It may be convenient to summarize here the tergiversations of all parties during this period. The Blois faction, with Louis's support, aided Geoffrey of Anjou in an attempt to strip his brother of his continental possessions in 1152 (Torigni, 165; Gervase of Canterbury, I, 149–50). Henry came to terms with Louis in 1154 (Torigni, 180). Thereafter his affairs prospered; he was successful against Geoffrey in 1156, and was entrusted with the control of Flanders in 1157, when the count was in Palestine (Torigni, 189–93). He was on the best of terms with Louis in 1158 (Torigni, 196–7; *Continuatio Beccensis*, 319–20; Gervase of Canterbury, I, 166), by whose influence Blois and Anjou were reconciled (Torigni, 198; *Continuatio Beccensis*, 320). Theobald V then supported Henry during the abortive struggle for Toulouse (Torigni, 203; *Continuatio Beccensis*, 324). But the Angevin was now becoming too strong. He acquired the castles of the count of Évreux (Torigni, 206), and had the prospect of control of the Vexin in sight. Blois strengthened their position by marrying Adela to Louis, at which Henry broke his terms with the consequences already noticed. In 1161 Theobald was largely responsible for the continuance of the war (Torigni, 211).

[2] Bouquet, XII, 330; John of Salisbury, *Historia Pontificalis*, ed. R. L. Poole App. IV. Octavian (later Victor IV) and Guy of Crema (later Paschal III) had been active in the cause of Stephen of England in 1148 (*ibid.* 45). For some comment on Guy of Crema, see Newburgh, I, 120.

[3] See above, p. 23, n. 3.

[4] *Si Octaviano palam auderent pro voto suffragari, libenter cederent in partem ejus*, John of Salisbury to Rannulf of Sarre (Letter no. 59, *Opera*, ed. J. A. Giles, I,

ostentatious delays and known contacts with the emperor, Alexander approved the hasty but politic match of Margaret and the young Henry, which was solemnized in November 1160, and at the end of the year the king declared for the pope.[1] Perhaps Puiset was with Henry during this period as one who might be presumed to have a useful knowledge of, and even some control over the ways and opinions of his cousins of Blois. He was the representative of an influence the Angevin at first hoped to exploit, and thereafter to control.

Sometime in the spring of 1162, whilst still in Normandy, the bishop was present when the papal legate, Henry of Pisa, confirmed a grant by Archbishop Roger of York of a prebend at Southwell to Master Roger, brother of Martin de Capella.[2] He was again with the king in 1163 at Westminster, when the dispute between St Albans and the bishop of Lincoln was ended, and possibly once more in 1165.[3] He moved with great caution through the opening stages of the Becket dispute. His attitude in the initial sessions of the synod at Westminster (October 1163), which Henry summoned to consider the question of criminous clerks, is uncertain, though from later evidence it might be presumed that he supported the archbishop. There is no evidence for his presence at Clarendon in January 1164, notwithstanding good testimony for the attendance of the whole episcopate and the story of the Durham chronicler that he subscribed to the 'outrageous royal constitutions'.[4] It may be that he was in fact at Clarendon, though in view of the insignificance of his role his name escaped the publicists, for on 19 April he was with the king at the consecration of the abbey church of Reading. This was the last public function attended by Henry and his primate, and Puiset, in common with several other bishops, granted an indulgence.[5]

63–71). The events of these years are examined by F. Barlow, 'The English, Norman and French councils called to deal with the Papal Schism of 1159', 264–8; see Foreville, *L'Église et La Royauté en Angleterre*, 94–5.

[1] Bouquet, xv, 700; Barlow, *art. cit.* 266–7; L. Delisle in *Journal des Savants* (1902), 47. [2] *PU*, ii, no. 106.

[3] See below, App. iii, *sub annis*.

[4] *Materials*, iv, 206–7; v, 72. But compare *ibid.* iii, 278; Newburgh, i, 141; *Scriptores Tres*, 10.

[5] See below, App. ii, no. 12.

There is no indication of his behaviour thereafter until 1169. By this date the quarrel, having passed through a series of abortive meetings and mediations, had developed extensive ramifications. The bishop of London, Gilbert Foliot, had become in a sense leader of a regalist party of opposition to his exiled metropolitan. After a further futile conference at Montmirail in January 1169, the attitude of both sides had hardened. Foliot, to avert an anticipated sentence from the archbishop, prepared to lay his own counter-appeal to Rome. To this end he was especially anxious to gain the support of the bishop of Exeter, whom with others he summoned to a conference at Westminster in May. Despite lack of wide backing, London's case, aided by able exposition, received a favourable hearing. He again attempted to secure something of what has been described as a 'united opposition' among the English episcopate, but in vain.[1] Puiset, like Henry of Winchester, declined, giving the sufficiently discreet answer that he would consult his metropolitan, *et quidquid liceret, salvo ordine Dei et suo, se consulte facturum.*[2] But within the next few months his policy took a rapid swing, and on 14 June 1170 by royal command and in the face of papal prohibition he joined Roger of York, Foliot, Salisbury and Rochester in the coronation of the young king.[3] Alexander, on receiving news of what had happened, suspended York and Durham, with all who had sworn to the customs of Clarendon (16 September 1170), whilst Foliot and Jocelin of Salisbury were anathematized.[4] These bulls were modified at Becket's request, out of a regard both for the facts of the case (for there appears to have been no oath about the royal customs) and the Angevin temper. Chester, Rochester, St Asaph, Llandaff and Durham were suspended until they should have satisfied the apostolic see, London and Salisbury

[1] Stubbs, 61; Morey, *Bartholomew of Exeter*, 27–8; Foreville, *op. cit.* 192–3; Knowles, *The Episcopal Colleagues of Archbishop Thomas Becket*, 98–9.

[2] *Materials*, VII, 57.

[3] *Gesta*, I, 5–6; Hoveden, II, 5; Torigni, 245; Diceto, I, 338; Foreville, *op. cit.* 302–6.

[4] *Materials*, II, 315–6; VII, 360–3, 364–7; Hoveden, II, 6–9; *Collectio Sangermanensis*, ed. H. Singer, Lib. III, xiii, 8; J. C. Davies, *Episcopal Acts Relating to Welsh Dioceses, 1066–1272*, II, no. 151.

were suspended and excommunicated, and York was likewise suspended and excommunicated and his case reserved for the pope (24 November 1170).[1] Becket, hearing the course of events in England following his reconciliation with Henry, issued the original, and not the modified bulls before he left the Continent for the last time in December 1170.[2]

After some vain royal and episcopal attempts to persuade the archbishop *ut...latam in archiepiscopum Eboracensem et alios episcopos sententiam relaxaret*, Puiset, like York, London and Salisbury, eventually sent to Rome to seek absolution, waning spirits having been revived, so it was alleged, by the aggressive counsels of Archbishop Roger.[3] At the *Curia* the proctors of York and Durham, who appeared at the same time as the royal ambassador, Master John Cumin, evidently enjoyed some initial success until their task was rendered almost impossible by news of the murder of Becket.[4] Alexander refused audience to all Englishmen, with a consequent total suspension of business. It was known that the Angevin lands were on the verge of interdict, and the martyr's last sentences about to be confirmed. The royal envoys were equal to the situation. After a hasty conference, a distribution of cash and the intercession of a group of cardinals, they exceeded their mandate and gave Alexander to understand they had power to swear the king would put himself at the pope's disposition, and would himself take an oath to that effect. Thereafter both the royal and episcopal clerks were received in audience, the matter being reported thus: *Nuntii vero Eboracensis archiepiscopi et Londoniensis et Saresberiensis episcoporum juraverunt...quod domini sui stabunt precepto ejus* (i.e. Alexander), *a nuntio vero Dunelmensi qui presens aderat nullum juramentum exactum est nec praestitum.*[5]

The final settlement was made a little after Easter 1171, having been preceded by much diplomatic activity and the

[1] *Materials*, VII, 386, 397-9; *Gesta*, I, 9-10; *Scriptores Tres*, 9-10; Foreville, *op. cit.* 316.
[2] *Materials*, I, 97; III, 117, 471; IV, 68; VII, 410; Newburgh, I, 160-1; Diceto, I, 339-40; Foreville, *op. cit.* 317, n. 3; Knowles, *op. cit.* 137.
[3] *Materials*, I, 99, 105; III, 121; VII, 405.   [4] *Materials*, VII, 476.
[5] *Materials*, VII, 474-7; Newburgh, I, 164; Gervase of Canterbury, I, 232-3; Diceto, I, 346; Foreville, *op. cit.* 324-5.

flow of gold. London and Salisbury, both aged and decrepit, were to be absolved if legates had not crossed the Alps within a month, having first taken the oath that they would obey papal commands.[1] Durham's proctor secured his complete absolution after what is described as much difficulty and delay.[2] Roger of York appeared before the archbishop of Rouen and the bishop of Amiens at Aumâle in December 1171, swearing with co-jurors that he had not confirmed the customs of Clarendon, nor knowingly provoked the king to the murder of Becket, and that he had been unaware of papal letters forbidding the coronation of the young king.[3] He was thus absolved, and accordingly announced his restoration to his suffragan.[4]

Puiset, as much involved as any of the other minor participants in the coronation of the young king, escaped the consequence of his actions with that agility he generally displayed in embarrassing situations. This is somewhat difficult to explain. His initial conduct, whatever its motives, had been less compromising than that of most of his colleagues. He was, as the Durham chronicler puts it, 'more innocent than most', so much so in fact that his name was often omitted from the publicists' narratives, even if he did not qualify as one who might be solicited to give some material aid to the exiled metropolitan.[5] At the same time the family of Blois had given adequate proof that they no longer hankered after the ways of Henry the Liberal, and for one reason or another outstripped the pope in their concern for Becket. On the other hand, the events of 1170–1 fall into that typical pattern of rash action followed by graceful redemption. The bishop's character was compounded, as is not uncommon, of arrogance and that disarming charm and easy eloquence which were once perhaps the soul of diplomacy. This plausibility, and, maybe, a measure of that amiability which all had marked in his uncle, Stephen, may have influenced Becket himself, and taken with Henry of Winchester's good standing with the archbishop, are possibly at the bottom of the Durham

---

[1] *Gesta*, I, 23 n.; Hoveden, II, 32–3.
[2] *Materials*, VII, 478.
[3] *Materials*, VII, 502; Diceto, I, 348; Foreville, *op. cit.* 332.
[4] *Materials*, VII, 504–6.
[5] *Scriptores Tres*, 10; *Materials*, II, 407; IV, 66.

story that the primate had intervened in Puiset's favour after the coronation.[1] His ambassador in 1170 was also presumably schooled to finesse and versed in the ways of what Newburgh called 'Roman subtlety'.[2] Yet no doubt the bishop's road to grace was shortened, here as elsewhere, by the reputation and influence of his wealth, and perhaps the delays were not unrelated to the calculation of the just price of repentance.

His policy throughout the dispute diverged equally from that of his family and his former colleagues. Hilary of Chichester supported the king; Jocelin of Salisbury, originally sympathetic to Becket, lived to feel—almost by accident—the blast of his archbishop's disapproval.[3] Henry of Winchester, however, consistently favoured the primate, by whom he was held in the highest esteem, whilst Theobald of Blois found the archbishop's distress a convenient opportunity and pretext to revenge his own misfortunes at the hands of the Angevin.[4] He supported Becket at Amboise in October 1170 and urged the pope to strong measures following the murder.[5] Archbishop William of Sens, the chief adviser of Louis VII, was likewise an intransigent opponent of Henry. He was in contact with Becket from the beginning of his exile, and aided some of his *familia* after their patron's death. Herbert of Bosham dedicated his revision of the Lombard's *Magna Glossatura* to Archbishop William,[6] and it was the Canterbury clerks, Master Alexander and Master Gunter, who were sent to the pope with news of the murder.[7] It was also through William's influence that the celebrated John of Salisbury eventually became bishop of Chartres.[8] Following Becket's death the archbishop of Sens interdicted Henry's continental lands, justifying his action by reference to a papal mandate designed to meet different con-

---

[1] *Scriptores Tres, loc. cit.*; this may of course merely refer to Becket's general concern at the tenor of the bulls issued in September 1170 (see above, p. 31).

[2] Newburgh, I, 79.   [3] Knowles, *op. cit.* 111-12.

[4] In 1160 and 1169 Henry had taken the castles of Montmirail and St Aignan, both of which were desired by Theobald (Torigni, 243; *Gesta*, I, 15; Hoveden, II, 20-2).

[5] Newburgh, I, 164; *Gesta*, I, 8, 15; Hoveden, II, 20.

[6] Glunz, *The Vulgate in England*, 341; Boase, *English Art, 1100-1216*, 186.

[7] *Materials*, VII, 433.

[8] *Materials*, VII, 429-33; Diceto, I, 410-12; *PL*, vol. 202, 567, no. CXVII.

ditions, and notwithstanding the refusal of his colleague of
Rouen to support him.[1] Thereafter he carried his enthusiasm
into an agitation for the martyr's canonization.[2]

Puiset, it seems, shared neither Theobald's opportunism nor
William's principles. His attitude was, indeed, not far removed
from complete indifference, and at the very climax of the
quarrel he appears to have been fully occupied in a vigorous
dispute of his own with a cell of St Albans lying in his diocese.[3]
Possibly he had something of Winchester's sympathy for
Becket (to whom he later dedicated a church),[4] but his own
essentially political outlook and his position at Durham no
doubt led him to regard the jurisdictional clash with a measure
of that indifference with which he apparently treated one aspect
of its outcome.[5] Before the exile of the primate and his party,
and the effectual retirement of Winchester and others of the
episcopal bench, he had little real weight or scope in politics.
He had none of Foliot's grievances against Becket, and no
reason, as Roger of York had, to hope for greater dignities for
his see. By 1170 the situation had changed; he had, for one
thing, no option but to obey the royal mandate. But it is also
quite probable that he regarded the coronation not only as an
opportunity to indulge his ostentatious tastes,[6] but, in view of
the clearer field, to gain the goodwill of the two kings and so
to enter the inner circle of royal esteem. The indifferent outcome
of this move may well explain his attitude to the rising of 1173.

The rebellion of the young king, engineered to some extent
by the able and unscrupulous Eleanor, was founded on the
discontent raised by Henry's vigorous rule and the rivalries and
selfishness of the royal children.[7] It was supported in England

---

[1] *Gesta*, I, 16-19; Hoveden, II, 18-20; *Materials*, VII, 442-4.

[2] Foreville, *L'Église et La Royauté en Angleterre*, 363, n. 2.

[3] See below, pp. 156-7. [4] See below, pp. 108, 113.

[5] See below, pp. 118, 172.

[6] Thus Reginald of Durham writes how it came to pass *ut dominus Hugo
Dunelmensis episcopus ad curiam regis coronandi, vel mandato urgente seu fama nobilitatis
instigante iter expediret* (*Libellus...Godrici*, 178-9). It is not certain to what date
this applies, but it was during the reign of Henry II, and since Puiset was probably
not present in 1154 (see above, p. 27), 1170 would seem to be indicated.

[7] Torigni, 256-7; *Gesta*, I, 34, 41-5; Newburgh, I, 171; Ralph of Coggeshall,
Chronicon Anglicanum, 17; Jordan Fantosme, *Chronique* (in *Chronicles*, III), 202-8;
Diceto, I, 350, 371; Poole, *From Domesday to Magna Carta*, 333-7.

by the great Anglo-Norman earls of Leicester, Norfolk and Chester, and on the Continent by Louis VII and the interrelated counts of Flanders, Champagne, Blois and Boulogne.[1] In the north of England it provided the opportunity for William of Scotland (a relative of the earls of Chester and Leicester)[2] to assert the traditional claims of his country to Northumberland and those counties of the north-west which his predecessor had been forced to abandon in 1157.[3]

Balanced against these forces were the whole of the episcopate, except Durham, who joined the general Blois opposition[4] —an interesting parallel to William of St Calais's earlier support of Odo of Bayeux against Rufus (1087); earls of the blood, such as Reginald of Cornwall, Hamelin of Warenne and William of Gloucester; the lesser baronage, such as the Kymes; and above all the sheriffs and professionals of the royal administration, such as the justiciar Richard de Luci, once a loyal servant of the house of Blois.[5]

Puiset's main concern was naturally with events in the north, where, after some delay—whilst he auctioned his support— William declared for the young king.[6] The Scots crossed the Tweed in the late summer (20 August); a large, ill-equipped and polyglot army, hamstrung by incompetent and divided leadership.[7] The castellan of Wark, Roger Stuteville, was allowed a truce, during which time he was able to fetch aid from farther south.[8] It was probably at this stage that the bishop of Durham, like the chapter of Hexham, perhaps

[1] The count of Boulogne had a claim on Mortain by reason of his marriage to Mary, one-time abbess of Romsey, a daughter of Stephen of England (cf. Diceto, I, 303).

[2] Robert II of Leicester (d. 1168), was a half-brother of Ada, mother of William the Lion. William and Robert III were cousins. Roger Beaumont, William's chancellor and later (1189) bishop of St Andrews, was a son of Robert III (*Early Sources*, II, 155, 494).

[3] *Gesta*, I, 45; Fantosme, 226; Torigni, 192; *Chronicle of Melrose*, ed. A. O. and M. O. Anderson, *sub anno* 1173.

[4] For a contact between Archbishop William of the White Hands and the young Henry, see J. R. Williams, 'William of the White Hands and Men of Letters', 373.   [5] *Gesta*, I, 51 n.

[6] *Gesta*, I, 45; Fantosme, 226–42.

[7] *Chronicle of Holyrood*, ed. A. O. and M. O. Anderson, 153; Fantosme, ll. 380–90, 640–3; *Melrose Chronicle*, *loc. cit.*

[8] Fantosme, ll. 483–530; *Melrose Chronicle*, *loc. cit.*

waiting surer indications of how the tide ran, and doubtless well-informed as to the habits of the more primitive elements of Scottish armies, came to terms with William, promising him unopposed passage through his lands.[1]

The Scots, having failed before Wark and Alnwick, were able to take the undefended Warkworth, and advanced to fail again before the great fortress of Newcastle. After some hesitation, natural enough in view of the list of unsubdued castles on their line of retreat, they turned west up the Tyne gap, by-passing yet another stronghold at Prudhoe, and eventually reached Carlisle.[2] There they remained before the walls until the news of the advance of Richard de Luci, fresh from his victory over the rebels at Leicester, sent them with undignified haste to Roxburgh. Luci burned Berwick as he rolled up the retreating army, and soon brought William to a truce which was to last until 13 January 1174.[3]

The cause of the young king, despite wide support, had shown few signs of prosperity in 1173. Reginald of Cornwall and Richard de Luci had captured the town of Leicester in July, and the earl of Leicester, an indifferent son of a great father, was taken at St Edmunds in October. On the Continent Brittany was cleared by the end of July, and the earl of Chester a prisoner. Louis VII was incapable of more than the sack of Verneuil, and after the fortuitous death of Matthew of Boulogne the forces which had taken Aumâle did no more.[4]

Thus far Puiset's attitude had been a mixture of caution and opportunism, with the former predominant, but all of which might be charitably interpreted as a desire to spare his diocese the pains of devastation. He had fought nobody, and, in the narrowest sense, committed himself to nobody. He was presumably in good favour, though nothing higher, with the

---

[1] *Per fines itaque Hugonis episcopi Dunolmensis securum transitum habens*...(Diceto, I, 376; Fantosme, ll. 532–7; *Scriptores Tres*, 10). This clearly means no resistance was offered at Norham, the episcopal castle on the Tweed.

[2] See PR *19 Henry II*, 113, for the expenses of the defence.

[3] *Gesta*, I, 61; Hoveden, II, 54; Fantosme, l. 835; Diceto, I, 376; Newburgh, I, 177–8. The course of the fighting is detailed in Fantosme, ll. 563–807; *Melrose Chronicle, sub anno*; *Gesta*, I, 50–61.

[4] For a general narrative, see Lady Stenton in *Cambridge Medieval History*, v, 569–71.

Scots for his inactivity in the autumn. He was included as a loyalist in the truce Luci negotiated with William the Lion. When this had almost elapsed he met the king of Scotland and secured an extension, *usque ad clausam Pasche* (i.e. the end of March), by a payment of 300 marks raised from the nobility of Northumberland. In this he did no more than bring the northern truce into line with that which Henry and Louis had negotiated at Caen, and he may have acted on royal instructions.[1] He was still waiting; perhaps he wished to see the drift of the opening campaigns; perhaps he needed the time to raise sufficient strength for a belated attempt to hold the balance in the north. He fortified Northallerton, in Yorkshire (where there seems to have been a fair amount of petty disaffection to Henry II),[2] and sent to his relatives for troops.[3] Beneath all this there is a sense more of weakness than grandiose opportunism; the Scots had to be bought off and mercenaries imported.

The pattern of events in 1174 was much the same as in the preceding year. William the Lion, now reinforced by Flemings, came south after Easter, and was again untroubled by the episcopal castle of Norham. Having once more failed before Wark[4] he sent raiders through Northumberland before retiring to Roxburgh. With another effort he advanced to establish a close siege of Carlisle, whilst other detachments took Liddel, Harbottle, Warkworth, Appleby,[5] Brough-under-Stainmore, and probed towards Richmond.[6] But this was isolated success. Already, in May, the royal bastard Geoffrey Plantagenet, with an energy and decision worthy of his father, had raised an army and taken Kinard Ferry, in Axholme, a stronghold of Roger Mowbray, who was then endeavouring to assist the Scots.[7] Thereafter he came north and, presumably somewhere in the vicinity of Bowes or Northallerton, compelled Puiset, then 'on

[1] *Gesta*, I, 64; Hoveden, II, 57. [2] Cf. *PR 21 Henry II*, 179–80.
[3] Hoveden, II, 57.
[4] The garrison in Wark was ten knights and forty sergeants (*PR 20 Henry II* 105). There were probably also various ancillaries.
[5] See *PR 22 Henry II*, 119 for the fines subsequently levied on those who were parties to this surrender.
[6] *Melrose Chronicle*, *sub anno* 1174; Fantosme, ll. 1156–514; Gerald of Wales, IV, 365–8; *Gesta*, I, 64–5; Newburgh, I, 182.
[7] Diceto, I, 379; Gerald of Wales, IV, 364–5.

the point of swerving to the opposite side', to take an oath of
loyalty. This accomplished, he joined Archbishop Roger of
York in the capture of Mowbray's remaining castles at
Malzeard and Thirsk, thus depriving the Scots of any opportunity for a contemplated drive to the south through the Vale
of York.[1] William drew off from Carlisle, struck a passing blow
at Prudhoe, and burned his way back through Northumberland
at the news of the approach of an English army which advanced through Durham and Newcastle to take the un-
suspecting king at Alnwick on 13 July.[2] Inopportunely for
Puiset, his allies landed at Hartlepool the very day William was
captured. It was no mere garrison force, but an army of forty
knights (that is four times the size of the knightly contingent
that had held Wark) and 500 Flemish mercenaries under the
command of the bishop's nephew, Hugh du Puiset, count of
Bar-sur-Seine.[3] The bishop hastily but wisely dismissed the
Flemings—having first provided them with pay and provisions
for forty days[4]—but sent the knights and their commander to
the new fortress of Northallerton.[5] By this time the rebels
were finished; Huntingdon surrendered on 21 July, the earl of
Norfolk shortly after, and when Henry returned to France
Louis VII briskly abandoned the siege of Rouen.

It might be said, somewhat unhistorically perhaps, that
Puiset was the only member of the English episcopate not
openly hostile to a retrogressive movement essentially the
work of those great feudatories who made sport of the Capetians. It may be that he was not unwilling to see the royal
authority in England similarly relaxed, for the traditions of his
relatives, with no record of service, were hardly in its favour.
As in the Becket dispute, his policy, with its apparent

[1] Diceto, I, 384; Newburgh, I, 182; Fantosme, ll. 1326–36; Hoveden, II, 58;
Gesta, I, 68–9; Gerald of Wales, IV, 366–7.

[2] Fantosme, ll. 1705–820; Hoveden, II, 63; Newburgh, I, 183–5; *Gesta*, I,
65–7; *Libellus...Cuthberti*, 272.

[3] It is interesting to note that in *PR 21 Henry II*, 180, Fulk of Selby was fined
£10 for sending his ship to Flanders.

[4] This precise mention of forty days, though of no feudal significance, is of
interest in relation to the terms of military service (cf. Stenton, *The First Century
of English Feudalism*, 176).

[5] Hoveden, II, 63; *Gesta*, I, 67.

opportunism, is difficult to assess. It may have been inspired by
sheer timidity or by excessive caution and that indecisiveness
which was such a chronic political weakness of the house of
Blois. As it was he took no active part on either side, though
there are some extremely tenuous indications of actual contact
with the English rebels. He was a friend of the family of
Walterville, or Watteville, one of whose members was an
important official of his household.[1] It was Abbot William de
Watteville whom Richard of Canterbury deposed from Peterborough in 1175, on account of certain military operations
against his monks, whilst at the same time, and perhaps more
significantly, he had incurred the royal animosity *eo quod ipse
receptaverat Radulfum de Walterville, fratrem suum, qui fuit cum
inimicis regis apud Huntendonam*. Following his deposition William
retired to Durham, where he was given a comfortable fee at
Newton, 'by the accommodation and alms of the lord bishop'.[2]
Beyond this there is nothing but circumstantial evidence of
even lighter weight; the fortification of Northallerton; the
presence of the bishop in Yorkshire in 1174, and the assumption
of Geoffrey Plantagenet that he was about to enter into active
alliance with the Scots. But inactivity in 1173 and a general
failure to resist the Scots—the prelude to one of the main
themes of the history of the bishopric—were sufficient evidence
of disloyalty to those less righteous and more critical than
Gerald of Wales. Coggeshall had no doubts as to the bishop's
guilt, and to Fantosme, who was particularly well informed, he
was 'all one with King William'.[3] Yet the Durham chronicler,
who was no blind devotee of Puiset, suggests he was more
maligned than guilty.[4] It may be that he originally desired
nothing more than to protect his diocese—seeking only peace,
as Fantosme reports it.[5] He was at this stage engaged not only
in the reform of his estates, but also in a fair measure of
domestic and ecclesiastical building, all of which must have

[1] *FPD*, 247.
[2] *Gesta*, I, 106; Diceto, I, 402; *PU*, II, no. 249; *PR 23 Henry II*, 104; *BB*, 2. For
further light on Abbot William, see *Selby Coucher Book*, nos. 85 and 86; *VCH
Northants*, II, 87.
[3] Ralph of Coggeshall, *Chronicon Anglicanum*, 17–18; Fantosme, l. 1604.
[4] *Scriptores Tres*, 10.   [5] Fantosme, ll. 535–7.

affected his revenues and perhaps moderated his political ambitions. But then other factors came into play. It was his misfortune to be nearest to the most active member of the rebel alliance, and he was probably impressed by the spasmodic successes achieved by the Scots. He seems to have contemplated declaring for William at a time when the greatest fortresses in the north, Newcastle, Carlisle and Richmond were all in danger, and when the ravaging of the Flemish-Gaelic armies was at its worst.[1] The rebellion was, in fact, on the point of collapse, though whether Puiset knew of the set-backs in the south and on the Continent is a different matter. His situation in May 1174 was that Northumberland was overrun and the county of Durham almost encircled by Scottish armies. Henry II considered the north as good as lost, and his officers were even more pessimistic.[2] There is, again, the possibility that his desire to play some conspicuous role in national politics, which seems to have influenced him in 1170, led him to pay more attention to the views of his Continental relatives who were behind the rising of 1173. In this connexion it is worth recalling that in 1172 Burchard Puiset, Hugh's son and intimate counsellor, was in the company of Henry the Liberal of Champagne.[3] It has been suggested that the bishop, free from the restraint of Winchester's caution and disgruntled by the failure of his policy in 1170, aimed to re-enact something of Winchester's role of the 1140's in 1174.[4] This overrates his abilities if not his ambitions, and the death of his uncle did little to relieve him of that reverence for the Angevin will so marked in 1160 and 1170. In any case there was now no room for a mediator, and no real candidate for Henry's throne. Puiset's military strength, until the arrival of his Flemings, must have been too slight to be of consequence to either side. Although he was in a position to raise an army, his indecision was such that it was only available when the war had ended. He had displayed himself as successively intimidated by the Scots and the English, and had never been capable of giving

[1] *Gesta*, 1, 66.
[2] Gervase of Canterbury, 1, 248; Diceto, 1, 381.
[3] See above, p. 23.   [4] Stubbs, 213.

either William or Henry the north. He had, in fact, done little but demonstrate his own irrelevance to its successful defence. He missed the opportunity, so ably seized by Roger of York and Geoffrey Plantagenet, to command the northern forces, and to deal with William's ill-equipped assortment of Celts and Flemings, who were incapable of taking a well-maintained castle and who showed no competence in the face of any determined opposition.

As it was his policy lacked almost equally the benefits of caution or committal; 'his temporizing...', as Stubbs wrote with the grandeur of his century, 'had redounded to his own confusion'.[1] His failure to resist the Scots was sufficient evidence of his motives for the loyalists; he had served the king *male et ficte*.[2] His negotiations with William were of questionable value. It is a strange reflection on his political sagacity that he could have contemplated exchanging the rule of the distant Angevin in Northumberland for that of the proximate Scot, even assuming that he had realized the indifferent qualities of the Lion. He may have saved Durham (though not Northumberland, where his church had many estates) the pains of invasion. Yet it is doubtful whether William intended to cross the Tyne so far east, or whether, had he so wished, he would—or could —have spared the bishopric.

In July Puiset, now knowing how matters stood in the north, and being no man for vain martyrdom, met the king at Northampton, and there, as if a defeated rebel, surrendered the castles of Durham, Norham and Northallerton into his hands. Durham and Norham, it would appear, were thereafter committed by Henry to the care of Roger Conyers and William Neville.[3] The reception at Northampton was scarcely friendly. Only with great difficulty could the bishop secure permission for his nephew, the count of Bar, to return to France.[4] Jukel of Smeaton, one of the episcopal *familia*, was fined over £67 for communing with the king's enemies, and the bishop's vill of

---

[1] Stubbs, *Constitutional History*, I, 481.
[2] *Gesta*, I, 160–1; *Scriptores Tres*, 10.
[3] *Gesta*, I, 73, 160–1; Hoveden, II, 65; PR *21 Henry II*, 165.
[4] *Gesta*, *loc. cit.*; Hoveden, *loc. cit.*

Northallerton paid 40 marks for the same offence. In York a number of families with whom Puiset was in contact were fined for selling goods and weapons to the rebels.[1] It is worthy of comment that no tenants from the county of Durham itself figure amongst those amerced. Whether this was fortuitous, or whether it indicates a loyalty which may have influenced the bishop's hesitations, cannot be decided.[2]

Durham's favour was at a low ebb. He followed the king during the next few years seeking to expedite *negotium suum*— presumably the return of his castles. He paid the enormous fine of 2000 marks (*immensam pecunie quantitatem*, as the Durham chronicle describes it[3]) that they might stand, and that he might again know the king's love.[4] In the event Durham and Norham were not dismantled, but Northallerton, like most other rebel strongholds, was eventually demolished in accordance with clause eight of the Assize of Northampton. There was, however, some delay (the work being recorded under 1177), which, though not uncommon, perhaps indicates an amelioration in the bishop's fortunes.[5] It is not clear when the two surviving castles were restored, though certainly later than 1177, when the king was advised not to return them, and accordingly made arrangements for their disposal in the event of either his own, or the bishop's death. Should he die first the castles were to be handed back to the bishop on the orders of either Richard de Luci, Richard, bishop of Winchester, or Geoffrey, bishop of Ely. Should the bishop die first they were to be returned to the church of Durham 'that its right be not diminished'.[6] The move was eminently fair. Moreover Henry, like his son after him, respected the episcopal wealth, and if Puiset did not enjoy the speedy success of the earl of Chester, who regained all his confiscated lands in 1177, he was not, on the other hand, treated

[1] PR 21 Henry II, 174, 179-80.
[2] The fact that Roger Conyers should have taken custody of one of the forfeited castles is important. He was the hereditary constable of Durham, and there are contemporary indications that he was involved in some dispute with the bishop, or had suffered some infringement of his fee, all of which may have some bearing on the views expressed in the text, cf. below, p. 192.
[3] *Scriptores Tres*, 10.
[4] *Gesta*, I, 160-1; Hoveden, II, 133.
[5] *Gesta*, I, 178; Hoveden, II, 101; Diceto, I, 404.   [6] *Gesta*, I, 178.

with any exceptional severity. As Stubbs pointed out, the king took into his hands all the castles of England and Normandy, not excepting Ongar, belonging to the faithful Richard de Luci, in 1176–7, and though lands were gradually returned to their owners, the custody of castles was withheld and they were, in general, subjected to a much closer supervision than hitherto.[1] Again, whilst great fortresses like Leicester, Groby and Thirsk were destroyed, Puiset lost only Northallerton, which he had hardly had time to develop, and by 1176 was restored to sufficient favour to be able to purchase the Yorkshire fee of Market Weighton for his son, Henry.[2]

Durham was returned in time to be seized again in 1182 when the king was moved to wrath by Hugh's refusal to surrender 300 marks, a legacy of Roger of York, who had died the previous year. The archbishop had left the money that it might be distributed among the poor and sick, and in various other pious causes. This was not to the liking of the avaricious Henry. Royal officers were sent to demand the money from Hugh, who replied, *non minori constantia animi quam verbi*, that he had employed it as the archbishop had directed to the benefit of the halt, lame and blind, and in the repair of churches and bridges, and if the king wanted it he must seek it.[3] Thereupon the royal disfavour once more descended on Durham. Norham Castle was again in the hands of a royal constable in 1185, and from thence to the end of Henry's reign.[4] The episode need not be taken at its mere face value. Its real significance lies in the tightening royal grasp on private strongholds and Henry's caution when threatened with renewed rebellion in 1183. Something similar appears to have occurred in Yorkshire without any such dramatic fiscal provocation, and the Pipe Rolls of 1186, 1187 and 1190 show that the king retained an interest in both Richmond and Bowes castle, and an important part of the Honor of Richmond even after the remarriage of the duchess, Constance.[5]

---

[1] Stubbs, 120; *Gesta*, I, 124.
[2] *Gesta*, I, 160–1; *PR 22 Henry II*, 100.
[3] Hoveden, II, 265–6; *Gesta*, I, 289; Diceto, II, 12.
[4] *PR 32 Henry II*, 125; *PR 33 Henry II*, 20; *PR 34 Henry II*, 2.
[5] *EYC*, IV, 112.

Although obviously regarded with suspicion, Puiset was active in political life from 1177 onwards, a prelude to his brief prominence under Richard. He was with the king from March to July in 1177, being one of the bishops present at the introduction of regular canons to Holy Cross, Waltham, in June, a reform Henry accomplished as part of his projected penance for the fate of Becket.[1] He was again in the royal presence in December 1178 and August 1181. It was at this stage that the old problem of the Latin Orient once more impinged on the politics of the west. By 1183 the energies and superb strategy of the great Sultan Saladin had created a Moslem empire which stretched from Cyrenaica to the Tigris, embracing the wealth of Egypt and the great cities of Damascus and Aleppo. He over-awed the Seldjuks of Anatolia and the East, and was supported by the Caliph at Baghdad. The Christian empire of Byzantium was no longer a danger, and it only remained for the Sultan to suppress the alien intruders whose possession of Palestine and the Syrian littoral he found such a dishonour to Islam.[2] In the Frankish kingdom of Jerusalem, thus encircled, there reigned but the blind and crippled leper, Baldwin, unable to move without assistance and racked with the pain of decay. Beyond him there loomed the fatal prospect of an anarchical minority. It was in these circumstances that Heraclius, the Patriarch, and Arnold of Toroga, the Grand Master of the Temple, were dispatched to preach the Crusade in western Europe. The history of their disappointing embassy is of no direct concern here, for Puiset, despite the traditions of his house, showed no more concern for the fortunes of Jerusalem than had his cousin Stephen in 1170.[3] He may have been at Reading in the spring of 1185 when all wept to hear from the Patriarch the great trials of the Holy Land. Henry was momentarily moved to accept the keys of Jerusalem,[4] but in a less emotional moment, having Philip Augustus before his eyes, returned them. It was after the subsequent assembly at London, in March, according to Howden, that the bishop, like many other magnates, took the

---

[1] *Gesta*, I, 134–5, 173–4; see below, App. III, *sub annis*.
[2] Runciman, *The Kingdom of Jerusalem and the Frankish East, 1100–87*, 435.
[3] See above, p. 23.   [4] Hoveden, II, 299; Gerald of Wales, V, 360–1.

cross.[1] But Henry was now concerned with more local matters, and Puiset accompanied him abroad in April on his way to deal with his refractory son, Richard, and to consult with Philip. One pressing question was that of the Vexin,[2] reopened by the death of the young Henry in 1183, and the consequent demands of the French king for the restoration of his sister Margaret's *maritagium*.[3] Puiset was the senior English bishop present at Gisors in March 1186, when the matter was discussed and settled.[4]

He returned to Durham before Easter the same year, his presence being necessary for the spiritual wellbeing of the north, since *nec erat aliquis episcopus qui officium episcopale faceret in archiepiscopatu Eboracensi nec in episcopatu Dunelmensi.* He joined the king at Carlisle early in the summer, when Henry, the active overlord of Scotland since 1174, was dealing with a rebellion in Galloway. Together with William of Scotland, Earl David, and Rannulf de Glanville he was dispatched to attempt to bring in the intractable Roland, son of Uctred, whose energy and ingenuity had so far defeated the slender abilities of the Lion and his local officials. The ambassadors guaranteed Roland a safe-conduct and brought him with them to Carlisle, where he duly made his peace with Henry.[5]

In September of the same year Puiset was present at Marlborough in a council especially convened for elections to the sees of York, Salisbury and Exeter. The chapter of York offered the king five names, those of the dean, Hubert Walter; the cantor, Hamo; Archdeacon Laurence of Bedford; Master Roger Arundel; and Bernard, prior of Newburgh. But as at Lincoln in May, none was acceptable to Henry, who in the chastening days of misfortune was showing a more canonical attitude in these matters than had hitherto been apparent.[6]

He was once more with the king in February 1187, and having accompanied him to France, probably returned in January 1188 to rejoin him at Geddington in February. It was here, after the

---

[1] Hoveden, II, 302; Diceto, II, 33; but cf. below, p. 47. The year 1188 is the more probable date.   [2] Above, pp. 27–8.

[3] *Gesta*, I, 343; Diceto, II, 40; see below App. III, *sub anno*.

[4] *DB*, II, 275..   [5] *Gesta*, I, 348–9.

[6] *Gesta*, I, 352. For Hubert Walter, see below, p. 176, n. 4.

kingdom of Jerusalem had been overwhelmed by the disaster of Hattin, that Puiset really seems to have taken the cross. He lived thereafter (or at least for a short time, according to William of Newburgh, who found his secular splendour and ambitions cause for reflection on the shortcomings of the episcopate) in unaccustomed austerity, even wearing a hair shirt under his fine delicate garments, *pro castigandis peccatis suis*.[1]

He was again sent to Scotland sometime in 1188 to collect the new tithe from which it was proposed to finance the Third Crusade and the defence of what was left of the Holy Land. William the Lion apparently hoped to negotiate on the basis of the restoration of those castles he had surrendered in 1174. It seems that he met Hugh near Wark, and there forbade him to enter the country. He then perhaps offered a lump sum of 4000 or 5000 marks which was to cover both the tithe and the castles. This, according to Howden, was rejected. The *Gesta* contains a more elaborate statement, suggesting that Henry accepted the proffered sum and gave a promise of restoration conditional on the tithe being raised. William accordingly agreed to pay, provided that he could persuade his tenants to support him. It was at this stage that Puiset and his colleagues met the Scottish king and his barons near Wark. But neither eloquence nor threats could move the Scots to consent to the tithe, and the royal ambassadors consequently withdrew from their unfruitful mission.[2]

It was only at the end of Henry's life that Puiset achieved any office that was demonstrably 'official'. He was perhaps a royal justice in 1179–80,[3] and in 1188–9 was an itinerant justice in Yorkshire, Cumberland and Northumberland, together with William de Stuteville, William fitzAudelin, Master Roger Arundel and others who clearly supplied the necessary expert knowledge.[4] There is some trace of the activities of the circuit

---

[1] Newburgh, I, 275; II, 438; *Gesta*, II, 33.

[2] *Gesta*, II, 44–5; Hoveden, II, 339; Foreville, *L'Église et La Royauté en Angleterre*, 451.

[3] BM, Wolley Charter, I, 46, mentions a plea *in curia domini regis apud Westmonasterium, coram justiciis domini regis, scilicet Rannulfo de Glanvill', Hugone Dunelmensi, Johane Norwicensi, Galfrido Heliensi, episcopis.*

[4] See below, App. III, *sub annis*.

in the records of those 'new pleas and new conventions' levied before, or by the bishop and his colleagues, during the course of which duties he appears to have received an allowance of 18*d*.[1] Thus a fine was taken at York on 1 February 1189, between the prior of Guisborough and the daughters of Aluered of Hutton, concerning land in that vill, whilst Nicholas, son of Richard, son of Roald, quit land in Guisborough to the canons which he had previously claimed of them in a plea moved before the same justices.[2]

The reasons for these late favours, which led the author of the *Gesta* to number Hugh among the royal familiars,[3] are not far to seek. It may be that the king, chastened by the death of the young Henry, the persistent ingratitude of his remaining children and the general harshness of life, felt somewhat more charitable towards another old man, whom, on the whole, he had treated with respect.[4] But there were other more prosaic factors. The death of the young king in 1183, and the accession of Philip Augustus to the throne of France in 1180, brought the question of the Vexin back to political prominence. At the same time a momentary change in the fortunes of the house of Blois, with the paralysis and death of their creature, Louis VII, put the family and Henry II into alliance, if not friendship. In 1180 Counts Theobald and Stephen appealed for Angevin support when the young Philip sought to break from the close circle which had governed the country in the preceding reign.[5] It was by Henry's mediation that some form of peace was reached, and consequently, in 1181, the count of Champagne, at the king's request, checked Philip's contemplated invasion of the empire.[6] Again, in 1182, the same French interest attempted to give some assistance to Henry the Lion, Duke of Saxony and Bavaria and son-in-law of the Angevin, during his renowned troubles with Frederick Barbarossa.[7] In view of these relations,

---

[1] PR *1 Richard I*, ed. J. Hunter, 158.

[2] See below, App. III, *sub anno*.   [3] *Gesta*, II, 44.

[4] For a mark of royal favour, cf. Hoveden, III, 246.

[5] *Gesta*, I, 244–5; Hoveden, II, 196; Diceto, II, 6; *Cambridge Medieval History*, VI, 291–2.

[6] d'Arbois de Jubainville, *Histoire des Ducs et des Comtes de Champagne*, III, 110.

[7] Hoveden, II, 201.

which prevailed till *c.* 1182, and the diplomatic uncertainty thereafter, it is not surprising that the most distinguished English member of the house of Blois should achieve a certain eminence, or that others of the family should make a number of appearances in England. Count Theobald was graciously received in 1184,[1] and Archbishop William of Rheims on other occasions.[2] But finally, perhaps, Puiset owed his reinstatement with the crown to changes less momentous. He was a convenient man to send into Scotland now that William the Lion was subdued, and in this and other matters Henry's choice amongst the hierarchy was limited since death had thinned away many of his old servants.[3] So it was that he came to make use of Puiset's obvious abilities and wide experience, the merits of which were emphasized by present necessity.

With the accession of Richard I, Hugh leaped to that prominence for which he had clearly always longed. The king's needs and the bishop's ambition were attractive poles. He joined the duke as soon as he arrived in England, took what was to become Durham's traditional role at the coronation, and was thereafter almost continuously in Richard's company until March 1190.[4] His wealth, which inspired what was described by the fulsome as a filial affection in Richard, ensured him an adequate share of the great harvest of privilege and liberty reaped as the king prepared for his crusade.[5] On 18 September 1189 he received the manor and wapentake of Sadberge (a detached portion of Northumberland, lying in what is now the south-east corner of County Durham), with all appurtenances and regalian rights, and with the service of certain knights holding of the crown between Tyne and Tees.[6] In return he quit to the king six episcopal fees in Lincolnshire, and promised 600 marks.[7] On 25 November he received the

---

[1] *Gesta*, I, 313.   [2] *Gesta*, I, 281; Hoveden, II, 167.

[3] Roger of York died in 1181, Foliot in 1187, Richard of Ilchester in 1188, and Geoffrey Ridel in 1189, to mention only a few.

[4] See below, App. III.

[5] *Scriptores Tres*, 14; *Gesta*, II, 85; Hoveden, III, 15.

[6] See below, pp. 187–8.

[7] DC Durham, Cart. I, fo. 248, printed in *Scriptores Tres*, App. no. XL; *CChR*, III, 393; *Gesta*, II, 87; Hoveden, III, 13–15; PR 2 *Richard I*, 21 (*Hugo episcopus Dunelmensis debet DC m. pro escambio de Satberge*).

earldom of Northumberland for life, with all regalian rights therein, but without the valuable mines of Carlisle, despite the terms of his charter.[1] For this he promised 2000 marks.[2] His subsequent investiture with the office, which was by sword and ring, provoked a feeble royal witticism which was duly retailed by several chroniclers. It would seem that somewhat earlier he had also proffered a further 1000 marks that he might be justiciar and quit from his crusading vow.[3] From this latter he was indeed released by Clement III (in a bull dated 4 December) under the most favourable conditions *ad preces...karissimi in Christo filii nostri Ricardi*.[4]

The details of his appointment as justiciar are obscure. It would appear that at the council of Pipewell (16 September) Puiset and earl William de Mandeville were jointly nominated to succeed the famous Glanville.[5] In view of their complete lack of legal training it seems reasonable to accept Howden's statement that there were associated with them for judicial purposes William Marshal, Geoffrey fitzPeter, William Brewer, Robert de Whitfield and Roger fitzReinfred.[6] It is not clear who was the senior partner, or whether some form of diarchy was seriously proposed. The claims of the two magnates were nearly balanced; the bishop was a relative of Richard, the earl a distinguished servant of the late king. It is, however, worthy of comment that it was Mandeville who was sent abroad on an important diplomatic mission the same year, whilst Puiset was retained in England.[7]

[1] Cf. *PR 3 Richard I*, 55.

[2] DC Durham, 3. 13. Pont. E 1 (copy), printed in *Scriptores Tres*, App. no. XLII; *Scriptores Tres*, 14; Newburgh, II, 438; Hoveden, III, 15; Devizes, 386, says the king took £10,000 from the bishop, and the Durham chronicle makes it £11,000, but cf. *PR 2 Richard I*, 21 (*Hugo episcopus Dunelmensis debet MM m.pro comitatu Northumbrie habendo*).

[3] *Gesta*, II, 87, 90–1; Hoveden, III, 16; Newburgh, I, 304–5. Puiset paid a fine for something unspecified at this time (*PR 2 Richard I*, 59).

[4] A copy of the exemption is preserved in DC Durham, Cart. III, fo. 153ᵛ. It is a bull of Clement III, but has the caption *Celestini Papa* (followed in *Scriptores Tres*, App. no. XLIV). The date is correct for Clement (see *JL*, II, 559). It might be noticed that Puiset's relatives, Theobald of Blois and Henry II of Champagne (son of Henry the Liberal) rendered distinguished services in the crusade, the latter, with Richard's support, becoming king of Jerusalem in 1192 (R. Grousset, *Histoire des Croisades*, III, 36, 93, 125).   [5] *Gesta*, II, 87, 90–1; Hoveden, III, 16.

[6] Hoveden, III, 16; cf. *Gesta*, II, 101.   [7] *Gesta*, II, 92; Hoveden, III, 19.

On 12 December Earl William died at Rouen.[1] Contrary to what is generally assumed it would seem that there was no redistribution of office, though Howden refers to both Puiset and the chancellor, William de Longchamp, as chief justiciars.[2] On the whole it is more probable that, as stated by the *Gesta*, Durham alone was chief justiciar, in which position he was subsequently replaced by Longchamp (March 1190).[3] The king departed for France on 12 December, together with his chancellor, leaving Puiset established in the castle of Windsor in effectual control of the country, though assisted, as already noticed, by the above-mentioned royal officers.[4] The chancellor was absent until 17 December, whereafter he and Puiset jointly administered the kingdom, with Durham in nominal control,[5] notwithstanding his failure to obtain the royal seal of absence.[6] In this context, and in view of subsequent events and the undisguised rivalry of the two bishops, it is important to note that of the sixteen writs and charters (so far known) issued by the administrators during this period (*c.* 15 December 1189– *c.* 5 March 1190), only six appear to have been witnessed by Hugh Puiset, and only one issued on his sole authority.[7]

The chancellor and justiciar were summoned to the royal presence in March, and joined the king at Bonsmoulins on the twelfth of the month. In the ensuing council Longchamp was promoted chief justiciar and Puiset's initial commission reduced to that of justiciar of the north.[8] Shortly after this victory the chancellor returned to England (*c.* 2 April) and Durham followed about a fortnight later. His authority in the north was now weakened by Longchamp's invasion of his nominal sphere of influence when, early in May, he visited York to punish those responsible for the attack on the Jews the pre-

[1] Ralph of Coggeshall, *Chronicon Anglicanum*, 26.
[2] Hoveden, III, 28; cf. *Gesta*, II, 101. These events are examined by B. Wilkinson in *The Government of England during the absence of Richard I*. His conclusions (5–6) do not favour Puiset's authority, but cf. Stubbs, 209, n. 1.
[3] *Gesta*, II, 101.
[4] *Gesta*, *loc. cit.*; Hoveden, III, 28; it cost the constable of the Tower 7s. 3d. to supply the bishop with wine (*PR 2 Richard I*, 3).
[5] *Gesta*, II, 101.   [6] Wilkinson, *op. cit.* 6 n.
[7] See below, App. III, *sub annis*.
[8] *Gesta*, II, 106; Hoveden, III, 32; Stubbs, 210.

ceding March.[1] Worse was to come. When Hugh claimed office he was grossly outwitted in a series of incidents which cast a sad light on his political sagacity. Expelled from the Exchequer he sought his rival, whom he met at Blyth, returning from York. He greeted him with mistimed arrogance and talked of his powers with all the grand indiscretion of offended dignity. Longchamp, strong in the knowledge of his own authority and its recent manifestations, disguised his intentions and expressed his willingness to admit Puiset to his new office. The two agreed to meet the following week at Tickhill, or Southwell according to Howden and Gerald.[2] On the appointed day Hugh went unescorted into the castle, there to find that his rival had a more recent and extensive commission which he was thereupon forced to announce. He was seized prisoner and so taken in shame to London, where he was stripped of all his great honours so recently received, and obliged to give hostages (his own son, Henry, and a Durham knight of the episcopal entourage, Gilbert de Laley) as security for his good behaviour. He was then allowed to withdraw to his Yorkshire manor of Howden, but scarcely had he arrived when Osbert de Longchamp, the chancellor's brother, and William de Stuteville appeared at the head of an armed force, under instructions to take the bishop should he refuse to give security to remain there. Puiset complied, promising not to move except by licence of the king or the chancellor.[3] He then sent messengers to Marseilles to explain his woes to Richard, who, displeased at the news, ordered (5 August 1190) the restitution of Northumberland and Sadberge, and recouped the bishop for his loss of Windsor Castle and its appurtenant manors by a somewhat unconsoling allowance of £24. 15s. a year in Pickering.[4] There was no mention of office.

[1] Newburgh, I, 323; Gesta, II, 107; Stubbs, 218–19.

[2] Hoveden, III, 35; Gerald of Wales, IV, 428.

[3] Devizes, 389–91; Gesta, II, 109; Hoveden, III, 35; Gerald of Wales, IV, 428; Stubbs, 219–20.

[4] Hoveden, III, 38–9; Gesta, II, 110; Poole, From Domesday to Magna Carta, 352. The charter for the regrant of Sadberge is preserved in a fourteenth-century copy at Durham (3. 1. Reg. no. 27, printed in Scriptores Tres, App. no. xli, cf. CChR, III, 394). Puiset's loss of Northumberland can be seen in PR 2 Richard I, 18, where Reginald Basset accounts for the county for half a year, and cf. ibid. 19 for

Puiset was thus restored to honour if not to power. But it was not long before the chancellor was driven into exile, and then the course of events and the ageing bishop's persistent and undiscerning ambition drew him back to the centre of politics. His greatest chance had gone and new names came to positions of responsibility, but his diplomatic experience, wealth and enormous strength in the north were gladly employed by the royal officials who struggled to hold England against the king's brother John. Thus Puiset's enforced retirement ended at the fall of the chancellor. Thereafter he appears as a justice in a final concord made at Westminster in March 1192, and again in a concord in the Exchequer in October 1193.[1]

The year 1191 was largely filled by John's attempts to overthrow Longchamp.[2] The chancellor, though patently not free from greed and ambition, had sought to fulfil a difficult task with indelicate vigour. But such was his standing in the royal confidence that not until the queen mother, Eleanor, herself went to Messina in February, would Richard give credence to the complaints against his servant. Thereupon Archbishop Walter of Rouen was commissioned as an additional justiciar and dispatched to England. He arrived in April, but either from policy or timidity took no action for the time being.[3] John strengthened his party, whilst Longchamp, uncertain as to Rouen's commission, and anxious for succession to the vacant see of Canterbury, imported foreign mercenaries. Trouble flared up when the chancellor, for proper reasons, attempted to dismiss one of John's men, Gerard de Camville (a tenant on the Durham fee in Lincolnshire),[4] from the shrievalty of Lincoln, and replace him in that vital castle by his

---

the loss of Sadberge. The loss of Windsor is similarly recorded (*ibid.* 31), where the bishop owes for the farm of the appurtenant manors for 'three parts of the year' only. The allowance in Pickering first appears in *PR 3 Richard I*, 61.

[1] See below, App. III, *sub annis*.

[2] Stubbs, 224–5, 226.

[3] Newburgh, I, 337; *Gesta*, II, 158; Hoveden, III, 96–7; Gervase of Canterbury, I, 497; Gerald of Wales, IV, 400–1; Stubbs, 230, n. 2.

[4] Gerard de Camville married Nicholaa, eldest daughter of Richard de la Haie, whose family held two fees of the old enfeoffment of the bishop of Durham in Lincolnshire in 1166 (*LR*, 416). The descent of the fee may be seen in *Rotuli de Dominabus*, ed. J. H. Round, 12 and *PR 7 Richard I*, 156.

own nominee, William de Stuteville.[1] John, spoiling for a show of strength for which he probably knew the chancellor had no mind, seized Tickhill and Nottingham, and ordered Longchamp out of Lincoln, where he had gone to deal with Camville. Walter of Rouen intervened, and a truce was eventually patched up at Winchester in July, when Puiset, now released from his confinement at Howden, was amongst the mediators.[2]

John, having measured his opponent, and urged on by Hugh de Nunant, bishop of Coventry, now moved to break the chancellor. He assumed a certain righteousness by airing the grievances of those Longchamp had offended by his brusque methods and greedy activity. He made much of the trials of his brother, Geoffrey of York, who having improperly arrived in the country with his encouragement, had been indecorously thrust into prison by one of the chancellor's relatives, amid scenes which inevitably evoked memories of Becket.[3] Longchamp was summoned to meet the barons and justices at Loddon Bridge, near Reading, but, alarmed at the strength of his opponents, retreated to the Tower. On 8 October, at a great meeting at St Paul's, at which Puiset 'and nearly all the magnates of the realm' were present, his numerous shortcomings were detailed. He was then stripped of his office and castles, and after various humiliations, including some of indelicate humour, allowed to leave the country.[4]

Thereafter Eleanor, assisted by 'the community of the realm', maintained such peace as there was. She prevented John from going to France in the spring of 1192 to intrigue with Philip Augustus, recently returned disgruntled from Palestine.[5] When, in March 1192, the chancellor, once more legate, landed at Dover, she would have temporized, but the council preferred

[1] Newburgh, I, 338; Devizes, 406; Hoveden, III, 134; *Gesta*, II, 207.

[2] Newburgh, I, 339; Hoveden, *loc. cit.*; *Gesta, loc. cit.*; Devizes, 407–8; J. H. Round, *The Commune of London*, 207–18.

[3] Devizes, 410–11; Gervase of Canterbury, I, 504–5; *Gesta*, II, 210–11; Diceto, II, 96–9; Gerald of Wales, IV, 392; Stubbs, 235–6.

[4] Newburgh, I, 341–3; Diceto, II, 100–1; Devizes, 413; Gervase of Canterbury, I, 507–8; *Gesta*, II, 212–20; Hoveden, III, 140–50; Gerald of Wales, IV, 398–407; Stubbs, 239–45.

[5] Devizes, 432; *Gesta*, II, 237; Stubbs, 248–51.

to bribe John rather than have Longchamp back.[1] At this time,
though his energies were largely absorbed in his disputes with
his archbishop, Puiset was edging his way back to power.[2] The
alignment of parties was still uncertain, and it is just possible
that he was contemplating an alliance with John. It was John
who had disposed of his worst rival, Longchamp, and who was
a potential lever under Archbishop Geoffrey. As already noticed
Gerard de Camville, whose activity in Lincolnshire had pre-
cipitated the crisis of 1191, was a Durham tenant. At Christmas
the same year John had joined Puiset at Howden, although the
bishop was then under a sentence of excommunication from
his metropolitan.[3] But for one reason or another the flirtation
got no further. Geoffrey's consecration had removed John's
last effective competitor for the crown, and the two brothers
were for the time reconciled.[4] Puiset, perhaps influenced by
that resurgence of loyalty to Richard effected by Eleanor, or
perhaps merely anticipating more support for his cause from
the queen, notoriously no friend of the unfortunate Geoffrey,
at least acted with less hesitation and more discretion than he
had shown in earlier crises. He seized his chance to establish
his position as a supporter of the existing régime in the summer
of 1192 when the royal administrators were glad to make use of
his well-known ability as a mediator to ease their problems in
Normandy. There the zeal of two papal legates and the shrewd
opportunism of Philip Augustus threatened to raise serious
trouble.

Celestine III had sent the legates, Octavian, bishop of Ostia,
and Jordan, cardinal priest of S. Pudentiana, into Normandy to
mediate in a dispute between Longchamp and the archbishop
of Rouen. They were refused admission to Gisors by William
fitzRadulf, seneschal and almost viceroy of Normandy, who, as
a good Angevin servant, pleaded he could receive no one without the king's permission. The cardinals urged the peaceful

[1] Devizes, 433; *Gesta*, II, 239; Hoveden, III, 188; Newburgh, I, 345-6; Gervase
of Canterbury, I, 512.
[2] Cf. below, pp. 176-81.
[3] See below, App. III, *sub anno*, and pp. 178-9.
[4] *Gesta*, II, 235-6; Hoveden, III, 179.

nature of their mission, but neither protests nor threats moved the citizens of Gisors (no doubt aware of forthcoming financial demands), who threatened them with violence unless they withdrew. As a result of these demonstrations Octavian interdicted Normandy and excommunicated the seneschal. Jordan, however, who was a friend of the king's, was unwilling to take such strong measures, much to the disgust of Philip Augustus, who thereupon ordered his expulsion from France.[1]

Puiset was dispatched to secure the remission of these sentences. He crossed from Dover to Wissant, and thence to Paris, where he met the ruffled cardinals and somewhat alleviated their distress by suitable blandishments (*blando sermone*). He persuaded Octavian to lift his sentence on certain conditions; William fitzRadulf and his militant supporters were to stand to ecclesiastical law on the injuries they had done the cardinals; the legates were to be allowed to come to Rouen, *non ut cardinales sed ut advenas*, where the clergy of Normandy were to find their expenses, and those of their retinue of fifty men and forty horses for ten days; the cardinals were to submit to the arbitration of Hugh of Durham and John, dean of Rouen, in all matters concerning the peace. But William fitzRadulf held to his original position and refused the legates entry—indeed it would seem there was little to be hoped for from the terms Puiset had negotiated, since they gave the legates practically all they had ever demanded. So the sentences remained, though the bishop, at fitzRadulf's request, followed the cardinals to Vézelay in a vain attempt to secure peace. Puiset returned to England, and the sentences were subsequently lifted by the pope.[2]

By January 1193, the news of Richard's capture and imprisonment in Germany was known. Hubert Walter, who had replaced Rouen in control, wrote to the bishop of Durham to

---

[1] The case achieved a certain celebrity, finding its way into canon law where it occurs in the work of the Anglo-Norman circle associated with John of Tynemouth (S. Kuttner and E. Rathbone in *Traditio*, VII (1949-51), 319; *Repertorium der Kanonistik*, 251-2).

[2] *Gesta*, II, 246-50; Hoveden, III, 193-4; Devizes, 419-20. It may have been by reason of this mission that Puiset received an allowance of £50 drawn on the farm of the mines of Carlisle (*PR 5 Richard I*, 77).

inform him of the event, sending a copy of the letter in which the Emperor Henry VI had conveyed his good fortune to Philip Augustus. Puiset was summoned to a council to be held at Oxford on 28 February, and was requested to order prayers throughout his diocese for the safety of the king.[1] John, gladly assuming that Richard would now never return, hastened to Philip to arrange a division of the spoils.[2] When he returned to England (about mid-Lent) and demanded the kingdom and homage it was decided to attack his two chief strongholds of Windsor and Tickhill. The justiciars themselves directed events at Windsor, whilst Puiset, replacing Archbishop Geoffrey of York, whose zeal and power were crippled by the disaffection of the royal officers, Hugh Bardolf and William de Stuteville, besieged Tickhill. The operations went well and the castle was on the point of surrender when, much to the bishop's disappointment, a general truce was arranged.[3] The amount of the king's ransom was probably known, and the justiciars, never men of great courage, no doubt felt it wise to concentrate on raising the enormous sum required, and so secure his speedy return, rather than bear the added expense of an attempt to contain John by force. Among the various expedients employed to secure the ransom it was ordered that the plate be taken from churches. Puiset, unwilling to see the cathedral he had but recently beautified thus denuded, legally redeemed its ornaments for 100 marks, and sent instead £2000 to the king, who, so we are given to believe, drew but small consolation from such a gift.[4]

In February 1194, Adam of Bury arrived in England with letters from John (who had retired to France at the news 'that the devil was unloosed') to his castellans ordering them to prepare to hold against the king. As soon as John's plans were known from Adam's liberal indiscretions, Hubert Walter held a council in which it was decided to strip John of all his lands.[5]

---

[1] Hoveden, III, 196–7.

[2] Hoveden, III, 204; Diceto, II, 106; Newburgh, I, 384–5; Stubbs, 251.

[3] Hoveden, III, 206–8; Newburgh, I, 390–1; Gervase of Canterbury, I, 515; Stubbs, 252–3.

[4] Hoveden, III, 210–11; *Scriptores Tres*, 14. Redemption of ornaments was allowed (Newburgh, I, 400).

[5] Hoveden, III, 236–7; Gervase of Canterbury, I, 523.

Puiset, in command of a great army drawn from Yorkshire, Northumberland and his own lands, and lavishly equipped with siege engines, once more appeared before the walls of Tickhill, whilst the earls of Derby and Chester attacked Nottingham, and Hubert Walter himself dealt with Marlborough.[1] On 13 March Richard arrived in England and summoned his barons to meet him at Southwell.[2] His presence inspired at first incredulity and then timorous reverence in those defending Tickhill, who sent two knights to offer him the castle, but he refused to consider anything but unconditional surrender. Puiset showed more moderation, and in parley with the constable, Robert de la Mare, promised him and his garrison *vitam et membra*—though on what authority and with what security does not appear. This had its effect, and by 27 March the castle had fallen and the bishop set out to meet the king at Nottingham, bringing his prisoners with him. Richard came out to greet the aged warrior, and both having dismounted, king and bishop met, each receiving the other with ostentatious affection.[3] The next day Nottingham surrendered, and John's rebellion was ended.

A great council held after the capture of Nottingham decided the fate of John and his guiding spirit, Hugh Nunant, and regulated the affairs of the kingdom with some regard for justice, but more for the needs of the royal purse.[4] Thereafter Richard moved south, accompanied, amongst others, by the bishop of Durham.[5] Puiset's service brought a momentary glow to Richard's heart, but these affectionate days soon sped. The bishop, in characteristic fashion, insulted the king of Scotland, who was then enjoying the Angevin favour as a potential bidder for Northumberland. Richard had left Northampton (12 April), whilst Hubert Walter and Puiset set out for Brackley, where Durham had a long-established hunting lodge. The episcopal servants, who had gone on ahead, were

---

[1] Hoveden, *loc. cit.*; Newburgh, I, 406–7; Gervase of Canterbury, I, 523–4; PR 6 *Richard I*, 145 (*in his que necessaria erant ad machinas et petrarias ad expugnationem castelli de Tickhill*, £20. 5. 1d).

[2] Hoveden, III, 238; PR 6 *Richard I*, 176.

[3] Hoveden, III, 239; Newburgh, I, 407.

[4] Hoveden, III, 241; PR 6 *Richard I*, 68, 102, 132, 145.

[5] See below, App. III, *sub anno*.

there preparing for the arrival of their master, when an advance party from the household of William of Scotland also arrived and unsuccessfully attempted to eject them. After this set-back William's servants moved to some inferior dwelling, whilst the Durham household awaited further developments. The bishop then arrived, and with his unfortunate determination in the face of smaller men, ordered that his tables be erected and spread, ignoring the advice of Hubert Walter that it might be tactful to leave the lodge to William. When the king of Scotland appeared, he was insulted to find himself thus dispossessed. He commanded that such food as had been prepared for him be given to the poor, and made off to complain to Richard, who was greatly displeased by what he heard.[1]

Durham's days of favour were over. The king, who needed the episcopal wealth, was put in mind of the bishop's unsatisfactory contribution to his ransom, and was no doubt able to recall instances of unwonted independence, or had such matters brought to his attention.[2] He probably intended to exploit a rivalry between Durham and Scotland for Northumberland to drive up the auctionable price of the county. Puiset, doubtless aware of his debts, the general revocation of favours then in progress and the ominous change of atmosphere, sought to oil the seas of the royal emotions by offering to surrender Northumberland on 19 April. He was ordered to give it into the hands of his one-time colleague, Hugh Bardolf,[3] but when Bardolf demanded possession after Richard had departed to France in May, the bishop, probably as a result of William of Scotland's bid and the manner in which it was played, had already offered 2000 marks (i.e. the original price) to retain seisin. In July Richard, obviously under the impression that the surrender had taken place, wrote from overseas commanding Bardolf to give up the shire if he could get security for payment. Bardolf, with what was either a bureaucrat's

---

[1] Hoveden, III, 245–6; *Libellus...Godrici*, 178.

[2] *Scriptores Tres*, 14; Newburgh, II, 416, 438.

[3] Hoveden, III, 249. Northumberland and Sadberge had been restored to Puiset in September–October 1190, after his clash with Longchamp. According to Devizes, 415, Northumberland was not returned until October 1191, but the royal officials were not accounting for it after 1190.

reverence for the letter of his instructions or an experienced suspicion of Puiset (for the bishop was still holding the shire), demanded that Hugh should surrender the county and be reseised on payment. This was not to Durham's liking, who replied, with untimely arrogance, that what he had he held. The words were duly reported to Richard, who, *in furore irae suae*, ordered that Northumberland and Sadberge be seized, and the 2000 marks with them, *et factum est ita*.[1]

Again the bishop strove to buy his way to favour. The king played on the old man's undying ambitions, accepted the episcopal offerings, but retained the county.[2] He made some concessions, however, granting the service of certain knights who held between the Tyne and Tees, and promising that with his debts settled, the bishop might join Hubert Walter in supreme office, *tanquam pater patriae*.[3]

Early in 1195 Puiset set out for London, pausing at York in February to strike a final blow at his old enemy, Geoffrey Plantagenet.[4] He celebrated his arrival at the manor of Crayke on Shrove Tuesday with such customary feastings as surpassed the failing digestive powers of his old body, thereby defeating the resources of contemporary medicine, and supplying the critical Newburgh with matter for reflection.[5] He fought back at death with a vigour worthy of his greatest moments, refusing to make his will until almost the end—possibly from some superstition that he had yet several years to live.[6] So he struggled on to Doncaster, and then no longer able to ride, was taken by water to the great Durham manor of Howden, where he died on 3 March. The removal of this great figure from the

[1] Hoveden, III, 261; *PR 6 Richard I*, 132, where Hugh Bardolf accounts for the farm of Northumberland (and Sadberge) for half a year. In Yorkshire the sheriff was allowed *in Pikeringa £12. 7. 6d. quibus Hugo Bard' debet respondere* (*ibid*. 145). This is half the amount Puiset had received as compensation for the loss of Windsor Castle, and shows that this last mark of royal favour went the way of Northumberland and Sadberge.

[2] *Scriptores Tres*, 15; Newburgh, II, 439.

[3] Newburgh, II, 439. The royal charter in favour of Durham was given at Brionne, 9 January 1195 (BM, Stowe MS. 930, fo. 146; see below, pp. 187-8).

[4] Hoveden, III, 284.

[5] Newburgh, II, 439-40, 436-7.

[6] According to Newburgh (II, 436-7) Puiset expected to live ten years in blindness, but this smacks of the chronicler's zeal for suitable allegory.

field of politics so impressed contemporaries in places as diverse as Rouen and Stamford that occasional private charters may be found dated 'in the year in which Hugh, bishop of Durham, entered the way of all flesh'.[1] His body was returned for burial in the chapter-house of his church, where already the royal officials under the direction of Hugh Bardolf had commenced their organized plunder. The keys of Durham Castle were deposited at the feretory and thence surrendered by the prior; those of Norham were resigned by the castellan, Henry of Farlington.[2]

On the whole Puiset failed to realize the opportunities offered in the last years of his life, and died unsuccessful in Durham and the kingdom at large.[3] In 1189 he was superficially at the height of his power; wealthy, experienced and strong in royal favour. He was lord of a principality stretching from the Tees to the Tweed, exercising in Northumberland powers equalling, or perhaps exceeding those he had long used in Durham. The sweeping terms of Richard's charters fully justify criticisms of the heedless nature of the royal policy. The grant of the earldom, it is true, was for life only, and the recipient's age should, by current standards, have ensured brief tenure. Its extent, however, equals and in some points outstrips those privileges earlier sold by Stephen and Matilda. Thus when the notorious Geoffrey de Mandeville received the hereditary justiciarship of Essex in 1141, he could at least expect the occasional company of a peer in the administration of royal justice.[4] Puiset was to enjoy an absolute monopoly. His franchise was comparable only to that created for John in the Midlands, and had the added advantages of traditional and geographical unity. In the fortress of Newcastle he acquired one of the finest and best maintained strongholds in the country, which together with Durham and Norham should have made

---

[1] Hoveden, III, 285; *Scriptores Tres*, 15; Newburgh, *loc. cit.*; Stubbs, 255-6; see below, p. 183.

[2] Newburgh, II, 440; *Scriptores Tres*, 15-16; Hoveden, *loc. cit.*; Bardolf was in possession of Durham by 26 February, i.e. five days before the bishop's death (*Chancellor's Roll 8 Richard I*, 261).

[3] See below, pp. 135-6, 181-2.

[4] J. H. Round, *Geoffrey de Mandeville*, 105.

him all but invincible. In sum he had achieved that ideal of the great feudatories of an earlier generation; the control of justice in those shires where their power was strong and the chances of oppression and profit proportionately large. But his ambitions went further. He had a powerful interest in the metropolitan chapter of York. His own son held the wealthy, influential and almost family office of treasurer, and his supporters came to include most of those alienated by the rancours apparently inseparable from the unfortunate Geoffrey Plantagenet: Henry Marshal, the dean; two canons of famous name, Hugh Murdac and Adam Tourneur; and Peter de Ros, archdeacon of Carlisle. With this weight, his own wealth and the encouraging fluctuations of papal policy he momentarily fought free of his archbishop.[1] He had plans for a family succession to both sees, and was almost in a position to create a new Northumbria such as Richard planned for Otto of Brunswick in 1195.[2] But the opportunity had come too late and Puiset was against an ebbing tide of fortune. Man for man Longchamp was more than his equal. At the same time he was harassed by the claims of his own convent under one of its ablest priors,[3] and his energies in part diverted into a running fight with his metropolitan. He was an old man, and as with many who hold the stage too long, the last act obliterates the glories of earlier scenes. His misfortunes and errors of judgement were such that both contemporaries and subsequent historians have assumed that Richard deceived him from the beginning; an old bishop made a new earl to be duped and buffeted whilst the gold fell from his pockets.[4]

In a passage of brilliant analysis Stubbs writes of 1189 that Richard's 'policy was to work the governmental machinery by men who were not likely to be dangerous, to bribe by large benefactions those whose claims might have made them so, to bind those who had invested their treasure so largely in public appointments to the maintenance of public security, to carry

---

[1] See below, pp. 178–80.
[2] Hoveden, III, 299, 308.
[3] See below, pp. 135–6.
[4] Devizes, 386; Newburgh, II, 438–9; Stubbs, 214, n. 1.

away with him as much as possible of the money which might
have sustained private wars, and as many as possible of the
feudal baronage whose possessions were so large or their
traditions so continuous as to render them jealous of royal
authority. But before he left England he had reason to see that
all this would be futile. The death of William de Mandeville in
November[1] left the justiciarship vacant, for Hugh de Puiset
could not be trusted to act alone—nay, it was a question
whether the king ever seriously intended him to act in this
capacity at all.'[2] This noble sweep of language seems unduly
generous to Richard's sense of responsibility. The king cared
little for England, except as a large privy purse to finance his
military ambitions. He probably never expected to return from
the Holy Land and rashly set impossible problems for others to
solve. It appears that when all was for sale the power as well
as the glory was included. Puiset was rich, and so came swiftly
and easily to an office that was far more than nominal. Until
his fall in the spring of 1190 he was as active in national affairs
as his colleague's jealousy would allow, appearing not only as
a witness to charters but also in his capacity of justiciar in at
least two final concords.[3]

Stubbs, followed by Poole,[4] suggests he went as a debtor in
1190. Yet Longchamp stripped the bishops of Winchester and
Coventry of privileges for which they had paid, and the debt
was only seven months old in April 1190—hardly a day in the
sight of the medieval administration which optimistically
recorded debts over decades. Puiset went because he was no
match for Longchamp. Neither was a man to welcome partners
in power, and they quarrelled from the beginning.[5] The
chancellor, secure in the royal favour, and with a parvenu's
relish for the realities of power, was generally a move ahead of
his opponent. He was not the man to be stayed in his course by
either a respect for persons or the all-reducing gold. He was
capable of stretching both the spirit and the letter of his

---

[1] For the correct date see above, p. 51.
[2] Stubbs, 209.   [3] See below, App. III, *sub anno.*
[4] Stubbs, 209; Poole, *From Domesday to Magna Carta*, 352.
[5] *Gesta*, II, 101; Hoveden, III, 29; Devizes, 389.

instructions as occasion demanded. His return to England in April 1190, a fortnight ahead of Durham, gave him the initiative, and it would seem that he had deliberately left his colleague to be entertained with idle words. Puiset's inept conduct in the subsequent meeting at Tickhill was a sad comment on his reputed diplomatic skill.

Richard was probably converted to a more sober view of the situation in England at Nonancourt in March of 1190, and the measures he took for the safety of his kingdom presumably reflect Longchamp's opinions. Geoffrey Plantagenet and John were made to take an oath that they would not enter England within the next three years.[1] At the same time the futile rivalry occasioned by the uncertain relationship of the justiciar to the chancellor was ended by Longchamp's combining both posts and the limitation of Puiset's authority to north of the Humber. This is probably less an echo of Richard's suspicions than the chancellor's able manipulation of the royal favour. It is difficult to accept Stubbs's contention that the king had never intended Durham's office to be anything more than nominal. The chroniclers' story that his position was merely a pretext for financial extortion is very largely a *post factum* gloss to point a moral, and is in effect vitiated by the comparatively small sums actually realized by the Crown.[2] It is true that the post once held by Glanville was initially committed to two magnates assisted by a large group of assessors, but in part this must have been dictated by the difficulty in replacing the knowledge and experience of the former justiciar. Moreover, if Puiset's colleague, Earl William de Mandeville, was, as Round put it, an honoured servant of the late king, he was hardly in a different category from the bishop, whose record of service from *c.* 1185 was little less distinguished than his own. In sum, Durham's appointment in 1189 had been in company with a group of professional administrators with whom he clearly acted, as is evidenced not only by records but also by the less didactic passages in Newburgh and Devizes.[3] The situation was accepted by the crown, if not by the chancellor. Puiset was left

[1] *Gesta*, II, 106; Hoveden, III, 32.   [2] See below, p. 66.
[3] See below, App. III, *sub annis*; Devizes, 386; Newburgh, I, 303.

in sole charge of England for a period in December 1189, and although, as has been noticed, he had a colleague in Earl William of Essex, Essex died in December and there was no redistribution of office until the following March, by which time the jealousies of the chancellor and justiciar had generated a fair heat. Longchamp had the royal ear at Nonancourt and made the best of his opportunity. Thereafter he generally seems to have assumed that it was Richard's wish he should be sole viceroy.[1] Possibly he was empowered to act alone in the king's business (*negotia regis*) which mandate temperament and convenience extended to cover all matters (*negotia regni*) to the exclusion of his colleagues.[2] He may have returned in April with instructions to displace—though not to dispossess—Durham, which, by Fortune's permission, he was able to interpret in the most convenient sense.[3] When Puiset returned to England in 1190 he met the chancellor coming south after dealing with those who with opportune zeal had seized Jewish houses at York and burnt them, together with the bonds by which embarrassing debts were secured. Longchamp, at the express royal command, had handled the offenders severely, for the Jews were then of especial financial value to the crown.[4] The Puiset faction, if not the instigators of the trouble, were nevertheless prominent among those punished, and the chancellor may have decided he had just cause to be rid of an unwanted colleague.[5]

Yet Puiset, who failed before Bardolf in 1194 much as he had earlier failed before Longchamp, though lacking the unscrupulous distinction of his younger associates, was not, as Stubbs deduced from chronicle evidence, 'cruelly plundered' by the king. If he was somewhat overawed by Longchamp after the events of 1190, he was again active in national politics by 1191, and might have been more so but for his quarrels with Geoffrey Plantagenet. He obtained Northumberland and

[1] Newburgh, 1, 337; Devizes, 389.
[2] Cf. Wilkinson, *The Government of England during the Absence of Richard I*, 8–9.
[3] Cf. above, p. 51.   [4] Newburgh, 1, 323.
[5] Those punished included the bishop's relatives William and Picot de Percy and Hugh Puiset, and Richard Malebisse, Alan Malecake and Marmaduke Darel of his household (Stubbs, 219; Poole, *op. cit.* 353; Colvin, *The White Canons*, 165–7).

Sadberge without paying for them, which was certainly not due to inability to do so, for after his death £3000 was removed in bulk from the bishopric, in addition to sums he had left to meet his debts.[1] The lands thus obtained he held, except for one small break, until 1194, during which time he enjoyed all the valuable perquisites which went with such office.[2] He apparently never paid the £90 ferm of the manors attached to Windsor Castle, yet when he lost the latter he received an allowance in compensation.[3]

Yet he was never as he wished, for it was his constant ambition to be at the centre of political life. He might not unnaturally have seen 1189 as the herald of a return to the ways of Stephen's reign, and burst forth with a zest sharpened by years of power at Durham and the long frustration imposed by the rule of the Angevin. He was one predestined by birth and temperament to govern, but not to assist in a humble role. His arrogant confidence, untaught by age, and his failing powers blinded him almost as he was blinded in Newburgh's allegory.[4] He was impervious to experience; he overestimated himself as he underestimated the abilities of his chief opponents. Before he recovered from his errors of 1190 he was against Geoffrey Plantagenet: his opportunity had gone and he had made no mark. From 1190 he struggled for his power at York and Durham, and bungling his affairs, was beaten by his own prior.[5] His unceasing ambition for office had led him to neglect his greatest opportunities in the north after 1189, and created a situation in his own diocese which defeated the abilities of such practised politicians as Philip of Poitou, Richard Marsh and Richard Poore. Perhaps his conduct in 1195 was the best comment on how little a long life can teach.

[1] Poole (*op. cit.* 352), like Richard himself (*Scriptores Tres*, App. no. XLI) is mistaken in assuming that Sadberge was paid for (cf. *Chancellor's Roll 8 Richard I*, 93). The case was the same with Northumberland, though after the bishop's death 1000 marks was paid towards the promised price out of a sum of 2000 he had left for the purpose (*Chancellor's Roll 8 Richard I, loc. cit.*; *Scriptores Tres*, 15). His total debts on *PR 6 John*, 42 are £1160. For the sums extracted by the royal custodians during the vacancy after Puiset's death, see *Chancellor's Roll 8 Richard I*, 253, and below, p. 194.

[2] See below, p. 201.

[3] *PR 2 Richard I*, 21; *PR 3 Richard I*, 160; *PR 4 Richard I*, 275; *PR 5 Richard I*, 128; *PR 6 Richard I*, 251; *PR 7 Richard I*, 81.

[4] See above, p. 60.   [5] See below, pp. 135–6.

CHAPTER III

THE BISHOP AND
ECCLESIASTICAL POLITICS

THE age of Henry II and Philip Augustus was equally that of Alexander III and Innocent III. The definition and enforcement of authority which characterized the period were, on the whole, achieved with greater rapidity, and justified with finer ability, at Rome than elsewhere in western Europe. The policy indicated by Gregory VII was vigorously developed by his successors, and Rome was rebuilt to power. As the grinding claims of rival authorities and the growing prosperity of the west created an age of jurisprudence and litigation which has been aptly compared to the classical days of Roman law, the papacy intervened with increasing frequency in a variety of local problems, defining its position in a developing common law which ranged from the details of canonization to the just definition of Christian marriage. The general significance of this movement for England has been demonstrated by Professor Brooke, its practical application detailed by Dom Adrian Morey, and the concurrent efforts of English canonists to pass on the swelling volume of papal law to church dignitaries revealed by Professors Holtzmann and Kuttner.[1]

Puiset's role in all this was slight. He was not one of such character, bearing or learning as to become a pillar of papal authority. He had no legal training comparable to that gained empirically or academically by such contemporaries as Roger of York, Bartholomew of Exeter, Gerard Pucelle or Baldwin of Ford. He lived as a great baron, with a magnificence which put Stubbs in mind of 'those grand stern figures that look down from the walls of the cathedrals of Mentz, Wurzburg and Bamberg',[2] but which was small qualification to become a luminary of the English Church. Yet he was by no means isolated from

---

[1] Z. N. Brooke, *The English Church and the Papacy*; Morey, *Bartholomew of Exeter*, 44–54; see below, pp. 68–70.   [2] Stubbs, 214.

         5-2

the current trends in ecclesiastical life, and like other clerical feudatories heeded the voice of the papacy in many things. He was a reasonably active diocesan, knew many great men of religion, and submitted for papal consideration what might fairly be called conscientious doubts (though few in number) on points of administration.[1]

The Papacy was not reluctant to employ men of obvious natural ability, as appears in Puiset's own career, or that of Samson of Bury. Such dignitaries, albeit 'nought textuel', could find amongst their clerks those of a learning more than sufficient to remedy the defects of their own education.[2] Durham, as the Church in England as a whole, was well abreast of contemporary canonical developments in the later twelfth century. An early list of conventual books (c. 1165–85) mentions, in addition to the outmoded Ivo of Chartres, those typical collections described as *Decreta Pontificum*, *Excerpta Canonum* and *Exceptiones Decretorum*. On another page we read of two copies of Gratian, a *Summa* on the same author, and the *Excerptiones Decretorum Gratiani*. The same spirit is revealed in the fact that one Guarinus possessed a copy of the *Liber Pauperum*.[3] Further evidence of this learning comes from surviving works, which if somewhat later than the period of Puiset's activity, at least postulate prior training or experience in their authors. The work of the canonists falls into two classes; the assembly of collections of decretals subsequent to Gratian, and the various forms of gloss on these or existing compilations. Professors Holtzmann and Kuttner have drawn attention to the large number of 'primitive' collections (i.e. those which string their material together without dissecting it into titles) produced in England in the half-century before the appearance of Bernard's *Compilatio Prima* (c. 1190).[4] There are three Durham compilations in this category, containing material drawn largely from the pontificate of Alexander III,

[1] See below, pp. 122–3.
[2] Cf. Jocelin of Brakelond, *Chronicle concerning the acts of Samson of Bury* (ed. Butler), 33–4.   [3] *Catalogi Veteres Librorum Dunelmenses*, ed. B. Botfield, 1, 7, 9.
[4] Kuttner and Rathbone in *Traditio*, VII (1949–51), 282; Holtzmann in *Nachrichten der Akademie der Wiss....in Göttingen* (*Phil.-Hist.Kl.*), 1945, 15–36; Kuttner in *Traditio*, VI, 1948, 345–51.

whose legal eminence made his opinions particularly valuable.[1] This same activity continued, or rather increased, after the appearance of the *Compilatio Prima*, and the English school was especially prominent in its attempts to remedy the defects in Bernard's work. At the turn of the century there was published the great systematic *Collectio Sangermanensis*, for which a Durham origin has been claimed, and about the same time there appeared a primitive collection which has been tentatively described as a precursor of the *Compilatio* of Alan the Englishman (1206).[2]

The Durham school, like many others of the later twelfth century, looked to France rather than Bologna for its direct inspiration. This influence may be detected in a series of glosses on Gratian by an unidentified Master B, which occur in conjunction with glosses on Rufinus in a one-time Durham manuscript. Work of a similar order, possibly of the time of Becket, is to be found in the *Notabilia clericus apud civilem*, surviving at Durham and Cambridge.[3] The same French school was likewise responsible for a group of writings related to the *Summa omnis qui juste*, described by experts as the most elaborate of all the commentaries on Gratian prior to Huguccio. This learning colours two Durham manuscripts, C II, 1, and C III, 1 which have been analysed by Professor Kuttner.[4] The former he relates to the *Glossae Stuttgardienses*, produced in the province of Sens, *c.* 1181–5, whilst in the latter there are citations of John Faventius and the celebrated Anglo-Norman canonist, Gerard Pucelle.[5] Other influences of this group, as represented by John of Tynemouth and Simon of Southwell, are perhaps to be found in a gloss on the *Decretum* preserved at Durham, wherein there appears the siglum S.[6]

[1] Kuttner, *Repertorium der Kanonistik, 1140–1234*, 280–1, *Collectio Dunelmensis I*, etc., DC Durham C III, 1. Cf. M. Cheney, 'The Compromise of Avranches of 1172, and the spread of canon law in England', 182.

[2] W. Ullmann, 'A Scottish Charter and its Place in Medieval Canon Law', 231–2; *ibid.* 'A Forgotten Dispute at Bridlington Priory', 456–73; H. Singer in *Sitzungsberichte der Kaiserlichen Akademie der Wissenschaft (Phil.-Hist. Kl.)*, CLXXXI (1914), 114.

[3] DC Durham, C IV, 1; Sidney Sussex College, Cambridge, MS. 101; Kuttner and Rathbone, *art. cit.* 294; Kuttner, *Repertorium*, 24, 26–7.

[4] Kuttner and Rathbone, *art. cit.* 296; Kuttner, *Repertorium*, 26.

[5] Kuttner and Rathbone, *art. cit.* 297–303; Kuttner, *Repertorium*, 195–7.

[6] DC Durham, C II, 1; Kuttner and Rathbone, *art. cit.* 320, n. 47.

The means and routes whereby this knowledge was transmitted to Durham are largely a matter of conjecture. We hear, however, amidst the many curiosities retailed by Reginald's Life of Godric, that a certain clerk from Durham, one Gervase, went to Paris *causa disciplinae secularis vel scholasticae perquirendae*, where he became a favourite pupil of Pucelle, who, as already noticed, is cited in the glosses in DC Durham, C III, 1.[1] There is other evidence of contact with the same schools, though on the whole the interests seem to be of a theological or humanistic character. Prior Absalon, who was educated abroad, remains an elusive figure.[2] Master Robert of Haddington, who died at St Victor (whence there had earlier come Master Laurence),[3] was a Paris-trained theologian of the period 1170–90.[4] Master Herbert *medicus*, who owned a formidably impressive medical library, might possibly be the scholar of that name who was recommended to Alexander III as a man of letters deserving preferment.[5] For the rest there is a strong probability that some considerable influence was exercised by the schools of Lincoln, where Bishops Walter and Hugh patronized such men as John of Tynemouth and Simon of Southwell. In this context it is worthy of note that Puiset's *familia* included a number of *magistri* originating from or beneficed in Lincoln; Master William of Blois, Master Henry of Lincoln, Master Richard of Lindsey and Master Stephen of Lincoln.[6]

The extent to which the bishop utilized this canonistical learning—and since it was in no sense 'official', hesitations would have been justified—remains a matter of assumption rather than demonstration. Again, whilst it is obvious that he was in a position to rely on the assistance of the learned, even if his clerks lacked the distinction of those of Becket or Hubert Walter, it is equally clear that this did not make him a canonist in the eyes of the papacy. On the whole the causes

---

[1] *Libellus...Godrici*, 452–4; see above, p. 69.

[2] *Scriptores Tres*, 7.   [3] See above, pp. 15, n. 5; 20.

[4] DC Durham, A III, 16; R. A. B. Mynors, *Durham Cathedral Manuscripts to the end of the Twelfth Century*, 78.

[5] *Catalogi Veteres*, 7. I owe this suggestion to Dr Eleanor Rathbone.

[6] Kuttner and Rathbone, *art. cit.* 321; see above, p. 69; see below, pp. 104, 235. I hope to discuss this subject more fully elsewhere.

so far known in which he acted reveal no specialization, and required no remarkable legal knowledge for their solution. This being so they are described in approximate chronological order.

In 1165–8, certain lay brethren of Sempringham, feeling unjustly bruised by the severity of their Rule, and the recent appearance in their Order of a new grade of canons, expressed their dissatisfaction by suggesting the existence of immorality in high places. Alexander III, supported it would seem by the exiled Becket, took action without further examination. His letter, however, was not delivered to the Master of the Order. Following protests from distinguished members of the English hierarchy denying the existence of scandals, the pope appointed judges delegate to investigate the accusations. The bishops of Norwich and Winchester were nominated for the southern houses of the Order, and the archbishop of York and the bishop of Durham for the northern. The two inquiries were duly held, Gilbert and his opponents being present at both. Matters were simplified in the north by the fact that there was only one house, Watton, containing nuns and canons alike. The lay brothers here were not in revolt, and consequently free from excommunication, whilst the charge of having been compelled to make a profession to Savigny was easily rebutted. The papal commands were then given to Gilbert, namely that he was to be reconciled to the lay brethren who were in revolt, and that in future only two or three canons were to attend the nuns' church to celebrate mass, to all of which the Master willingly submitted. There then arose a charge that he had refused to receive the first papal letters. Over this there was some delay, and the case was adjourned whilst the brethren improved their brief. At the resumption, from which Puiset was absent, the proof against Gilbert entirely failed. The future saint, having now convinced the judges of the decorous morality of his convents, promised to receive the delinquents with paternal affection, and to modify certain hard points of observance in the rule. The unrepentant leader of the agitation, Ogger,[1] was not, however, satisfied, and demanded radical modifications.

[1] *PU*, III, no. 231.

Eventually the king intervened, and with papal approval assisted in the re-establishment of order.[1]

A case of somewhat similar flavour concerned the Augustinian priory of Bridlington. A canon of the house had appealed to Rome, complaining of the uncanonical election and incontinent life of his prior, probably that Gregory who ruled *c.* 1160–80. In reply Alexander III had delegated the case to the bishop of Durham and the abbot of Fountains, who subsequently reported (early in the 1160's) that they found the prior innocent. Thereafter one Walter, apparently another canon of the house, again appealed, adding to his list of complaints the accusation that the judges delegate, having put the house on oath, then absolved the prior without hearing the community's evidence. Thus aggrieved, the appellant was moved to an eloquent and detailed exposition of the trials of his brethren. The prior was no master, but a tyrant, terrifying the feeble and whipping the obdurate. The weak dare not disclose their ailments; sinners were deprived of confession. He lived apart from his community in such company as distressed his canons, whose grief was the greater since he treated their property as his own. As a result of this appeal the case was redelegated (in the 1160's) to judges of proved capability and experience; Archbishop Roger of York, Bartholomew of Exeter, and the abbot of Ford. They were to inquire into the methods used by Durham and Fountains, and should their conduct have been as was alleged, Walter was to be paid the expenses of his journey to Rome and the new judges were to rehear the case. If, on the other hand, the prior had been absolved after due process of law, the matter was to be closed, to which end there were added minute instructions on strictures and precautions.[2]

Together with his metropolitan, Puiset was commissioned in a case of forgery in 1175–6. The papal legate, Hugh de Sancto Angelo, informed Alexander III that a certain Master H. of Southwell had presented forged letters to Roger of York—

---

[1] This dispute has been examined at length by Knowles, 'The Revolt of the Lay Brothers of Sempringham', 465–87.

[2] Morey, *Bartholomew of Exeter*, 55; *Comp. II*, lib. II, tit. 18, c. 2 in *Quinque Compilationes Antiquae*, ed. E. Friedberg; *JL*, 13891; Ullmann, 'A Forgotten Dispute at Bridlington Priory', 456–73.

presumably to secure induction to livings. This the accused had denied, but had been found guilty, and the cardinal had accordingly wished to condemn him as a forger. The culprit thereupon appealed to Rome, whilst the legate, under pressure from some of the great of the land, withheld his sentence. Alexander, disapproving of the lenient way in which the case had been handled, was unwilling to see such a sinner go unpunished. He therefore ordered Roger of York and his suffragan to strip Master H. of his churches of Epperstone and Shelford, *contradictione et appellatione cessante*, and thereafter dispatch him to a monastery, *ubi possit, quod tam nequiter egit, lamentis penitentie emendare*. In course the two delegates wrote to inform Bishop Roger of Worcester, that they had so far deprived the offender of his churches and would duly complete the rest of their mandate.[1]

A case of greater importance and delicacy had been delegated to Jocelin of Salisbury and Hugh of Durham in October 1174. When peace should have been re-established between Henry II and his son, the two bishops were to examine the disputes of the legates, Richard of Canterbury and Roger of York, on primatial rights, cross-bearing and other matters. They were to summon the two archbishops before them, hear their cases, take depositions which were to be forwarded to Rome, and fix a date by which the litigants were to appear before the pope.[2] This was an echo from the venerable quarrel of York and Canterbury, then in one of its more vigorous phases. Roger, restored to his see after his activities in 1170, ambitiously sharp as ever for his rights and pretensions, had been regranted the right to carry his cross before him throughout England until the whole question should have been investigated.[3] At the same time the election of Richard of Dover was accompanied by a wave of papal favours for Canterbury which naturally swept the two metropolitans into collision.[4] Roger's officials

---

[1] See below, App. II, no. 1. For the legation of cardinal Hugh, see Tillmann, *Die Päpstlichen Legaten in England*, 73–7.

[2] *PU*, II, no. 141 (6 October 1174); Foreville, *L'Église et La Royauté en Angleterre*, 519.

[3] *Materials*, VII, 568; Foreville, *op. cit.* 517, n. 2.

[4] *PU*, II, nos. 134–7.

at St Oswald's, Gloucester, refused to recognize Richard as their metropolitan at his primary visitation, and York appealed to Rome.[1] A truce was negotiated by the king in 1175, but at Northampton in the following year Roger inflamed the strife by his desire for jurisdiction over the Scottish Church.[2] In March of the same year a struggle for precedence in a council at Westminster ended by York being assaulted and trampled on by Canterbury's servants.[3] There is no evidence that the bishops acted on their mandate, which in the circumstances is hardly surprising. Jocelin was old and infirm, with an ill health which had often stood him in good stead. He had painful experience of the results of clashes with lay and spiritual authorities. Puiset was smarting from the effects of a considerable political error, and doubtless the two bishops, seeing where the wind lay, felt it both invidious and indiscreet to probe such a festering sore.

As ordinary and judge delegate Puiset was involved in a number of cases concerning the Cistercians of the northern province. At this time the Order generally was experiencing great difficulties.[4] In England Gerald of Wales and Walter Map accused them of boundless greed, and an unscrupulous zeal in the ways of Mammon. The theme and its development are worthy of the indignation of a More. Yet it must be remembered that Gerald and Map were moved to that immoderate eloquence characteristic of the offended Celt; that the former was greatly influenced by his unfortunate dealings with the backwood brethren of Wales, and that neither of these distinguished clerks was particularly well acquainted with the northern province. Nevertheless, the spirit of their criticisms is significant and echoes a general complaint. Archbishop Richard of Canterbury wrote to the abbot of Cîteaux reproaching the Order with greed, and pointing out that privileges dating from the days

[1] *Gesta*, I, 80–1; Diceto, I, 395–6; Foreville, *op. cit.* 518.

[2] *Gesta*, I, 111–12; Hoveden, II, 92; Foreville, *op. cit.* 510.

[3] Diceto, I, 405–6; *Gesta*, I, 112–13; Hoveden, II, 92–3; Gervase of Canterbury, I, 258; II, 398.

[4] Jean-Berthold Mahn, *L'Ordre Cistercien et son Gouvernement, 1098–1265*, 110. For the withdrawal of monks and *conversi* from Rievaulx, see *PU*, I, no. 192 (1171–81). For trouble at Fountains, see below, p. 75, n. 5 and *PU*, III, no. 160.

of poverty should now be used with greater moderation.[1] Alexander III admonished the abbots of Swineshead and Furness on their flagrant breaches of the Rule.[2] In 1173–6 Hugh of Durham and Hamo, dean of Lincoln, were commissioned to investigate the evidence of Roger of York that the convent of Swineshead was in possession of the advowson of the church of Cotgrave. The monks were either to surrender the living, or demonstrate to the delegates (*si poterunt*) how this ownership was to be reconciled with the pristine Rule. Should such proof not be forthcoming within twenty days the church was to be abandoned.[3]

Cîteaux was moving to some variety of those luxurious Cluniac ways against which Bernard had once fulminated. The munificence of donors, an unpleasant alliance of godliness and economic success, and a streak of meanness and sharp practice in business, had built a temporal mansion perhaps more splendid than was fitting. The prosperity of the Order was a temptation to the unruly and a target for the wits. Cistercian privilege and smugness were an annoyance to the hierarchy,[4] whilst their considerable popularity as an object for pious donations combined with their undoubted economic efficiency to make them a thorn in the flesh of their rival brother Orders.

As a friend of Rievaulx[5] and as an ordinary with jurisdiction in Yorkshire, Puiset was concerned in a number of cases which were of common form throughout western Europe; complaints of oppression and quarrels over property and privileges. Quite

---

[1] *PL*, vol. 207, col. 252.

[2] *PU*, II, no. 174. Cf. Knowles, *Monastic Order*, 350–1, 354–5, 656–9. For the Continental parallel, see Mahn, *op. cit.* 112–13.

[3] *PU*, II, no. 154. For Cistercian laxity on this point, see Mahn, *op. cit.* 48. The first example there noticed is *c*. 1145. For similar evidence from the Premonstratensians, see Colvin, *The White Canons*, 25.

[4] Bishops of the northern province, it might be noticed, showed an aggressive willingness to excommunicate monks or *conversi* occupying property in defiance of papal prohibitions (*PU*, III, no. 252).

[5] See below, pp. 109, 259. It might be noted that whatever Puiset's relations with Rievaulx were, those with Fountains seem to have been less happy. At one stage the abbot excommunicated some of his monks and *conversi* 'for disobedience and rebellion', whereupon the bishop took it upon himself to absolve them. He received a sharp letter from Alexander III ordering him to respect the sentence (*PU*, III, no. 160).

early Rievaulx was troubled by encroachments on her lands. A mandate of Alexander III (23 November 1160), addressed to Roger of York, Hugh of Durham, their archdeacons and (rural) deans, instructs them to deal with any under their spiritual jurisdiction who should thus disturb the brethren in their rights and possessions; *eos ad restitutionem et satisfactionem...faciendam vel ad plenam justitiam exhibendam infra triginta dies postquam querela...ad vos pervenerit convenire et commonefacere studeatis. Si vero ipsi malefactores neutrum facere forte voluerint, ipsos ex tunc excommunicationis vinculo innodetis.*[1] Another mandate of somewhat later date (11 November 1167–9) ordered the archbishop and his suffragan to check any attempts to wrest property from Rievaulx by actions in lay courts.[2] It is extremely doubtful whether such injunctions or their execution—if indeed they were executed—had much effect. The language of a subsequent letter suggests not. The archbishop and the bishop of Durham were given power over those outside their ordinary jurisdiction (*si aliqui parrochianorum vestrorum aut alii*, etc.). Those interfering with property belonging to Rievaulx were to be brought to reason through anathema. No disputes over possessions *eis pia devotione collatis* were on any account to go to a lay court, but were to be heard by the archbishop and his suffragan, and should they prove remiss justice would be done by others.[3]

But the trouble continued, even extending to physical assaults on monks and *conversi*.[4] A mandate of 14 March 1174–6, addressed to the bishop of Durham and the abbot of St Mary's, York, shows the house at strife with neighbours both lay and ecclesiastic. The complaints against laymen, most of whom were one-time patrons, probably reflect disorders rising out of the revolt of 1173–4.[5] The quarrels with the religious sprang in part from the Cistercian demand for solitude,[6] which made their

---

[1] *PU*, 1, no. 83. Cf. nos. 82 (23 November 1160) and 132 (14 March 1174–6).

[2] *PU*, 1, no. 106.

[3] *PU*, 1, no. 107 (1167–9).

[4] *PU*, 1, no. 195 (1171–81); Foreville, *L'Église et La Royauté en Angleterre*, 425.

[5] Cf. *PU*, 1, no. 191, and the names there mentioned, which include Robert de Stuteville and his son, William; Roger Mowbray, and his son, Nigel; Everard de Ros and other lesser persons.

[6] Thus Alexander III in favour of Meaux (18 December 1172): *ne quis prope monasterium vestrum ad dimidiam leucam sibi habitationem faciat* (*PU*, 1, no. 116).

houses particularly intolerant of neighbours, and in part from a jealous competition for land, aggravated by the vagueness of early pious gifts.[1] Rievaulx had already complained that other Orders ignored her boundaries, and as early as 1164 the Cistercians and Gilbertines had entered into a formal agreement to secure Christian harmony in these matters.[2] The monks now complained that the canons of Malton (Gilbertines) had filched the *vastum de sub Picaringe*;[3] the canons of Sempringham (Gilbertines) cast lustful eyes on other lands, and the canons of Kirkham (Augustinians) had helped themselves to an over-generous portion of the *pascua de Helmesleia*, which had been given to the two Orders jointly.[4] The judges, having summoned the parties before them, were to order Malton and Sempringham to desist from aggression, though should either house claim title in the disputed property the case was to be heard and ended. Kirkham was to be admonished to abide by its legal rights.[5]

Another group of mandates is concerned with Cistercian problems of tithe. Two important bulls, one for Furness,[6] the other for Rievaulx,[7] are of the family *Audivimus et audientes*, common throughout Europe at this time by reason of an important swing in papal policy.[8] The early Cistercians had been generally exempt from the payment of tithe through the enthusiasm and generosity of their patrons, especially the episcopate.[9] This largesse was not, however, shared by those to whom tithe was a source of revenue rather than an investment for ancestral souls. The monks soon acquired sufficient wisdom from un-spiritual buffetings to realize that it was best to sacrifice some-thing of the letter and spirit of their privileges and compound

---

[1] Cf. the long process of defining Pickering, covering at least the entire reign of Henry II (*EYC*, 1, nos. 402, 404–7).

[2] *Cartulary of Rievaulx*, ed. J. C. Atkinson, no. CCXLVI.

[3] For their title, see *EYC*, 1, no. 408.

[4] For Kirkham's title, see *Rievaulx Cartulary*, no. CCCXLVII.

[5] *PU*, 1, no. 132.

[6] *PU*, 1, no. 157 (4 April 1166–79), addressed to the archbishop of York and the bishop of Durham.

[7] *PU*, 1, no. 161 (1 May 1166–79), addressed to York and Durham.

[8] Cf. *PU*, 1, no. 160 (1 May 1166–79), for Rufford; *PU*, 1, no. 175 (3 November 1176–86), for Quarr.

[9] Mahn, *L'Ordre Cistercien*, 103.

for tithe.[1] During the pontificate of Adrian IV, and probably in response to a general wish, Cistercian exemption was limited to *novales* (i.e. tithes on land newly brought under cultivation as opposed to land already under cultivation, or *labores*).[2] This ruling was not upheld by Alexander III, who maintained that his predecessor had given a personal view which was accordingly without value.[3] The Cistercians were entirely exempt *a solutione decimarum tam de terris illis quas deduxerunt vel deducunt ad cultum, quam de terris cultis, quas ipsi propriis manibus vel sumptibus excolunt.*[4] Those already taking tithe suffered no speedy conversion, and by suggesting an error in papal diplomatic sought to establish that *labores* should read *novales*, and so return to the more favourable position of Adrian IV. In *Audivimus et audientes* and other related bulls, Alexander announced in firm language that he was no innovator and that papal privileges were not to be subject to perverse interpretation. The liberties of the Cistercians were plain to all men of good will and sound mind, and his ruling was correct as it stood. Had he only intended to exempt the Cistercians on *novales* he would not have spoken of *labores*, and the episcopate must accordingly ensure that the privileges of the Order were respected.[5]

Despite frequent papal intervention the monks remained in trouble.[6] The exemption of *labores* was studiously ignored, as by the clergy of York who publicly maintained the contrary.[7] Archbishop Roger and his suffragan were duly and vainly warned against the common sin of putting *novalia pro laboribus*,[8] and were subsequently enjoined to ensure that the brethren of Fountains were not vexed *super decimis de laboribus suis* by any such duplicity.[9] Somewhat earlier York, together with the

---

[1] Mahn, *op. cit.* 106; Knowles, *Monastic Order*, 355.

[2] Adrian IV to Ulrich of Halberstadt, 11 June 1156, *JL*, 10189a, cited Mahn, *op. cit.* 107.

[3] Mahn, *op. cit.* 109.

[4] *PU*, I, no. 157, for Furness; cf. p. 77, nn. 6, 7 and 8.

[5] *Nam si de novalibus voluissemus intelligi ubi posuimus de laboribus, de novalibus poneremus, sicut in privilegiis quorumdam aliorum apponimus* (*PU*, I, no. 157).

[6] Cf. the number of mandates concerning Continental houses noted by Mahn, *op. cit.* 108, n. 3.

[7] *PU*, III, no. 244.

[8] *PU*, III, no. 251.   [9] *PU*, III, no. 156 (1167–9).

bishops of Lincoln and Coventry, had been urged to check similar improper demands on the monks of Roche and Rufford.[1] But Roger, notoriously no lover of regulars—at least in the eyes of William of Newburgh—was presumably little affected by these injunctions. At some uncertain date he interdicted Rievaulx and threatened the monks with excommunication to secure payment of tithe to one of his clerks.[2] Such practice, or variants thereof, was apparently common. Priests of the northern province were alleged to deny mass *et cetera ecclesiastica beneficia* to servants of the monks that the latter might be constrained to pay tithe.[3] Such abuses, wrote Alexander to the diocesans, were not to be tolerated. A further mandate of 14 March 1174–6, addressed to York and Durham, points out that notwithstanding the liberties of the Cistercians, certain ill-regulated clerks, and more especially those of Welburn, were brazenly demanding tithe of Rievaulx. Since such behaviour *non mediocriter nos et Romanam ecclesiam offendunt* the offenders were to be ordered to desist, and if they refused, were to be excommunicated.[4] Even when the monks had agreed to compound, trouble continued. On a complaint from Rievaulx, Alexander wrote to Roger of York and Hugh of Durham that considering the privileges of the Order, *ut nulli decimas teneantur persolvere de laboribus*, some gratitude should be shown when the monks, of their grace, allowed a composition. The archbishop and the bishop must look to it that such agreements were maintained undisturbed.[5] But in this Durham was equally guilty, and the bishop and his church were in turn admonished for breaking the terms they had once made with Rievaulx concerning the tithes of Cowton.[6]

These frequent mandates, of great importance for Cistercian history, affected Puiset mainly as an ordinary and as the only surviving suffragan of his archbishop. They reflect also some-

---

[1] *PU*, III, no. 151.
[2] *PU*, I, no. 188 (1164–81).
[3] *PU*, III, no. 271 (1170–80).
[4] *PU*, I, no. 133.
[5] *PU*, I, no. 193 (1171–81).
[6] *PU*, I, no. 194 (1171–81). Cf. a case relating to Fountains where a priest named Taurinus was accused of cutting growing crops *occasione decimarum*, though there was already an agreement between the parties (*PU*, III, no. 270 (1170–80)).

thing of a friendship with Rievaulx, whose monks perhaps regarded the bishop as a man of sufficient consequence and affluence to protect their interests and balance the suspected hostility of Roger of York.[1] To what degree these aims were achieved it is difficult to say. The edifice of papal justice was often more impressive than effective, and the northern hierarchy was no more disposed than its colleagues elsewhere to be a guardian of the privileged regulars. The rapid succession of papal missives would seem as much an indication of their ineffectiveness as of Rievaulx's good favour at Rome. Under Lucius III Cistercian abbots were still complaining of their difficulties over tithe.[2]

In July 1181, Puiset, as suffragan of York, supported his archbishop in an intervention in Scotland.[3] Following the death of Bishop Richard of St Andrews in 1178,[4] the chapter, without consulting the king, elected John the Scot, whilst William the Lion nominated his own chaplain, Hugh.[5] Alexander III quashed the election of Hugh,[6] who was removed from office, and eventually excommunicated by the legate Alexius.[7] Meanwhile John, although consecrated, was unable to gain possession of his see by reason of William's opposition. Acting on papal advice he and the legate therefore sought the aid of Henry II, Scotland's overlord since 1175.[8] Early in 1181 Henry summoned the parties, including the king of Scotland, before him in Normandy and attempted to arrange a settlement, but the pope refused to admit any agreement which obliged John to relinquish St Andrews.[9] It was probably at this stage that Roger of York was appointed legate in Scotland, with orders that together with Hugh of Durham he should excommunicate William and interdict the kingdom were John not given possession of St Andrews.[10] In July William returned to England, and on passage to the north was met by the Scot and Puiset, but to no purpose. John excommunicated the royal

[1] EYC, II, no. 952.
[2] PU, III, no. 370 (1185).
[3] Gesta, I, 282.
[4] Melrose Chronicle, sub anno.
[5] Gesta, I, 250; Hoveden, II, 208.
[6] PU, I, no. 181.
[7] Gesta, I, 264; Hoveden, II, 209–10.
[8] Gesta, I, 263–5.
[9] Gesta, I, 276–7; Hoveden, II, 259–60.
[10] Gesta, I, 281; Hoveden, II, 211.

chancellor and others of the Lion's household. The bishop of Durham, with papal authority, exhorted the clergy of St Andrews to submit to John, whilst the archbishop addressed a similar message to all clerks of the kingdom. William replied by sequestrating the property of those who made any show of recognizing the Scot, whereupon Roger excommunicated him and together with Puiset interdicted the kingdom.[1] The sentences were pronounced before November 1181 (when Roger of York died), but do not appear to have been confirmed by Alexander III, who died on 30 August of the same year. Through the intervention of Henry II, William was absolved by Lucius III in March 1182.[2] The case, which no longer concerned the province of York, dragged on until after the death of Hugh the chaplain in 1189. John eventually compromised and was appointed to Dunkeld, whilst the royal chancellor, Roger Beaumont, was given St Andrews.[3]

Hugh again acted on a papal mandate in 1181 in a dispute between the archbishop of Canterbury and the convent of St Augustine's, whose abbot, claiming exemption from the ordinary, refused to make profession and demanded benediction in his own church.[4] The claim is characteristic of the period —a complaint against an episcopate which was defining and enforcing its authority with unwonted vigour. Hence sprang similar disputes between St Albans and Lincoln, Battle and Chichester, Malmesbury and Salisbury, Bury and Norwich, Evesham and Worcester;[5] hence too collisions of bishops with the wealthy conservatism of their regular chapters, as at Canterbury, Coventry and Durham. Thus privileges of venerable ancestry were stirred from lengthy hibernation, and somewhat refurbished in the awakening, set forth by their owners to justify their independence.

The Benedictines of the cathedral chapter of Christchurch were naturally jealous of the oldest English house of their

---

[1] *Gesta*, I, 281-2; Hoveden, II, 212 and 263; *Holyrood Chronicle*, 164, n. 4, where a satisfactory chronology of the case is established.

[2] *Gesta*, I, 286-7; Hoveden, II, 268-9.

[3] Foreville, *L'Église et La Royauté en Angleterre*, 511-12.

[4] Gervase of Canterbury, I, 274-5.

[5] Cf. Knowles, 'The Growth of Monastic Exemption'.

Order, whilst the archbishops often found the same foundation something of an embarrassing neighbour. In the time of Becket the abbot, Clarembald, reputed father of seventeen children, refused to profess, and in addition to other misdemeanours, became a firm supporter of Foliot.[1] Following his deposition in 1173 Roger, a monk of Christchurch, was elected.[2] He in turn refused to profess and was eventually blessed by the pope.[3] Since it was to the interest of king and pope alike to restrain the archiepiscopal authority, the new abbot was able to obtain bulls granting him the right to excommunicate malefactors should the episcopate refuse to act; forbidding the archbishop to excommunicate the monks or interdict the convent, except by papal mandate, and finally the celebrated *Filium specialem, nullo mediante*.[4] Archbishop Richard, complaining that St Augustine's had beguiled the world by forged originals, appealed to Rome. In reply Alexander appointed the bishop of Hereford and Baldwin of Ford to examine the documents, but their proceedings were allegedly too favourable to the archbishop, and the monks accordingly appealed.[5] The case was then redelegated to the bishop of Durham and the abbots of St Albans and Bury; three of the greatest ecclesiastical immunists of the country. In the presence of Richard and twelve experts of his choice the St Augustine's primitives were to be individually produced (some suitably secluded place having been chosen), inspected, and, if need be, transcribed. In the meanwhile the archbishop was to be given the opportunity to present his case against the documents at the *Curia*. Should he fail to do so there was to be no further discussion of the charters.[6] Puiset and Simon of St Albans (for the abbot of Bury was already dead) accordingly summoned the parties to meet them on 26 May 1181 in the monastery of Bermondsey, where the privileges in question were to be examined.[7] After

---

[1] John of Salisbury, *Opera*, II, 268–73.
[2] Gervase of Canterbury, I, 77 and 256; Diceto, I, 354.
[3] Gervase of Canterbury, I, 274–6; *Gesta*, I, 208–9; Diceto, I, 428–9.
[4] Thomas of Elmham, *Historia Monasterii Sancti Augustini Cantuariensis*, ed. C. Hardwick, 433–9.
[5] *PU*, I, nos. 201 and 202.   [6] *PU*, I, no. 201 (23 January 1181).
[7] *PU*, I, no. 202; Gervase of Canterbury, I, 296.

some trouble from Richard,[1] who knew certain evidences he wished to see to be at Rome, the litigants appeared. The monks produced two privileges, allegedly granted by Augustine and Ethelbert, which were transcribed for dispatch to the scrutiny of the *Curia*. There was difficulty with the rest of the evidence. The archbishop cited certain charters which the monks held they had never mentioned. They were uncertain as to whether or not they possessed others. The bull of Pope Agatho, which Richard had requested, was at Rome, as also that of Boniface, with which he was not at the time concerned. After this vain pursuit of dubious antiquity the archbishop demanded to see the privileges of recent popes, for which there was no time.[2] The Christchurch party were not impressed by suggestions of venerable age, and noted signs of native industry in the ancient evidences; erasures, modern formulae, incorrect sealing.[3]

The case, which no longer concerned the bishop of Durham, was decided by Lucius III in June 1183. The abbot of St Augustine's was always to be blessed in his own church, and was not to profess to the archbishop. The decision was confirmed by Urban III and Celestine III, and the abbey removed from the jurisdiction of the archbishop, even in his role as legate.[4]

A number of other disputes on which there is little evidence were also handled by the bishop during the closing years of Alexander's pontificate. A quarrel between Nicholas, prior of Lancaster, and Norman, a clerk, over the church of Melling (Lancs) and its chapel was settled to the effect that these were to be held by Norman of the priory at an annual pension of twenty shillings.[5]

Meanwhile, in Yorkshire, an important layman, Reiner the Fleming, had presented one of his clerks to the church of *Wodeham*. The nominee, one William, was refused admission to the living by Archbishop Roger of York. He therefore departed to Rome, returning in due course with a mandate instructing the bishop of Durham to admonish the metro-

---

[1] *PU*, I, nos. 203 and 204.
[2] *PU*, I, no. 205; Foreville, *L'Église et La Royauté en Angleterre*, 526–7.
[3] Gervase of Canterbury, I, 296–7.
[4] Knowles, *art. cit.* 414–15.
[5] See below, App. II, no. 2.

politan to admit him. Should the archbishop refuse, Puiset, having first ascertained William's canonical fitness, and that his initial presentation had been to a vacant church, was to eject the intruder, admit the plaintiff, and restore to him such fruits as he might have lost by appeal after his first presentation.[1]

About the same time Hugh sat with the famous civilian, Master Vacarius,[2] in a dispute between the canons of Bridlington and Odo the Knight and his son, Matthew, concerning the church of Eston. It was eventually agreed that the prior should demise the presentation to Matthew and his heirs, with the stipulation that every future parson should pay the canons a yearly pension of half a mark. It was further covenanted that no parson be presented until he had sworn his willingness to pay, and that presentations should take place in the presence of the prior or one of his canons. On the other hand, Matthew and his heirs promised that they would not make over their rights in the church of Eston to any other body. The record of the agreement was witnessed by a large and impressive group of ecclesiasts, amongst whom the Durham *familia* was especially prominent; William du Puiset, Masters William of Howden and Henry of Lincoln, an unidentified Master William—perhaps William of Blois—and the elusive William, son of the archbishop.[3] Whether these latter had taken any active part in making the concordat, or whether they had assisted their master as assessors on points of law, must remain matters for speculation. It is, however, worthy of note that a very similar body is to be found with the bishop at another arbitration which he effected at approximately this date.[4]

It would seem that Puiset only acted once as a papal judge delegate after the time of Alexander III. In 1183, together with Sylvanus, abbot of Rievaulx and Clement, abbot of St Mary's, York, acting on a mandate of Lucius III, he settled a dispute on

[1] Mansi, XXII, col. 423. William, the clerk of Reiner the Fleming, appears *c.* 1175–85. For Reiner, a tenant of the Skipton and Percy fees (*c.* 1160–1200), see *EYC*, VII, 196–7.

[2] For Vacarius, see Liebermann in *EHR*, XI (1896), 305–14; Kuttner and Rathbone, 'Anglo-Norman Canonists of the Twelfth Century', 287.

[3] *An Abstract of Charters and other Documents contained in the Chartulary of the Priory of Bridlington*, ed. W. T. Lancaster, 426.   [4] See below, p. 85.

the rights of a mother church against a chapelry—a frequent source of litigation at the time. The quarrel, between Abbot Samson and the convent of Bury on the one hand, and the nuns of Stixwould on the other, over the church and chapel of Wainfleet, ended with an agreement that the nuns were to remain in possession of the church, paying Bury forty sesters of salt a year. Bury was to retain the chapel, but not thereby to injure the rights of the mother church of Wainfleet. The monk, or monks, serving the chapel were not to exercise any parochial rights outside its ancient boundaries, and no secular priest was to officiate there without the consent of the mother church. It was further agreed that none except the religious should receive eucharist or penance there, unless denied them by the priest of the mother church, and threatened by imminent death. It was also agreed that Robert, the clerk, who held the church of the nuns, should retain it for life, paying them twenty sesters of salt a year, and the abbot of Bardney, who was an interested party, ratified the form of agreement.[1]

There remains a group of adjudications of uncertain provenance. It may be that the papal documents initiating the cases have left no trace, or that the bishop was acting in a private capacity, exercising in a wider sphere that bent for conciliation with which he was currently credited and which he displayed in some measure in his own see. During a cause in the thirteenth century the nuns of Swine produced writings which appear to have embodied some form of episcopal arbitration.[2] Sometime between 1174 and 1181 a controversy relating to Hood, involving the canons of Newburgh and Adam Fossard, was settled by the bishop,[3] whilst in 1189 he witnessed the record of a compromise negotiated by the abbot of Tewkesbury and others, exempting the priory of Bradenstoke from the abbey of Cirencester.[4]

---

[1] See below, App. II, no. 3; *Feudal Documents from the Abbey of Bury St Edmunds*, ed. D. C. Douglas, no. 221.

[2] *The Register of William Greenfield, Archbishop of York*, v (ed. A. Hamilton Thompson), 198–9.

[3] *Mon. Ang.* VI, 322; *EYC*, IX, no. 121, where dated 1166–83. The presence of William Puiset as archdeacon indicates a date after 1174.

[4] The Register of Bradenstoke, BM, Stowe MS. 925, fo. 34ᵛ.

Puiset, like any other of his colleagues, was by convention among the natural councillors of his king, and accordingly liable to be involved in those difficult ecclesiastical cases which found their way, rightly or wrongly, to the royal presence. Of these two were outstanding, the dispute between the abbot of St Albans and the bishop of Lincoln, and that of the convent of Christchurch with Archbishop Baldwin of Canterbury. The great St Albans suit for exemption was ended by Henry II at Westminster in 1163, when Durham was amongst those present. Prior to this he had twice intervened on his own initiative —much to the satisfaction of the monks. The first occasion was in 1156, shortly after Robert of Lincoln had refused to accept a group of privileges recently acquired in Rome. It was then that Puiset, *partes suas interponens*, arranged a meeting at St Neot's, where, with the assistance of the bishops of London and Hereford he was largely responsible for what was in the event only a momentary truce.[1] Shortly thereafter Lincoln was incensed by bulls granted to the convent by Adrian IV, who, he alleged, had a natural domestic affection for St Albans. Once again (1159) Puiset arranged a suitable meeting-place and with the aid of the bishops of Chichester and Hereford brought the parties to some form of peace.[2]

Canterbury was a matter of greater notoriety. The immediate cause was a project of Archbishop Baldwin to endow a college of secular canons at Hackington. This, for a variety of reasons, met with the strenuous disapproval of the monks of Christchurch.[3] The dispute, played to an accompaniment of much public propaganda, moved through an epic of appeals, sieges and miracles, relieved at times by interludes of low comedy. Each party sought supporters at home and abroad, 'and the state of Europe was such that neither...had any difficulty in finding them'.[4]

After some vain attempts to heal troubles arising out of Baldwin's initial administrative actions, Henry II himself

---

[1] *Gesta Abbatum Monasterii Sancti Albani*, ed. H. T. Riley, I, 131.
[2] *Gesta Abbatum Monasterii Sancti Albani*, I, 134–5.
[3] Stubbs, 366–438; see below, p. 137.
[4] Stubbs, 386.

visited Canterbury in February 1187. Details of the course of events have been preserved by the Christchurch chronicler. The king and his archbishop entered the chapter-house (11 February), leaving strict orders that none be admitted except those they summoned. They then called in the bishops of Norwich and Durham, Hubert Walter and Peter of Blois, together with the subprior and a group of monks. Henry attempted to mediate, suggesting that the monks should abandon their appeal to Rome and abide by his ruling. They welcomed the proposal, but wished to pursue the appeal. Thereupon the king suggested the arbitration should be conditional on the consent of the prior, to which the monks replied that they could do nothing in his absence. There was some further manœuvring, but nothing of any purpose was achieved.[1]

The quarrel continued and expanded. A Christchurch party became more apparent in the kingdom and especially among the episcopate. As at St Albans Puiset was regarded as a monastic champion—a curious irony in that it made him the opponent of a scheme identical to that which he was pursuing in his own see.[2] His services were solicited by the chapter, and, as in the earlier dispute, they were freely given. Early in 1188 the convent wrote to the bishops of Worcester, Ely, Durham and St David's, putting them on their guard against 'false information', and describing what were allegedly the archbishop's new oppressions. Accordingly, in a series of individual letters, the monks begged the bishops to persuade the primate to abandon his plans for a new church.[3] Nothing resulted but more appeals and counter-appeals, together with some near-military operations against the chapter. At the coronation of Richard I both parties were manœuvring for support. The convent was represented by eight monks, whilst the bishops of Durham and Bath were said to be prepared to resist any petition that Baldwin might make for his new church.[4] Nothing of this order occurred, but the archbishop, finding himself comparatively

---

[1] Gervase of Canterbury, I, 354–5; Stubbs, 389.
[2] See below, pp. 110, 136.
[3] *Epistolae Cantuarienses*, ed. W. Stubbs, 148.
[4] *Epistolae Cantuarienses*, no. CCCXXIV; Stubbs, 407.

untrammelled, 'resolved to proceed to extremities'. One measure in this notable policy was the appointment as prior of that Roger Norreys who was to earn subsequent notoriety in a number of fields. The monks appealed to the king, and on 8 November 1189 their proctors were received at Westminster. There was much unseemly argument over a wide range, but in the end a form for discussion was suggested which involved the delicate phrase 'saving their ancient charters and privileges'. This, as applied to the charters of Richard of Dover, formerly a Canterbury monk, was more than Baldwin would tolerate. It was at this stage that Puiset, seeing that yet another day was likely to be wasted in futilities, suggested that the charters from the time of Richard should be examined, and only those consonant with reason held relevant. This evasion appears to be of small merit, though perhaps no worse than other ambiguities which have eased political consciences. As it was it came to nothing. The bishops of Bath and Durham and the master of the Temple urged the monks to accept royal mediation. Richard, tired of discussions, empanelled a jury of eight bishops (including Durham), five abbots and the prior of Merton. This again proved abortive, notwithstanding the violence of the royal language.[1]

Late in November the king and his whole court came to Canterbury. Another attempt was made at arbitration and this time, after a false start, with success. The king suggested that the archbishop should surrender his college and the prior, and the monks would allow him to decide other points by his own sense of justice. The convent felt this to be attractive, but still hesitated. They consulted their friends, amongst whom was the bishop of Durham, and on their advice agreed to submit. The cause was for the time terminated and a deed drawn up recording the settlement.[2]

On the whole this evidence illustrates known details of royal and canonist procedure, of greater significance for papal and monastic history than for the individual career of the bishop of

---

[1] Gervase of Canterbury, I, 468; Stubbs, 408.
[2] Gervase of Canterbury, I, 477-9; *Epistolae Cantuarienses*, no. cccxxxv; Hoveden, III, 24; Stubbs, 408-10.

Durham. It is, for example, worthy of comment that the papal mandates cited traverse almost the entire reign of Henry II, showing no remarkable increase stimulated by the compromise of 1172. At the same time they reveal a picture of pope and bishops co-operating in matters of discipline and privilege throughout the upheavals of the Becket dispute. Puiset appears in a more uncertain light. Possibly his public solicitude for monks, strongly contrasting with his behaviour in Durham, should be taken as political opportunism—his concern for the chapter of Canterbury might even suggest an eye to the archiepiscopal throne. His skill as an arbitrator must remain no more than an assumption, but of his reputation and weight there can be no doubt. His services were sought by a number of communities and clearly respected by Richard's government; he was employed by Alexander III within a year of having opposed his recognition as pope.[1] For the rest, though he was in some measure influenced by that general working of the canonist leaven which marked the pontificate of the greatest pope since Gregory VII, he was no scholar and hardly the man to be interested in the subtleties of technical law. There is no evidence to suggest either his knowledge or ignorance of current law. The clerks of his household must have been able to remedy his academic shortcomings. His family, connexions and office combined to give an eminence and authority to which parties in dispute might submit without objection, whilst his own natural charm, wide experience and recognized skill as a mediator allowed him to share—albeit without distinction—in the routine operation of the elaborate machinery of papal justice. Compared with some of his more learned colleagues he was rarely employed as a judge delegate, nor did he often act in causes of great moment or complexity—perhaps his behaviour in the Bridlington case was warning of a spirit more cavalier than judicious. He probably appeared for Rievaulx on the nomination of the house. Otherwise he was doubtless commissioned as an immunist who might well act in such a case as that of Canterbury; as one well versed in the affairs of the north; and as the only suffragan of York who could be

[1] See above, pp. 29–30.

employed either in Scotland or the southern province. The testimonial is somewhat ambiguous, but at least it demonstrates that in this, as in other aspects of his career, Puiset was less the abnormality, the isolated grandee that he seemed to earlier historians, but like others of humbler inclination, clearly exposed to the tendencies of his age.

CHAPTER IV

THE BISHOP AS DIOCESAN

I. THE BISHOP IN HIS DIOCESE

THE English bishops who were Puiset's contemporaries were distinguished men in a distinguished age. On the Continent Peter Comestor and Maurice de Sully had been rivals for the see of Paris, whilst Rainald of Dassel, chancellor to Barbarossa, and archbishop elect of Cologne, was patron of a poet who can well stand comparison with the English lyricists of the seventeenth century. In England Robert of Melun, author of a *Summa Theologica* and a theologian of European reputation who had taught in Paris, was bishop of Hereford, whilst Henry of Winchester anticipated the tastes and interests of a Medici pope.[1] If, as has recently been observed, the colleagues of Archbishop Becket formed the ablest bench in English medieval history, perhaps much of their distinction lay, if not in spiritual qualities, in intellectual and administrative abilities revealed in the routine of diocesan life, as well as in the direction of national affairs, or the operation of those legal and administrative reforms which marked the reign of Henry II.

The period was one of especial importance in diocesan history. Uniformity, such as it was, was increasing. Traditional liberties were threatened as authority was defined and enforced. The ancient vagaries of the Celtic churches of Ireland, Wales and Scotland fell before the common pattern, whilst monastic and episcopal peculiars felt the efforts of the ordinaries to unify and extend their jurisdictions. Expanding authority and papal diplomacy raised hopes and disputes. Bishops were frequently at law with their chapters, metropolitans with their suffragans. With this, and other more laudable activities, there came an inevitable expansion of the machinery of diocesan administra-

---

[1] V. Mortet, *Maurice de Sully, passim*; Helen Waddell, *The Wandering Scholars*, 152–8; Edmund Bishop, *Liturgica Historica*, 392–401.

tion. Fine grades of office—the ancestors of the immense officialdom of succeeding centuries—appear among the witnesses to episcopal *acta*; clerks, chaplains, notaries and a wide variety of secular colleagues. The 'official' emerges before the end of the century, whilst the territorial archdeaconry was firmly established, and archidiaconal powers so extensive that by 1190 a preacher could find no more effective parable to demonstrate the mutability of human fortunes than to declare to his congregation that even popes and archdeacons died.[1]

The condition of the diocese of Durham at this time, and the nature and extent of the bishop's authority therein are difficult to define and describe. Certain significant features may, however, be noticed, the most important of which was the unique and dominant position of the cathedral chapter. It was then at the height of its literary and intellectual distinction, magnificently housed in one of the most superb churches of western Christendom, and endowed with the enormous prestige of the name of Cuthbert and the wealth of a patrimony containing the best part of the one-time kingdom of Northumbria.[2]

Apart from the outlines of a number of disputes with Puiset himself, and indeed with the majority of the neighbouring diocesans and religious, little is known of the history of the convent.[3] Individual monks are often named, such as Henry and Reginald, 'dwelling at Finchale', and despite the gloomy logic of the law books, frequently test charters. Some, like Alan, Robert son of Udard, William of Nunwick, Ralph and Geoffrey, use their own names. Others have names in religion of a good patristic flavour; Samson, Hilary, Augustine, Patrick, and that Chaucerian 'sir Silvanus, monk of Durham', who seems to have ridden forth on many a mission.[4] Little can be dis-

---

[1] Mortet, *op. cit.* 162.

[2] *Two Lives of St Cuthbert*, ed. B. Colgrave, 2; Sir Maurice Powicke, 'Maurice of Rievaulx', 17–25. Walter Daniel (in his *Vita Ailredi*) described Maurice, who was a product of Durham, as one known to his contemporaries as another Bede, *tam vite quam sciencie*, cf. Knowles, *Monastic Order*, 229 and 499. For other notices of Durham learning in this period, see above, pp. 68–70, and below, pp. 102–3.

[3] See below, pp. 130–6, 159–60.

[4] DC York, Register of St Mary's, new foliation, fo. 305; DC Durham, 2. 3. Sac. no. 5; *Abstract of Charters and other Documents contained in the Cartulary*

covered of either the origins or social status of the professed of the house. During Puiset's episcopate the community contained, in Thomas de Muschamps, a member of the Northumbrian aristocracy. Bertram, the ablest prior of the period, was descended from the intermarriage of one of Rannulf Flambard's many relatives with a family of conventual sergeants holding at Ferryhill. The subprior, Henry, was either a Scandinavian or a German. Adam of Moorsley—the earliest life corrodian mentioned at Durham—who before 1198 had surrendered his lands to the convent in return for the corrody of a monk, again appears to have been of the status of a sergeant or lesser knight.[1]

A number of the major officers and obedientiaries of the house appear from time to time, suggesting in their designations a fully developed administration of the usual type. The priors had their own officials and a clearly defined household. In this relatives played their customarily important role. So under Germanus (1162–89) we hear of the *nepotes* Walter and Master Richard, whilst in the time of Bertram (1189–1212) there is the ubiquitous family of Ferry, one of whose many members, Henry, nephew of the prior, later held the church of Herrington.[2] These were as a rule accompanied by a limited number of obedientiaries and a select body of monks, clerks and sergeants. In the time of Germanus there was Adam *de camera prioris*, or *de camera Germani prioris*, and Robert, chamberlain of the prior, whilst under Bertram there appears Adam, the prior's 'sergeant of the cellar'. John the clerk, nephew of the prior (either Absalon, or his successor, Thomas), witnessed a deed before 1162, and Alan, clerk of the prior, occurs before 1189.[3]

Henry, the subprior, *natione Teutonicus*, and apparently a man

---

of Fountains, ed. W. T. Lancaster, 208; DC Durham, Cart. ii, fo. 265ᵛ; *Liber Cartarum Sancte Crucis de Edwinesburg*, 10, no. 9; DC Durham 4. 7. Spec. no. 7, printed in *FPD*, 128 n.; DC Durham, Cart. ii, fo. 54; *FPD*, 295. There is a list of the books of William of Nunwick in *Catalogi Veteres*, 8.

[1] DC Durham, 4. 7. Spec. no. 15, printed in *FPD*, 127 n.

[2] DC Durham, 3. 7. Spec. no. 1; Cart. iii, fo. 247ᵛ. For the family of Ferry see the index to *FPD*, *sub nomine*. For Master Richard, see below, p. 146.

[3] DC Durham, 1. 4. Ebor. no. 25; Cart. Elemos. 89–90, printed in Surtees, ii, 206; DC Durham, 2. 1. Ebor. no. 14, printed in *EYC*, ii, no. 950; *EYC*, ii, no. 981; DC Durham, 4. 7. Spec. no. 1, printed in *FPD*, 128 n.

of parts, attested a charter in 1154–8. A successor, Patrick, possibly the aforementioned monk of that name, appears *c.* 1190.[1] Two sacrists, Godfrey and Laurence, occur in the 1150's, and towards the end of the century the office was held by Alan, Adam, Arnaldus and Elyas, and we hear of the responsibilities incumbent on them following the death of some local magnate.[2] William the feretrar also appears *c.* 1190.[3] Robert of Howden, 'monk and priest', who sealed charters (*manu sua propria*) with the seal of St Cuthbert was clearly some form of chancellor—such an office being mentioned in 1190— just as John de Insula was one of the many conventual scribes.[4] Roger the cellarer tests charters as early as 1155 and as late as 1190, and Robert the hostiller occurs within the same period.[5] Before 1180 there is a reference to Alan, clerk of the cellar, who is accompanied by Robert the cook, and many others, often so curiously named as to recall the companions of Falstaff, generally described as servants of one or other of these pleasant and indispensable offices.[6] Hugh the cellarer, who appears about the same time, was one party to a friendly agreement which resulted in the episcopal forester being offered salmon in return for timber for repairing one of the monastic fish kidells.[7]

The infirmary, almonry and hostelry were all well established with separate endowments and considerable control of their own affairs by the end of the episcopate. At the same time the priory churches of Coldingham, Finchale, Stamford and Holy Island had started on their way to what was to prove to be the troublesome independence of the status of cells. Stamford is described as the *monasterium* of St Leonard in 1146, and again so

[1] DC York, Register of St Mary's, new foliation, fo. 305; *Libellus...Cuthberti*, 107; Symeon, I, 326, 329; *EYC*, VIII, no. 117; *Register of Wetherhal*, ed. Prescott, no. 119.

[2] DC Durham, 3. 9. Spec. no. 12, printed in *FPD*, 141 n.; 3. 8. Spec. no. 4, printed in *FPD*, 132 n.; 4. 7. Spec. no. 9, printed in *FPD*, 127 n.

[3] DC Durham, 2. 6. Spec. no. 10.

[4] *FPD*, 299–300. The office of chancellor of the monks of Durham is mentioned in *EYC*, VIII, 117.

[5] DC Durham, 1. 8. Spec. no. 34, printed in *FPD*, 121 n.; *EYC*, VIII, no. 117.

[6] DC Durham, 3. 9. Spec. no. 12, printed in *FPD*, 141 n.; Reg. I, fo. 93, printed in *FPD*, 23 n.; Reg. I, fo. 72ᵛ, printed in *FPD*, 16 n.; Reg. I, fo. 11.

[7] *FPD*, 244.

in 1196.[1] In 1186 Coldingham, Stamford and Holy Island are all termed cells, though the meaning of the word is nowhere defined, and it is only in relation to Coldingham that its practical significance is revealed.[2] A prior of the house occurs in the address of a papal privilege (1159–81), and a certain Herbert is mentioned in that office in the convention of Falaise (1175).[3] The appointment of both prior and monks was described, in 1157, as being *sub ecclesie Dunelmensis potestate*, though it is clear that there was not always a prior in residence. The writs of the Scottish kings, Malcolm (1153–65) and William (1165–1214), usually assume the house would enjoy a fair control of its own secular affairs, and at one stage there appears the *plena curia prioris de Coldingham*.[4]

The monopolistic policies of the cathedral chapter, and the generally intractable nature of such land as had escaped the church of Durham, left little space for other communities. Thus the diocese, and more especially what is now Co. Durham, contained few houses of religious, and none of any consequence. There were a number of small hospitals at Durham, Witton Gilbert, Sedgefield and Newcastle.[5] The traditions of an earlier asceticism lingered on at Finchale (where dwelt Godric, repentant of a life of either commerce or piracy), Ebchester, Yearhaugh and Farne.[6] Rievaulx held at Sheraton, the nuns of St Bartholomew's, Newcastle, at Stella, and Holme Cultram at Hartlepool.[7] Carlisle, Nostell, Lanercost, Nun Monkton,

---

[1] *PU*, II, nos. 51, 278.

[2] *PU*, II, no. 238.

[3] *PU*, II, no. 205; *Gesta*, I, 96, and cf. *Liber Cartarum Sancte Crucis de Edwinesburg*, 41, no. 51. Herbert first appears *c*. 1147.

[4] *PU*, II, no. 94; DC Durham, Cart. Misc. no. 605.

[5] DC Durham, 4. 1. Pont. no. 4, printed in *FPD*, 198 n.; 2. 6. Spec. no. 69; 2. 1. Elemos. no. 19; *Early Newcastle Deeds*, ed. A. M. Oliver, 55, no. 73; *Libellus ...Godrici*, 376–7; *VCH Durham*, II, 114.

[6] For Finchale, see DC Durham, 3. 1. Pont. no. 6, printed in *Priory of Finchale*, 21, and the *Libellus...Godrici, passim*. For Ebchester, see Surtees, I, 283–4; Hutchinson, II, 591–601; Colgrave, *Two Lives of St Cuthbert*, 318; Symeon, I, 300. For Yearhaugh, see *FPD*, 240 and 277. The hermit in question was a descendant of Flambard. For Farne, see the life of St Bartholomew in Symeon, I, 300, 309–10 and cf. Knowles, *Monastic Order*, 170.

[7] Surtees, I, 283–4; PRO, Augmentation Office, Ancient Deed E 326/B 11537; *The Register and Records of Holm Cultram*, ed. F. Grainger and W. G. Collingwood, 43–4.

St Albans and St Mary's, York all had churches in the diocese.[1]
At Hexham (whose canons also held in Durham), there was a
peculiar of the see of York, where Puiset seems to have attempted to exercise unsolicited influence in the selection of a
prior.[2] In Northumberland there were Cistercians at Newminster, who held at Chopwell and Elvet, and Austin canons
at Brinkburn, who had land at Whickham by Puiset's gift.[3]
Guisborough, the powerful Bruce foundation of the same order,
held Trimdon, and had possessions at Castle Eden, Hart,
Stranton and Hartlepool, but its attempt to establish a cell
at Baxterwood, near Durham, was speedily quashed by the
convent.[4] During Puiset's episcopate the order of St John of
Jerusalem was introduced into the county by private benefaction, and the great families of Vesci and Bolbec founded houses
of Premonstratensians at Alnwick and Blanchland.[5]

The fortunes of parochial life are obscure. Some 150 churches
and chapelries are mentioned during the later twelfth century,
though the number must have stood much higher, and was
certainly increasing as new lands were opened up and new
populations came into existence. So great were these changes
and their fiscal potentialities that the bishop himself had papal
licence to carry out extensive building, *propter raritatem
ecclesiarum et densitatem habitantium*, a privilege which needless to
say he endeavoured to exploit to the fullest.[6] During the
episcopate Peter of Sedgefield and Thomas of the buttery each
had Puiset's permission to build chapels, the one at Rowley, the
other near Bushblades.[7] Earlier Papedus had founded one at
Ancroft, as also John de Amundeville at Nun Stainton, in the
parish of Aycliffe, where services were held three times a week,

[1] See below, pp. 97–8.
[2] *Historians of the Church of York*, ed. Raine, III, 80; DC Durham, Cart. Misc.
no. 6590.
[3] *Newminster Cartulary*, 45–6; DC Durham, Cart. II, fo. 251, printed in *FPD*,
199 n.; *Brinkburn Cartulary*, no. CCXXIV; *BB*, 34; *PU*, I, no. 237.
[4] *BB*, 9; *Reg. Pal. Dun*, II, 1135; *EYC*, II, nos. 652 and 655. See also below,
p. 110.
[5] *Early Newcastle Deeds*, 112; *Mon. Ang.* VI (2), 867, no. 3; *Reg. Pal. Dun*, IV,
105; *Mon. Ang.* VI (2), 886, no. 1; Colvin, *The White Canons*, 98.
[6] *PU*, III, no. 330.
[7] DC Durham, 4. 1. Pont. no. 3; *Calendar of the Greenwell Deeds*, ed. J. Walton,
no. 6.

and wherein the locals were baptized and confessed, and had all sacraments *que Christianus habere debet*. These arrangements Puiset found satisfactory in view of the perils awaiting the traveller between Stainton and Aycliffe, and from a similar consideration of the environs of Durham, himself founded a chapelry at Witton, within the monastic parish of Elvet.[1]

The churches of the see ranged from wealthy cells, such as that at Tynemouth, belonging to St Albans, or Holy Island, with its five dependent chapels, to the new foundations, and private chantries or chapelries, like those maintained by local aristocrats at Hardwick, Hylton or Presson.[2] At least half the total, including most if not all the plums, was owned in some fashion or other by the religious. Thus, if the somewhat optimistic figures of papal and episcopal confirmations be accepted, forty belonged to Durham, fourteen to Tynemouth, six to Carlisle, two to St Mary's, and at least two to Hexham.[3] As was general, a fair selection of these monastic churches was appropriated, or at least awaiting the death of the incumbent and the goodwill of the diocesan that the financial lot of the brethren might be eased. At Durham it would seem that Jarrow, Monkwearmouth and Holy Island were the only livings which had been appropriated before Puiset's accession. The number was not increased during the episcopate, though the convent, in addition to generally phrased licences, hoped to devote the revenues from Norham, Merrington, Northallerton, Howden, Monk Hesledon, Elvet, Bishop Middleham, Aycliffe and Pittington to purposes of its own.[4] The canons of Nostell

---

[1] *FPD*, 225; DC Durham, Cart. IV, fo. 8, printed in *FPD*, 163 n.; see App. II, no. 5.

[2] DC Durham, I. 8. Spec. no. 41, printed in Surtees, I, 282; Cart. II, fo. 82; *NCH*, XI, 92 n. For the appearance of chantries in the twelfth century, see Kathleen Edwards, *English Secular Cathedrals*, 293, n. 1.

[3] For Durham, see *PU*, II, nos. 94, 212. For Tynemouth, see *PU*, III, no. 110; *NCH*, VIII, 63, n. 1. For Carlisle, see Brand, I, 238, note t. For St Mary's, see DC York, Register of St Mary's, new foliation, fo. 5 (noticed in *EYC*, I, 440). For Hexham, see DC Durham, Cart. Misc. no. 6590. This does not purport to be a comprehensive survey of monastic churches in the diocese. It must be further noticed that the appearance of a name in a papal or episcopal confirmation was no guarantee of seisin. This, it is hoped, will be made clear in the following pages.

[4] F. Barlow, *Durham Jurisdictional Peculiars*, 19; *PU*, II, nos. 149, 212; see also below, pp. 133–4.

had episcopal permission to appropriate at Bamburgh, *ad ecclesie sue promotionem et hospitalitatem augmentandam*, though the opportunity to implement this licence was lacking.[1]

Where monastic churches were not so treated, nor in the hands of farmers or custodians, they were, either in part or whole, held by incumbents who economically, if not legally, were tenants at a quit rent. Thus Ednam rendered 16 marks a year, Earlston and Eden 1 mark, and Bishop Middleham two pounds.[2] In this context it is perhaps worth noting the rough parallel between what, for lack of a better term, might be called quasi-leases, and the arrentation of demesne common in the earlier twelfth century, on the one hand, and that growth of appropriation and direct exploitation which characterized the turn of the century on the other.[3] The position of the pensioners was often merely the expression of a compromise between lay and ecclesiastical interest, and meant, for the most part, that hereditary parsons were required to make such payments as recognition of their subjection. Thus, for example, *c.* 1154–8, Ralph de Caugi, renewing an earlier donation by his Greinville ancestors, granted Ellingham to Durham, *salvo iure et possessione Gaufridi persone eiusdem ecclesie dum vixerit*. The condition was added that after Geoffrey's death the church should go to the 'most suitable' of the Caugi heirs, paying the convent an annual pension of 5s., and only after his death was Durham to enjoy the parsonage. These terms were renewed in slightly more decorous phrases in 1171–4, when the convent was promised Ellingham as freely as their other churches *in feodo alicujus baronis*. In practice this meant that although Puiset confirmed Durham's 'free disposition' of their gift, it was in fact Adam de Caugi he inducted at a pension of 5s. a year.[4] Again, at Ednam, the convent granted the church, with all its lands, appurtenances, and three chapels, to one Robert, son of Goze, to hold at an annual pension of 16 marks, with the reservation that whilst

---

[1] See below, pp. 198–9. [2] See below, pp. 116–17.
[3] Cf. Knowles, *Monastic Order*, 598–9.
[4] DC Durham, 3. 1. Pont. no. 11, printed in *FPD*, 100; DC Durham, 3. 1. Pont. no. 11*, printed in *NCH*, 11, 268, n. 2; DC Durham 3. 1. Pont. no. 12, printed in *FPD*, 103 n., *NCH*, 11, 272, n. 4. Some material on the families of Greinville and Caugi is gathered in *NCH* and *FPD*, *loc. cit.*

Goze was living, *et in seculo esse voluerit, habebit custodiam eiusdem Roberti et eiusdem ecclesie.*[1] The practice was common, and this particular mode of ensuring the hereditary transmission of livings was one of the shortcomings Alexander III endeavoured to remove from the English Church.[2]

This same lay grip is reflected in the number of cases where the benefice was divided, usually the result of paternal solicitude or the outcome of some general partition of property, wherein the church and its appurtenances had received the same treatment as any other items. In 1174 there were three parsons at Hartburn and two at Coniscliffe. Corbridge had two in 1193, and in 1196 there was an unspecified number at Norton and Washington, and at least two at Easington.[3] From later evidence it appears that Ponteland had long been divided *in tres porciones equales*, which had satisfactorily maintained three brothers. This situation Puiset had attempted to end by ordering that as the portions became vacant they should be united.[4]

The diocesan clergy, numerous though they were, have, with certain great exceptions, left little mark. Several, by need or inclination, held land and appear among the lesser freemen of the Liberty.[5] Others, to the peril of their souls, took employment among the temptations of lay households and occasionally perform as the somewhat rustic scribes of private charters.[6] There seem to be but two references to the discharge of any pastoral duties. The chaplain of Ancroft is mentioned as hearing confessions from four vills, whilst at the end of Puiset's episcopate Roger of Weardale, custodian of the vacant church of Heighington (then in dispute between bishop and convent), went forth to visit the sick, having first entrusted the key of the church to his clerk as a precaution against attempted

[1] DC Durham, Reg. 1, fo. 108ᵛ.

[2] Cf. Foreville, *L'Église et La Royauté en Angleterre*, 395 and references.

[3] *NCH*, VIII, 64–5; Brand, 1, 238, note t; *Chancellor's Roll 8 Richard I*, 257. Cf. Knowles, *Monastic Order*, 564.

[4] Merton College Archives, Deeds nos. 562, 578. The brothers were apparently William, Gilbert and Elias (*NCH*, XII, 408 n.).

[5] *Priory of Finchale*, 6; *BB*, 2, 28.

[6] *Libellus...Godrici*, 226; *Northumberland and Durham Deeds*, 120–1, no. 2; DC Durham, 3. 8. Spec. no. 5, printed in *FPD*, 132 n.

monastic intrusions.[1] Monks were possibly serving some churches—as for example Finchale—or acting as custodians of such vacant livings as the priory could claim. Thus in the much disputed Heighington John of Reading, ably supported by three laymen, was pleasantly established *in domo persone*, wherein, during his brief tenure of office, he was observed by those with an attentive eye for such matters making merry *cum quibusdam parrochianis suis*.[2] In most of the better preferments there were clerks from either the bishop's or the prior's household. In livings on the baronial fees there were the inevitable relatives of the local magnates—Caugi, Balliol, Hansard, Laley and Conyers.[3] Pluralism was common. Burchard Puiset was archdeacon of Durham and treasurer of York. Peter de Ros, canon of York and archdeacon of Carlisle, had half Corbridge. Master Richard of Coldingham held at least two churches, and the parson of Brantingham was a canon of Beverley.[4] It is, of course highly improbable that either the grandees or such great clerks, most of whom were busy men, did any more than draw a revenue from their livings. At Bishop Middleham, which Master Richard of Coldingham held of the priory, there was *quidam firmarius (qui) tenuerat ecclesiam illam ad firmam de predicto Ricardo*.[5]

A large number of livings continued to descend from father to son, despite the fulminations of reformers and the intervention of the papacy, and many clerks, from the bishop downwards, had relapsed in some degree or other from what, after the inevitable lag, was now coming to be regarded as virtue. One of the miracles of Godric concerns a daughter of the priest of Embleton, and another a worthy matron whose husband was in some grade of orders.[6] A mute cripple, effectively cured by the saint's ministrations, joyfully announced to the admiring spectators that his sire was a certain *Willelmum sacerdotem*. On

[1] *FPD*, 228, 261, see also below, p. 198.

[2] Newburgh, 1, 150; *Libellus...Godrici*, cap. cix; Barlow, *op. cit.* xii, n. 1; *FPD*, 287–8, 296–7.

[3] DC Durham, 3. 1. Pont. 12, printed in *FPD*, 103 n.; *Chancellor's Roll 8 Richard I*, 256–7; *Priory of Finchale*, 76; Surtees, 11, 168; *FPD*, 246.

[4] For Burchard Puiset and Master Richard of Coldingham, see below pp. 146, 234. For Peter de Ros see Brand, 1, 238 note t; *Gesta*, 11, 248. For Philip of Beverley see DC Durham, 2. 1. Archiep. no. 30; *FPD*, 295.

[5] *FPD*, 250.   [6] *Libellus...Godrici*, 376, 409 and 463.

one occasion there is mention of John, son of the parson of Aycliffe, whilst the wife of the parson of Lanchester, and William the priest, and James his son, all appear in Boldon Book.[1] Somewhat more surprising, in view of the frequent association of the dissemination of a stricter papal morality with the widespread appearance of *magistri*, is the fact that Master Walter of Haddington, a distinguished clerk of the priory in the later twelfth century, had a daughter, Agnes, to whom he bequeathed land in Elvet.[2]

Though papal decrees and the legislation of various councils on the subject of clerical celibacy were known and recorded at Durham, and the monk, Symeon, writing in the early twelfth century, shows a keen awareness of the merits of chastity, the prevailing situation caused little local consternation.[3] This indeed would have been difficult considering the bishop's own position as a successful paterfamilias, and the paternal solicitude shown by some of the greatest clerks in watching the interests of their progeny. So bishop and priors freely recognized hereditary influences—as at Ednam or Ellingham—and well into the thirteenth century we find Robert Stichill, son of a local priest, as bishop of Durham.[4]

Such was the typical background against which Puiset discharged his office of diocesan. A few wealthy communities, of which only Durham itself could show any appreciable learning, the informed ability of the clerks of his entourage, and for the rest huge distances, sparse populations, and a clergy largely ignorant and for the most part scarcely differentiated from the flocks to whom they ministered. The bishop's recorded reflections on his duty are characteristically limited to a few platitudes derived from the current jargon of the papal chancery.[5] In practice these were generally belied by qualities scarcely those of the patristic centuries; greed, magnificence, ostentation and a limitless ambition. In the spiritual, as in the secular field the most conspicuous signs are of deliberate efforts to consolidate

[1] *BB*, 28, 31; *Priory of Finchale*, 79–80.
[2] DC Durham, Cart. Elemos. 135–6. For other examples, see below, pp. 145, 235–6.   [3] Symeon, i, 93; ii, 207, 240, 256, 270, 280.
[4] *Scriptores Tres*, 45; cf. M. Gibbs and J. Lang, *Bishops and Reform, 1215–1272*, 8.
[5] *EYC*, ii, no. 937.

authority, which need no subtle reason for their explanation. The episcopate was punctuated by a series of clashes with the convent of Durham, and with the two great immunists of the see; York at Hexham and St Albans at Tynemouth.[1] But there are no episodes which show Puiset, like Bartholomew of Exeter or Hugh of Lincoln, in constructive contact with his clergy, though on the lowest plane economic necessity must have sent him on periodical tours of his see—there is even a reference to a visit to Holy Island, *hospitandi gratia vel...ibi divina celebranda misteria*.[2] Contemporaries found little to commend in his discharge of the pastoral office; the natural simile was of the shearer rather than the shepherd.

His tastes were not in such fields, nor in those of learning, for his intellectual interests were of a modest order. Like his uncle of Winchester he was less a scholar than a connoisseur, and more at home in politics than the traffic of ideas.[3] His library contained little written after *c.* 1160–70, and nothing speculative, unique, or even rare, suggesting on the whole the well-informed but conventional tastes of the earlier years of his episcopate, for which subsequent events and opportunities had perhaps left neither leisure nor inclination. Its range is disappointing in one who probably grew up in the shadow of the fine classicism of Chartres, yet pleasantly surprising in comparison with the more obvious features of his general mode of life.[4]

The classics and their near associates were conservative and weak, especially when compared with the remarkable humanism of the Durham chapter.[5] There was a more or less complete

[1] See below, pp. 156–7, 170.   [2] *Libellus...Cuthberti*, 117.
[3] *Sine multis literis eloquentissimus* (Newburgh, II, 437).
[4] Puiset's collection of books, which passed to the convent of Durham, compares favourably in numbers with most contemporary episcopal libraries. In content it surpasses the literary interest of Alexander the Magnificent and Robert Chesney of Lincoln (cf. Gerald of Wales, VII, App. 168–9). It does not seem that Hugh was a bibliophile of the order of his uncle of Winchester, who gave fifty books to Glastonbury alone (Knowles, *Monastic Order*, 524). Nor again can it be said that his tastes were anything scholastic when his collection is compared with that of the able, but by no means intellectually distinguished, Thomas Becket (cf. M. R. James, *The Ancient Libraries of Canterbury and Dover*, xli–xlii, 82–5).
[5] *Catalogi Veteres*, 1–10, and the comments of J. de Ghellinck, *L'Essor de la Littérature Latine*, II, 69, where he holds the classical wealth of Durham comparable to that of Bec, Corbie, Cluny, Lorsch, etc.

collection of the works of Claudian, whose 'intolerable wit' found such small favour with Gibbon,[1] Cicero's *Rhetorica*, the influential *De Amicitia*, which coloured a great deal of Christian exposition of the same theme, and the *Ad Herennium*.[2] There were two copies of Priscian, presumably the universal *Institutiones Grammaticae*,[3] Solinus's popular collection of curiosities, the *Res Memorabiles*,[4] the unexciting works of the Christian classic, Caelius Sedulius,[5] and the indispensable compilations of Isidore of Seville, 'toujours très consulté et écouté'.[6] Among the moderns Alan de Insula dedicated his *Historia Bruti* to the bishop with the traditional apparatus of fulsome praise—*tu mihi Maecenas, tu Caesaris aemulus unus*—and much else in the same vein,[7] whilst Reginald of Durham expressed himself with greater moderation.

There was a heavier selection of theology, generally showing (as might be anticipated) little interest in works of edification or hagiography, but something of that usual keen awareness of the exegesis current in the middle decades of the century. Patristics were represented by St Ambrose's *De Officiis Ministrorum*, and Gregory the Great's *Moralia* (in three volumes), the latter significantly accompanied by Garnier of St Victor's *Gregorianum*, a comparatively handy subject index to the copious Biblical allegories in the saint's works.[8] More recent were the immensely popular *Libri Sententiarum* of Peter Lombard, together with his glosses on the Pauline Epistles and the

[1] Puiset's books are listed in *Wills and Inventories...of the Northern Counties of England*, ed. J. Raine, 3–4, and *Catalogi Veteres*, 118–19. Claudian is now MS. O. 3. 22 of Trinity College, Cambridge (R. A. B. Mynors, *Durham Cathedral MSS.*, no. 155).

[2] The *Rhetorica, De Inventione* and *Ad Herennium* are DC Durham C iv, 5 (Mynors, *op. cit.* no. 154). For Cicero's popularity, see de Ghellinck, *op. cit.* i, 8, 186, ii, 79; J. E. Sandys, *A Companion to Latin Studies*, 648–9.

[3] For the importance and popularity of this, see de Ghellinck, *op. cit.* ii, 44.

[4] For the wide appeal of Solinus's works, see de Ghellinck, *op. cit.* i, 152, ii, 238.

[5] The nature of Sedulius's work is discussed by F. J. E. Raby, *A History of Christian Latin Poetry*, 108–10. For his wide popularity, and his influence on Laurence of Durham, see de Ghellinck, *op. cit.* ii, 144, 220.

[6] De Ghellinck, *op. cit.* ii, 253.

[7] *Dialogi Laurentii Dunelmensis Monachi et Prioris*, ed. J. Raine, 89.

[8] DC Durham, B iii, 13 (Mynors, *op. cit.* no. 150); cf. de Ghellinck, *op. cit.* i, 100.

Psalter,[1] and the equally influential *Historia Scholastica* of Peter Comestor, again complete with an abridgement[2]—in all a group of books of which copies were spreading through Europe by about 1170, and which few monastic or cathedral libraries were without by the end of the century. In addition there were a large number of glosses, probably mainly by the Lombard, on various books of both Testaments,[3] and the ubiquitous letters of Peter of Blois, of whom Puiset was seemingly a helpful patron following the death of Henry II.[4] Amongst other identifiable works were the popular sermons of Peter of Ravenna, a *Mappa Mundi* (i.e. a verbal description, perhaps that of Hugh of St Victor),[5] and the *Eulogium ad Alexandrum III Papam* of John of Cornwall, a pupil and critic of the Lombard, written *c.* 1175-7. The presence of this latter work in the episcopal library perhaps suggests some interest in current theological controversy, but is in any case further testimony of the contact, already noticed, between Puiset's *familia* and that distinguished intellectual circle at Lincoln in the late twelfth century, of which John of Cornwall was a member.[6]

Ecclesiastical law appears to have been weak—some uncertain *Decreta*, though possibly recent compilations—and the outmoded collection of Ivo of Chartres.[7] Service books, on the other hand, were abundant, and included five antiphoners, four graduals, three benedictionals, a missal and a pontifical.

[1] The Sentences are discussed by de Ghellinck in *Revue d'Histoire Ecclésiastique*, XIV (1913), 511-36, 705-19. The Pauline Epistles are DC Durham, A II, 19 (Mynors, *op. cit.* no. 149; E. G. Millar, *English Illuminated Manuscripts from the Tenth to the Thirteenth Century*, 36 and plate 51). The Psalter is DC Durham, A III, 7 (Mynors, *op. cit.* no. 148), cf. de Ghellinck, *L'Essor de La Littérature Latine*, I, 96-7. The spread of the Lombard's works in England in the middle decades of the century is analysed by H. Glunz, *The Vulgate in England*, 231-2, 255.

[2] Cf. de Ghellinck, *op. cit.* I, 95.

[3] A gloss on Isaiah is perhaps to be identified with MS. no. 50 of Jesus College, Cambridge (N. Ker, *The Medieval Libraries of Great Britain*, 39). The gloss on Leviticus is DC Durham, A IV, 1 (Mynors, *op. cit.* no. 152). Numbers is University of Durham Library, Cosins V II, 1 (Mynors, *op. cit.* no. 153). Matthew, DC Durham, A IV, 10 (Mynors, *op. cit.* no. 151).

[4] *Petri Blesensis Opera*, ed. J. A. Giles, I, 392-3.

[5] De Ghellinck, *op. cit.* I, 52.

[6] DC Durham, A II, 21. For John of Cornwall, see Morey, *Bartholomew of Exeter*, 107-8; de Ghellinck, *op. cit.* I, 73-4; E. Rathbone, 'John of Cornwall', 46-60.

[7] Cf. Kuttner and Rathbone, 'Anglo-Norman Canonists of the Twelfth Century', 295.

Whatever was lacking in content—and the gaps are considerable—was almost amended in format. Among Puiset's books are two Bibles and a number of glosses, which in their writing, binding and illumination—a last and glorious reflection of Northumbrian traditions—equal those great Bibles so characteristic of the later twelfth century, and are perhaps only excelled in their own church by the fine simplicity of the St Calais books.[1]

But Puiset was a maker of castles rather than churches, and churches rather than books. He was in all things a man of opulent magnificence. His own seals show him superbly clad in vestments encrusted with elaborate embroidery.[2] An inventory of these splendours reveals that of his many chasubles, one was of red velvet, 'nobly embroidered' in gold and bezants, and studded with great pearls and precious stones, whilst another was in black, emblazoned with a bizarre assortment of jewels, golden stars and griffons. The stoles and maniples were in the same taste, and included two in red *cum regibus et turribus brudatae*, whilst the albs were, if anything, even more splendid. One was red, decorated with twin-headed golden eagles *in parvis rotis*, a second, in the same basic colour, had the inevitable griffons, this time enhanced with flowers *in magnis rotis*, and another, *indici coloris*, added a further display of griffons, flowers and symbolic lions.

Every detail of worship, and every manifestation of episcopal power, expressed in some way or other this same impressive magnificence. In the bishop's private chapel—which required several horses for its transport—there were a cross and chalice *ex auro puro*, a great thurible of precious metal, and two small silver candelabra. Among a number of altar cloths there was one of especial merit, with a frontal on which were worked

---

[1] Cf. above, p. 104, n. 3. The great Puiset Bible, in four volumes, is DC Durham, A II, I (Mynors, *op. cit.* no. 146). The manuscript is discussed and illustrated in Millar, *op. cit.* 36 and plate 50 (cf. Glunz, *op. cit.* 194; Boase, *English Art, 1100–1210*, 229–30, 232, where there are comments on the binding). The two-volume Puiset Bible is DC Durham A II, 2 (Mynors, *op. cit.* no. 147), the text of which is that of the St Calais Bible (Glunz, *op. cit.* 193). For the general character of late twelfth-century Bibles see Glunz 173, 177, 183; Millar, *op. cit.* 33–5, 40–1; Boase, *op. cit.* cap. VI.

[2] *Durham Seals*, ed. W. Greenwell and C. H. Blair, II, 443, no. 3114*a*, and n. 28.

golden representations of the Trinity and the Apostles, *circa quorum capita sunt perli insuti*.[1]

When he prepared for his crusade in 1189 he ordered a collection of precious paraphernalia and domestic utensils, together with what appears to have been a small fleet for their transport, the combined glories of which were to set him before all others. Some slight record of one of this squadron, 'the great ship of the bishop of Durham', has survived. After Puiset's death she was seized by the royal officers, refitted, and sailed by an east coast skipper and crew from (probably) Gateshead to London, and there moored in the Thames with a watch aboard. Her size may be gathered from the fact that when she reached port and was laid up, it was necessary to hire a house to stow her ample gear, and that whilst on passage she carried a prize crew of thirty-two, whereas a royal galley in full commission had only sixty, the average ship of the southern magnate forty, and those of the Cinque Ports twenty-five.[2]

The episcopal largesse was consistently of this magnificent and ostentatious order, with 'mere charity' seemingly in a subordinate role. There were in Durham, it would appear, only seven tenants who held under any shelter system, with no rent or duty demanded, and by no means all of these were of that class of unfortunates to whom such generosity is traditionally offered. So William, one-time abbot of Peterborough, had Newton-by-Durham 'by the accommodation and alms of the Lord Bishop'.[3] At Carlton there was Summina, a widow, 'with 2 bovates quit of rent and service for her life', and in Stanhope three widows, each with a toft in alms. At Hartburn one Eva held 6 acres whilst on a portion of the episcopal waste at Satley there was a certain Brother John (later described as a hermit), 'restored to health by God's grace and the merits of St Cuthbert'.[4]

---

[1] *Wills and Inventories*, 3–4. Puiset's style was by no means individual in the matter of sacerdotal robes (cf. Morey, *Bartholomew of Exeter*, 83; Boase, *op. cit.* 90, 203).

[2] *Scriptores Tres*, 13 (the number of ships ordered is not given); *Chancellor's Roll 8 Richard I*, 18, 253; *PR 2 Richard I*, 8–9.

[3] *BB*, 2. William was deposed from Peterborough in 1175 by Archbishop Richard of Canterbury (*Gesta*, 1, 106; Gervase of Canterbury, 1, 256; see also above, p. 40).

[4] *BB*, 15, 30; DC Durham, Cart. Elemos. 83; *FPD*, 240; *BF*, 1, 30.

From piety and some care for public health, and no doubt with the added encouragement of the decrees of the Third Lateran Council, Puiset founded hospitals at Kepyer and Sherburn. Both, as later canonists had it, were *loci religiosi*, with their own churches and chapelries, directly subject to the episcopal jurisdiction, and like the run of such foundations, more fitted to guard the soul than cure the body.[1]

The leper house of Sherburn, founded *c.* 1183 for the benefit of the soul of Henry II 'and the eternal rest of those who raised us to the episcopate', was probably an enlargement on some earlier foundation.[2] It was based on the normal, and, indeed, the only expedient known to a society devoid of medical knowledge. The unfortunate sufferers were completely segregated from their fellows—a policy condemned by the distinguished historian of medicine as 'one of the dark incidents of man's inhumanity to man'.[3] Following what seems to have been the general haphazard practice of convenience, it was set, to the entire satisfaction of the local chronicler, in the midst of an area of rich and populous demesne.[4] It was intended to house the forbidding figure of sixty-five lepers in five 'cells'—the usual arrangement, somewhat resembling the *domunculae* of the hospitals of Christian antiquity—thus giving the settlement the nature and appearance of a small hamlet. The lepers were to be tended, as was customary, by an Order containing both men and women, of whom, however, nothing more is said. In accordance with recent legislation the hospital had its own church, in addition to an inner chapel, which were to be served by three priests and four other clerks. The whole establishment was under the direction of a procurator in priest's orders, appointed by, and responsible to the bishop.

[1] Mansi, xxii, col. 230; cf. Jean Imbert, *Les Hôpitaux en Droit Canonique*, 156.

[2] The text of the instrument of foundation is known only from later sources. There is an *inspeximus* by Bishop Hatfield, dated 1349, of a deed from the lost register of Antony Bek in DC Durham, Reg. ii, fo. 323ᵛ (printed in Surtees, i, 283–4; Hutchinson, ii, 591–601). In a charter dated 1183, Race Engaine refers to the hospital as 'newly constructed' ('A Second Calendar of the Greenwell Deeds', no. 41).

[3] Charles Singer, *A Short History of Medicine*, 79.

[4] *Scriptores Tres*, 11–12; cf. Imbert, *op. cit.* 116, 154 and notes; Morey, *Bartholomew of Exeter*, 99.

The dower, *pro pauperum sustentatione*, was munificent. It included Sherburn itself, with its mill and other appurtenances (all of which had recently benefited from the bishop's careful attention), licence to assart 160 acres on the Derwent near Ebchester, 10 bovates at Whitton, the vill of Garmondsway, a carucate nearby purchased from Race Engaine, and another at Sheraton, recovered at 50 marks from Rievaulx before the expiration of its lease. In addition there were the churches of Kelloe and Grindon (the latter newly built by Puiset in honour of Becket), and those of Sockburn and Bishopton, granted by Roger Conyers, in all of which the procurator, with the advice of the bishop, was to institute vicars.[1] It might be noted, however, that of all these endowments, only Sherburn itself came from the episcopal demesne, the remainder being either waste or purchase, whilst the acquisition of Garmondsway was perhaps of that order of proceeding which so incensed William of Newburgh. [2] Of the subsequent history of the foundation there is little trace, beyond the fact that towards the end of his episcopate the bishop granted one of his sergeants, Reginald of the chamber, *custodiam porte leprosorum de Shirburn*.[3]

It was also about 1180 that Puiset refounded Flambard's hospital at Kepyer, damaged during the fighting for Durham in the 1140's.[4] The new establishment was of some size, and of the usual quasi-monastic pattern employed in the care of the sick and the poor. It had its own infirmary, church, hall and court (*Curia*), wherein confessions were to be heard. It was given a staff of thirteen brethren, described as *conversi*,[5] who were to live the common life under a master and prior appointed by the bishop. Six were to be chaplains celebrating for the souls of Flambard and Puiset, the seventh a steward, the eighth in charge of the infirmary, the ninth a fisher, the tenth a miller, the eleventh to supervise the ploughs, the twelfth instauror, and

---

[1] See above, p. 107, n. 2, cf. Imbert, *op. cit.* 155.

[2] For Garmondsway, see below, pp. 199, 264. Newburgh's comment (II, 437–8) is: *ex parte minus honesta largitione construxit; alieni quippe juris non modicum huic devotioni per potentiam applicans, dum propria sufficienter impendere gravaretur.*

[3] *Reg. Pal. Dun*, II, 1299–1300 (1190–5).

[4] Symeon, I, 159; see above, p. 8, and below, p. 129.

[5] *quod sint in domo de Kepyer tresdecim conversi.*

the thirteenth in charge of the general business affairs of the house.[1]

The bishop confirmed the hospital in possession of Flambard's gifts, exempted its church from archidiaconal exactions, and granted in addition a borough at St Giles (Durham) a turbary at Newton, and a toft in each vill in which it had tithes of his demesne—Houghton, Ryhope, Easington, Darlington, Sedgefield and Boldon.[2] In another charter he granted land at Whitelees and mines at Rookhope (Weardale), which were to supply lead to roof the church and infirmary, and iron for use in ploughshares.[3] Furthermore he gave the brethren the vill of Cleadon, and a thrave of wheat[4] from every carucate of his demesne *sicut datur hospitali Sancti Petri in Eboracshire*. To these were added tithes from the episcopal *novalia* in Durham and Howden—which involved not only an uncertain and difficult point of canon law, but also the abrogation of a charter of Bishop Flambard in favour of the convent, and brought strong protests from the priory's church of St Peter of Howden and its distinguished incumbent.[5]

At the same time, as befitted the traditions of his house in England, Puiset was in general a generous patron of the religious. He was a known supporter of Rievaulx, a close friend of its most famous abbot, Ailred, and, as might be deduced from the presence of the abbots of Newminster, Rufford and Rievaulx at his deathbed, a steadfast believer in the then languishing Cistercian spirituality.[6] His friends included William, one-time abbot of Peterborough, Richard, prior of

---

[1] DC Durham, Reg. III, fo. 11ᵛ; Reg. II, fo. 325; Hutchinson, II, 300; *Memorials of St Giles's, Durham*, ed. J. Barmby, 196, n. 1; cf. Imbert, *op. cit.* 275–7.

[2] PRO Durham Cursitor Roll 43, m6, no. 31; *Memorials of St Giles's*, 195–6; *Mon. Ang.* VII, 732.

[3] Durham Cursitor, *loc. cit.*; *Memorials of St Giles's*, 199–200; BB, App. x; *Mon. Ang.* VII, 733.

[4] A thrave was apparently two small stooks of sheaves made in a cornfield before the corn was removed to the granaries. Coulton (*The Medieval Village*, 77 n.) holds the thrave to have been a score of sheaves. Much valuable information on the subject is gathered and discussed by J. W. F. Hill, *Medieval Lincoln*, 68–9.

[5] PRO Durham Cursitor Roll 43, m6; *Memorials of St Giles's*, 196; *Mon. Ang.* VII, 732; *VCH Durham*, II, 111. See also below, pp. 146–7.

[6] *EYC*, II, no. 958, see also above, pp. 75, 80, and below, pp. 258–61.

the Augustinian house of Newburgh, and the celebrated, if unfortunate, Simon, abbot of the great Benedictine community of St Albans, at whose request he dedicated a chapel to St Cuthbert *juxta claustrum Sancti Albani*.[1] He was a benefactor of the Templars, the monks of Newminster, the canons of Marton and Brinkburn, and the nuns of Moxby and Neasham, and like his uncle of Winchester, well remembered for his gifts to St Albans.[2] In Durham he gave land at Landieu (in Weardale) to a certain brother Rannulf and his brethren, and to one brother John, a hermit, 90 acres at Yearhaugh on the Derwent *ad quamdam cellam religionis...in honore dei et beate marie faciendam*.[3] He also founded, or restored, a college of secular canons at Darlington, where a new church was built (but apparently not completed during the episcopate)[4] and, greatly to the disgust of the monks of Durham, supported his son Henry in an attempt to introduce the Augustinians of Guisborough into a cell at Haswell and later at Baxterwood, almost a suburb of the city. This settlement was to have been endowed largely from those fair acres Henry had acquired at the expense of his less fortunate knightly neighbours—Haswell from Geoffrey of Haswell, Wingate from Hugh Burel, Hetton from the homonymic Bertram—to which were to be added 120 acres of the episcopal waste at Aldin Grange. These large hopes, however, speedily foundered on the uncompromising vigilance of the community of St Cuthbert, who quickly converted such pious largesse to their own benefit.[5]

To his own cathedral, 'the finest and most perfect achieve-

---

[1] Above, p. 40; *Gesta Abbatum Monasterii Sancti Albani*, I, 184–94, especially 190.

[2] B. A. Lees, *Records of the Templars in England; the Inquest of 1185*, 126; *Newminster Cartulary*, 45–6; *Chancellor's Roll 8 Richard I*, 261; *Brinkburn Cartulary*, no. ccxxiv; *BB*, 34; Surtees, III, 259; *VCH Durham*, II, 106; BM, Cotton MS., Nero D VII, fo. 89.

[3] DC Durham, 2. 3. Sac. no. 5; *FPD*, 240; DC Durham, Parv. Cart. fo. 122ᵛ.

[4] *Scriptores Tres*, 14. There was a tradition at Durham that some members of the community reformed by Bishop St Calais in 1083 had withdrawn to Darlington, amongst other places (Symeon, I, 123 n.). A Master Peter, canon of Darlington, occurs *c.* 1174–90 in DC Durham 2. 1. Ebor, no. 14 (printed in *EYC*, II, no. 950).

[5] *Scriptores Tres, loc. cit.* DC Durham, I. I. Finch. no. 14; 2. 2. Finch. no. 3, printed in *Priory of Finchale*, 3; 3. 6. Spec. no. 28, printed in Surtees, I, sec. II, 213; 3. I. Pont. no. 9, printed in *Priory of Finchale*, 8; *VCH Durham*, II, 109. See also below, pp. 136, 223. The property destined for Baxterwood largely passed to Finchale.

ment of the Anglo-Norman school',[1] Puiset gave a golden cross and chalice, together with a feretory of exceptional value, design and beauty, wherein were rehoused the remains of the venerable Bede *cum multorum aliorum sanctorum reliquiis*.[2] In addition he was responsible for much stained glass work *circa altaria*, granted an eighty-day indulgence for the maintenance of the church fabric, and arranged for the lighting of the choir. Three silver lamps, with revenues appropriated *ad luminare ante corpus pii patroni*, were hung by the altar, there to burn perpetually to the honour of St Cuthbert. Others, hanging *instar coronae*, were lit on great feast days, their supply of wax candles being sustained by the profits of the church of Rounton (obtained from the families of Conyers and Surtees), part of the revenues from the churches of Bywell and Edlingham (acquired from St Albans), and the rent of a sergeanty at Bradbury.[3]

But above all he was a great and lavish builder in an age of magnificent building,[4] and it is some expression of this spirit which raised his most durable memorial. Not to be outshone, so it was said, either by the elders of his church, or by his own contemporaries, Hugh rebuilt Durham Castle (destroyed by fire in the early years of his episcopate), where the Norman gallery, with its double range of windows and elaborate doorway still stands as a monument to his splendour.[5] At the same time he renewed an uncertain area of the city walls, and bridged the Wear at Elvet to join his usurped suburb there.[6] But most important, and constituting his greatest benefaction to Durham,

[1] A. W. Clapham, *English Romanesque Architecture after the Conquest*, 25–6.

[2] Symeon, I, 168. The gesture was not unique; compare, for example, the list of relics which Roger of York acquired in Rome (*Historians of the Church of York*, III, 109–10).

[3] Symeon, I, 168; *Scriptores Tres*, 11; DC Durham 1. 11. Spec. no. 4, printed in Surtees, III, 393–4, *EYC*, II, no. 951; 2. 1. Ebor. no. 19, printed in *EYC*, II, no. 948; 2. 2. Spec. no. 16, printed in *NCH*, VI, 104 n.; *Calendar of the Greenwell Deeds*, no. 6; DC Durham, 3. 1. Pont. no. 9, printed in *Priory of Finchale*, 8. Similar arrangements were made by Henry of Winchester at St Swithun's (*PU*, II, no. 125).

[4] Symeon, I, 168; Newburgh, II, 437; Clapham, *op. cit.* 80, 85, 87; Mortet, *Maurice de Sully*, 210.

[5] *Scriptores Tres*, 12; *Libellus....Godrici*, 182; *VCH Durham*, III, 65, 70, 78; Boase, *English Art, 1100–1216*, 227.

[6] *Scriptores Tres, loc. cit*; *VCH Durham*, III, 13, 63. The remarks in this latter concerning the chronology of Puiset's work have no basis in fact.

was the building of the Galilee chapel, for which the marble was specially imported—in all probability from Normandy. The erection of such large axial lady chapels was one of the architectural innovations of the later twelfth century, and other examples have been noticed at Chichester, Great Malvern and Glastonbury.[1] At Durham work was commenced at the east, only to be cast down (so it was rumoured) by the ill will of St Cuthbert. Hopes and efforts were thereupon transferred to the west, where, with the saint's good favour, was raised up the beauty of the present Galilee, from whence unprivileged femininity might gain solace by contemplation of more distant holy places.[2] Work appears to have been in progress early in the 1170's—or so it might be gathered from a report of Godric's successful ministrations to a youth injured through the slackness of a fellow-labourer—and the chapel was completed about 1180.[3] It has been described by a competent authority as 'a notable example of late Romanesque building', unique in its design of five equal and parallel aisles (doubtless inspired by a precipitous lack of longitudinal space) with their slender twin marble columns and semicircular arches.[4] It is further remarkable as containing one of the few examples of twelfth-century wall painting where it is still possible to form some idea of the complete scheme. The surviving work, originally in bright greens, blues, reds and yellows, is in an altar recess on the northern side of the old west door. It consists of a band of conventional leaf ornament running round the recess at the level of the springing, a larger pattern of a similar nature on the soffit, and a panel on the inside face of each jamb. On the panels on the north and south sides are the rigid and clumsy figures of a king and bishop (locally identified as St Oswald and St Cuth-

---

[1] Clapham, *op. cit.* 92.   [2] *Scriptores Tres,* 11.

[3] *Scriptores Tres, loc. cit.*; Symeon, I, 168. Cuthbert's misogyny (cf. Symeon, I, 59–60), a frequent embarrassment to honest and noble ladies, was respected as well as known in the late twelfth century. When, *c.* 1180–9, Radulf Surtees and his wife and son quit the church of Rounton to Durham, Radulf and Richard confirmed their gift on the high altar of the cathedral, whereas Beatrice advanced no farther than *altare beate marie in occidentali parte eiusdem ecclesie que Gililea vocatur* (DC Durham, 2. 1. Ebor. no. 16, printed in Surtees, III, 393; *EYC,* II, no. 949).

[4] Clapham, *op. cit.* 94; Boase, *op. cit.* 226–7.

bert) set in architectural canopies—all very much of an order familiar to the less ambitious illuminated page. The back of the recess, below the ornamental band, is occupied by another favourite convention, the representation of hanging drapery, with borders at top and bottom, but the middle part, which, according to tradition, was 'our ladye carryinge our Saviour on her knee as he was taken from the cross', has been defaced.[1]

Other work by Puiset is more difficult to trace. Although the best part of his building was certainly done under the direction of one architect and one master mason, whose hands may also be seen in a number of conventual churches, he himself lacked that almost professional flair and enthusiasm which left a characteristic stamp on the architectural interests of Flambard. He is said to have built or rebuilt a number of episcopal residences in various places where the existing domestic arrangements were not to his taste.[2] Of these, as with Sherburn, Kepyer and the projected priory of Baxterwood, nothing of substance remains. He may have been responsible for the fine north and south doors of the cathedral, which have certain general features in common with the work in Durham Castle.[3] Local antiquarian zeal, at a period before the great 'restorations', claimed, and perhaps rightly, the churches at Auckland and Darlington for him, and it is known that he built another at Grindon in honour of Becket, but whether this can be identified with the existing ruin is uncertain.[4]

It is inevitable that a description of Puiset's diocesan career should be largely concerned with those things that show him in his glory. He was a great lord, a relative of kings, and the most splendid holder of a see to be known by the magnificence of its bishops. Like Henry of Winchester he employed admini-

---

[1] Clapham, *op. cit.* 146–7 and pl. 35; *VCH Durham*, III, 119–20. The Rev. J. C. Dickinson points out that it is unlikely that there was a *pietà* in existence in the twelfth century.

[2] See below, p. 233. *Scriptores Tres*, 12; Newburgh, II, 436–7.

[3] Clapham, *op. cit.* 130.

[4] W. H. Longstaffe in *Transactions of the Architectural and Archaeological Society of Durham and Northumberland*, I (1862), 2–8; J. F. Hodgson, 'The Churches of Darlington and Hartlepool', 146; Boase, *op. cit.* 257. The building of a church at Grindon in honour of Becket is mentioned in the charter for Sherburn (Surtees, I, 283–4, cf. *VCH Durham*, III, 253).

strative and financial abilities necessarily diverted from wider spheres to reorganize the lands and enhance the beauty of the churches of his see. His gifts to his cathedral, and his buildings at Durham, Sherburn and Kepyer are manifestations of that same spirit in which Henry of Winchester rebuilt Glastonbury, re-established Cluny, founded the hospital of Holy Cross, and decorated his cathedral with the most precious and varied works of art. Yet no man is without his world, and Puiset, like his colleagues and his own church, was clearly in touch with Europe and with Rome. He visited the *Curia* at least twice, in 1153 and 1179, and was present at the Council of Tours in 1163.[1] He was to some, and perhaps a surprising extent, influenced by the current concern for diocesan affairs, and that pervasive papal power which had been its inspiration, directly or indirectly, since the beginning of the century.

Occasionally he appears in the role of head of the conventual chapter of Durham. So, for example, he admitted Ralph de Caugi to the benefits of fraternity with the house,[2] and his authority was necessary, and his advice sought, in matters touching the convent in relation to its ecclesiastical neighbours.[3] Thus, when in 1174 a settlement was reached with St Albans over the position of the cell of Tynemouth, it was *de assensu et auctoritate venerabilis patris nostri Hugonis*.[4] So too an agreement between Bishop Roger Beaumont of St Andrews, and Prior Bertram of Durham (1193/4), concerning the status of Durham's Lothian churches, was made *cum consilio et assensu domini Hugonis*.[5]

His *acta* contain a number of deeds, usually of no particular importance, in favour of various religious houses situated or holding within his diocese; Guisborough, Brinkburn, St Mary's, York, Nun Monkton, Nostell, Newminster, Carlisle, Kirkham and two small priories in Newcastle.[6] He took cognizance—

---

[1] See below, App. III, *sub annis*.

[2] DC Durham, 3. 1. Pont. no. 11, printed *FPD*, 100 n. For this procedure see Knowles, *Monastic Order*, 412, 476.

[3] *Dec. Greg. IX*, lib. II, tit I, cap. IX; *JL*, 13166.

[4] DC Durham, 2. 2. Spec. no. 15.   [5] *North Durham*, no. CCCCLXII.

[6] *Guisborough Cartulary*, ed. W. Brown, II, no. MCLXXV; *Brinkburn Cartulary*, nos. CCXXV and CCXXVII; DC York, Register of St Mary's, fo. 305; DC Durham,

perhaps more as feudal lord than spiritual father—of those gifts to the religious by which local grandees and others sought to guarantee the future safety of their souls; *ut hic et in futuro nobis proficiant ante deum*, as the great William de Vesci commented on one of his own benefactions.[1] On one occasion, of which Madox has preserved a record, a layman, Tok, son of Tok, apparently a burgess of Durham, is to be found embracing the religious life before the bishop.[2] So, too, James of Bolam, and his son, Gilbert, granted land at Cowpen to Brinkburn in the presence of Puiset and Archdeacon John,[3] Geoffrey of Otterington quitclaimed Crosby to Rievaulx before Hugh and Abbot Ailred,[4] and William de Vesci addressed a charter in favour of Alnwick to the bishop and his archdeacons.[5] Puiset himself confirmed a grant by Gilbert de Laley to the almonry of Durham, another by William of Thorpe in favour of the convent, and a gift of land to Kirkham given by Orm of Presson.[6] The spiritual aspect of this authority is somewhat stronger in a charter of Walter Bolbec for the Premonstratensians of Blanchland, wherein it is stated that the number of canons serving the house should not exceed twelve, *nisi consilio domini episcopi et advocati eiusdem loci*.[7]

Beyond this seigneurial world there lay a humbler field of routine duty in which the bishop laboured perhaps spasmodically and profitably, but nevertheless with more zeal than he or his contemporaries are sometimes allowed. Ordinations find incidental reference in an agreement with York in 1163–6, when it was admitted by the archbishop that clerks and canons from his peculiar at Hexham *ab episcopo Dunelmensi ordines recipient*.[8] Puiset licensed the erection of new chapelries, as at Rowley and

Cart. IV, fo. 8, printed in *FPD*, 163 n.; BM Cotton MS. Vesp. E XIX, fo. 118ᵛ; *Newminster Cartulary*, 45–6; Brand, I, 238, n. t; *PU* III, no. 427; *Early Newcastle Deeds*, 55; Brand, I, 206, n. v.

[1] DC Durham, 1. 1. Spec. no. 3; *NCH*, I, 200 n.; II, 49 n.
[2] Thomas Madox, *Formulare Anglicanum*, 50, no. XCII.
[3] *Brinkburn Cartulary*, no. CXCVI.
[4] *EYC*, II, no. 953.
[5] *Reg. Pal. Dun.* IV, 105; *Mon. Ang.* VI (2), 867, no. 3.
[6] DC Durham, 2. 6. Spec. no. 69; 3. 1. Pont. no. 22, printed in *FPD*, 133 n.; *NCH*, XI, 92.
[7] *Mon. Ang.* VI (2), 886, no. 1; Colvin, *The White Canons*, 49 and 98.
[8] *Historians of the Church of York*, III, 79.

Bradbury,[1] and defined such services and sacraments as might be celebrated and received in private churches.[2] Much against the will of the monks of Tynemouth he endeavoured to consecrate chapels within certain of their parishes,[3] and dedicated new cemeteries at Witton, Horton, Seaton and Yearhaugh.[4] Similar activity was contemplated for Rowley, the local lord meanwhile being allowed to bury his deceased tenants wherever he wished.[5] Likewise the canons of Brinkburn received the valuable pecuniary licence—for burials meant benefactions —to bury their patron, Roger Bertram, together with his wife and such other good persons as should wish to be buried there.[6]

In parochial affairs there are interesting traces of the troubled history of the benefice. In place of the *dominium* of the church-owner there was emerging, under papal and episcopal guidance, the compromise of patronage, leaving him his right of presentation, but endowing the diocesan with the authority to institute. It was, nevertheless, still common practice, against which Puiset himself complained, for laymen to institute and deprive clerks without the consent or authority of the ordinary, or for clerks and religious to claim churches by no other title than lay gift.[7] Such activities received a renewed condemnation in the Lateran Council of 1179, but already before that date there is some evidence that, in a few cases at least, episcopal authority had, for one reason or another, made itself felt. At Whitfield (Northumberland), Robert, chaplain of Ada, queen-mother of Scotland, presented his nephew to the living, *c.* 1165–74, and Puiset duly instituted him, *salvis in omnibus episcopalibus consuetudinibus*.[8] About 1170 Prior Germanus of Durham 'gave' the chapel of Castle Eden, with all its appurtenances, to William, clerk of the infirmary, at an annual pension of one mark.

[1] DC Durham, 4. 1. Pont. no. 3; *Calendar of the Greenwell Deeds*, no. 6.

[2] DC Durham, Cart. IV, fo. 8, printed in *FPD*, 163 n.; Cart. II, fo. 82; I. 8. Spec. no. 41, printed in Surtees, I, 282.

[3] *PU*, III, no. 179; see also below, pp. 156, 199.

[4] See below, App. II, no. 5; *NCH*, VIII, 66 n.; DC Durham, Parv. Cart. fo. 122ᵛ (new fol.).   [5] DC Durham, 4. 1. Pont. no. 3.

[6] *Brinkburn Cartulary*, no. CCXXVIII.

[7] *Comp.* I, Lib. III, xxxiii, c. 28 (*Quinque Comp. Ant.*); *JL*, 13868; Foreville, *L'Église et La Royauté en Angleterre*, 392 and 467.

[8] Hutchinson, I, 179.

Shortly afterwards the bishop confirmed the gift (somewhat inevitably, since William was his own clerk), and duly instituted him, just as earlier he had inducted Peter de Ros archdeacon of Carlisle, into half the portioned church of Corbridge, at the presentation of the canons of Carlisle.[1] There was a more complicated situation at Ellingham, where the great families of Greinville and Caugi had granted their church to Durham with important reservations in their own favour. Thus, as required by the terms of their charters, the convent presented 'the fittest' son of Ralph de Caugi, who was accordingly instituted.[2]

Where, however, by happy chance, diocesan and patron were identical, there flourished an almost Hildebrandine zeal which paid scant attention to the recent claims of the crown, or its supposed authority to enforce them. So Puiset apparently laid claim to the chapels of Otterington, Warlaby and Worsall (Yorks), and came into collision with the Yorkshire family of Stuteville over presentation to Cowesby, desired by bishop and magnate alike. The first clash was settled (in one of those often overlooked private mediations) by Archbishop Roger of York, to the effect that Hugh allowed something of Stuteville's claims, and granted the chapel to a clerk of his nomination, whilst reserving—in that favourite medieval phrase—his own future rights.[3] Towards the end of the episcopate the quarrel was renewed, but this time closed (1189–92) with Stuteville's admission that he had no rights whatsoever in the patronage.[4] In Durham there was similar trouble with the great family of Conyers concerning the church of Rounton. This again was settled in the bishop's favour, with Roger and his son apologetically surrendering *omne jus patronatus quod nos habere credebamus in ecclesia de Rungetona*.[5] Such prowess, successfully emulated by the convent, did not pass unmarked, and in 1184 the crown

---

[1] DC Durham, Reg. 1, fo. 113, printed in Surtees, I, 45; see below, p. 237; Brand, I, 238, note t.

[2] See above, p. 98.

[3] See below, pp. 169, 171; DC Durham, 1. 1. Archiep. no. 5, printed in *EYC*, IX, no. 14 (1164–74).

[4] DC Durham, 3. 1. Ebor. no. 1, printed in *EYC*, IX, no. 71.

[5] DC Durham, 2. 1. Ebor. no. 19, printed in Surtees, III, 394, *EYC*, II, no. 948. The family of Surtees was also involved and made a similar surrender (2. 1. Ebor. no. 17, printed in *EYC*, II, no. 947).

endeavoured to levy a fine of 500 marks on the bishop for hearing a case of advowson in court Christian (contrary to the constitutions of Clarendon). But in typical style nothing was ever paid—a point missed by many appraisers of Angevin 'autocracy'.[1]

Where, in the hands of the religious, a new and more exclusive proprietary church was being nourished by the favourite device of appropriation, it was the bishop's duty to supervise the process, watch his interests therein, and, with more detachment, those of incumbents and parishioners. Puiset's formulae vary from church to church, and are, on the whole, more occupied with the security of the episcopal customs than the unfortunate lot of the vicars. Gainford and its chapelry of Barnard Castle went to St Mary's, York at the beginning of the episcopate with no further stipulation than *salva reverencia Dunelmensis ecclesie*.[2] An early privilege concerning the Durham churches in Yorkshire (where Puiset's authority was doubtful) states that the convent should put in vicars with 'adequate portions' to serve the livings and pay the episcopal dues.[3] Later, in a charter for Sherburn, the formula runs that the proctor of the house, with the advice of the bishop (who was in any case patron), should choose *perpetuos et idoneos vicarios*, who were to serve its churches and bear all episcopal exactions.[4] A licence for Nostell of about the same time merely states the canons might have Bamburgh, with all its fruits, obventions and possessions, for their own uses 'saving the episcopal customs and dignity'.[5] An imperfectly known charter for Lanercost, concerning the church of Old Denton, provides for the presentation of a perpetual vicar who was to pay the episcopal customs and an agreed pension. In this case alone there appears the vital condition that the impropriators were not to raise the pension without the prior consent of the bishop.[6] Towards the end of the century, however, with the

---

[1] PR 30 Henry II, 37.
[2] DC York, Register of St Mary's, new fol. fo. 305 (1154–8).
[3] DC Durham, 1. 1. Archiep. no. 19, printed in *EYC*, II, no. 937 (1154–6).
[4] Surtees, 1, 283–4 (c. 1183).
[5] BM, Cotton MS., Vesp. E xix, fo. 118ᵛ (1185–9).
[6] *A Breviate of the Cartulary of Lanercost*, ed. M. E. C. Walcott, sect. VIII, no. 16.

strengthening of the theory and practice of episcopal authority, and under the influence of those neat *clausulae* expressing an increasing papal concern with the progress of appropriation, Puiset's charters assume greater clarity and detail, though, as seems to have been usual, without any concurrent larger consideration for the position of the vicars. Thus (1193) the canons of Carlisle were to retain the fruits and profits of their churches, and appoint vicars to serve with the cure of souls, the canons themselves bearing the burden of the episcopal dues.[1] At Elvet the monks of Durham were to have the church *in manu sua*, pay *episcopalia* and other exactions, and put in suitable priests, removable at will.[2]

The strength of Puiset's episcopal power, and the respect with which, for one reason or another, it was regarded, are, however, perhaps most clearly revealed in the number of local arbitrations which he undertook. Trouble might be between neighbouring houses of religious, as in 1171 between Durham and Kelso concerning the ownership of the chapel of Earlston,[3] or between the laity and the religious, as with Stephen of Newton in Glendale and the canons of Kirkham. In this latter case agreement was reached, after a long dispute, in the second half of the twelfth century. Stephen resigned all his right in the chapel of Mindrum, which the bishop confirmed to Kirkham with all tithes and parochial dues from the vills of Mindrum and Downham, and in return the canons abandoned their claims against Newton.[4] There were echoes of this same quarrel somewhat later, when Puiset, perhaps acting this time on a papal mandate, adjudged the advowson of Newton to Kirkham against the influential royal clerk, Hugh Murdac, his sentence being confirmed by Clement III *c.* 1187–91.[5]

In November 1172 the bishop mediated between the convent of Durham and a local baron, Alexander of Hylton, in one of those frequent collisions concerning the rights possessed by a

[1] Brand, I, 238, n. t.   [2] See below, App. II, no. 5.
[3] In this case he appears to have confirmed the decision of papal judges delegate (DC Durham, Cart. Misc. no. 1354, *North Durham*, III, no. DCXLIII; *ibid*. no. CCCCIX; *PU*, II, no. 208).
[4] *NCH*, XI, 15; *Northumberland and Durham Deeds*, 268, no. 2.
[5] *PU*, III, no. 427.

mother church over the chapels founded within its boundaries. It was agreed that Alexander and his heirs should choose a suitable chaplain for Hylton, who was to be presented to the prior. They were to give all the tithe of their own demesne for his upkeep, but were to pay the mother church of Wearmouth a thrave of wheat on every bovate, and revenues from other lands were similarly divided. Alexander and his household were to attend the mother church with customary alms and offerings on the great feast days—Christmas, Easter, Pentecost and the feast of Peter and Paul (saints of the Wearmouth dedication). If the chaplain of Hylton in any way infringed these closely guarded financial rights of the parent church, then, it was ordained, *cessabit capella per matrem ecclesiam usque ad satisfactionem*.[1] A dispute of an identical nature between the church of Monk Hesledon, and a chantry at Hardwick, belonging to Ralph of Fishburn, another local aristocrat, was settled to much the same effect in the bishop's presence in March 1184.[2]

Tithes were another perpetual source of friction, one of the main causes of trouble being, as already noticed, the Cistercian claim to exemption. As a rule the brethren found it better to compound with the parochial clergy or their patrons, rather than endeavour to enjoy the uncomfortable letter of their privilege. Thus a dispute between Newminster and the church of Mitford, concerning the tithes of Highlaws, was ended by Puiset with the arrangement that the monks should pay two marks a year as commutation.[3] He likewise ratified a similar rate between Rievaulx and Leake for Crosby,[4] whilst Durham compounded at three marks with the same house for certain tithes due to the church of Northallerton.[5] A more complicated case arose from the bishop's own ambiguous generosity in his endowment of the hospital of Kepyer, and the tortuous law governing such tithes. In 1189 he admitted an agreement between his convent and the new foundation, by which Durham quitclaimed tithes on the crops of Cleadon (formerly

[1] DC Durham, Cart. II, fo. 82.
[2] DC Durham, I. 8. Spec. no. 41, printed in Surtees, I, 282.
[3] *Newminster Cartulary*, 42.   [4] *EYC*, II, no. 954.
[5] *Rievaulx Cartulary*, 29.

belonging to their church of Elvet), and in exchange Kepyer undertook to pay the same church 2*s*. a year on St Oswald's day, together with two sheaves from the tithe of their demesne of Newton.[1]

It might be objected that such notices, sparsely scattered across the best part of half a century, amount to little. In a number of instances where the church of Durham was involved Puiset was the inevitable tribunal. For the rest it is uncertain at whose instance such mediations were undertaken; whether disputes automatically came before the bishop as ordinary, or merely reached him in the last resort, or that some compromise already effected might have the weight of his authority. Yet here, as elsewhere, there are many hints as to the volume of such business. The high quality of the episcopal *familia*, together with the bishop's imperious character and well-known experience and repute in such matters, probably rendered it as proper as discreet that he should be consulted. Here too, as in other sees, there is often no trace of royal or papal intervention; signs of a local independence in many such matters which has perhaps been unjustly obscured by the modern stress on the rapid centralization of secular and ecclesiastical justice. The argument must not, of course, be pressed too far. The solutions produced were of a pattern common to the church—composition for tithes, care lest local claims to independence should jeopardize the rights of a *matrix ecclesia*—all strengthening previous suggestions of the extent to which Puiset was in touch with general ecclesiastical policy. Above all there is clear evidence of the high standing of the episcopal office and the competent vigour of diocesan life. Perhaps this latter reflected more the spirit than the letter of papal teaching, yet, by a curious irony, in part explains the modest concern of some of the episcopate with the principles and events of the Becket dispute.

What seems most remarkable about Puiset's diocesan career, in view of his subsequent reputation, is the suggestion that he had some conscience in what he did. His activities were some-

---

[1] DC Durham, 4. 16. Spec. no. 45*, printed in *Memorials of St Giles's*, 213–14; see below, App. II, no. 6. For the canonical problem, see Imbert, *Les Hôpitaux en Droit Canonique*, 88–90, 294.

thing more than the grudging discharge of an inescapable minimum of routine. His household contained learned men, and whilst the support of learning has unfortunately never been any automatic guarantee of competence, honesty or wisdom, their presence at least suggests something of the bishop's realization of his responsibilities. Moreover, like many of his less secular contemporaries, he voluntarily appealed to the pope on questions of canonical interpretation which probably came before him as judge ordinary or delegate.[1] The significance of all this has been variously interpreted, though it now seems generally accepted that it witnesses the great weight of papal influence under the distinguished Alexander III, and the unformed nature of a law which thus needed individual explanation. To these there might be added the anxiety of the episcopate (or perhaps, more strictly, their advisers, though this remains a problem beyond solution), to be sure of their grounds in cases abounding with guile, and evidences enmeshed in obscurities and ambiguity.

Like many others Puiset sought advice from Alexander on the vexed question of preventive appeals. It was apparently common practice that when some aggrieved party, having appealed to Rome, set out for the *Curia*, their opponents would take no action to justify themselves. When, however, they learned that the appellants had returned with papal letters, they in turn appealed and departed for Rome—a process which might go on indefinitely—so that it became impossible for the judges to open the case. Therefore, wrote Alexander in one of his many important definitions of delegate powers, should anyone attempt to delay the course of justice by such guile, the bishop should neither forward the counter-appeal, nor should he hesitate to settle the dispute in question on the lines of the mandate already received.[2]

[1] Morey, *Bartholomew of Exeter*, 75; Cheney, 'The compromise of Avranches of 1172, and the spread of Canon Law in England', 183–97. Mlle Foreville (*L'Église et La Royauté en Angleterre*, 391) would attribute most of such activity to the period 1173–9. This does not seem to be substantiated by the evidence in hand (but cf. M. Morgan, 'The Organization of the Scottish Church in the Twelfth Century', 135–49, esp. 139, n. 2).

[2] *Dec. Greg.* IX, Lib. II, tit. xxviii, c. 15; *JL*, 13870, cf. Foreville, *op. cit.* 544.

Again Hugh sought a papal ruling on the inevitable problem of the sons of priests. To this Alexander replied, *super eo quod nobis tua devotio postulavit,* that such individuals, unless brought up in a monastery, or amongst canons regular, and of a good life, ought not to be admitted to the diaconate or priesthood.[1]

Sometime between 1179 and 1181, he inquired whether one who, when under twenty-five years of age, had been presented to a church before the Lateran Council (1179) ought, by reason of the decrees of that council, to be ejected from his living, even when the presentation had been confirmed by the diocesan after 1179. To this knotty point, suggesting both the free style of contemporary presentations, and an episcopal conscience perhaps slowly stirred by lawyer's doubts, Alexander replied that unless there were some other urgent reason, the clerk need not be deprived *occasione minoris etatis aut decreti quod in concilio promulgavimus.*[2]

A problem concerning the delegate and ordinary alike was that of the means whereby a conventual church might seek to disavow an agreement made by its abbot or prior acting with its written authority. In answer to a question from Durham, Alexander ruled that when an abbot or prior, fortified with a capitular mandate, entered into an agreement, then the chapter should be bound to honour it *si fuerit aliquot annis servata,* whether or not they had consented to it.[3]

Yet by no means all, nor the best part, of Puiset's activities were marked by this caution, and neither could, nor did, commend themselves to the papacy. He freely admitted his own son's proprietary interest in the projected house of Baxterwood.[4] Earlier, in 1174, 'out of consideration for the honesty and religion known to flourish at St Albans', he granted that the abbot might increase the pensions from his churches in the

---

[1] *Comp.* 1, Lib. 1, tit. ix, c. 5 (*Quinque Comp. Ant.*); *JL,* 13869. Cf. Foreville, *op. cit.* 394 for another example of a similar query from the southern province.

[2] *Comp.* 1, Lib. 1, tit. viii, c. 7 (*Quinque Comp. Ant.*); *JL,* 14348. For other examples of such presentations, see Foreville, *op. cit.* 465.

[3] *Dec. Greg.* ix, Lib. 1, tit. xxxvi, c. 3; *JL,* 13868.

[4] Henry Puiset's rights were subsequently transferred to cover the election of a prior of Finchale (*Priory of Finchale,* 24). For the acquisition by Finchale of the property destined for Baxterwood, see above, p. 110.

diocese of Durham by 40 marks a year—a policy condemned by the Lateran Council five years later.[1] Again, neither Puiset, nor indeed many of his colleagues, would or could keep pace with the zeal that flourished in high circles. Thus the papacy, in addition to giving guidance on difficult points of law or major issues of policy, was frequently obliged to draw the attention of the hierarchy to certain irksome aspects of legislation, and admonish lesser clerks to conduct themselves in ways more fitting to their stations. Hence canons and decretals dealing in dreary reiteration with illicit financial exactions, usury, the problem of the Jews, and a large variety of moral lapses.

So Alexander III, in a letter to the archbishop of York and the bishop of Durham, declared that the iniquities of certain clerks of their dioceses had come to his knowledge. They had refused to bury the dead until they had taken their own handsome choice from the possessions of the deceased. This disingenuous circumvention of the prohibition of fees *pro sepultura* was declared to be contrary to the traditions of the Church, the decrees of the fathers, *et decreto nostro quod in concilio Turonensi iam pridem edidimus.* The ordinaries were to warn their clergy against such profitable sin and its violation of the weight of honest tradition, and point out that it was only lawful to accept such gifts as the deceased or their relatives might care to offer. If any further complaints of such a nature reached Rome, *nos tante presumptionis excessum gravissime auctore Deo vindicare curabimus, ita quod in pena officii et ordinis illorum quos talia perpetrasse constiterit, id procul dubio durius a vobis requiretur.*[2]

A long letter (probably dating 1179–81), addressed to the bishop of Durham, deals with the misdeeds of the Jews,[3] and the kindred problem of usury. Jews, so it was said, proceeded at law with an unfitting contempt for their opponents, taking clerks, and even the bishop before lay courts, and using the testimony of one person, or unwitnessed deeds as evidence, whilst refusing to admit the validity *adversum se magnorum et*

[1] *NCH*, VIII, 64–5; Mansi, XXII, col. 222.
[2] *Collectio Sangermanensis*, Lib. II, i, 15. Canon 6 of the Council of Tours had forbidden burial fees (Mansi, XXI, col. 1178).
[3] For Jews at Newcastle, see *PR 1 Richard I*, 242.

probatorum virorum...testimonium. The pope accordingly ruled that on no account was the bishop to heed a summons to appear in a secular court in any such dispute. Furthermore, he emphasized that when such cases were heard in ecclesiastical courts the evidence of at least two or three people was required as legal proof, for it was written *in ore duorum vel trium testium stat omne verbum*, and whilst there were many cases which required the evidence of more than two, *nulla est tamen causa que unius tantum testimonio...rationabiliter terminetur.*[1]

Moreover, in accordance with the increasing anti-Semitic zeal of a period which was to witness some of the worst massacres,[2] the bishop was to forbid Christians from certain specified contacts with Jews. They were not to enter the service of Jewish households, and Christian nurses were not to tend Jewish children, lest, by the machinations of the devil, simple souls be converted *ad superstitionem et perfidiam.*[3]

The letter concludes with one of the periodical condemnations of usury. Christians should not walk in the paths of such unrighteousness, *quia usurarum crimen utriusque testamenti pagina detestatur.* Clerks who persisted in such practices heedless of warning were to be suspended from their livings, the laity brought to suitable repentance *vinculo excommunicationis.*[4]

Of the machinery of diocesan administration, through which routine was discharged and these numerous exhortations presumably spasmodically translated into action, there is but the slightest evidence. The Durham court Christian is only mentioned incidentally to its amercement for usurped jurisdiction.[5] At times the bishop is reputed to have consulted his clergy, and on one occasion a grant with quittance from tithe was properly made *concedente ecclesia...in cujus parochia eadem (villa) sita est.*[6]

---

[1] *Dec. Greg.* IX, Lib. II, tit. xx, c. 23. The ascription to Durham is in the *Collectio Cheltenhamensis* (BM, Egerton MS. 2819). I owe these references to Dr Holtzmann.

[2] Newburgh, I, 294–9; 309–13; *Gesta*, II, 83–4.

[3] *Dec. Greg.* IX, Lib. V, tit. vi, c. 8. Cf. the legislation of the Third Lateran Council (Hoveden, II, 180), and the comments of Dr Roth in *Cambridge Medieval History*, VII, 642.

[4] *Dec. Greg.* IX, Lib. V, tit, xix, c. 7; *JL*, 13974.

[5] PR 30 *Henry II*, 37; see above, p. 118, and below, p. 172.

[6] *Newminster Cartulary*, 46; see also below, p. 220.

Diocesan synods, on whose composition and functions it would be dangerous to generalize, receive passing mention. It was, for example, in such an assembly that Puiset mediated between Stephen of Newton in Glendale and the canons of Kirkham, a settlement being reached 'in the presence of the synod and under its witness'.[1] Synods again form one item in an agreement with York (1163–6), when it was stipulated that the prior of Hexham should attend at Durham, whilst the assembly of 'clergy and people', by which Puiset was elected into the see, is described as *synodum* by the Durham chronicler.[2] It is also probable that certain impressive gatherings in the cathedral church, when solemn pledges were made on the high altar before lay and ecclesiastical magnates, were in fact such, though they are nowhere so described.[3] In all, synods were clearly a regular and important feature of local ecclesiastical life, important enough, in fact, from matters of finance and prestige for the prior and archdeacons to dispute who should preside in the absence of the bishop, and adjudge *de querelis et aliis Christianitatis officiis*.[4] Ruridecanal chapters, without, however, any suggestion as to their functions, are noticed from time to time. It was perhaps one that witnessed Adam de Caugi's induction to Ellingham, for in addition to the archdeacons, those present included a dean and a variety of local clerks.[5]

A number of officials are vaguely and comprehensively mentioned, such as 'archdeacons and other officers', or 'archdeacons and deans and their officers'. Their functions, as opposed to their much resisted financial exactions, are suggested rather than disclosed. The archdeacons held chapters, sequestrated livings, suspended unlicensed incumbents, and, if need be, excommunicated them. On one occasion the prior and archdeacon of Durham are found settling a dispute as to the

---

[1] *NCH*, XI, 15, 124; cf. above, p. 119. At an earlier synod, held in the time of William of St Barbara, the bishop, assisted by the abbot of St Albans and the prior of Guisborough, mediated between Tynemouth and Guisborough, (*Guisborough Cartulary*, II, no. MCXLVIII).

[2] See below, p. 170; *Scriptores Tres*, 4.

[3] See above, p. 112, n. 3, and below, pp. 220–1.

[4] DC Durham, 1, 1, Pont. no. 1, printed in *FPD*, lii–lvi.

[5] DC Durham, 3. 1. Pont, no. 12; *NCH*, II, 272, n. 4.

ownership of a church.[1] Where, as in Northallertonshire, the bishop had established a peculiar and possessed archidiaconal rights, we hear of his appointment of deans, and their holding of chapters (from which the convent of Durham made every effort to withdraw its clerks).[2] From other evidence it seems that such archidiaconal chapters were attended by all the clergy concerned, whether beneficed or not. Proceedings therein are largely unknown, though it characteristically appears that a clerk might there be criticized for unbecoming resistance to fiscal demands. There was clearly some form of preparatory activity before the more formal gathering, and on one occasion we hear of the archdeacon admonishing some unfortunate *in camera sua ante capitulum*.[3]

Deans, who were seemingly busy officials and the frequent amanuenses of the archdeacons, are often named; Solomon, Master Walter, dean of Pittington, and Walkelin, dean of Wearmouth. In 1196 Henry, dean of Northumberland, who first appears *c.* 1160, was held responsible by the royal custodians of the see for the profits of hospitality in the archdeaconry of Northumberland.[4] Elsewhere there is mention of the distribution of chrism at Newcastle by this same officer *in septimana Paschae*, whilst one of his clerks discharged the same duty at Alnwick.[5]

As a bishop, Puiset was patently not of that dedicated class of good pastors, and more than one of his contemporaries saw his life as an epitome of the current shortcomings of the hierarchy. Yet, as was proper to a man of such administrative talents, his episcopate was clearly more than the achievement of an unavoidable minimum. Perhaps the most outstanding feature of his career as diocesan is less its obvious reflection of his magnificent ambitions and tastes, than that a man of such inclinations should have had some interest in contemporary theology, and have been involved, not only with certain inescapable routine duties, but with other more difficult matters either voluntarily submitted or summoned to his hearing. Such

---

[1] *FPD*, 222–3, 227; DC Durham, 3. 2. Spec, no. 9, printed in *NCH*, VII, 145.
[2] *FPD*, 251. [3] *FPD*, 222–3, 227.
[4] DC Durham, 2. 4. Spec. no. 6; 3. 8. Spec. no. 1; *FPD*, 157; 1. 2. Pont. nos. 8, 16; Brand, I, 206, note v; *Chancellor's Roll 8 Richard I*, 257.
[5] *FPD*, 222.

activity, varying in merit and efficacy, was indeed general, as is witnessed in the scope of papal advice and intervention, and the resultant expressions of royal concern. It illustrates the wide influence of those Roman policies that could so affect a man who was in all things primarily a superb secular prince. But it must be admitted that time, distance and interest brought distortions of perspective, and that a bishop such as Puiset moved in a different world to the lawyer and publicist. A knowledge, or even an awareness of the letter of reform, were other matters than its detailed application. Inconvenient papal claims might be ignored, and this, in view of Puiset's conduct concerning advowson, hardly from any timorous respect for the royal authority, which fared no better when opportunity offered. Problems were at times settled with more regard for practical convenience than the latest dicta of the learned. There were scholars at Durham well abreast of current developments in ecclesiastical law, but their influence was at best of an indirect and limited character in local affairs. In general Puiset's attitude was that of an earlier age; his zeal required encouragement rather than moderation. He was, not unnaturally, slow to check his flock from unrighteous greed. He joined his distinguished metropolitan in a convenient oversight of a decree of the Council of Tours, and it is interesting to note that he was anxious to secure a liberal reading of a Lateran decree which he had already interpreted with a certain freedom.

II. THE BISHOP AND HIS CONVENT

By 1154 the church of Durham had been served for some three-quarters of a century by Benedictine monks. These, the successors of the one-time Congregation of St Cuthbert, had been introduced into the cathedral by Bishop William of St Calais in 1083. After the initial denigration of their immediate spiritual ancestors they had absorbed and intensified an earlier veneration for the incorrupt body of that saint whose name and deeds were so intimately linked with the history of the see.[1] In the

---

[1] For the pre-Conquest reverence for the name of Cuthbert, see Knowles, *Monastic Order*, 165–6. For the changes made at Durham by St Calais in 1083, see *FPD*, xii–lxxxi; Knowles, *op. cit.* 169–70.

twelfth century the story of this heroic age was studied, copied and rewritten with a skill and enthusiasm not unworthy of the golden days of the Northumbrian renaissance.[1] At the same time events of the years 1083–1154 contributed a less literary and more aggressive tint to this just and enormous corporate pride. The early bishops of the reformed foundation, William of St Calais (1081–96), Rannulf Flambard (1099–1128) and Geoffrey Rufus (1133–40), were all distinguished royal servants,[2] and accordingly much absent from the diocese. Flambard, like his predecessor, was exiled for political misdemeanours, and in addition there were long vacancies in 1096–9 and 1128–33. The death of bishop Rufus in 1140 saw the immediate and determined attempts of David of Scotland to round off his considerable northern acquisitions by intruding his creature, William Cumin, into the see.[3] The outcome was two years of civil war, accompanied by the usual stories of the wasting of lands, the desecration of churches and the destruction of property. In a way these were the most superficial effects of the whole episode, for a simple agrarian economy had remarkable resilience. But the same events sharpened the political wits of the convent, taught it the benefits and efficacy of Roman assistance, and in various crises threw up chances easily transmuted to some of those precedents which underlay later claims.

Thus, with the partial exception of Flambard's pontificate, Durham had never known the sustained grip of a capable administrator. By necessity and opportunity the will of the convent had hardened to a masterful independence. This was indiscriminately shown in the uncritical adulation of the saints of the see, the refutation of supposed calumnies on the 'restorer' of 1083, and the zeal with which freedom had been sought and defended in 1142 and 1153, not only against secular grandees, but also against the redoubtable Bernard of Clairvaux

[1] Cf. Knowles, *op. cit.* 499, and see above, pp. 68, 70, 102.

[2] For St Calais, see Knowles, *op. cit.* 169; for Flambard, see below, p. 219. Geoffrey Rufus was the chancellor of Henry I, cf. below, p. 220.

[3] William Cumin was a relative and former clerk of Bishop Rufus. At the time of his attempt to secure Durham he was archdeacon of Worcester and chancellor of Scotland (Symeon, I, 143; II, 314). For the story of his intrusion, see Symeon, I, 143–4, 161–4, and for his subsequent behaviour, *ibid.* 146–60, 163–7. See also above, pp. 8, 13.

and his many and able northern disciples.[1] Such determination, as has been shown, stood Puiset in good stead in the troubled months of his election, but was an ill omen for the future.

On his return to England in 1154 the new bishop was as yet moved to some sense of gratitude by the transient memory of the sacrifices of his chapter. He conducted himself with a measure of that charm native to the house of Blois, and with such discreet restraint that the Durham chronicler, writing in the heat of later battles, recalled common talk of a second Daniel.[2] But events shortly took a turn which required less pleasant allusions. The bishop realized the opportunities of his position, the advantages thereof, so it was suggested (and doubtless rightly), having been rendered more plain by the efforts of local opportunists and intriguers. It is, moreover, noteworthy that at this critical moment death or resignation removed the restraint of a number of the elders of both the chapter and the episcopal *familia*. Prior Laurence had died in France, his namesake had departed to St Albans about the same time, and Flambard's able descendant, archdeacon Rannulf, had at last been replaced by 1155.[3] From the longevity of their successors it may be deduced that the chapter was confronted by a bishop advised by a body of counsellors as youthful as himself.

The unanimity which had given Puiset the see was ripped, and a rift opened between the prior and his monks. From about 1155 to the end of the episcopate there was almost continual trouble of varying intensity. The questions at issue are clear in principle but difficult in detail. The bishop died with something of that remorse dear to the monastic chronicler, and his form of repentance is a brief abstract of Durham's grief, more elaborately chronicled in a group of spurious charters of contemporary manufacture.[4] The disputes were of a familiar order, ranging from minor accusations of theft, encroachment and uncertain boundaries ignored, to pleas of immunities infringed and ancient liberties overthrown. Monastic tithes and churches

---

[1] See above, pp. 12–21.　　　　[2] *Scriptores Tres*, 7–8.
[3] See above, pp. 15, 17; and below, p. 234.
[4] *Monachis autem terras et libertates quas eis abstulerat, restituit (Scriptores Tres,* 15). In DC Durham, 3. 1. Pont. no. 8 Puiset speaks of the wrongs *que ecclesie beati Cuthberti intulimus* (App. 11, no. 7). For the Durham forgeries see below, App. iv.

were said to have been unjustly alienated—as at Howden.[1] In criminal and fiscal matters the conventual court had been deprived of its proper parity with that of the bishop.[2] A number of properties had found their way into the bishop's hand, including the borough of Elvet, lands at Norham and Aycliffe, and between Boldon and Hedworth, Rainton and Houghton-le-Spring, and Pittington and Sherburn.[3] In some cases trouble had arisen concerning either title to some particularly delectable or useful preserve, as at Heworth, Brackenholme and Woodhall,[4] or an uncertain forest boundary, as at Hemingbrough.[5] Where monastic demesne, and more especially monastic wood, and episcopal forest reputedly coincided there was difficulty with pannage and forest dues, and over pasture rights and other forest liberties. The bishop, or, more properly, his numerous officers, were, like their colleagues elsewhere, quick with accusations of waste. The priory and its tenants were naturally reluctant to pay for what they regarded as customary liberties.[6]

In a field which has attracted more attention, the convent sought the free election of its prior,[7] who was not to be de-

[1] DC Durham, 3. 1. Pont. no. 4, printed in *FPD*, 198; DC Durham, 3. 1. Pont. no. 1 (App. II, no. 10); 4, 1. Pont. no. 12 (App. II, no. 6). See also below, pp. 146–7.

[2] The priory's claims for its court, as defined in an alleged charter of St Calais, read: *curiam suam...libere et honorifice...sicut habemus nostram* (DC Durham, 1. 1. Pont. no. 1, printed in *FPD*, lii–lvi). The phrase is re-echoed in a spurious charter of Henry I (DC Durham, 2. 1. Reg. no. 4), and in another attributed to Henry II, with, however, the significant addition of *omnia habeant que ad coronam regis pertinent* (DC Durham, Parv. Cart. fo. 48, new fol.). The claim to parity was accepted by Puiset (3. 1. Pont. no. 1, printed below, App. II, no. 10). For disputes on criminal jurisdiction see *FPD*, 225, 226, 231, 285; for wreck, *ibid.* 279, 285; for commercial rights *ibid.* 241, 253, 270.

[3] DC Durham, 3. 1. Pont. no. 4, printed in *FPD*, 198; 4. 1. Pont. no. 5, printed in *FPD*, lxxxvi.

[4] *FPD*, 108, 254–5, 290, 292–3, 295.   [5] *FPD*, 254–5, 260.

[6] Quittance from pannage and foresty appear in an alleged charter of St Calais (*FPD*, lii–lvi). There the phrasing is *de forestagio et pasnagio in omnibus dominicis maneriis suis, et similiter clerici qui tenent ecclesias de eis*. This clause is repeated in what purports to be a charter of Henry I (see above, n. 2). It was admitted by Puiset in these words (*FPD*, lxxxvi). The right to take 'necessary timber' first appears in the above charter of St Calais, and from there was also recognized by Puiset. Evidence on the details of these quarrels is in *FPD*, 230–2, 263, 264, 268, 271–2.

[7] *Liberam semper electionem prioris habeant* (*FPD*, lii–lvi). This was the form confirmed by Puiset (see below, App. II, no. 10). Other versions are in the supposed privilege of Gregory VII (*PU*, II, no. 2) and other charters attributed by the convent to St Calais (*FPD*, xlvii–l, l–li, lxxii–lxxiii).

posed, except at its united wish, and then only *pro certa et rationabili causa*.[1] He was, according to one version of history, the second dignitary of the church, with an abbatial stall in the choir; abbot, in fact, in all but name, standing in the same relation to his bishop as did the dean of York to the archbishop.[2] The prior and monks claimed full control of the cathedral church, with the right to appoint and dismiss obedientiaries,[3] and custody of vacant conventual churches, with their free appropriation.[4] Such churches, it was held, had ever been quit of episcopal and archidiaconal exactions,[5] with the prior himself exercising archidiaconal rights therein.[6]

Such was the nature of the dispute. Its chronology is uncertain. There was a short lull following the election, before, as the chronicler has it, the wicked came down from Israel. From this period there date a small number of episcopal *acta* in favour of the convent; grants of land at Wolviston, Follingsby and York.[7] Thereafter came a trial of strength. There were the

---

[1] *FPD*, xxxviii–xliii, lxxvi–lxxix; DC Durham, 2. 1. Reg. no. 1.

[2] *Sit secundus ab episcopo, in omni dignitate et honore abbatis, nomine prioris, infra ecclesiam* etc. (*FPD*, lii–lvi). This was accepted verbatim by Puiset (see below, App. II, no. 10). Other forms and details appear elsewhere. Thus in a spurious charter of William I there is the elaboration: *secundum antiquam Lindisfarnensis ecclesie dignitatem priori dexteram episcopi sui et primum locum et honorem in omnibus post episcopum . . .* (*FPD*, lxxii–lxxiii). The reference to an abbatial stall is common. So Puiset admitted that the prior might have *stallum in sinistra parte chori, sicut abbas* (see below, App. II, no. 10), which was but a rephrasing of the ubiquitous *sedem abbatis in choro sinistro* (*FPD*, lxix–lxxi, lxvii–lxviii). For the equation with the dean of York, see *FPD*, lxvii–lxviii.

[3] *Et omnia officia et jura abbatis super monachos* (*FPD*, lxxii–lxxiii). *Facultatem plenariam cum consilio capituli sui ordinandi domum suam in interioribus et exterioribus agendis suis, tam in ecclesiis quam in terris et ceteris possessionibus suis* (*FPD*, lii–lvi; *EYC*, II, no. 926). The clause was accepted verbatim by Puiset (see below, App. II, no. 10). For the conventual control of obedientiaries, see *FPD*, lxvii–lxviii, lxix–lxxi.

[4] *Ecclesias autem quascumque . . . in sua manu et donatione liberas habeant, et honestis clericis deserviendis committant* (*FPD*, xxxix–xl). For Puiset's acceptance of these claims, see below, App. II, nos. 8, 10.

[5] *Quietus sit . . . de hospitiis et auxiliis episcoporum et archidiaconorum et ceteris gravaminibus et vexationibus* (*FPD*, lii–lvi). This was admitted by Puiset in the form that the prior and monks be free *ab hospiciis et auxiliis et omnibus grauaminibus episcoporum, archidiaconorum et omnium officialium . . .*, see below, App. II, no. 10.

[6] St Calais was alleged to have granted that the prior be *archidiaconus omnium ecclesiarum suarum in episcopatu dunelmi* (*FPD*, lii–lvi; *PU*, II, no. 2; *FPD*, lxxiii–lxxiv). This Puiset apparently refused to accept.

[7] DC Durham, 3. 1. Pont. no. 14, printed in *FPD*, 141; Cart. II, fo. 79ᵛ, printed in *FPD*, 10; 3. 1. Pont. no. 18.

usual complaints of faction, and that the privacy of the chapter was violated. The custody of cells and conventual lands, together with other offices, were allegedly going to episcopal partisans *in contemptum prioris*, whilst the bishop's opponents were stripped of their possessions. Prior Absalon (1154–8), *sub quo nutabant libertates ecclesie*, had nothing of the wayward will of his Biblical namesake. There was none to resist the bishop, and simple monks, so it was said, did not dare to speak their minds. Nevertheless the convent seized the opportunity to record the view that the prior was second only to the bishop, and at the same time produced a charter of Flambard, whose oppressions were recalled by present tribulations, securing Puiset's confirmation *ut ad disposicionem omnium rerum suarum liberam in omnibus habeant facultatem.*[1] By 1157 they had papal confirmation of his grant of the free disposition of their churches,[2] and before October 1162, of Flambard's dying repentance.[3]

Thus far the issue had been one of administration. In this, it is fairly clear, the bishop had successfully asserted his will, much to the chagrin of those who could remember days when matters had been differently regulated. With the death of Absalon an attempt was made to halt what was regarded as episcopal aggression. The eventual unhappy outcome was a widening of the field of dispute. Thomas, the new prior, was elected by the brethren, though whether with, or despite the bishop's will is unknown. Within a few years (*c.* 1162) this unfortunate was apparently goaded by the discontent of his chapter, or perhaps more strictly its politicians, into making a dramatic stand. He attempted to resist Puiset *super quibusdam libertatibus*, and more especially concerning the church of Northallerton. As might be anticipated the monastic promises of unity and support melted 'as wax' before the heat of the episcopal ire, leaving Thomas, ejected from office, to retire to the solitude and safety of the Farnes.[4]

[1] *Scriptores Tres*, 7; DC Durham, 4. 1. Pont. no. 14, printed below, App. II, no. 4.   [2] *PU*, II, no. 94.   [3] *PU*, II, no. 107.

[4] *Scriptores Tres*, 8. This important incident, which had an obvious bearing on the content of the Durham forgeries, is ignored by Barlow, *Durham Jurisdictional Peculiars*, 78.

The bishop now freely set his sickle to the conventual harvest. The cautious Prior Germanus (1162–89), *summe simplicitatis et patientie monachus*, having the spectacle of Thomas before him, wisely tempered a will to resist by due appreciation of the ineffectual loquacity of his brethren.[1] There was, nevertheless, clearly a party of stalwarts in the chapter who continued the battle, their hopes perhaps sustained by the growing disposition of crown and papacy to intervene in the affairs of the diocese. In 1165 the convent secured Alexander III's confirmation of some unspecified variety of a charter of William of St Calais, which, it might be suggested, marks the beginning of that policy of redocumenting the early history of the see in the light of modern needs.[2] The attempts of the priory to gain effective control of its Yorkshire and Durham churches, as against both bishop and lay owners, are reflected in a stream of papal privileges. Northallerton, the root of Thomas's discomfiture, was confirmed in 1163.[3] Free disposition of the conventual churches was guaranteed by Alexander in 1164, and again by Urban III in 1186–7.[4] Control of the revenues of Northallerton and Norham was granted in 1160–76, together with the liberty to appropriate.[5] At the same date Alexander again confirmed possession of Northallerton and Norham, adding thereto Hesledon, Howden, Elvet, Aycliffe, Pittington and Middleham.[6] Norham, Northallerton and Hesledon were once more confirmed in 1171–81, together with the hermitage of Finchale.[7]

The dispute appears to have reached a climax in 1186–9—a period, it will be recalled, when for various reasons Puiset's authority in the kingdom at large was fairly strong. It would seem that he then sequestrated the total revenues of the priory, and took the administration of its lands and churches into his own hands.[8] The convent sought the defence of an appeal to a selective version of the history of the see, to which end a great series of charters was prepared. These documents contain in

---

[1] *Scriptores Tres, loc. cit.*   [2] *PU*, II, no. 120. See also below, App. IV.
[3] *PU*, II, no. 111.   [4] *PU*, II, nos. 119 and 245.
[5] *PU*, II, no. 148; *EYC*, II, no. 979.   [6] *PU*, II, no. 149.
[7] *PU*, II, nos. 211 and 212.   [8] Hoveden, II, 360; *Gesta*, II, 60.

expanded form the very points on which Puiset was brought to surrender, and were in fact eventually presented to the dying bishop for his confirmation.[1]

The energy behind this industry and ingenuity was one of the forces that restored the conventual fortunes. The tide had already turned before 1189. The bishop, sumptuously preparing for his crusade, returned the *custodiam et curam prioratus* to his monks for a handsome payment in 1188.[2] Germanus secured some 'liberties' including the recognition of his title to an abbatial stall, but apparently failed to implement them.[3] In 1189 there followed the episcopal admission of a compromise between the hospital of Kepyer and the monastic church of Elvet.[4] With the death of Germanus the convent was allowed, or secured, the free choice of its prior, and once again, as with the earlier election of Thomas, a champion of what might be called the extremist party was put forward. Thereafter the will of this new prior, Bertram, and Puiset's own preoccupation with large political schemes, led to the complete episcopal surrender of 1195. It was now, as the chronicler wrote, that the church of Durham resumed its 'pristine liberty'. What this meant in practice may be seen in the aforementioned charters and the events of the next quarter-century. Within a few brief years Bertram secured episcopal, papal and royal confirmations of the documents wherein the conventual aspirations were so amply described. Puiset admitted practically all that was asked of him, and what little was rejected by his moribund acumen, or unrecorded through the haste of his last short days, was successfully submitted to the uncritical scrutiny of two of the most advanced chanceries in Europe.[5] His surrender was greater than that of any of his predecessors. His action, and especially its written record constituting a sort of bill of rights, helped to create a situation which almost defeated the abilities of his

---

[1] See below, App. IV, and pp. 259, 263.
[2] Hoveden, *loc. cit.*   [3] *Scriptores Tres*, 8.
[4] See above, pp. 109, 120, and below, p. 147.
[5] *Scriptores Tres*, 7–8. Celestine III confirmed the concocted bull of Gregory VII on 16 May 1196 (*PU*, II, no. 278). An extensive charter of Richard I, reciting elements of Puiset's surrender, was issued in February 1196 (DC Durham, Cart. I, fo. 50; *CChR*, IV, 323).

successors, bishops Poitou and Marsh, and which had a permanent influence on the medieval history of the church of Durham.

Disputes such as these were common. On the Continent there were celebrated controversies between bishops and capitular archdeacons, and between ordinaries and important houses in their dioceses.[1] In England, just as Durham, attempting to secure peculiars in Yorkshire, Scotland and Durham, was in trouble with the episcopate, so too, in 1183, St Augustine's Canterbury had to abandon the privileges of a peculiar in the churches of Thanet.[2] St Albans, more fortunate in its clashes with Robert of Lincoln in 1153–63, was confirmed in its liberties in Hertfordshire, where priests of its churches were to attend an abbatial synod, and were to be amenable in matters spiritual to the abbot's archdeacon, and not the archdeacon of Lincoln.[3] Evesham, with an exemption as great as St Albans, was at law with the bishop of Worcester at the turn of the century on its churches in the Vale, where its rights were eventually confirmed by papal judges delegate.[4]

The cases in cathedral monasteries have certain features in common. After some forty years of strife with his chapter Puiset attempted to introduce canons regular from Guisborough into the close vicinity of his church, and at the same time restored and rehoused a community of secular canons at Darlington.[5] There is no evidence that either, or both, of these foundations were cast as rival chapters, but events elsewhere were ominous, and Durham clearly had its suspicions of Baxterwood. At Christ Church, Dublin, a regular chapter had been established by Laurence O'Toole in about 1163. This was at first enlarged by Archbishop John Cumin, the distinguished servant of Henry II. Within the course of a few years, however, he took over the church of St Patrick and re-endowed it as a secular collegiate house for thirteen prebendaries, presumably to be clerks of his own *familia*. About the same time, at St

---

[1] Knowles, *Monastic Order*, 274; Mortet, *Maurice de Sully*, 183–5.
[2] Knowles, 'The Growth of Exemption', 414–15.
[3] *Gesta Abbatum Monasterii Sancti Albani*, I, 145–8; Knowles, *art. cit.* 216–17.
[4] Knowles, *Monastic Order*, 605–6.   [5] See above, pp. 110, 113.

Andrews, Roger Beaumont and his successor had commenced a process which was to convert a community of Culdees into a separate collegiate church, and so in fact strengthen the bishop's hand against his chapter of regulars.[1]

Similar events in other sees have attained a greater notoriety. At Coventry, Hugh Nunant, nephew of Arnulf of Lisieux, worked up divisions amongst his monks by methods such as the brethren of Durham later attributed to Bishops Poitou and Marsh. Following a scuffle in which he was apparently injured, Nunant wished his community to hell, and thereafter promised the king that within two months there would be no monk in any cathedral in the land. The action fitted the word, and in 1190 his chapter was dispersed, being replaced by seculars until 1198.[2] At Canterbury, where there had already been similar troubles in the time of Theobald, Archbishop Baldwin clashed with his monks on the administration of property and what he, with the eye of a Cistercian, alleged were their delinquencies. He seized the revenues from a number of churches appropriated to the convent, and eventually proposed to establish a college of canons at Hackington (1186). Through the unbending opposition of the monks this grandiose scheme, by which king and bishops were to have prebendal stalls in a foundation staffed by learned clerks, eventually came to nothing.[3] There were also less spectacular disputes at Rochester, where Bishop John of Séez granted away churches without the consent of his chapter, and there was again trouble with Bishop Gilbert. Likewise Worcester was in difficulties with Bishop Simon, and again at the end of the century.[4]

These disorders were sufficiently widespread for it to be suggested that there was something of an organized conspiracy against monastic chapters. Gerald of Wales, no impartial witness, affects to give glad credence to a story that Hugh

[1] G. W. S. Barrow, 'The Cathedral Chapter of St Andrews and the Culdees in the Twelfth and Thirteenth Centuries', 36–8.

[2] Gervase of Canterbury, I, 488–9; Newburgh, I, 394–6; Devizes, 387, 392, 441–3; Knowles, *Monastic Order*, 322–3.

[3] Gervase of Canterbury, I, 332–4, 337–46; Knowles, *Monastic Order, loc. cit.*; Foreville, *L'Église et La Royauté en Angleterre*, 536–7.

[4] Knowles, 'The Growth of Exemption', 213–31; *Monastic Order*, 630.

Nunant endeavoured to persuade his colleagues, *qui monachos in sedibus suis habebant*, that he should be financed as a proctor at Rome to secure the general dismissal of such communities.[1] The value of this evidence is uncertain. It is, however, noteworthy that such disputes were not limited to monastic cathedrals, or indeed to monastic houses. There were clashes between abbot and chapter on the appointment and dismissal of obedientiaries at Bury and Westminster in the later twelfth century.[2] Couched in other terms similar problems had earlier troubled the churches of Lincoln and London. In the former the canons had obtained, by about 1150, 'an almost complete immunity from episcopal, and its corollary, archidiaconal control, not only in their church and chapterhouse, but also in the lands and churches of the common and the prebends'.[3] At London the chapter of St Paul's disputed with their bishop patronage in prebends, the control of vacancies and jurisdiction in prebendal lands, whilst in the time of Richard Belmeis I the archdeacons had been forbidden to meddle with the priests or men of the manors belonging to the convent.[4]

The evidence for Durham is far from explicit. The documents manufactured in 1189–95 may perhaps be regarded as an optimistic gloss of custom. The moment of their production suggests that hitherto there had been no call for such detail; earlier bishops, though erring, had been less adamant, earlier opportunities of lesser moment. A similar conclusion might be drawn from the language describing the trials of previous crises. Flambard repentantly restored specific holdings, many of which seem to have been of little merit, and granted the priory *ut ad dispositionem omnium rerum suarum infra ecclesiam et extra in omnibus liberam habeant facultatem*.[5] Bishop Rufus was also

---

[1] Gerald of Wales, IV, 66–7.

[2] Knowles, *Monastic Order*, 414–15; BM, Cotton MS., Faust. A III, fos. 229ᵛ and 231.

[3] *Registrum Antiquissimum of Lincoln*, ed. C. W. Foster and K. Major, I, xviii.

[4] *Early Charters of the Cathedral Church of St Paul, London*, ed. M. Gibbs. xxiv–xxv, xxix. Cf. the situation at Salisbury (*Register of St Osmund, Salisbury*, ed. W. Rich-Jones, I, 213), and at York (*Historians of the Church of York*, III, 35; Edwards, *Secular Cathedrals*, 126).

[5] DC Durham, 2. 1. Pont. no. 1, printed in *EYC*, II, no. 934; 2. 1. Pont. no. 2, printed in *Scriptores Tres*, App. no. xxi.

eventually persuaded to recognize something of the like, though no details of the settlement have survived,[1] whilst under St Barbara the trouble had been limited to points of precedence between the prior and the archdeacon of Durham.[2]

The exact position established by the priory before it was assailed by Puiset's resumption of the 'old vexations' cannot be ascertained. Some of its subsequent claims, equitable no doubt in view of prevailing conditions, had little justification in history and the same, or less, in law. Free election of a prior, likewise coveted by many other houses, including Bury and Evesham, was sanctioned by neither the Benedictine Rule nor the generality of current practice. Indeed, in 1186–7, Urban III, guided admittedly by the *ex parte* statements of Hugh Nunant, declared that it was customary in England for the priors of regular chapters serving cathedral churches to be episcopal nominees.[3] The selection of obedientiaries was, with 'the advice and consent of the chapter', the prerogative of the abbot, which at Durham meant the bishop, whose abbatial rights were apparently only freely admitted in such comparatively unimportant matters as admissions to confraternity.[4] Local lore is obscure, but it is at least certain that in the almost patristic age of St Calais, here as in other matters a disappointing exemplar, the celebrated Prior Turgot had himself been nominated by the bishop, as also the prior and sacrist of 1083.[5] There is no trace of an election until the time of Thomas, chosen *communi consilio fratrum*, of whom Puiset speedily disposed, but it is hard to believe that earlier champions of capitular rights could have been episcopal placemen.[6] On the whole it would seem that when circumstances allowed, as in

---

[1] Symeon, I, 142.

[2] DC Durham, I. I. Archid. Dun. no. 2, printed in *FPD*, lxii–lxiii. See also below, pp. 140–1.

[3] Knowles, *Monastic Order*, 626; *PU*, II, no. 243; Foreville, *op. cit.* 483. In 1174 the monks of Canterbury received a papal privilege allowing them free election of a prior *sede vacante* (Smith, *Canterbury Cathedral Priory*, 29).

[4] Knowles, *Monastic Order*, 414–15, 626; cf. *Chronicon Abbatie de Evesham*, ed. W. D. Macray, 206; see above, p. 114.

[5] Symeon, I, 111 n., but as recorded (*ibid.* 127) the bishop is said to have acted *communi fratrum consilio* (*ibid.* I, 123; II, 204).

[6] See above, pp. 19, 129.

1158 or 1189, the chapter would 'freely elect' its prior. For the rest bishops had probably nominated on the advice of the convent in moments of comparative peace—a compromise accepted elsewhere—and in less happy times followed the dictates of will and interest, as indeed they were entitled to do by the strict letter of law.

Of the prior the convent held that, *jure decani*, he should have the 'first voice' in the election of a bishop, and should be the second dignitary of the church of Durham, superior in the local hierarchy to the archdeacons.[1] Here some prescriptive title had been recognized by a body of arbitrators who, in 1147, having heard the testimony of local worthies, recorded the verdict that the prior had always occupied an abbatial seat in the choir, and had, in all things, *sedem primam et vocem et locum primum post episcopum*. The memories of such ancients were impressive, but in detail their narrative is subject to correction from other sources. The bishop at the time, it is worthy of comment, was St Barbara, the only candidate of the chapter who had thus far held the see. His assessors were two abbots, Ailred of Rievaulx and Robert of Newminster, aided by three northern priors. It is not perhaps surprising, therefore, that the ambitious Archdeacon Wazo withdrew his appeal to Rome, *convictus et confusus*.[2]

The view accepted in 1147 was substantially that held or recorded by the Durham chronicler, the monk Symeon, who, perhaps with the policies of Bishop Flambard in mind, treats the position of Prior Turgot in some detail. He stresses his nomination as archdeacon by St Calais, and again rehearses the office when describing the events which accompanied the founding of the new cathedral.[3] Identical phrases appear at a similar point in that curious tract *De Iniusta Vexacione Willelmi Episcopi Primi*,[4] whilst the *Historia Regum* introduces a clumsy and almost irrelevant sentence into one episode that Turgot's preferments may be fully appreciated.[5] The happenings of 1093, as recorded by Symeon, were duly transferred to the

---

[1] See above, p. 132, n. 2.
[2] DC Durham, 1.1. Archid. Dun. no. 2, printed in *FPD*, lxii–lxiii; 1.1. Archid. Dun, no. 1*a*, printed in *FPD*, lx–lxi.
[3] Symeon, I, 129. [4] Symeon, I, 195. [5] Symeon, II, 198.

Liber Vitae, where they took their place amongst other fundamental writings.[1]

The capitular opinion, evidently, from its literary ubiquity, highly valued if much challenged, finds a certain confirmation in the early history of the reformed see. The prior was named before the archdeacon in a mandate of Innocent II for an episcopal election in 1142.[2] Turgot appears to have ruled in spiritualities during St Calais's exile in 1088–91, and it is quite probable that he, or his community, secured some official definition of his status from the bishop at his restoration, since such an exercise of power had presumably raised difficulties. The same role may or may not have been filled by subsequent priors in ensuing vacancies, but once the office had been held and the record thereof indited it was only a matter of time before a claim was made to independent jurisdiction.[3] The course of events gives but dubious support to this title. Durham tradition admitted that 'pristine liberty' had perished under Flambard, and although there were clearly resurgences in every episcopate their practical success before the time of St Barbara is doubtful. An examination of such early Durham deeds as are free from suspicion shows that the prior finds no place in the writs and charters of either Flambard or Rufus. Only thereafter do there appear two charters, in one of which Prior Roger heads the list of attestations, whilst in the other Prior Laurence precedes Archdeacon Rannulf.[4] The situation, then, if its complexities may be summarized, seems to be that under St Calais the priors had enjoyed considerable administrative and political prominence. This, together with such title as was attendant thereon, had come near to extinction by the rule of Flambard and Rufus, but had been in large measure restored by the opportunities of the years 1140–53. When, therefore, in 1147 the above-mentioned arbitrators gave precedence to the prior they were doing no more than record the prevailing situation. Its history, however, was a different matter.

---

[1] *Liber Vitae Dunelmensis*, ed. A. Hamilton Thompson, fo. 46ᵛ.
[2] *PU*, II, no. 29; Symeon, I, 148–9.
[3] Symeon, I, 128; Barlow, *Durham Jurisdictional Peculiars*, 3–4, 15.
[4] PRO, Augmentation Office, Ancient Deed B 11535; DC Durham, 1. 2. Pont. no. 3*.

Within a few years this victory was found wanting in practical merit. Puiset accepted the formal superiority of his priors,
as may be seen in his *acta*, but canon law and the affections of
kinship strengthened the hand of the archdeacons, whom the
convent found dangerous as administrators rather than rival
claimants to presidency in solemn masses. An ingenuous
corollary was accordingly deduced from the position reputedly
recognized to Turgot and his successors, claiming that the
prior was thereby entitled to enjoy archidiaconal rights in the
conventual churches.[1] Such bifurcation of office was not unknown. Bury, St Albans and Evesham all maintained similar
liberties, and the position prevailing in the prebends of the
great dignitaries at London, Lincoln and York was clearly
appreciated in Durham.[2] But there was the weakness of a necessary afterthought. Until at least 1147 the prior had been
equated, and probably rightly, with the dean of a chapter.
Turgot's position, or so it was understood by early glossators,
was not that of an administrative officer. Rather he and his
successors were thought of in those majestic terms of *decani et
archipresbiteri*, governing the whole diocese in the bishop's
absence, or, like their alleged predecessors, Boisil and Cuthbert,
preaching to their parishioners, or presiding in synod or at
mass.[3] There is no suggestion of the discharge of any specifically
archidiaconal functions. On the other hand it seems fairly clear
that archdeacons of the normal pattern were present in the
diocese from the very date of its reorganization. The existence
of Thurstan, who occurs under St Calais, is significantly
ignored by Symeon, and has been misdated or flatly denied by
subsequent historians.[4] Moreover, William II, in a writ which
may be dated 1092–5 —that is the very period in which Turgot's
powers reputedly flowered—ordered his lieges of Carlisle and
all those dwelling beyond the Lowther to accept the spiritual

---

[1] See above, p. 132.

[2] *FPD*, 287, 290; see above, pp. 132, 138.

[3] 1. 1. Archid. Dun, no. 2, printed in *FPD*, lxii–lxiii; *Liber Vitae*, fo. 46ᵛ;
Symeon, I, 129; Barlow, *op. cit.* 13.

[4] *Turstinus dunelmensis archidiaconus* was included in a confraternity agreement
between St Calais and Vitalis, abbot of Westminster (*Liber Vitae*, fo. 48 and also
xviii). The date is therefore 1081–5 (cf. Flete, *History of Westminster*, 141).

jurisdiction of the bishop of Durham and his archdeacon.[1] This latter was obviously not the prior of Durham, for the convent made no attempt, at least until the fifteenth century, to exploit the potentialities of this same document. It may, therefore, be suggested that there is little reason to accept the conventual statement that its prior was as an archdeacon *ab initio*, and there is equally no need to postulate the devolution of archidiaconal jurisdiction from the Congregation of St Cuthbert to its reformed successors.

There is little to suggest that the riders of this claim—the exemption of conventual churches from episcopal dues, custody of vacant livings and control of their 'disposition'—enjoyed any practical prescription or success. It is by no means certain that St Calais had envisaged any form of peculiar, or that he exempted any priory churches from the payment of *episcopalia*. Such a step was not impossible, and might indeed be deduced from the language in which Symeon describes the segregation of the monastic lands from those of the bishop in 1083. Such as went to the convent were to be quit of all episcopal service and custom. In all this there is an unmistakably feudal ring, but even if it be accepted in an ecclesiastical sense the quittance was specific, and thereby limited to a fee by no means extensive, as may be seen in the list preserved in the *Liber Vitae*, which seems to represent something of the true state of affairs prevailing immediately after 1083.[2]

In 1128 Flambard admitted that the prior might have 'free disposition of all (monastic) things, both within the church and without'. The phrase is so vague as to mean almost anything or nothing, but in the context of the surrender of a number of specified properties and churches there is the acknowledgement of an independent secular and ecclesiastical fee.[3] The fact, however, that the phrase was subsequently amended suggests it failed to express conventual hopes with sufficient force. This in itself is important, for the deathbed of a bishop was the most

---

[1] *Mon. Ang.* I, 241, no. vi; Sir Edmund Craster, 'A Contemporary Record of the Pontificate of Rannulf Flambard', 33–56. There is a similar writ of slightly later date (1096–9) in *Mon. Ang.* I, 241, no. vii (Craster, *art cit.* no. v).

[2] Symeon, I, 123; *Liber Vitae*, fos. 49–50.

[3] See above, p. 138.

opportune place to record the largest claims. It would seem, then, that in 1128 as in 1083, the priory fee in Durham was neither large nor highly privileged. Thereafter circumstances which have already been noticed led to some uncertain extensions. In 1168–9 Alexander III stated that the church of Holy Island *et ceteras ecclesias* had been exempt from episcopal custom for the past forty years.[1] Once again there is a suspicious modesty, suggesting a limited immunity which was far removed from that monastic ideal of a liberty which grew concurrently with every new acquisition.

There is little in other sources to throw any light on the real status of the convent's churches. In Lothian it seems fairly clear that episcopal dues were drawn by the bishops of St Andrews in Earlston and Ednam.[2] If, in Yorkshire and Durham, some measure of quittance had been secured during, or since the time of Bishop Geoffrey Rufus,[3] there was no immunity against Puiset. The Yorkshire livings, he ruled, were to be given suitable vicars with 'adequate portions', who were to pay *episcopalia*.[4] The scene is even clearer in Durham. Pressure appears to have been put on Holy Island, whilst at Elvet the burden of payment certainly fell on the monks themselves, a situation which the bishop assumed to be both general and proper: *Prior vero Dunelmensis tanquam persona synodalia et episcopalia solvet, sicut alie persone episcopatus facere solent.*[5]

The related quarrels over 'free disposition' are less obscure. The priory's claim was in a sense equitable and probably just. Apart from whatever had been granted in 1083, it had acquired by 1157–8 some form of title in a fair number of churches. It could reasonably be assumed, as was commonly done, that ownership was sufficient warrant for any policies pursued in these. Despite the current increase in episcopal authority there remained a tendency for powerful ecclesiastical corporations to

[1] *PU*, ii, no. 124; Barlow, *op. cit.* 20. The period of forty years was required by canon law to establish prescriptive title (cf. *PU*, ii, no. 115; *PU*, iii, no. 190, where the governing text is given). The period was not, therefore, as has been suggested, a 'favourite' with Durham.

[2] DC Durham, Reg. i, fo. 108ᵛ.   [3] See above, pp. 141, 143.

[4] DC Durham, i. i. Archiep. no. 19, printed in *EYC*, ii, no. 937.

[5] DC Durham, 3. i. Pont. no. 3 (printed below, App. ii, no. 5); Barlow *Durham Jurisdictional Peculiars*, 20–1.

take the law into their own hands in such matters as institution and appropriation. The dean and chapter of Lincoln were admonished by Alexander III (1173–6) for instituting to their Yorkshire churches without consulting the archbishop, whilst about the same time (1174–8) it was alleged that regular canons were appropriating without the licence of the ordinary.[1] There is nothing to suggest that Durham saw the chance or possessed the courage to take such steps. But proprietary rights, in addition to their disfavour with the papacy, had their own peculiar failings. Very often all the convent possessed, apart from the grandiose titles of a papal confirmation, was some magnate's promise of eventual parsonage, as for example at Ellingham,[2] whilst at Ednam, Earlston, Dinsdale and Howden son succeeded father without the voicing of even a formal objection, except, in the latter case, by the papacy.[3] The priory, with the patience of immortality, was prepared to await the fruition of its title, the more willingly perhaps since the absence of vacancy at least had the merits of defeating episcopal claims to custody, and since the 'incumbents' were, as a rule, men strongly connected with the priory fee.

It was not, however, the restrictions of this relative freedom which galled the convent. Its opponent was the diocesan rather than the lay owner. It was the bishop who sought possession of a living that was vacant, or of which the advowson was uncertain. On such occasions, as is shown elsewhere, Puiset moved with determined alacrity. In a number of instances he improved on the moment, and emulating the policy of Flambard put his own nominees into churches where the priory had better right. Thus the chapel of Castle Eden, granted to the monks of Durham by Robert II Bruce (1143–52) was given to the episcopal clerk William of the infirmary c. 1171–4.[4] Much the same happened at Billingham. The vill was reputedly the gift of its founder, Bishop Ecgred, and despite a romantic history of subsequent alienation, figured in the earliest list of

---

[1] *PU*, II, nos. 153 and 169.   [2] See above, pp. 98, 117.

[3] For Ednam, see above, pp. 98–9. For Dinsdale, see *FPD*, 249–50. For Howden, see below, pp. 146–7.

[4] DC Durham, 3. 8. Spec. no. 9, printed in *EYC*, II, no. 649; DC Durham, Reg. 1, fo. 113, printed in Surtees, 1, 45.

priory possessions. The church, though repeatedly confirmed to the monks (1157, 1162, 1186) was held throughout Puiset's episcopate by one of his most important officers, Simon Chamberlain.[1] Again Bedlington, where there was some trouble *c.* 1156, was in the hands of Ralph Harang, though acknowledged as a priory church in 1146,[2] whilst Heighington, albeit of uncertain pedigree, was occupied during his lifetime by Burchard Puiset, who evidently endeavoured to acquire a family interest therein.[3]

But in at least two cases Puiset may be exculpated. Master Richard of Coldingham, simultaneously rector of Elvet and Bishop Middleham,[4] was not, as has been supposed, an episcopal clerk intruded into conventual livings. He was a man of great local standing, a forerunner of that later aristocracy of graduates so influential in ecclesiastical administration, his services desired by bishop, prior and private lord alike.[5] But his strongest connexions were with the priory. Germanus, in the grant of the church of Bishop Middleham, describes him as 'our clerk'.[6] It might be felt that no especial significance attaches to this, except perhaps as a stylistic nicety to cover that episcopal pressure the prior already knew. Yet a little later the inflexible Bertram granted Richard's 'nephew' land at Woodhall, and there is a fair probability that Richard himself was a relative of Germanus. On one occasion there is a reference to 'Master Richard, nephew of the prior', and on another to 'Master Richard, nephew of prior Germanus'.[7]

The other case concerns Master Roger of Howden, almost certainly the chronicler and royal servant of that name. It was

---

[1] Something of the early history of Billingham is in Symeon, I, 53, 108; II, 102. It appears as a possession of the priory in *Liber Vitae*, fo. 49ᵛ. For confirmations of the church see *PU*, II, nos. 94, 107 and 238. See also below, pp. 154, 235.

[2] *PU*, II, nos. 51 and 94; *FPD*, 296.

[3] DC Durham, Parv. Cart. fo. 51 (new fol.); Cart. I, fo. 50ᵛ; *FPD*, 238, 243.

[4] See below, p. 223; DC Durham, 3. 1. Pont. no. 3 (see below, App. II, no. 5); 3. 12. Spec. no. 16; *PU*, II, no. 164, which may now be dated 1162–78, in view of the previous mention of Prior Germanus.

[5] Cf. Barlow, *op. cit.* 19 and 25; see below, p. 223.

[6] The grant is to *magistro Ricardo de Coldingham, clerico nostro* (3. 12. Spec. no. 16; *PU*, II, no. 164).

[7] DC Durham, 4. 2. Ebor. no. 14, printed in *EYC*, II, no. 999; 3. 2. Spec. no. 3; Reg. I, fo. 90ᵛ.

suggested by Stubbs, and has been accepted by Professor Barlow, that Roger was of Puiset's *familia*, and so owed both his career in national affairs and his local advancement to the bishop's influence.[1] This seems improbable. Roger, though admittedly a busy man, was scarcely ever with his supposed patron. His official career, which commenced in 1174, coincided with the lowest ebb of Puiset's political fortune.[2] His great and wealthy Durham living, with its *curam tot animarum*, he acquired by simple hereditary title, succeeding his father, Robert, in the church of Howden *c.* 1173–6. This transaction, opposed by the papacy, was completed by Germanus and the archbishop without the participation of the bishop of Durham.[3] There is no reason to attribute Roger's unfortunate reticence on Durham affairs to any supposed hostility towards the convent arising from this matter. On the contrary it may be presumed that the chapter were anxious to secure his succession, and so in a sense 'retain' an able clerk, just as earlier they had 'retained' another distinguished royal servant, Hugh de Morwick.[4] Roger's subsequent career, if it shows no signs of close association with the convent, shows even less trace of any marks of episcopal favour. His church appears to have been particularly exposed to the bishop's depredations. So, on his deathbed, Puiset quit St Peter of Howden from an annual payment of £10, which, as he confessed, he had taken for a number of years against the dictates of his conscience.[5] Somewhat earlier he had also restored tithes hitherto diverted to the hospital of Kepyer.[6] Here it seems there had been a violation of the will of Flambard, who had granted the monks *de toto meo dominico rectam decimationem de omnibus rebus unde decimatio fieri debet*.[7] Whether or not

---

[1] Stubbs, in the introduction to vol. I of the *Gesta*, liv; Barlow, 'Roger of Howden', 359; *Durham Jurisdictional Peculiars*, 89.

[2] *Gesta*, I, 80; see above, p. 42; it is also worth noting that while Puiset withdrew from the Third Crusade, Roger went to Palestine (see Lady Stenton in *EHR*, LXVIII (1953), 574–82).

[3] *FPD*, 279; DC Durham, 1. 1. Archiep. no. 6, printed in *EYC*, II, no. 978; *PU*, II, no. 148. I hope to discuss the family of Howden more fully elsewhere.

[4] DC Durham, 1. 5. Spec. no. 1, printed in Surtees, II, 103; *PU*, II, no. 112.

[5] DC Durham, 4. 1. Pont. no. 1 (see below, App. II, no. 9).

[6] DC Durham, 4. 1. Pont. no. 12 (see below, App. II, no. 6); *PU*, II, no. 269.

[7] DC Durham, 2. 1. Pont. no. 3, printed in *EYC*, II, no. 977, *Scriptores Tres*, App. no. xviii.

they enjoyed seisin is a different matter, but in any case, since Kepyer was re-endowed after Roger's institution to Howden it can scarcely be claimed that Puiset's conduct shows respect and favour for an important friend and protégé.[1]

The conventual claim to the custody of its vacant churches reveals a fundamental weakness in the position of the priory. Apart from uncertain titles to advowson, it may be doubted whether such rights could ever have been enjoyed, except on the smallest scale. Even in the late twelfth century churches were passing from father to son *nulla vacancia*—a situation presumably almost universal at an earlier date.[2] It is true that in the eleventh century, had opportunity arisen, it would have been neither improper nor illegal for the owner of a church to retain wardship during vacancy. This view prevailed in the priory as late as 1218, when, for example, a witness testified that in the time of Puiset a Durham monk had had the custody of Heighington *quod ecclesia eorum* (i.e. the monks) *est*.[3] This might have done for an earlier age, but by the last quarter of the twelfth century custody of vacancies was, by common law of the Church, an episcopal, or more strictly speaking, an archidiaconal, right.[4] The priory felt its weakness, and accordingly sought to reclothe whatever proprietary title it may have had in styles more fitting the time. So Anketill, *monachus et sacerdos*, giving evidence on the same living, based himself on the spurious charters and argued that custody belonged to the monks, *quod prior sit archidiaconus ecclesiarum suarum*.[5] Legally this was better, but it still remained to be demonstrated that there was in law or fact a monastic peculiar.

In secular matters the evidence is similarly slender. It is known that Puiset's forest administration operated with a zeal well calculated to heighten the distress usually experienced by those dwelling within such preserves.[6] To what extent he overrode his convent is uncertain. Local geography, which caused sufficient confusion in its own day, is now irrecoverably remote. If there is a suggestion that the bishop encroached on the

---

[1] See above, pp. 108–9.   [2] *FPD*, 249–50; Barlow, *op. cit.* 34.
[3] *FPD*, 288.   [4] *Dec. Greg.* IX, iii, 7, c. 6.   [5] *FPD*, 296.
[6] See below, p. 188; cf. Poole, *From Domesday to Magna Carta*, 29–31.

priory at Woodhall, where the monks had long possessed at least one carucate *cum bosco*, and clearly had seisin,[1] there is also evidence that they in turn were endeavouring to divest the forest of Howden of a limb at Brackenholme.[2]

Apart from such territorial questions it is a matter of speculation as to what forest liberties the convent had originally enjoyed, and where and how they had multiplied or been destroyed. The claims to have pasture in the woodland of their fee within the episcopal forest, and to take 'necessary timber' (i.e. for building and repairs) therein were not in themselves unreasonable. The canons of York had similar privileges in the royal forest itself.[3] The collection of 'necessities' was a liberty Puiset usually allowed his major forest tenants. It is noteworthy, though, that this right was almost invariably governed by the proviso that such activities should take place 'without waste' and under the supervision of the episcopal foresters, of whom there is no mention in the spurious *Venerabilis*.[4] The corollary that conventual vicars and demesne manors be quit of pannage and foresty is again not unreasonable. The bishop allowed as much to his own undistinguished foundation at Yearhaugh.[5] The dispositions of his predecessors are unknown. In all probability St Calais had admitted such exemptions in that fee with which the chapter had been endowed. These were doubtless ignored by the like of Flambard, Rufus and Puiset as occasion demanded. The age was not marked by nice scruples in such matters, and even under Flambard himself we hear complaints that Northumbrian grandees were hunting through the episcopal forests and removing such timber as they claimed was customary. At the same time it would seem that the monks hoped to amplify whatever rights they possessed, and to extend them to cover that considerable Honor which they were erecting.

---

[1] *FPD*, 254–5, 294–5; *PU*, II, no. 51; *EYC*, II, no. 998. Prior Bertram made a grant at Woodhall, which was confirmed, but not licensed, by Puiset (DC Durham, 4. 2. Ebor, no. 16, printed in *EYC*, II, no. 1000).

[2] *FPD*, 254–5, 292, 293. [3] *EYC*, I, no. 136.

[4] *BB*, App. VII; DC Durham, Reg. I, sec. II, fo. 6, printed in *BB*, App. V; Reg. I, sec. II, fo. 47ᵛ, printed in *BB*, App. III; *FPD*, lii–lvi.

[5] DC Durham, Parv. Cart. fo. 122ᵛ (new fol.).

The position of the conventual court is equally difficult. Inherently the monastic claims were feasible, for immunities of varying extent were tolerated at other great shrines. A priory fee had been in existence since 1083. In the vacancy preceding the election of Flambard the Crown is reputed to have drawn £300 a year from what were presumably the episcopal lands, whilst those of the monks were left untouched.[1] Early writs of William II speak of the monastic possessions as they had been the day St Calais was alive and dead, and Flambard talks of these same holdings *tam in ecclesiis quam in villis et terris*.[2] For all this some form of court had been maintained. So Henry I, in a writ addressed to the archbishop of York, the bishop of Lincoln and all sheriffs, ordered that the convent should have its court as fully as in the time of his ancestors, and his words were re-echoed in subsequent royal, though not episcopal, confirmations.[3] Potentially then, in the early twelfth century, the position of the priory was strong. Henry's wife, Matilda, in a grant at Empingham, freed the land from all work and service, 'as freely as my demesne', and equated the situation with that prevailing in other properties of St Cuthbert.[4] Yet, in fact, the monks had nothing more explicit than the old jingle of 'sake and sok, toll and theam and infangentheof', which, as may be seen from episcopal experience, constituted no regality.[5]

What was meant in practice is unknown. At times there emerges an assembly of priory tenants transacting business concerned exclusively with the priory fee, such as minor grants made by Prior Laurence at Monkton and Pittington.[6] Somewhat earlier, in 1131, Prior Algar granted, or perhaps confirmed, the whole of Staindropshire to Dolfin, son of Uctred, at an agreed rent. The resultant record is a remarkable document.

---

[1] Symeon, I, 135.

[2] DC Durham, Cart. I, fo. 46, printed in *Scriptores Tres*, App. no. xvii; *Scriptores Tres*, App. no. xv; DC Durham, 2. 1. Pont. no. 2.

[3] DC Durham, 2. 1. Reg. no. 8; cf. a writ of Stephen 1136/8 (DC Durham, 1. 1. Reg. 13, printed in *Scriptores Tres*, App. no. xxvi); a writ of Henry II, 1155/8 (DC Durham, 3. 1. Reg. 2, printed in *Scriptores Tres*, App. no. xxxiii).

[4] DC Durham, 1. 3. Ebor. no. 13.

[5] DC Durham, Cart. 1, fo. 46, printed in *Scriptores Tres*, App. no. xvii; see above, n. 3, and below, p. 189.

[6] DC Durham, Reg. 1, fo. 48; Cart. Misc. no. 6324.

Dolfin became the 'liege man' of the convent with the provision that he should appear, after due summons, *ad placita Sancti Cuthberti et monachorum*. This distinction, accompanied as it was by numerous reservations of fidelity, would seem to recognize the independent status of the conventual court.[1] It is, however, worthy of note that this arrangement was made during a vacancy. But perhaps at best all it showed was, as the monk Radulf later put it with astonishing modesty, *quod prior habet curiam suam et sectam ad ipsam de hominibus suis, et defaltas si non venerint*.[2] There is nothing to suggest an exclusive jurisdiction over conventual tenants. From what little there may be seen of civil pleas it is clear that from an early date the mediatized shire court controlled by the bishops had no rival in Durham. It was there that the greatest pleas affecting priory lands were settled. Thus, although the above-mentioned agreement between Algar and Dolfin was said to have been reached *in pleno capitulo*, those present included the two archdeacons and Geoffrey Escolland, one of the royal keepers of the vacant see. Again in a suit in 1148, concerning the ownership of a living in Lincolnshire, notwithstanding the fact that the issue was between the prior and Robert de St Martin, those amongst the *multitudine hominum tunc ad placitum in Dunelmo existenti* included the bishop, the archdeacon of Northumberland and the sheriff of Durham.[3] So too when Roger of Kibblesworth, a priory tenant, surrendered his drengage at Wolviston to the convent, it was done at a solemn assembly of the shire court, *in presencia Domini Hugonis...in pleno placito apud Dunelm*.[4] In less dramatic moments it would seem that smaller issues were regulated by the episcopal sheriff.

The evidence for other matters is obscure. At best the monks might assume that the segregation of lands entailed a segregation of jurisdiction, and that they were thereby entitled to follow the episcopal example of impounding wrecks or levying commercial tolls. On the whole the assumption was weak. There is a slight possibility that a title to wreck had been established by 1158, when it appears in what purports to be a

[1] DC Durham, Cart. II, fo. 186ᵛ.   [2] *FPD*, 281.
[3] DC Durham, Parv. Cart. fo. 59ᵛ (new fol.).   [4] See below, pp. 220-1.

charter of Henry II.[1] This text, unfortunately, is not above suspicion. It was not subsequently cited, and the alleged liberty finds no place in a genuine writ of the same king.[2] As far as port rights in the Tyne were concerned, the Crown apparently considered them as possessions of bishop and convent alike, and at the same time admitted the priory's independent commercial interests elsewhere.[3] But if early royal charters were generous with quittances, the bishops were more discreet. Thus the least tendentious statement of the monastic claims, that contained in the *Liber Vitae*, whilst holding that the merchant community of Elvet should be free from all episcopal levies, at the same time acknowledges that this exemption does not extend to murage.[4] The later testimony of witnesses on all these points is flatly contradictory. As a rule it suggests that conventual claims rested most securely on the opportunities offered by vacancies or the wandering wits of dying bishops.[5]

There is no good evidence of the monastic court handling a criminal plea before 1196, and it seems unlikely that such jurisdiction had been previously enjoyed.[6] It found no recognition in 1166, when the royal justices entered the lands of St Cuthbert (*in terram Sancti Cuthberti*) by the counsel of the king's barons and with the consent of the bishop. The prior was not mentioned.[7] It is therefore probable that he appropriated the methods of the Assize of Clarendon by Puiset's licence, or more feasibly by simple usurpation following the bishop's death. It is noteworthy that the convent was not in possession of a gallows and pit in Durham until 1195/6, when these were introduced at Elvet with significant haste.[8]

Initially, it may be suggested, the priory had a court which, given the opportunity, might have developed in a way comparable to that of the bishops'. Royal writs and charters handled both jurisdictions in the same limited terms, neither creating

---

[1] DC Durham, 3. 1. Reg. no. 1.

[2] DC Durham, 3. 1. Reg. no. 2, printed in *Scriptores Tres*, App. no. xxxiii.

[3] *CChR*, III, 393; *Scriptores Tres*, App. no. xxxv; DC Durham, 3. 1. Reg. no. 4, printed in *Scriptores Tres*, App. no. xxx.

[4] *Liber Vitae*, fo. 49^v.   [5] *FPD* 226, 231, 238, 279, 285.

[6] *FPD*, 225, 226, 227–8, 231, 285.

[7] See below, p. 191.   [8] *FPD*, 227, 269, 283.

nor denying immunity. Events, despite lengthy vacancies, allowed no such growth, which doubtless found little favour in the eyes of diocesans (and their relatives) drawn from the Anglo-Norman bureaucracy. Puiset's episcopate, which clearly weighed heavily on conventual tenants, did not deprive the priory of some pre-existing right, but rather displayed a tantalizing example, the emulation of which was gallingly forbidden.

The purely territorial disputes were perhaps of the least moment, and the spurious charters accordingly show little in excess of the genuine conventual endowment. By about 1158 the priory had acquired an extensive fee in Northumberland and Durham, in addition to such lands as were held in Lincolnshire, Yorkshire and Scotland. This demesne, like that of the bishops, lay in a number of definable areas; some ancient *mansiones*, retained or regranted in 1083, others the subsequent endowments of pious or repentant benefactors. In Northumberland there was a small area on the Tyne, at Wallsend and Willington, and a little farther north at Bedlington and Cramlington on the lower reaches of the River Blyth. Off the north-east shoulder of the shire lay the venerable territories of Holy Island and the Farnes, with some dependent property on the adjacent mainland at Fenham, Elwick and Ross. Nearer the Tweed was the vill of Shoreswood, unpleasantly close to the episcopal borough and castle at Norham.[1]

In Durham itself the main bulk of conventual property was in the north-east and the south of what is now the modern county. At the mouth of the Wear lay Monkwearmouth, of ancient fame, with appurtenant lands at Southwick, Fulwell, and Preston, now perhaps better known as suburbs of Sunderland. Farther north, on the Tyne, was the ill-fated Jarrow, with limbs at Westoe, Hebburn, Monkton, Harton, Hedworth, Follingsby and Heworth, rubbing on the one hand against the episcopal demesne at Gateshead, and on the other against that at Whitburn. In the immediate vicinity of the city of Durham were Elvet and Shincliffe, with the Pittingtons, Moorsley, Cocken and the Raintons lying to the north-east, on that road

[1] *PU*, II, no. 94.

to what is now Sunderland which passed through episcopal property at Houghton-le-Spring. South of the city, spaced along the Great North Road, there lay Tursdale, Ferryhill, the Merringtons, Woodham, Aycliffe, Ketton and Barmpton, adjoining the great demesne concentrations of the bishop at Auckland, Middleham and Darlington. There were two further blocs in the south. The one was roughly to the west of Darlington, at Burdon, Skerningham, Winston and Staindrop, the other in something of equal measure to the east, at Billingham, Blakeston, Cowpen and Wolviston. On the coast, and somewhat isolated, there was another group of lands at Hardwick, Dalton-le-Dale, Castle Eden and the two Hesledons.[1]

The fundamental assumption of the separation of the priory fee from that of the bishop was mutually accepted (at least in theory) and litigation thereon mostly occasioned by boundary disputes or alleged usurpations. Puiset and his partisans enjoyed the reputation of a successfully acquisitive society. His attitude, by no means unique, was that of the aggressive 'improver', and the chief monastic complaints of the violation of 'lawful boundaries' come from those very areas where his demesne was being reshaped; Houghton-le-Spring, Sherburn and Aycliffe.[2] But there were allegations of more radical interference with conventual property.[3] Elvet, to which the monks had impeccable title, was converted into an episcopal borough.[4] At Wolviston the priory holding had been increased by Flambard, Rufus and Puiset himself, who, c. 1163–74, had added thereto the one-time lands of a certain Robert de Hubreville. This apparent generosity was almost immediately followed by the intrusion of the bishop's own servant, Richard the Engineer, into the same property, *propter requisitionem domini nostri episcopi Hugonis*, as the charter of Prior Germanus delicately puts it.[5] At Norham Puiset admitted the unjust

---

[1] *PU*, II, no. 94.

[2] DC Durham, 4. 1. Pont. no. 5, printed in *FPD*, lxxxvi; see below, pp. 205–7.

[3] *FPD*, lii–lvi; DC Durham, 3. 1. Pont. no. 1 (see below, App. II, no. 10).

[4] DC Durham, 3. 1. Pont. no. 4, printed in *FPD*, 198. For the conventual title to Elvet, see *Liber Vitae*, fo. 49ᵛ; *PU*, II, nos. 51 and 94.

[5] DC Durham, 2. 1. Pont. no. 1, printed in *EYC*, II, no. 934; 4. 1. Pont. no. 15, printed in Surtees, II, 149; 3. 1. Pont. no. 14, printed in *FPD*, 141; Cart. Misc. no. 7126.

seizure of Whiteside, lying between Norham and Shoreswood, as also a turbary in the latter vill.[1] The merits of all this are uncertain, and it might be felt that the language shows only the weariness of a deathbed. Whiteside he had indeed earlier granted to his burgesses of Norham, though with what right is unknown.[2] At the same time there is some evidence that the convent's claim rested on nothing better than a title to common pasture.[3]

The causes of such trouble, in Durham as elsewhere, admit no single explanation. Litigation, it is a commonplace, appears to have been endemic to the age. Yet whilst it is perhaps worth recalling the extent to which Alexander III deliberately encouraged resort to Rome—*si vos vel monasterium vestrum in aliquo gravari presenseritis, libere vobis sedem liceat apostolicam appellare*, as he wrote to Durham—it is equally worthy of comment that Puiset and his chapter seem to have wrestled together for the best part of half a century without appearing before any tribunal, either royal or papal.[4]

Professor Knowles has written of the 'growth of a sentiment hostile to the monastic order', expressed in the strictures of a group of secular clerks, and the attacks by a number of bishops on various monastic claims and rights. This movement he somewhat unfairly equates with a decline in the ability of the episcopate, and more justly with the rise to office of members of a court party.[5] Such causes did not apply in Durham. Politically Puiset was isolated. At the same time he was well known in monastic circles, and for one reason or another enjoyed a good reputation in at least one major Cistercian house.[6] When occasion demanded, his own community was handled with beguiling tact. The result, which has somewhat misled modern historians, was that confused respect, compounded more of awe than love, expressed by the Durham

[1] DC Durham, 4. 1. Pont. no. 5, printed in *FPD*, lxxxvi.

[2] DC Durham, Reg. I, sec. II, fo. 2ᵛ, printed in Hutchinson, III, 395–6, *North Durham*, 257, n. h.

[3] In the charter cited in the preceding note the grant of Whiteside is conditioned by *quod homines monachorum de Schorisworth communem cum eis pasturam in eadem terra habeant sicut unquam melius habuerunt tempore Rannulfi episcopi.*

[4] *PU*, II, no. 149.   [5] Knowles, *Monastic Order*, 314, 317–18.

[6] See above, pp. 75, 80.

chronicler.[1] There is no reason to suggest that the bishop was moved by any fundamental antipathy to monasticism. His objections to his chapter, as to other persons and institutions, would seem to have been simply that they blocked both potential revenues and the free exercise of his will.

Durham was admittedly good tinder for any conflagration. Here, as elsewhere, every difficulty was aggravated by chronic vagueness and uncertainty. Territorial boundaries were often said to be unknown (though perhaps not without reason), and were in practice but ill marked.[2] The status of a church, and the nature of its incumbent's tenure were frequently indefinable. Even in the early thirteenth century there was no record of institutions to livings or custody of vacancies, and no certain knowledge of the ownership of advowson. The doings of minor secular officials often have an air of almost anarchical independence.[3]

But the matter went deeper. The diocese contained but few great religious houses or feudatories, thus setting bishop and convent to sharpen their tempers the one against the other. Moreover, to intensify those frictions unhappily native to a closed community, it happened that the unwished exigencies of his career constrained Puiset to spend more time in Durham than any of his predecessors. As his ambitions at large suggest, he was no tractable neighbour. He made deliberate attempts to consolidate both his secular and his spiritual authority, thereby clashing with the two great immunists of the see, York and St Albans. His brusque handling of the latter case, details of which have recently been made available, is worthy of close study. Trouble presumably arose from his exercise of unsolicited offices of consecration in a number of chapels and cemeteries where Tynemouth, as daughter of an exempt house, could claim discretion in the selection of a bishop.[4] The details of all this are largely unknown,[5] but merge with the dramatic misfortunes of one

---

[1] Cf. Barlow, *Durham Jurisdictional Peculiars*, 16–17.
[2] *FPD*, 255, 256, 258, 259.   [3] *FPD*, 251, 254, 257, 266, 295.
[4] *PU*, III, nos. 179 and 330.
[5] See below, p. 199; see also above, p. 116.

Turgisius, apparently the prior of Tynemouth who had resisted the episcopal authority. As a result he had been subjected to such pressure as obliged him to leave the diocese either excommunicated, or with a sentence pending, in either case a further violation of the rights of an exempt house.[1] Two papal mandates (15 August 1170) ordered Puiset to revoke any action he might have taken against Turgisius, and to receive him without hostility should he return to his priorate. At the same time Bishop William of Norwich was forbidden to publish the excommunication with which Puiset had entrusted him.[2] Alexander's injunctions were ignored, and the ex-prior, now a monk in the mother house of St Albans, duly excommunicated. The sentence was nullified by the pope in November, and it would seem that Turgisius, with papal backing, ventured to return to Tynemouth.[3] The bishop, unmoved by repeated mandates, continued to enforce his sentence. Burials were prohibited at Tynemouth, and there is mention of a chaplain who refused to celebrate mass in the presence of Turgisius.[4] Such behaviour was again condemned by the papacy in the summer of 1171, and Puiset once more ordered to issue an absolution.[5] At the same time Alexander empowered the bishop of Exeter, the abbot of Bury, and the prior and archdeacons of Durham to act in the event of the bishop's remissness.[6] With this, it would seem, the case ended. As Mr Pinch found of Mr Chuzzlewit, the episcopal determination was such that it must needs be defined in less flattering terms.[7]

The convent of Durham, on the other hand, like chapters elsewhere, had, in the course of years, become wealthy and privileged. Its aspirations were in a measure favoured by contemporary events and especially the policies of the papacy, which saw in the encouragement of capitular powers one way to 'free canonical elections'. But even without such timely support the priory was strong in the tenacious corporate pride of an undying community. Such loyalty was compounded from

[1] *PU*, III, no. 174.   [2] *PU*, III, nos. 173, 174 and 175.
[3] *PU*, III, no. 176.   [4] *PU*, III, no. 184.
[5] *PU*, III, no. 178.   [6] *PU*, III, nos. 180 and 181.
[7] Newburgh, II, 436–7, and cf. *Scriptores Tres*, 12, where it is said there were many *qui mentis fortitudinem dicerent fuisse tyrannidem*.

a variety of motives by no means all of a worthy order; the monks, with few and fleeting diocesan or secular duties, took an almost morbid interest in rights, privileges and retrospect. Recent events had intensified such tendencies. The election of Puiset closed a period of liberty. His accession came at the end of a decade which had shown the convent as a real and effective force in local politics. Twice had the claims and ambitions of Archdeacon Wazo been confounded; in 1147, when he had been obliged to withdraw an appeal to Rome, and again in 1153, when he had been deprived of his hopes of the see.[1] Twice, in 1142 and 1153, had free election been secured in the face of powerful opposition. If the earlier priors of the new episcopate proved but indifferent champions of capitular aspirations their shortcomings were more than compensated by the rule of Bertram. But even in the reputedly bleak years of the priorates of Absalon and Thomas there was no lack of determination, albeit academic. Every unpopular act of episcopal authority—or in the language of the forgeries every 'unjust vexation'—was met by an appeal to the history of the see. This, as remembered and recorded at Durham, was some five hundred unsullied years of monastic achievement (recent tarnish having been deftly removed) from which there shone forth the great deeds of monk bishops and those who might optimistically be identified as priors.[2] From the works of Bede, and especially from his writings on Jarrow-Wearmouth and Cuthbert (of which at least seven copies were made during the period in question), there might be culled many perorations, particularly on the virtue and necessity of free election. It

---

[1] See above, pp. 12, 140.

[2] Symeon, I, 9, suggests Walcher's study of Bede. St Calais and Rufus were also reputed to have read therein (*ibid.* I, 142, 171). The reformation of 1083 was consistently regarded as a return to the ways of Lindisfarne, which name frequently figures in the spurious charters. Thus in the alleged privilege of St Calais, the *Venerabilis*, the bishop speaks of his desire to revive *antiquum morem Lindisfarnensis monasterii*, and in his confirmation of rights, of the liberties *quas Abbates et monachi Lindisfarnensis monasterii segregatim ab episcopo suo prius habuerant* (FPD, liii). Another supposed charter of the same bishop alludes to the fact that his inquiries into *qualiter in initio apud Sanctum ageretur Cuthbertum* revealed the doings of a monastic community, which were corroborated by the *ecclesiastica gentis anglorum...hystoria* (FPD, xxxviii).

mattered little that in their context they concerned abbatial rights.[1]

This temper of the chapter is nowhere more clearly revealed than in the aggressive lauding of the peculiar merits of the saints of the community. St Cuthbert and St Godric complacently perform miracles which had defeated the powers of St Andrew, St James of Compostella, the combined resources of Scottish sainthood or the abilities of St Thomas of Canterbury. Occasionally the utter failure of the latter might be attributed to the inscrutability of divine judgement. At other times it could be allowed that he had at least been a party to some cure. But eventually 'the holy blissful martyr', whose popularity must have seriously affected monastic revenues at other shrines (and Durham had for some time experienced an almost modern difficulty in maintaining its fabric fund),[2] is represented as magnanimously advising the locals of the futility of journeying to distant holy places, *cum sanctum Cuthbertum multo me pretiosiorem, et sanctum Godricum mei consortem, in finibus vestris habeatis*.[3]

Translated to other realms this meant that in 1167 Croyland was brought to abandon claims on Edrom,[4] whilst Kelso surrendered Earlston[5] and between 1172 and 1174 there was a vigorous attempt to eject the monks of St Albans from their privileged cell of Tynemouth.[6] At the same time the convent was endeavouring to gain from the bishops of St Andrews liberties identical with those it sought in Durham and Yorkshire:

[1] For the dating of the MSS. of the lives of Cuthbert, see *Two Lives of St Cuthbert*, 21, 26, 27–8, 31–2. For Bede's statements on abbatial elections, see *Opera*, ed. Plummer; so the speech of Benedict Biscop (1, 375), that of Ceolfrid (1, 381), or the election of Hwadbert (as described in 1, 383).

[2] See the indulgence of Anastasius IV, 15 December 1153 (DC Durham, Cart. 1, fo. 40ᵛ, printed in *Scriptores Tres*, App. no. xxviii; *JL*, 9779) and the precept of Alexander III, 8 August 1164 (DC Durham, Lib. Sac., fo. 2ᵛ, printed in *Scriptores Tres*, App. no. xxxvi; *JL*, 11051).

[3] *Libellus...Godrici*, 374, 376, 379, 390, 397, 442 and 460; *Libellus...Cuthberti*, *passim*.

[4] DC Durham, 1. 4. Ebor. no. 9; Cart. Misc. nos. 609 and 612.

[5] DC Durham, Cart. Misc. nos. 1330 and 1354; *North Durham*, nos. ccclix–ccclxi, dcxliii.

[6] *PU*, III, nos. 190 and 203; *NCH*, VIII, 44–63; W. S. Gibson, *A History of the Monastery of Tynemouth*, II, App. no. xlv.

the exemption of its numerous Lothian churches from episcopal exactions, the right to appropriate, and the custody of vacant churches, though its success in these distant parts was limited, as may be seen from the concordats of 1193 and 1204.[1]

The priory, like its bishop (and doubtless encouraged by his reputed good fortune, so admired by the Durham chronicler),[2] was jealously defining its rights and possessions in a desire to enjoy a monopoly, spiritual, secular and financial, in as large an area as could be claimed for St Cuthbert. The age was one of legal and administrative experiment, and, as has been shown elsewhere, such developments were not unappreciated at Durham.[3] The authority of the diocesan was enhanced by the common law of the Church, the technique and efficiency of his secular administration continually improved by such royal innovations as he was able to appropriate or emulate. The convent attempted both to protect its revenues, and at the same time to share or subordinate new forms of power and their attendant rewards so revealed. In the ecclesiastical sphere this meant disputes over archidiaconal jurisdiction; in the secular field over the control of the procedure introduced by the Assize of Clarendon, or those new writs which were becoming familiar during the later years of the century.

The situation was aggravated both by an imperfect knowledge of the details of the 'reformation' of 1083, and the fact that where they did emerge they were of a pattern incongruous in the later twelfth century. In a sense the disputes which ran with such vigour from *c.* 1160 to 1228 were the expression of the impracticability of much of St Calais's work. His intentions, or so at least the convent believed, had never been fulfilled,[4] though it may be doubted whether this had much bearing on the outcome. In his time he had been a monk and abbot, and in his reform had accordingly used Lanfranc's 'customs', in which bishop and abbot were completely equated.[5] But

---

[1] Barlow, *Durham Jurisdictional Peculiars*, 117–38.
[2] *Scriptores Tres*, 9, 12.
[3] See above, pp. 68–70, and below, pp. 203–7, 221.
[4] Symeon, I, 124.
[5] C. H. Turner, 'The Earliest List of Durham MSS.', 122; J. Armitage Robinson, 'Lanfranc's Monastic Constitutions', 375–88; Barlow, *op. cit.* 3.

Durham, like other cathedral monasteries, was to enjoy a succession not of monk bishops, but of seculars sent to the north less as spiritual guides or heroic tenants of some mythical pro-consular office, than that their distinction in the royal service might find there that financial reward the see could so adequately bestow.[1]

As happened in other monastic houses the bishop or abbot, perhaps as much by inclination as necessity, withdrew from his community. His tastes, and his employment in national affairs, imposed a different design both on his life and on the administration of his property, but it was the convent much more than its nominal abbot that was forced to try to redefine its position. It was essential to ensure that the administration of the cathedral and its endowment should not be in the hands of the nominees of an unsympathetic alien, but should in some way reflect the views of the community. As long as it was admitted that the bishop was abbot he had an almost absolute control over the appointment of the major officers, and thereby, in fact, over their property. Thus from at least 1147 it became the policy of the convent to argue that the prior was abbot in deed if not in name, and accordingly they transferred to him all those rights canonically pertaining to the office. This theoretical readjustment contained more than the element of necessity. A parallel was drawn between the prior of Durham and the dean of York.[2] Perhaps this has no more significance than would be suggested by the physical proximity of York to Durham. Nevertheless the powers of the metropolitan chapter were singularly attractive and well calculated to commend themselves to more restricted regular brethren. Jurisdiction *sede vacante* belonged to the dean. The canons had early established archidiaconal rights in their own prebends, and York was the only English chapter to assert that the archbishop could not appoint to canonries without its assent.[3] There was little in such aspirations to recommend them to the bishop or his

---

[1] Knowles, *Monastic Order*, 624.   [2] See above, p. 132.
[3] The Register of Dereham, BM, Add. MS. 46353, fo. 310ᵛ; *EYC*, II, no. 1153; *Historians of the Church of York*, III, 35; Edwards, *English Secular Cathedrals*, 121. It is also worth noting that secular cathedrals had early established their right to elect deans (Edwards, *op. cit.* 122).

officers. They threatened his patronage and revenues and at the same time promised the near company of an unamenable self-perpetuating oligarchy.

Not only were there flaws in the original design, but of necessity it held no answers to many subsequent problems. The increasing powers and responsibilities of the episcopal office had entailed the creation of assistants, the archdeacons, whose position in the local hierarchy was uncertain. The clash of the prior with these new officials was a foregone conclusion. They were rival claimants over a wide field of spiritual jurisdiction. The increasing absence of the bishop from his cathedral not only raised administrative difficulties, but also meant that the reverence and honour due to the head of the church had to seek another focus. Again it was perhaps only logical that at Durham the convent should attempt to convert proprietary rights in various churches to a franchise, but there was little in this to appeal to those whose financial opportunities were thereby restricted.

The opponents were nicely balanced. The prior, important and often supreme in chapter, had the power and prestige which came from service of the church. The archdeacons enjoyed, as a rule, if not the kinship, at least the patronage of the bishop, and an office rapidly increasing in authority and responsibility. Tradition, more especially the spacious retrospect of the monks of Durham, supported the prior, canon law the archdeacon; *post episcopum...vicarium eius in omnibus*, as Gerald of Wales noted with an appreciation presumably general among his *confrères*.[1]

At Durham, as in England as a whole, a good measure of success lay with the convent. The archdeacons were excluded from chapter and thereby from any role in the internal government of the church. As was common they were obliged to reside—perhaps not unwillingly—outside the close (the Bailey apparently being the dwelling of the archdeacon of Durham by the end of the twelfth century).[2] But of far greater importance was the fact that within the same period a number

---

[1] *Dec. Greg IX*, I, xxiii, c. 1; Gerald of Wales, VIII, 113.
[2] DC Durham, Cart. Elemos, 158; cf. Edwards, *op. cit.* 249–53.

of priory churches were withdrawn from archidiaconal jurisdiction and spasmodically maintained as a form of franchise.
The capitular attitude to the archdeacons is strikingly illustrated in the history of the formulae for episcopal elections.
The bull of Adrian IV (1157) details the monks' right to elect
cum archidiaconis. By 1186 all reference to the latter has dis-
appeared, and when, in the early thirteenth century, the former
bull was transcribed an inevitable revision was made by erasing
the clause relating to the archdeacons.[1]

The problem of the division of the patrimony of St Cuthbert,
though in practice of a lesser consequence, had its own
peculiar difficulties. Bishop and convent rubbed together as
great landowners in Northumberland, Durham and Yorkshire.
Very often, as the outcome of earlier generosity, a conventual
church lay in the midst of episcopal demesne. It was clearly to
the interest of both parties so to regulate the position that both
tithe and manorial profit went to the same hand. Trouble,
therefore, fell largely in those areas where the episcopal power
was strongest, and of the churches most frequently mentioned
in the disputes it might be noted that Elvet, Pittington and
Finchale are immediate neighbours of Durham, Howden was
on a manor where the bishop was often in residence, and
Northallerton and Norham were both sites of episcopal castles.

In many places episcopal forest and monastic demesne and
wood either coincided or lay in close proximity. The exact
extent of Durham forest is unknown, though probably of the
same generous proportions prevailing in the kingdom at large.
Apart from Weardale there were preserves on the upper reaches
of the Derwent, and at Stella, Newton-by-Durham, Penshaw,
Gateshead, Crawcrook, Merrington and Ferryhill in Durham,[2]
and at Howden, Cotness, Brackenholme and Woodhall in
Yorkshire.[3] The friction inseparable from such regions was to
some degree aggravated by Puiset's policy of making grants
from waste. So, on one occasion, he gave Muggleswick to the

---

[1] *PU*, II, nos. 94 and 238; DC Durham, Parv. Cart. fo. 18ᵛ (new fol.).
[2] DC Durham, 4. I. Pont. no. 13, printed in *BB*, App. VIII; PRO, Augmentation Office, Ancient Deed E 326/B 11537, printed in Brand, I, 206, note v; DC
Durham, 3. I. Pont. no. 9, printed in *Priory of Finchale*, 8; *FPD*, 232, 279.
[3] *FPD*, 254, 260, 292–3; DC Durham, Reg. I, sec. II, fo. I.

priory in exchange for Hardwick, and thereby set it amongst the forest of Weardale.[1]

Beyond all this there lay a sense of profit and loss assessed with Johnsonian realism.[2] Wreck rights were the more valuable by reason of the increase in coastwise shipping,[3] forest liberties by the leaping demand for timber rather than any sudden proclivity for blood sports. Without timber early society could have neither fed, warmed, clothed nor armed itself. Its value was enhanced in the later twelfth century by a developing commerce, with consequent requirements in carts and ships, and by that remarkable activity in building which has already been noticed. The old almonry at Durham was a wooden structure. Timber was used not only to grace the towers of the cathedral, but *tam ad maneria quam ad curiam*. There is mention of monastic dwellings being built at Westoe and Jarrow, whilst prior Bertram raised some form of house at Pittington *de meremio capto in foresta episcopi*, and sought other material 'to make his chamber'.[4]

In this context the history of Gateshead is significant. It was an episcopal estate, to which there was attached Puiset's favourite 'chase' of Heworth. This, with its irksome forest restrictions, clashed with the convent's demesne, and with the alleged interests of its churches at Westoe and Jarrow. But Heworth, which was well wooded, was of especial economic value—assessed by a forester at 1,000 marks—since timber could easily be extracted and moved by raft on the Tyne.[5] Both bishop and convent saw its unique merit in relation to riparian property, with the result that ownership was hotly disputed. The monastic claim was initially weak, but a title was inserted in the spurious version of Henry I's confirmation of Flambard's surrender, and from there acknowledged by Puiset.[6] Seisin was another matter.

[1] Below, pp. 206, 209; DC Durham, 3. 1. Pont. no. 20, printed in *FPD*, 182, cf. *BB*, 32.

[2] Cf. Alexander III's criticisms of the activities of the religious in Yorkshire (*PU*, II, no. 151 (1173–6)).

[3] Below, pp. 215–16.   [4] *FPD*, 238, 273, 274, 285, 286.

[5] *FPD*, 238, 239, 245, 285, 295. For an earlier example of rafts on the Tyne, see *Two Lives of St Cuthbert*, 163.

[6] Heworth itself figured in papal confirmations of conventual property as early as 1157 (*PU*, II, no. 94). In DC Durham, 2. 1. Reg. no. 4, the phrase has

In all it is worth recalling that the last quarter of the twelfth century was a period of agricultural prosperity, accompanied by a price rise. On an average stock prices increased by some 50–60 % and grain by about 35 %.[1] Land and money were in demand. Estates were surveyed and consolidated for their better administration and the greater profit of their owners. The decade of Boldon Book brought similar inquests at St Paul's (1181), Bury (1182), and Glastonbury (1189), in addition to the Templars' Survey (1185) and the *Rotuli de Dominabus*.[2] How this movement affected the relations of bishop and convent as landowners will be shown below. In general there was a spirit of economic aggressiveness; disputes, as at Aycliffe, over the ownership of newly cultivated land, or as at Howden on tithes from land recently reclaimed from waste. The bishop clashed with his chapter, and the chapter with its neighbours. As early as 1155 Puiset mediated between the priory and Elias Escolland concerning Dalton, Seaham and Seaton.[3] About 1180 Germanus was at issue with the great family of Amundeville over boundaries at Aycliffe and Coatham,[4] and in Lincolnshire with Hugh de Cauz about land at Blyborough,[5] whilst a few years earlier (*c.* 1177) the convent had been fined 20 marks for unjust disseisin in the same county.[6] During the same period there were other disputes with Thomas, son of William, concerning 'the rightful divisions' between Elvet and Houghall,[7] whilst Germanus and Roger Conyers disputed Stainton and Ketton— a quarrel later renewed under Bertram.[8] On all sides there was expansion, assart and a desire for new land and new revenue, the inevitable friction, here as elsewhere, aggravated by the

become *boscum...de hewrthe ex orientali parte de mareburne quamdiu durat versus mare.* This does not appear in Flambard's charter, but in 1195 Puiset confirmed to his convent *Boscum suum de Hewurth totum desicut mareburna currit in Tinam versus mare* (DC Durham, 3. 1. Pont. no. 19, printed in *FPD*, 108).

[1] Poole, *From Domesday to Magna Carta*, 54; *Cambridge Economic History*, II, 166.

[2] Poole, *op. cit.* 55; for similar evidence from Rochester see R. A. L. Smith in *EHR*, LVI (1941), 587.

[3] See App. III, *sub anno.*   [4] DC Durham, 3. 11. Spec. no. 3.

[5] DC Durham, 4. 3. Ebor. no. 15.

[6] *PR 23 Henry II*, 112.

[7] DC Durham, Parv. Cart. fo. 80 (new fol.).

[8] DC Durham, 1. 12. Spec. nos. 2 and 13, printed in *FPD*, 156 n.

exceedingly obscure demarcations of boundaries, and questions of title.[1]

Similar considerations applied in matters ecclesiastical. An increase in revenue was largely considered in terms of the multiplication of sources rather than their more effective exploitation; the control of more churches, more tithe and other appurtenances. The benefits implied in the accumulation of saleable tithe in an era of agricultural prosperity need no demonstration. The endowment of the bishop's *familia* from the conventual advowson economically widened the field of episcopal patronage. Disputes over the custody and disposition of vacancies doubtless reflect changing conditions in the church as a whole, but there was a plain financial issue beneath the legal gloss.[2] The custodian enjoyed the revenues of the living—a liberty the convent could only achieve by claiming archidiaconal rights for its prior—whilst the corporal possession of a church was the essential practical step towards appropriation, increasingly regarded as the panacea for monastic financial distress. In this and other matters, as is shown elsewhere, Puiset, fortified by canon law, was more liberal with parchment than goodwill.[3] In all such things he had an acute awareness that when others gained he stood to lose.

No simple reason disposes of the troubles at Durham during Puiset's episcopate. The most obvious ingredient was a clash of personalities now too remote for analysis, though it may be suggested the situation was not without something of that monastic impasse immortalized by Browning. The rest were more fundamental. Both in the ecclesiastical and secular spheres there were movements to uniformity, encouraged by the demands and example of Crown and Papacy alike. Economically there was a general demand for increased revenue. The convent, like its bishop, influenced by these movements, was also faced, in view of current changes in the church, with the need to reclothe proprietary rights in more suitable form and thereby preserve and expand such liberties as it had acquired. At the same time new aspirations were formed by experience

[1] Cf. *Feudal Documents from the Abbey of Bury St Edmunds*, cxxxviii.
[2] Below, p. 198.   [3] Below, pp. 198–9.

of the nature and vigour of Puiset's own administration. The problem was insoluble except in terms of a series of uneasy truces. Between 1154 and 1228 the quarrel was but a violent phase in a struggle which ran through varying forms from the time of St Calais to the fifteenth century. The bishops, generally seculars and professional administrators of wide experience, found themselves confronted by what they considered the parochial conservatism of an undying corporation, sharp for its privileges and absorbed in a history bristling with precedent: in any case a stumbling-block to either the zealot or the politician.

III. THE BISHOP AND HIS METROPOLITAN

Conditions in the province of York and the diocese of Durham had a dangerous similarity in 1154. Territorially they were entangled, each possessing a peculiar within the bounds of the other's jurisdiction.[1] Each had recently experienced a period of ineffectual government: York through the tactless zeal of Henry Murdac and his Cistercian supporters, Durham through the political disputes arising from the Scottish intrusion of William Cumin into the see. Both had now come to the hands of young, able and ambitious men, ready to unify and, where possible, extend their authority.

Roger of York, trained in the active household of Theobald of Canterbury, and accordingly skilled as a lawyer and administrator alike, was, apart from Foliot, the most distinguished of Becket's contemporaries, and with the exception of Thurstan, the ablest archbishop of York since the Conquest. Whilst there is no reason to attach undue importance to the appearance of Master Vacarius in his household, or to suggest he was thereby better advised in canon law than his suffragan,[2] he was no man to suffer diminution of either his ordinary or his precarious metropolitan authority. With the spectacle of Becket before him, and abetted by that expediency which encouraged Crown

[1] See above, pp. 96, 126; below, pp. 169, 170–1.
[2] Barlow, *Durham Jurisdictional Peculiars*, 62–3, but cf. Kuttner and Rathbone, 'Anglo-Norman Canonists of the Twelfth Century', 287, for a severer view of Vacarius's standing.

and Papacy to implement the theoretical balance of Canterbury and York established in 1072, 'he pressed his claims and authority in every direction; to consecrate the archbishop of Canterbury; to carry his cross in the southern province; to crown kings'.[1] But despite his personal eminence and persistent efforts his powers were less than his titles. His legatine claims on Scotland were largely ineffective. In 1164, according to the Melrose chronicler, he retired from Norham 'in confusion' after an attempt to exercise his new jurisdiction.[2] Richard of St Andrews refused to seek consecration of him in 1165;[3] Jocelin of Glasgow was consecrated by the archbishop of Lund[4] and in 1176 Roger's Scottish legation was withdrawn.[5]

Relations with Durham are uncertain. Puiset, unlike at least two of his predecessors, professed to York.[6] Thereafter there are faint signs of harmony. Early charters of Henry II are often witnessed by the group, Roger of York, Robert of Lincoln and Hugh of Durham.[7] Some time in the same period Puiset and Chesney were present at an inquiry into York's Liberty in Nottingham.[8] But before 1166 a rift had opened. Alexander III, in the bull *Ad pastoralis officii* (for the bishop of Durham), wrote of *dissensiones que aliquando inter te et venerabilem fratrem nostrum R(ogerum) Eboracensem archiepiscopum orte sunt*, and accordingly, at Hugh's request, granted that during his lifetime *nemini liceat, excepto summo pontifice vel legato ab eius latere misso, personam tuam suspendere, aut excommunicationis laqueis innodare, vel ecclesiam tuam*.[9]

The cause of the dispute is unknown. Uncertain boundaries of title and jurisdiction offered opportunities neither party was

---

[1] Knowles, *The Episcopal Colleagues of Archbishop Thomas Becket*, 14; Foreville, *L'Église et La Royauté en Angleterre*, 64–71, 276–7, 509–16.

[2] *Melrose Chronicle, sub anno.*

[3] Dowden, *The Bishops of Scotland*, 7–8.

[4] Dowden, *op. cit.* 298–9; Foreville, *op. cit.* 507–8.

[5] Haddan and Stubbs, *Councils and Ecclesiastical Documents*, II, 245.

[6] *Gesta*, II, 241; Hoveden, III, 169. According to Symeon, I, 138, neither St Calais nor Flambard made any profession.

[7] See below, App. III, *sub annis.*

[8] *CPR, 1266–72,* 541; *The Register of Archbishop John le Romeyn*, ed. Marshall, I, 47–8.

[9] *Collectio Sangermanensis*, Lib. III, xv, 8. This was not noticed by Barlow, *Durham Jurisdictional Peculiars*, 67–8.

likely to neglect. In Yorkshire there had been trouble (presumably with lay patrons or archiepiscopal clerks) over the chapelries of Otterington, Warlaby and Worsall, where in one case at least the bishop held the field.[1] At the same time it seems that he may well have taken tithe in the deanery of Bulmer, to which he had no claim.[2] The most likely source of friction lay in those peculiars that both diocesans clearly wished to incorporate within their sees. At Hexham Puiset had apparently attempted to influence the election of a prior.[3] During the same period there was likewise a clash over Durham's jurisdiction in Yorkshire, where the church possessed a great franchise of that nature frequently associated with the shrine of a celebrated saint. It was in part pre-Conquest demesne, as Wycliffe and Cliffe-on-Tees, granted by bishop Ecgred *sancto confessori Cuthberto*, in part the bequest of early Anglo-Norman kings, as Welton and Howden.[4] It lay near the Durham boundary, in Allertonshire (Birkby, Cowesby, Leake, Osmotherley, North Otterington, Thornton-le-Street, Northallerton, Kirby Sigston, West Rounton); in Howdenshire, to the north of the Humber (Howden, Brantingham, Hemingbrough, Skipwith, Walkington, Welton); and in York City, with a detached portion north of Crayke, and another at Holtby.[5]

By the early twelfth century title to the majority of the churches on these lands was in the hands of the convent of Durham. The appurtenant rights are uncertain, though on the whole it appears that there was a strong conventual immunity, with the archbishops recognized—in a limited degree—as ordinaries. It was the metropolitans who supplied chrism (and took a fee of 6*d.* for so doing until the time of Thurstan). Under Thomas I attempts to levy *synodalia* were reputedly thwarted by the vigilance and foresight of St Calais.[6] Archbishop Thurstan

---

[1] *Historians of the Church of York*, III, 81; *PU*, II, no. 212.

[2] *Historians of the Church of York*, loc. cit.

[3] *Historians of the Church of York*, III, 80; for the Liberty of Hexham, see *NCH*, III.

[4] Symeon, I, 53; *EYC*, II, no. 919; *Liber Vitae*, fo. 50ᵛ; *EYC*, II, nos. 964 and 975; *Mon. Ang.* I, 238; *EYC*, II, no. 974.

[5] *PU*, II, nos. 51, 94, 107; DC Durham, 3. 1. Reg. no. 1, printed in *FPD*, lxxxiii, cf. Barlow, *op. cit.* 53.

[6] DC Durham, 2. 4. Ebor. no. 6, printed in *Historians of the Church of York*, III, 68.

granted freedom from aids, hospitality and 'other vexations' both of himself and his officers, whilst allowing that if a common aid were taken the convent might make a voluntary contribution without prejudice to its liberty. He further admitted that if either he or his successors had cause for complaint against any of the conventual clerks, they would accept such right as the priors might offer therein.[1] For the rest there is no evidence.

Puiset took the earliest opportunity to seize complete authority in the franchise. In a charter which may be dated 1154–6 he assumes the peculiar to be an integral member of his diocese (*Cum singularum ecclesiarum in nostra diocesi consistencium*), speaking in language which suggests innovation (*priori et conventui sancti Cuthberti damus et concedimus*), and entirely ignoring any claims of the archbishops. He lists the conventual churches in Yorkshire, confirms their patronage, and grants licence to appropriate.[2] There is no mention of any internal jurisdictional arrangement, but the implication from the tone of the document is that the bishop is ordinary, and he was hardly the man to regulate the payment of *episcopalia* for the benefit of another.

Such claims were doubtless little to the liking of either prior or archbishop, who may well have co-operated to secure their abrogation. In 1163–6 the bishop was obliged to abandon—at least in theory—the position he had previously attempted to seize. In a concordat between the two churches, regulating the status of their respective peculiars, it was agreed that York's liberty at Hexham should receive oil and chrism from Durham, as was customary. The prior of Hexham was to attend Durham diocesan synods, and clerks and canons were to receive orders from the bishops of Durham. The parishioners of Hexham might visit Durham at Pentecost, but were not to be subject to forcible encouragement from either side. In all Puiset had maintained existing rights, but had failed, it may well be suspected, in his desire to attach the liberty more closely to his

---

[1] DC Durham, I. I. Archiep. no. 7*a*, printed in *EYC*, II, no. 936; cf. Barlow, *op. cit.* 55–61.

[2] DC Durham, I. I. Archiep. no. 19, printed in *EYC*, II, no. 937; cf. Barlow, *op. cit.* 61–2.

see. In Yorkshire, on the other hand, he was forced to surrender by agreeing that if clerks of Durham churches, or laymen from Durham demesne, did anything meriting ecclesiastical punishment, they should appear before the archbishop though the bishop or his representative might be present. He likewise recognized that it was the archbishop who had jurisdiction in the disputes at Otterington, Warlaby and Worsall. Roger, it seems, negotiated with *de facto* authority. His allowance of immunity from synodals indeed admitted something of the liberty the convent itself had previously enjoyed, but basically he had consolidated his power in a manner which Puiset had failed to achieve.[1] Hints of disputes, and the bishop's subsequent behaviour, suggest an unwilling surrender made perhaps under pressure to an archbishop then strong in the royal favour.

The immediate outcome is uncertain. The trouble had probably been political rather than personal, and Puiset was eventually responsible for the burial of his metropolitan, of whose will he was also an executor.[2] To what extent the concordat was observed during the archbishop's lifetime it is difficult to say, though it seems that Durham, politically closer to York after 1170, moved with caution.[3] Roger mediated between his suffragan and the great family of Stuteville in a dispute concerning the advowson of the chapel of Cowesby, though in what capacity is unknown.[4] Hugh managed to salvage or retain an archidiaconal jurisdiction in Allertonshire, where there is mention of his holding chapters *c.* 1163–89, at which the convent showed little inclination to attend.[5] This was indeed far from the plenary ambitions of his early episcopate, but may have been an advance on the position of his predecessors, and at least respected the formal word of the agreement.

The death of Roger in 1181 renewed Puiset's opportunities. It might be argued that in response to current tendencies he hoped to consolidate and extend his diocese. Such influences

---

[1] *Historians of the Church of York*, III, 79–80; Hoveden, II, 70; *PU*, II, no. 193; Barlow, *op. cit.* 64–6.

[2] *Gesta*, I, 283; see above, p. 44.

[3] See above, pp. 31, 35.   [4] See above, p. 117.   [5] *FPD*, 251.

no doubt had weight, but on the whole it seems his interests
were less sociological and more purely concerned with finance
and politics embodied in large schemes for the absolute control
of the north. In 1191 the new archbishop, Geoffrey Plantagenet,
properly complained that for the past two years the bishop,
contrary to the rights of the church of York, had taken, and
retained in his own hand, Peter's Pence and Whitsuntide pro-
cessions and offerings from the (conventual) churches of
Howden, Hemingbrough, Skipwith, Holtby, Northallerton
and Walkington.[1] The period may well have been longer, for
after 1181 Hugh had tightened his grip on the north. He exercised secular, and possibly even spiritual, jurisdiction within the
church of York during the vacancy preceding Plantagenet's
election. He is to be found accepting the homage of one of his
tenants *in ecclesia beati Petri Eboraci*, surrounded by an assortment of York dignitaries and Durham vassals. Robert, son of
Alan de Torp, made a grant in favour of the nuns of Appleton,
'in the presence of Hugh, bishop of Durham and the chapter of
York'.[2] A Durham court Christian, probably sitting in Yorkshire, sought to ignore the Constitutions of Clarendon in
1183–4.[3] In 1186–7 the bishop secured a privilege that
ecclesiastical disputes from his diocese were not to be heard
outside the province of York.[4] He was a royal justice in the last
year of Henry's reign, and thereafter bishop and earl. It is not
surprising that in the face of this formidable concentration of
the means of extortion, wielded by a blindly ambitious old man,
the convent of Durham produced for papal inspection evidences
which included the spurious charter of Thomas I, designed to
secure the total exemption of their Yorkshire churches from the
financial exactions of the ordinary.[5]

The position occupied by the priory in the earlier skirmishes
is largely unknown. In detail it desired, in Yorkshire as in

[1] *Gesta*, II, 226; Hoveden, III, 168–9; for the justice of Geoffrey's complaint,
see W. E. Lunt, *Financial Relations of England and the Papacy to 1327*, 21–2.

[2] DC Durham, 2. 2. Finch. no. 17, printed in *EYC*, II, no. 986; *EYC*, III,
no. 1744.

[3] Above, pp. 118, 125.

[4] *PU*, II, no. 240; Foreville, *L'Église et La Royauté en Angleterre*, 544–5.

[5] DC Durham, 1. 1. Archiep. no. 8; *EYC*, II, 265; *PU*, II, no. 223.

Durham, control of the 'disposition' of its lands and churches, and financial immunity from the *de facto* ordinary, to which, indeed, it had good title. At the same time there were allied claims against the bishop of Durham relating to forest rights and court keeping, which have already been noticed.[1] The major struggle with Puiset was in Allertonshire, where it turned on exemption from his jurisdiction rather than matters of ownership, in which he had largely admitted the conventual title. In Howdenshire the issue was merely of the alienation of tithes and their subsequent restoration;[2] possibly the priory was already too deeply entrenched to be moved, though Puiset was initially willing to make the attempt. In Allertonshire, on the other hand, the bishop's authority was traditionally stronger, as may be seen in later depositions concerning the withdrawal of suit from episcopal chapters.[3]

It might be argued that in lieu of the totality of those claims rejected by Roger of York, Puiset was concerned to consolidate his power in an area more or less contiguous with his Durham property, and strategically placed on that superb route through the Vale of York, whose value is attested in his own and earlier fortifications at Northallerton itself.[4] It was in Allertonshire, it is further worthy of note, that he enfeoffed a number of his most important tenants; members of the families of Hairon, Howden, Wallsend and Coleville.[5]

In all it is fairly clear that the bishop exerted considerable pressure, and that his claims were vigorously resisted. Prior Thomas, it will be recalled, was exiled *super ecclesia de Alvertona*.[6] What happened is unknown. It may be that Puiset refused the licence to appropriate which he subsequently granted,[7] or more probably that he demanded some practical recognition of ordinary rights, as implied by his initial charter. In the same area he pressed claims to the advowson of Cowesby, which presumes he was an interested party in ensuring that the church

---

[1] DC Durham, 1. 1. Reg. no. 9; *EYC*, II, no. 990; Hoveden, I, 127.
[2] Above, pp. 109, 147; below, p. 196.   [3] *FPD*, 251.
[4] Above, p. 38; William Cumin had fortified Northallerton in 1142 (Symeon, I, 148).
[5] *BF*, I, 24–5; below, pp. 229, 236.   [6] Above, p. 133.
[7] *PU*, II, no. 111 (29 May 1163).

of Leake received its due pension, and he was similarly active in the case of West Rounton.[1]

The success of all this was doubtful. Conventual churches eventually secured exemption from 'exactions' and the attentions of episcopal officers.[2] As far as the priory was concerned the field was a better one than Durham or Lothian, for the presence of a third party, in the person of the archbishop of York, brought a desirable freedom of manœuvre. It would seem that the monks acquired some form of privilege from Roger at the beginning of his episcopate. Its contents—possibly a repetition of Thurstan's charter—are unknown, for it exists only in a corrupt text.[3] Relations, as might be expected, were seemingly friendly. A Durham monk, William of Nunwick, witnessed York's confirmation to Fountains of a Mowbray land grant in Nidderdale.[4] The archbishop's jurisdiction was apparently freely recognized in Howdenshire. It was into his hands that Robert of Howden surrendered his living, and it was to the archbishop that Germanus presented his famous successor.[5] In his charter of confirmation Roger was careful to reserve both his own rights and those of his officers, but nothing more may be deduced from this than that the affairs of Howdenshire were regulated by the archbishop and the convent of Durham. In all probability he had put some curb on the priory's franchise, possibly extending his jurisdiction in matters of delinquency, but despite this and the aforementioned reservations it is doubtful whether he or his officers received much therein.

Roger's death brought a rapid change, with Puiset renewing all his claims of 1154–6. The practical application of these is implied not only in the subsequent complaints of Archbishop Geoffrey Plantagenet, but also in the spurious charter of

[1] Above, pp. 117–18.

[2] FPD, 274; cf. Barlow, Durham Jurisdictional Peculiars, 80.

[3] DC Durham, 1. 1. Archiep. no. 4 (see below, App. 11, no. 14). By its witnesses the charter is dated 1154–66, and is probably based on an original of that date, though as it stands it is a forgery. The seal, similar to others of Roger of York, has been tampered with, and probably opened. The hand is that of those documents generally accepted to be spurious (see below, App. iv). The charter is accepted as genuine by Barlow, who did not, however, inspect the original.

[4] Fountains Cartulary, 208.   [5] Above, pp. 146–7.

Thomas I, a copy of which the priory sent to Rome *c.* 1186.[1]
According to this diffuse compilation, the church of Durham—
that is, the whole liberty—was to enjoy quittance from all
archiepiscopal exactions.[2] This might seem to have little
relevance, yet it may be suggested that at the time Puiset was
standing in the place of the archbishop, either claiming a
jurisdiction in spiritualities during the vacancy, or at least
exercising sufficient influence in the metropolitan chapter to
render such phraseology necessary.[3] In the event the statement needed reinforcement, conveniently supplied, so it
appears, by retouching Roger's original charter, significantly
not available in 1186. This new version of pristine liberty
alleged that the archbishop had granted the monks all their
Yorkshire churches (wisely unspecified) *in manu sua*. Moreover,
their vicars in these livings were not to be compelled by anyone
to attend synods or chapters (*nemo ad synodum vel capitulum
venire compellat*). The very generality of this clause, taken with
subsequent evidence on disputes over suit at chapters clearly
indicates against whom the charter was directed. It was further
held that the archbishop had ruled that neither archdeacons nor
deans should take aids, hospitality or other 'exactions' in conventual churches, unless they were voluntarily offered. Any
shortcomings were to be in the prior's jurisdiction, though if
the matter was of such an order that it could not be handled
without assistance, then the archbishop would give his help.
At the same time it is worthy of note that in this one instance
where there is any reference to such authority it is described
more in terms of fraternal aid than archiepiscopal prerogative
(*nisi nostro auxilio corrigi non potuerint*).[4]

Thus the bishop was to be excluded from the liberty. This,
together with the style of the document and the date of its
production, suggests the hand of prior Bertram, here, as in
Durham, the determined opponent of Puiset's claims. The
practical outcome is uncertain. There was no deathbed re-

[1] Above, p. 134; below, p. 301.
[2] DC Durham, 1. 1. Archiep. no. 1, printed in *EYC*, 11, no. 926; *FPD*,
lxxvi–lxxix; *Historians of the Church of York*, 111, 17.
[3] Cf. Stubbs, 264.
[4] DC Durham, 1. 1. Archiep. no. 4 (see below, App. 11, no. 14).

pentance concerning Yorkshire. Perhaps there was no need, for despite the profits and successes of 1181–90 it would seem that the episcopal powers had collapsed before 1195, and the reason is not far to seek.

With the accession of Geoffrey Plantagenet to York in 1189 there arose a quarrel of a less constitutional and more spectacular nature—an indication of the changed character of the episcopate, and the political decline which followed the death of Henry II. The archbishop elect, amply endowed with the energy and instability of his royal father, was no man to be content with the shadow of power, nor was his suffragan likely to welcome attentions necessarily diverted in his direction. Supreme in the north, independent since the death of Roger in 1181, Puiset had his own views on the future of York which he coveted for his own family. He had no wish to have such an energetic neighbour as the former royal chancellor who had met and known him in humiliating circumstances in 1174.[1]

So it was that he opposed Geoffrey's election 'to the extent of his power'.[2] It was soon suggested that the elect, whose masterful ways were well known, had prepared the path of promotion by an improper use of the royal seal.[3] Durham claimed that his own absence invalidated any proceedings, Hubert Walter pleaded prior election.[4] Together they appealed against the actions of those canons who had given a transeat to the supposed royal wish. For the time the *status quo* was re-established; the custody of spiritualities was returned to the dean, the royal officials retaining the temporalities. In the great council of Pipewell in September 1189 Richard formally granted the archbishopric to his brother. Geoffrey, with unfailing tactlessness, marred this occasional harmony with a series of just, but ill-timed, complaints against the royal distribu-

[1] Above, pp. 38–39.

[2] Gerald of Wales, IV, 374–5. The history of Archbishop Geoffrey of York has been told by Stubbs in the introduction to vol. IV of his edition of Hoveden, reprinted in Stubbs, 260–309.

[3] Newburgh, I, 300–1; Gerald of Wales, IV, 375–7.

[4] *Gesta*, II, 77; Gerald of Wales, IV, 373; for the validity of this claim see *Gesta*, I, 319. For Hubert Walter, then dean of York, a protégé and ward of Glanville, and later archbishop of Canterbury, see Poole, *From Domesday to Magna Carta*, 369; *Memoranda Roll I John*, lxii, n. 7.

tion of the dignities of his church.[1] Trouble followed over the installation of Richard's nominees, Burchard Puiset and Henry Marshal, in the treasurership and deanery. This earned the elect the royal displeasure, and the custody of the see was given into Puiset's hands, who thereafter styled himself—so Gerald would have us believe—*Dei gratia Dunolmensis episcopus, comes Northumbriae, et Eboracensis ecclesiae custos*, and referred to his metropolitan in unseemly terms.[2] At Canterbury, in December 1189, in the presence of the papal legate, John of Anagni, and a great assembly of ecclesiasts, Hugh and Hubert Walter (now bishop of Salisbury) appealed to Rome, repeating their previous claim that Geoffrey's election had been uncanonical in view of their own absence. Burchard Puiset and Marshal strengthened the case by denouncing the elect as a murderer and the son of a whore, but despite this weight of almost customary defamation, the legate confirmed the election. The strife was further embittered when Durham, at the king's request and flatly in the face of York's orders, blessed a new abbot of Selby. By this time Geoffrey had learned something of his lesson. He offered his brother £3000 *pro amore habendo*, and peace was speedily engendered. At Richard's command Durham, Hubert Walter, Henry Marshal and Burchard Puiset withdrew their appeals. Marshal was confirmed to the deanery, Puiset to the treasury, and the privileges of the church of Durham were ratified.[3] After being swindled by Richard, who, according to Gerald, substituted £2000 for 2000 marks in the actual agreement for the purchase of fraternal goodwill, Geoffrey returned to York in January 1190.[4]

Thereupon there arose undignified disputes in the minster. Burchard Puiset and Marshal, prematurely or punctually observing vespers, attempted to disregard the elect's summons to cease, and extinguished the lights when he in turn attempted to sing the service. The archbishop completed his office, despite these considerable embarrassments, and thereafter complained to the clergy and citizens of York of the insults he had suffered.

[1] Hoveden, III, 16–17.
[2] Hoveden, III, 17; *Gesta*, II, 91; Gerald of Wales, IV, 376–7.
[3] Hoveden, III, 27–8; *Gesta*, II, 99–101.
[4] Gerald of Wales, IV, 380; Hoveden, III, 31.

The following day (6 January) there was an effort to make peace, but Marshal and Puiset not only ignored the opportunity, but attempted to raise a hostile demonstration. For a while Geoffrey was able to prevent the people from mobbing the two recalcitrant dignitaries, but Burchard soon found it necessary to take refuge in the tomb of his ancestor, William fitzHerbert.[1] At the same time Hugh Puiset used his influence as justiciar to such effect that the archbishop, unable to collect his £2000, again forfeited the king's love.[2]

Burchard Puiset, together with Reginald of Bath and the dean of Le Mans, dispatched to Rome in April by Richard to secure his own absolution and papal disapproval of his master elect, laboured so well and generously in the family cause that Clement III refused to allow Geoffrey's consecration. Moreover, in the bull *Sincera devotio* he exempted Hugh and his church, *cum clericis et laicis tue diocesis et omnibus aliis ad ecclesiam Dunelmensem in Eboracensi archiepiscopatu pertinentibus a jurisdictione illius Eboracensis ecclesie donec vixeris*, reserving, however, the future rights of the church of York.[3]

The following year Celestine III, swayed, so it was said, by the arguments of Master Simon of Apulia,[4] revoked Clement's bull, ostensibly on the grounds that it had been obtained and granted by irregular means. Puiset, ordered to profess, immediately appealed to Rome, putting his person and church under papal protection, a move he repeated after the archbishop's consecration.[5] Geoffrey, once consecrated, and fortified by papal mandate, summoned his suffragan to a provincial synod (30 September) at which he was to profess and account for his unlawful detention of the procurations from the

[1] Hoveden, III, 31–2.
[2] Gerald of Wales, IV, 380.
[3] *Gesta*, II, 146; Hoveden, III, 74; Gerald of Wales, IV, 383; Newburgh, I, 371. For the bull, see *Collectio Sangermanensis*, Lib. III, xv, 9.
[4] For Simon of Apulia, 'the violent and unscrupulous Italian' (Stubbs, 287), see Kuttner and Rathbone, 'Anglo-Norman Canonists of the Twelfth Century', 306.
[5] *Gesta*, II, 209; Newburgh, I, 371; Gerald of Wales, IV, 383; *Historians of the Church of York*, III, 88. The preventive appeal was good law; it appears in the *Decretum*, and was used in a famous instance in 1169 by Foliot against Becket (*Dec.* C. II, 6, 16; cf. Foreville, *L'Église et La Royauté en Angleterre*, 295).

churches of Allertonshire and Howdenshire.[1] On receiving the summons Puiset again appealed, replying to a total of three citations by a sum of three appeals.[2] The archbishop, supported, it would seem, by many of his province, thereupon excommunicated him (December), and ordered the vessels he had used in celebrating Mass to be broken as unclean. But the bishop, ignoring the metropolitan eruptions (including another sentence of excommunication in February 1192), and claiming the special protection of Rome, prepared to pursue his appeal, *multa ut videbatur prosperitate gaudens.*[3]

Geoffrey's presence at York in 1192 raised the inevitable storms, and Burchard Puiset and Henry Marshal renewed their appeals. Both the papacy and the royal administrators now attempted to heal a quarrel rapidly assuming dangerous proportions. Eleanor and Hubert Walter summoned the archbishop and his reluctant suffragan to London (*c.* 15 March). Hugh was prepared to submit to the proposed arbitration, *salvis privilegiis suis*, but Geoffrey demanded a prior plea for absolution in the church of York, and a promise of obedience. Hugh refused, claiming that the metropolitan should acknowledge personally and publicly, and especially in York Minster, that his sentence was invalid. In the meanwhile the archbishop, with unfailing tactlessness, offended the would-be arbiters from the southern province by having his cross borne erect at the Temple.[4]

About the same time, as a result of Durham's appeals (or, according to Newburgh, on account of his lavish distribution of gold at the *Curia* and York's concurrent remissness therein),[5] Celestine III commissioned the bishops of Lincoln and Rochester, together with the abbot of Peterborough, to annul Geoffrey's rash sentences. Puiset, it was pointed out, had professed to York,[6] and had been consecrated at Rome. He had

---

[1] Hoveden, III, 168–9; *Gesta*, II, 226; Newburgh, I, 371.
[2] *Gesta*, II, 209 and 225; Hoveden, *loc. cit.*
[3] *Gesta*, II, 226 and 237; Hoveden, III, 169.
[4] *Gesta*, II, 238.   [5] Newburgh, I, 372.
[6] Above, p. 168. There is an analogy here with Alexander III's exemption of Foliot from renewed profession to Canterbury when he was translated from Hereford to London (cf. Foreville, *op. cit.* 552).

privileges from 'eight or more popes' (*sic*) that he was not to be excommunicated, except by the pope or his legate, and in this case he had been sentenced after appeal.[1] A further letter to the bishops of Lincoln and London and the abbot of Peterborough enjoined that if it were true that the archbishop had ordered the overthrow of an altar, *contra omnem potestatem et reverentiam Jesu Christi*, and the destruction of sacred vessels, then Durham should be exempt from the jurisdiction of York during the lifetime of the two protagonists. But Hugh, dissatisfied, sent once more to Rome to seek an unconditional freedom.[2] Little came of this beyond an unconsoling mandate at the end of the year (25 December) ordering the bishop of London and the abbot of Peterborough to ensure that Durham received 'satisfaction' from those abbots, priors and others of the province of York who had excommunicated him after his appeal had been laid *illis presentibus et audientibus*.[3]

The final stages of the dispute are obscure. The two opponents seemingly appeared before the delegates at Northampton in April or May (1192), but the hearing was adjourned to July after the judges had clearly experienced much difficulty.[4] It was then necessary to send Puiset to France. He demanded a settlement at York as the price of his services, and the government saw fit to pay.[5] Eleanor and the justiciars issued orders which even the stiff-necked Geoffrey thought wise to heed; he was to satisfy his chapter or the temporalities of the see would be seized. The momentarily chastened archbishop and his weary opponents came to terms. The dissentient canons were received with the kiss of peace, having first agreed (with proper security) that they would stand to the judgement of the chapter 'on all points hitherto at issue'. Geoffrey's nominee, Hamo, and Burchard Puiset satisfactorily arranged to share the revenues of the treasurership. Burchard gave Hamo the valuable church of Alne, whilst Hamo quitclaimed the office with the stipulation that he should receive it in the event of

---

[1] Hoveden, III, 170; *Gesta*, II, 240–1, 245–6.

[2] Hoveden, III, 171; *Gesta, loc. cit.*; Löwenfeld, *Epistolae Pontificum Romanorum Ineditae*, no. 424.

[3] DC Durham, Cart. III, fo. 154, printed in *Scriptores Tres*, App. no. xliii; JL, 16939.   [4] Hoveden, III, 172.   [5] See above, pp. 55–6.

Burchard's death, *vitae mutationem*, or promotion to a greater
dignity. Only Henry Marshal, 'not wishing to humiliate him-
self', remained without the archiepiscopal love.[1] Geoffrey and
Hugh were apparently reconciled by the judges delegate at
Northampton in October, when the bishop at last recognized
York's claims and submitted.[2]

The following year the archbishop was again at strife with
his chapter. He had temporarily appointed Simon of Apulia
dean to keep out a royal nominee, but the good Sicilian then
felt a natural reluctance to leave such a comfortable preferment.
He joined the extremists of his church, who were then resisting
the archiepiscopal requests for aid in raising a sum promised
for the royal ransom by pleas that thus would the liberties of
their cathedral be destroyed. Their conduct was remarkable
even by the indecorous standards of the time. They stripped
the altars, locked the archbishop's stall in the choir, and blocked
the doorway by which he entered the church. Geoffrey substituted a body of chaplains for the chapter and excommunicated the canons. The repertoire of anathema was mutually
recited, and the inevitable appeals flew forth.[3] In the autumn
of 1194 the bishop of Durham was commissioned by the pope
to declare the archiepiscopal sentences invalid, and to publish
the mandate for the restoration of the canons, which he did in
the minster in September.[4] The following year Simon of
Apulia, mobbed near York, retaliated by excommunicating his
assailants, and it was Hugh's last blow at Geoffrey when he
confirmed the sentence on his way to London in February 1195.[5]

Puiset's relations with York form one aspect of his general
ambition. He already possessed a considerable personal influence in Yorkshire in 1154, to which he would have added an
extension of his episcopal powers at the expense of the archbishops and the convent of Durham. In its early stages the
conflict had a deceptive juristic flavour, with Roger describing
the Durham liberty in terms of York archdeaconries and Puiset
talking as if it were but a section of his diocese. But his final,
and perhaps his initial, aim transcended anything that might be

---

[1] *Gesta*, II, 247–9.   [2] Hoveden, III, 172; Gervase of Canterbury, I, 513.
[3] Hoveden, III, 222–3.   [4] Hoveden, III, 273.   [5] Hoveden, III, 283–4.

attributed to changing conceptions of diocesan unity or episcopal functions. His hopes in 1154 were doubtless not those of 1189, but there was a common denominator of acquisitive ambition. As he clearly realized, the rule of Henry II precluded anything beyond aggressions in Durham and Yorkshire. The same opportunism put him in alliance with Roger of York, to whom he owed no debt of gratitude. The accession of Richard brought the return of ways more primeval. Puiset then sought to recreate what was almost a new Northumbria. To this end he endeavoured to control the York chapter, as was shadowed by his behaviour in the period after Roger's death, and to put his favourite offspring into the archiepiscopal see, or at least into some major capitular office. Fortune ran against him, but with customary resilience he reduced his ambitions to an attempt to free his see from the jurisdiction of York, and then to pass it on in hereditary succession to the same favoured Burchard Puiset.[1] These schemes likewise came to nothing, but even so the incidental profits, especially between 1181 and 1189, must have been pleasingly handsome. The plans were no doubt of a magnificent order, with more than a faint suggestion of the ancestral style, yet by comparison with those of Henry of Winchester or of John they were both mild and practicable. Under Henry II and Roger of York the bishop had little opportunity, but by 1189 he had too much in too many fields, when by contemporary standards he was an aged man, already fond and foolish, as the cynics and moralists were glad to demonstrate. But time was against him in another sense, for the kingdom under Richard, and the papacy under Celestine and Clement, moved with an inconsistency too abrupt for even the ablest opportunist. Perhaps, as in the generality of his career, Hugh lacked a sureness of touch, more especially after 1189. So by 1191 the Puiset family and their allies, now known as the supporters of discord, had lost the goodwill of the citizens of York, so valuable in 1153–4. For the rest, misjudgement and ill fortune set him in an ever closing circle of able opponents.

---

[1] *Scriptores Tres*, 18. Burchard, and his rival, Philip of Poitou, were in attendance on the king at Le Mans in June 1195 (*Reg. Ant. Linc.* I, no. 198; *CChR*, IV, 147).

CHAPTER V

THE LIBERTY OF DURHAM
1153–95

Hugh puiset was a man predestined to govern. The course of his massive ambitions across the reigns of Stephen, Henry and Richard has been epitomized in the magnificent phrases of Stubbs.[1] His death so impressed contemporaries (with the unpleasant exception of the visionary monk of Eynsham[2]) that occasional private documents may be found dated 'in the year in which Hugh, bishop of Durham, entered the way of all flesh'.[3] In detail the portrait may now be rendered less heroic and more conventional, yet Puiset remains an outstanding man of an outstanding age. His position was unique in England. He was prince and bishop; secular lord of a franchise favourably comparable to such fees as Chester, Lancaster or Richmond, an Honor which adequately endowed the episcopal style and provided some compensation for those opportunities lost when the English fortunes of the house of Blois foundered in 1154.

The great episcopal immunity, the area where, in local parlance, the bishop had 'the regality', was neither the diocese of Durham nor the patrimony of St Cuthbert—that vast agglomeration of lands reaching from the modern Berwickshire, through Northumberland and Durham, and by the Vale of York to Lincolnshire. The Yorkshire lands were apparently excluded, for in 1188 Northallerton was amerced by the Crown for concealing a royal plea.[4] The status of the Lincoln fees is doubtful, but to Puiset they were sufficiently remote to be considered a fitting instalment on the price of Sadberge.[5] The

---

[1] Stubbs, 211–14.

[2] *Cartulary of Eynsham*, ed. H. E. Salter, II, 340–1.

[3] *Documents Illustrative of the Social and Economic History of the Danelaw*, ed. F. M. Stenton, no. 450; *Cal. Doc. France*, no. 143.

[4] PR 34 Henry II, 92.

[5] For the episcopal lands in Lincolnshire see the *Lincolnshire Domesday* (*Lindsey Survey*) ed. C. W. Foster, and BF, I, 159, 161, 163–7, etc.; cf. above, p. 49.

core of the Liberty, apart from a small portion of Northumberland centred on Norham, was essentially the modern Co. Durham, an area variously described by royal officers and up-country monks as Haliwerfolc, Durhamshire or the Land between Tyne and Tees.

Durham was rich and remote. The long fingers of Angevin power touched the north at Carlisle, Newcastle and the well-maintained castles of Northumberland,[1] but never pressed too heavily on Durham *sede plena*. Puiset's nearest rival, his own convent, was all but politically extinct until the last decade of the episcopate, when it was revived by prior Bertram, *vir bonus et strenuus*[2]—a descendant of that Rannulf Flambard whose energies had earlier distressed the church of Durham. For the rest neither the county nor the diocese contained any great and wealthy houses of religious, such as divided the revenues and embarrassed the authority of many southern bishops. There were able neighbours in the archbishops of York, Roger of Bishopsbridge and Geoffrey Plantagenet, but though their claims were a frequent source of ecclesiastical friction, they were no threat to independence, for York lacked an authority and interest comparable to those with which Canterbury quashed the aspirations of the Welsh Church. The diocese of Carlisle was of a poverty unattractive to men of purpose, and not unnaturally remained vacant until 1218 following the death of its first bishop in 1157.[3] The Scottish monarchy, traditionally interested in advancing its borders to the Tyne, and on occasions to the Tees and beyond, was at one of its many low ebbs in the last half of the twelfth century. It was ruled first by Malcolm the Virgin (1153–65), a sore saint for his kingdom, whose energies were wrongly reputed to be absorbed in overcoming the temptations his mother scattered in his chaste path,[4] and secondly by William the Lion, generally more fortunate in name than deed.

---

[1] The amounts spent by Henry on the maintenance of the northern castles are worthy of note. They show, amongst other things, where he considered the effective defence of the area to lie. The sums on the Pipe Rolls are; Newcastle, £1144 (and cf. Round, *Geoffrey de Mandeville*, 340, n. 1); Carlisle, £69; Bamburgh, £76; Wark, £328.   [2] *Scriptores Tres*, 8.   [3] Hoveden, II, 309.
[4] Newburgh, I, 76–8, 148, but cf. *Scot. Hist. Rev.* XII (1915), 438.

There was little to detract from these timely opportunities of nature and politics. The obligations of the Liberty were few and light. It was generally quit of court services and common financial levies, and the monks had suitable anecdotes illustrating the depressing fortunes of the impertinents who would dare to tax St Cuthbert.[1] In criminal matters it became the royal policy to hold the bishop responsible for the arrest and return of accused persons who had taken refuge in the immunity. A case occurred in 1194, when a knight of the Honor was charged with rape, and the bishop was required to produce him in court. Nothing more was done.[2] Where the Liberty fused almost imperceptibly with the Honor the lord, as a tenant in chief, owed the Crown the service of ten knights.[3] Puiset, in common with others of the episcopate, refused to acknowledge more than his traditional *servicium debitum*.[4] He had, in fact, a surplus enfeoffment of over sixty fees, and a total of over seventy.[5] The Crown never appears to have realized any military service on this host, except that in 1195/6 Durham was represented in Normandy by a solitary warrior whose service saved him a five mark scutage.[6] There is no sign of that 'standing army of knights and sergeants continually exercised in warlike pursuits' which romantic imagination persistently associates with the Liberty and the defence of the border. When an army was required in 1173/4 it was hired from abroad.[7] For the rest, in some ten scutages and aids taken under Henry II and Richard I, the king received the proceeds from ten fees, the bishop the profits of sixty. He was, however, obliged to pay spasmodic *dona*, which cost him over £330 in 1159[8] and some

---

[1] For quittance from geld see *EYC*, II, nos. 929 and 930; *PR 8 Henry II*, 52; Symeon, I, 107–8; G. T. Lapsley, *The County Palatine of Durham*, 295. A confirmatory writ of Henry II (*c.* 1158) quits the men of St Cuthbert *de scyris et hundredis, tridingis et wapentacnis et auxiliis Vicecomitum et prepositorum* (DC Durham, 3. 1. Reg. no. 11, printed in *Scriptores Tres*, App. no. xxxiii). Puiset's position was confirmed in a number of charters issued at the same date (*CChR*, v, 292; *Scriptores Tres*, App. no. xxxiv; cf. Lapsley, *op. cit.* 161–2).

[2] Lapsley, *op. cit.* 225.   [3] *LR*, 416–18.

[4] J. H. Round, *Feudal England*, 243; H. M. Chew, *Ecclesiastical Tenants-in-Chief*, 21.   [5] *LR, loc. cit.*

[6] *Chancellor's Roll 8 Richard I*, 258; cf. S. E. Gleason, *An Ecclesiastical Barony of the Middle Ages, The Bishopric of Bayeux, 1066–1204*, 74.

[7] Above, pp. 38–39.   [8] *PR 5 Henry II*, 31.

£65 in 1165, whilst in his declining years he unavailingly contributed £2000 to Richard's ransom in a bid to retain the royal
favour.[1] Of castles and their upkeep little is said: an adulterine
was raised at Northallerton in 1173/4, and more legally Norham
and Durham were rebuilt.[2] Castle guard at the latter is occasionally mentioned in private charters, and the great families
of fitzMeldred, Hylton, Amundeville, Basset and Conyers all
had property in Durham connected with necessary periods of
residence *ad custodiam castelli*.[3] Such arrangements were, however, of long standing, as Flambard's creation of a fee at
Ancroft for the guard of Norham, or the duty of certain
episcopal manors to furnish peasants to act as castle watchmen.[4]

Such was the general extent of the bishop's obligations,
which neither politically nor financially weighed against his
enormous privileges. His own career brought other offices of
little moment. By his purchase of Sadberge he acquired an
interest in the guard of Newcastle (the wapentake being a
detached portion of Northumberland)[5] but there is nothing to
show how this was discharged. Of a more curious nature was
a duty that arose from Richard I's passing, mercenary friendship
with William of Scotland. This demanded suitable arrangements
for the Scottish king's progress to court. The bishop of Durham and the sheriff of Northumberland, supported by the local
barons, were to meet him on the Tweed and thence escort him
to the Tees, where he was to be received by the archbishop of
York and the dignitaries of Yorkshire, and so passed from shire
to shire until he reached the English court. How all this
worked in practice, and to what extent, and with what enthusiasm, the bishop of Durham participated, it is impossible
to say.[6]

In power and extent the Liberty was, and in many ways

[1] Hoveden, III, 210; *Scriptores Tres*, 14.
[2] See above, pp. 38, 111. The castle of Norham had been built by Flambard,
and was destroyed by the Scots in 1138. The rebuilding undertaken by Puiset was
at the royal command (Symeon, I, 168; II, 260, 291).
[3] *FPD*, 196 n., 197 n.; DC Durham, Cart. II, fo. 266; *VCH Durham*, III, 53.
[4] *North Durham*, 385; *BB*, 20, 22, 23, etc.
[5] *BF*, I, 203; *CCIR, 1337–9*, 39.
[6] DC Durham, Reg. I, sec. II, fo. 95ᵛ; Hoveden, III, 244; Poole, *From
Domesday to Magna Carta*, 280.

remained, inchoate. In comparison with the earldom of Chester, or the defunct palatine of Shropshire, its venerable prescriptive ancestry debarred it the assets of tenurial and territorial unity.[1] Whilst the greater part of the modern county was held in chief by the bishop, it yet contained patches of royal demesne and mesne holdings of great feudatories. The old Roman road crossing the county was 'the king's road'.[2] The body of Northumberland split Norham from Durham, and the mines of Weardale belonged to the Crown until 1154.[3] The king had demesne in Sadberge (forming an irregular wedge north-east of Stockton), where Henry II made a grant in favour of Durham's cell of Finchale.[4] In the same area the Balliols held five fees in chief,[5] and the Bruces two: a castle at what is now Castle Eden, and land at Hartness and Hartlepool, by nature destined to be an unending source of friction between the Crown and subsequent bishops.[6] There was another royal tenant at Ulnaby Hall, whilst Peter Carew held a fee in the sea-side resort now bearing his name, the Amundevilles in Coatham, the Baards in Middleton St George and Hartburn, and the great northern family of Bertram, lords of Mitford and founders of Brinkburn, at Greatham.[7] These defects Puiset carefully remedied with an acquisitive zeal that found its opportunity at the death of Henry II. His conduct recalls the earlier activities of his own ancestors, or the contemporary policies of some powerful 'state-building' German dynast. The mines of Weardale he had received as Stephen's last act of patronage.[8] He purchased the earldom of Northumberland in 1189 and held it more or less continuously until 1194. At the same time he bought out the royal enclave of Sadberge (which became a permanent member of the franchise), and in January 1195

---

[1] Cf. J. Tait, *The Cheshire Domesday*, 30–1; *VCH Shropshire*, 288. To the contrary, see Lapsley, *Durham*, 54, where he commits himself to the view that 'in the bishopric no land was held of the king'.

[2] *Libellus...Godrici*, 334.

[3] DC Durham, 1. 1. Reg. no. 16, *Scriptores Tres*, App. no. xxvii.

[4] *Libellus...Godrici*, cap. clix; Eyton, *Itinerary of Henry II*, 242; *Priory of Finchale*, 192.

[5] BF, 1, 25–6.   [6] *EYC*, 11, no. 649 and 11–16.

[7] BM, Stowe MS. 930, fo. 146; DC Durham, Cart. 1, fo. 248; *Scriptores Tres*, App. no. xl; BF, 1, 25–6.   [8] Above, n. 3.

belatedly secured the service of a number of the royal tenants noticed above.[1] He endeavoured to gain a guiding influence in the York chapter and secure the archiepiscopal throne for Burchard Puiset. Had this come to pass he would have rounded off a total exemption far greater than any other in Europe. As it was his hopes miscarried and the general run of these vast plans came to nothing, but at least during the last years of his life Puiset was within measurable distance of that revived Northumbria Richard planned for Otto of Brunswick in 1195.[2]

With the possession of what was at once a feudal Honor and a mediatized shire came a fluctuating body of powers. The bishop levied scutages, took aids and exploited the opportunities of wardship and escheat. He regulated disputes between his feudal tenants, licensed the alienation of lands to what was in fact mortmain,[3] adjusted boundaries, assisted in the creation of tenures more valuable to himself, and admitted the frequent mortgaging and broking which brought a liberal endowment to his own family. On the demesne his authority ran from the creation of boroughs to the control of assarting and hedging. But nearer to his heart were the interests of his forests, for he was as mighty a hunter as Osbaldeston's equestrian bishop, or that fellow Lancastrian who 'ate, drank wine, was merry, and to the field again'. Indeed, so dear did he hold the wood of Heworth that he begrudged any right of warren therein—or such at least were the memories of his hunting companion, Henry of Farlington.[4]

Beyond such conventional rights lay a scale of franchisal powers ascending from passing independence in what in more spacious days would have been called foreign affairs (as witness 1173–4), to an unsteady monopoly of civil and criminal justice. The position has been defined by subsequent writers as 'palatine', which raises more questions than it answers, for as has recently been said of another great Liberty, it is by no means easy to discover what the criterion of a palatinate in this period

---

[1] Hoveden, III, 14–15; *Gesta*, II, 87; *Scriptores Tres*, App. nos. xl, xlii; DC Durham, 3. 1. Reg. no. 27; *Northumberland and Durham Deeds*, 253, no. 1.

[2] Above, pp. 61–2, 182.

[3] DC Durham, 1. 1. Finch. no. 14.

[4] *FPD*, 234.

is supposed to have been.[1] The bishop's 'regalian jurisdiction', like his feudal obligations, was more a matter of prescription than charter, and as has been suggested of other northern Liberties, originated in ancient Northumbrian custom rather than post-Conquest grant or the hoary myth of border defence.[2] It rested on no document couched in the 'uncouth phrases' of Saxon law, though the writs of Henry II drive us back on these humble definitions in the charters of Stephen and Henry I, and local knights had the ingenuity to cover all fact by conventional jargon.[3] When, however, Richard I made the grants of Northumberland and Sadberge he admitted the bishop's 'regalian' position, and at the same time the insufficiency of the normal formulae to extend it. Thus in the Sadberge charter the prospective rights fall into three sections; *cum socha et sacha et tol et theam et infangenthefe*, to which is added *cum omnibus aliis libertatibus et liberis consuetudinibus et cum placitis ad coronam pertinentibus sicut nos ipsi in propria manu nostra habebamus et sicut ipse episcopus habet et tenet alias terras suas*, etc.[4]

But this was a far cry from unbridled liberty and profit. The real nature of these 'pleas of the crown'—a delusive territory disputed between bishops and priors from *c*. 1180 to 1228—emerges from depositions taken in the first quarter of the thirteenth century as attempts were made to patch up the quarrels. Under Marsh witnesses testified for the prior's claim to parity in such matters that from the time of Puiset 'to the present' (*c*. 1218) 'pleas of the crown were held in the prior's court'. Then follows a recital of one case of arson, two of rape, two of breach of peace and five of murder.[5] About 1221, Durham knights, some of whom could remember Puiset, claimed the bishop alone had cognizance of cases of theft, together with the right to punish (generally described as the exercise of team and infangentheof), 'since he alone has

[1] G. Barraclough, *The Earldom and County Palatine of Chester*, 10.
[2] The real march and defence of the north, as contemporaries well realized, was Northumberland, not Durham, cf. Bulmer's reply to Henry II in 1166 (LR, 440) and the royal concern for the Northumbrian castles noticed above. Cf. Barraclough, *op. cit.* 14-15 as to similar misconceptions concerning Chester's relations with Wales.
[3] Cf. p. 190.   [4] See above, p. 188, n. 1.
[5] DC Durham, 2. 4. Pont. no. 8, printed in *FPD*, 218-19.

regalian power'. Roger Audre and William of Layton both declared they had never seen *latrones judicari vel duellum fieri nisi in curia Episcopi*, and John of Thorpe was of the opinion that *nullus habet placitum de latrocinio nisi Episcopus*. Henry of Farlington was more explicit, and vigorously confirmed his neighbours' testimony, adding that it was impossible for the prior or anybody else to replevy the accused in a case of theft.[1] Delinquency was discovered—at least on one occasion—through those powers supposedly conferred by 'soke', and the practical operation of 'the search', or in the more formal language of one constitutionalist, 'the Assize of Clarendon'.[2] According to another witness 'the search was made' by the prior in his own fee during Puiset's episcopate, but only by the bishop's licence.[3] Such opinions were contraverted by the priory tenants, generally from later evidence, not to deny that royal pleas were in private hands, but to secure some share therein.[4]

It was further maintained that the bishop might emulate the crown in the employment of the writ of right, and that in sum his writ ran to the exclusion of that of the king.[5] Thus when, in 1204, Geoffrey son of Geoffrey argued that in the time of Henry II no freeman used to be impleaded in the bishop's court save by writ of the king or his chief justice, his views were flatly denied. The case got no further, and the royal clerks who eventually handled it confessed themselves defeated, ending its report with a misquotation from Horace.[6]

On the whole there is good reason to believe that the Durham knights spoke rightly of what they knew, though labouring to define the indefinable. Whilst the Assize of Clarendon was not perhaps the passing expedient it appears to Dr Hurnard, the legal reforms of Henry II lack the logical consistency Maitland found in them, and pay—at least in

---

[1] *FPD*, 231, 233–5. Richard of Auckland noted that the 'regality' covered both *Haliwerfolc et Norhamshire* (*FPD*, 238). Somewhat similar language had earlier appeared in Reginald's *Libellus...Cuthberti*, 210.

[2] *FPD*, 274, 275, 285.

[3] *FPD*, 274, 282. [4] *FPD*, 282.

[5] *FPD*, 231; Adam of Lumsden defined the situation as *currit breve Episcopi quando est Episcopus, et breve Regis quando vacat sedes* (*FPD*, 232).

[6] *Curia Regis Rolls*, III, 108–10; Lapsley, *Durham*, 313–16; C. T. Flower, *Introduction to the Curia Regis Rolls*, 94–5.

operation—a greater deference to the immunist than used to be admitted.[1] The writ *mitto hac vice*, in which the king announced his justices would visit Durham, is important evidence, not only of the existence of the franchise in 1166, but also of the respect with which it was treated. The royal officers were to enter the Liberty to take the assize *de latronibus, et murdratoribus et roboratoribus*, with the consent of the bishop, and their visit was not to constitute a precedent harmful to the episcopal rights.[2] It might be felt, as Round believed, that such guarantees were merely the politeness of clerical formulae, but no royal officers were permanently established in the Liberty, no justices were assigned the shire, and there is little record of Durham pleas in the rolls of Henry II and Richard.

But immunity was not autonomy. From later evidence there is a strong presumption that express royal consent was necessary for the introduction and employment of the new possessory assizes,[3] and, according to a charter of John of August 1208, freemen of Durham were not to be impleaded of their free holdings *nisi per breve nostrum et heredum nostrorum vel capitalis justiciarii nostri sicut fieri consuevit toto tempore Regis Henrici patris nostri et omnium antecessorum suorum.*[4] This agrees in some measure with the tenor of an early writ of Henry II, stating his right to intervene where, in a proprietary action, there had been a failure of justice, and with the views of Geoffrey son of Geoffrey already cited.[5] As a reading of recent history it was somewhat optimistic, having been inspired by the petition and payment of Durham knights then distressed by the militant policies of bishop Poitou.[6] But what was wrong in detail was right in spirit. The royal writ ran in Durham less as a matter of course definable in a lawyer's phrase than as the play of opportunity and character admitted. Henry I had licensed

---

[1] N. D. Hurnard, 'The Jury of Presentment and the Assize of Clarendon', 374-410.
[2] DC Durham, Cart. 1, fo. 50, printed in *Scriptores Tres*, App. no. xxxi, and Round, *Geoffrey de Mandeville*, 112.
[3] Cf. Flower, *Introduction to the Curia Regis Rolls*, 95; and see below, p. 222.
[4] DC Durham, Cart. 1, fo. 194; *Rotuli Chartarum*, 10 John, 182a.
[5] DC Durham, Cart. 1, fo. 61ᵛ, printed in *Scriptores Tres*, App. no. xxxii.
[6] Cf. Lapsley, *Durham*, 167.

Flambard's fair at Norton and ordered *ut omnès ad illud venientes et inde redeuntes habeant meam firmam pacem*, just as the equally powerful John allowed Poitou's at Howden in 1200—powers Puiset was able to arrogate to himself concerning Elvet during Richard's heedless reign.[1] Even Stephen had held that an infringement of the rights of the monks of Durham was a breach of the royal peace, emendable to the Crown.[2] So too Henry II never hesitated to violate or define the Liberty when occasion demanded, with the result that neither in the field of politics nor of justice did the bishop hold an absolute immunity.[3] Sometime before 1183 the episcopal mint, having declined in face of a more active rival in Newcastle, was suppressed by royal command.[4] About 1163 the king took Brother Rannulf and the cell of Landieu at Wolsingham in Weardale into his own peace and protection.[5] In *c.* 1176 he confirmed Radulf of Wolviston in possession of lands there, just as earlier Stephen had confirmed a fee at Plawsworth and Chilton to one William the chamberlain.[6] Sometime *c.* 1170 he inquired *per barones et milites in curia Dunelmensi* as to the rightful holding of the Durham grandee, Roger Conyers, ordering that in future Roger was not to be impleaded of his lands *sine precepto nostro, supra magnam nostram forisfacturam*—which is a particular anticipation of that general statement of Geoffrey son of Geoffrey.[7] In 1174 the castles of Durham and Norham were in the hands of royal officers, following Puiset's uncertain attitude to the rising of 1173. When the constables were relieved in 1177, their succes-

---

[1] R. W. Southern, 'Rannulf Flambard and early Anglo-Norman Administration', 123; DC Durham, 3. 1. Reg. no. 8; BM, Stowe MS. 930, fo. 142v; *FPD*, 199n.

[2] DC Durham Cart. 1, fo. 47v, printed in *Scriptores Tres*, App. no. xxvi.

[3] Cf. Barraclough, *The Earldom of Chester*, 10, for similar conditions at Chester. There is some evidence that Durham tenants sought, or were drawn into, the royal courts. In 1195—though possibly after Puiset's death—William of Chilton proffered 10 marks to have right of a fee in Chilton against two other Durham tenants, Jordan Hairon and Alan of Chilton (*PR 7 Richard I*, 25, and cf. *PR 30 Henry II*, 52). There is another indecisive entry relating to Daniel of Durham in *PR 16 Henry II*, 51.

[4] *BB*, 1-2.   [5] DC Durham, Cart. 11, fo. 98v.

[6] DC Durham Cart. 11, fo. 148v; *Calendar of the Greenwell Deeds*, no. 2.

[7] *EYC*, 11, no. 945; Surtees, 111, 407. No general conclusion can be drawn from this instance; Conyers was a man of great importance and a large part of his fee lay in Yorkshire (see below, p. 226).

sors swore that *ubicunque latronem, vel hujusmodi malefactores in terra episcopi Dunelmensis comprehenderent, caperent et ad justitiam perducerent*—possibly a reference to an enforcement of the Assize of Clarendon.[1] Durham Castle was returned in time to be seized again in 1182, when the king was moved to wrath by Puiset's immoderate refusal to surrender 300 marks, a legacy from Roger of York, who had died the previous year. Norham Castle was once more in the hands of a royal constable in 1185, and from then to the end of Henry's reign.[2] As Stubbs originally noticed, control of the northern strongholds was a distinct object of Angevin policy after 1176.

It is fairly clear that, had Henry so wished, he could have found adequate opportunity to break the franchise. Though it might well have been to his interest, it was not his wish, and so in 1177 he is found providing for the return of those castles Puiset's politics had lost, ordering that in the event of the bishop's death they should go to the church of St Cuthbert, *ne jus ecclesie Dunelmensis minueretur*.[3] Yet it is also clear that jurisdictional immunity, perhaps overrated in the work of legal historians, was no great hindrance to the will of a strong king. The niceties of legal right, the *jus ecclesie*, could be respected without detracting from the efficacy of royal power. It mattered infinitely less who hanged criminals than who kept castles, and on this there was no argument. Durham fell in 1174 just as St Calais bowed to William II, Flambard to Henry I, or Bek to Edward, and that implication which Professor Cam has noted under the latter, that Liberties 'were not held absolutely, but conditionally', can never have been far away in the England of Henry II. The most serious threats to Durham's independence came not from the unbending pressure of a consistent policy of legal reform, but from the king's reactions to Puiset's political indiscretions.

Authority paid good dividends, for Durham, *deliciis affluens*, was a wealthy see.[4] The combination of spiritual and secular jurisdiction, and the possessions of the church in Northumberland, Yorkshire and Lincolnshire compensated the short-

---

[1] *Gesta*, I, 178.   [2] See above, p. 44.
[3] *Gesta*, I, 178.   [4] Gerald of Wales, IV, 66.

comings of County Durham itself. The *donum* of the bishop in 1159 was 500 marks, an amount equal to that of the opulent Winchester. In 1166 the see had the greatest surplus enfeoffment among the religious—over 60 fees in excess of a *debitum* of 10: a sign of wealth rather than especial martial zeal,[1] as is suggested in the excess totals of Lincoln (44) and York (36), cities where the existence of considerable Jewish and Flemish populations postulated commerce and prosperity.[2]

In 1195–6 the Crown drew a revenue of approximately £5000 from the bishopric. This, however, was not the bishop's annual expectation, for it includes spasmodic levies and irregular windfalls, such as a scutage (£90), fines on sergeants (£677) and free tenants (£488), the revenues from ten vacant baronies (£326), a tallage of manors (£340), and a fine on clerks (£779).[3] Nevertheless, the bishop probably enjoyed an annual income from all sources rarely less than £3000: a figure that dwarfs the contemporary lay revenues quoted by Professor Painter, and compares as favourably with Winchester, Lincoln and Canterbury as with the profits of John's palatinate in 1189, or the later fortunes of Walter Marshal.[4]

Of the 1196 figure the item of smallest concern is the income from criminal pleas—just over £30, or 0·6 % of the total—a

---

[1] Miss Chew, *The English Ecclesiastical Tenants-in-Chief*, 8, argues that Durham's light assessment was due to its palatine status and peculiar responsibilities for border defence. The same reasons are cited to explain the large total enfeoffment (*ibid.* 119). This responsibility, if it ever existed, was more honoured by breach than observance.

[2] Chew, *op. cit.* 119. Cf. H. C. Darby, *Historical Geography of England*, 221; C. Roth, *A History of the Jews in England*, 11–12, 53; E. M. Carus-Wilson in *Ec. Hist. Rev.* XIV (1944), 32; Gleason, *The Bishopric of Bayeux*, 50.

[3] *Chancellor's Roll 8 Richard I*, 253–61. Although the account is not for a complete year, an annual figure may be calculated, since the majority of the totals are not terminal, and such as are may easily be adjusted for the remainder of the year.

[4] In 1208–9 Winchester had a revenue of £2700 from manorial sources (*Pipe Roll of the Bishopric of Winchester, 1207–8*, ed. H. Hall); in 1202 Lincoln, from similar sources and a scutage, produced £1700 (PR *4 John*, 277); Canterbury, from manorial sources, boosted by heavy sales (36% of the total), gave John £5169 over 23 months in 1205–7 (PR *8 John*, 54–5). Professor Painter, examining baronial revenues for the period 1160–1220, has shown the average income of the 54 laymen selected to have been £202 (without feudal increments). The greatest secular figures quoted are £5000 for John in 1189 and £3350 for Walter Marshal in 1245 (*Studies in the History of the English Feudal Barony*, 170–4).

position it was generally destined to hold among the resources of the franchise. Thus when under bishops Marsh and Poore the history of these 'royal pleas' was investigated, it was found that only some ten cases, ranging over the customary fields of moral turpitude from arson to murder, had been heard in the prior's court in nearly a quarter of a century. The situation was apparently no different on the episcopal fee, for one witness, questioned 'of toll and team and infangentheof'—the words colloquially covering the greatest immunity—replied that *episcopi habuerunt omnia predicta...nec recolit se unquam aliquod istorum vidisse accidere.*[1]

Of other profits of court there is little trace. Under Poore local memory could recall but three cases of wreck (later destined to provide the cell of Farne and the citizens of Hartlepool with a fair income), and the fact that a spar of uncertain dimensions once washed ashore had fetched 15s. 4d.[2] A case of treasure trove reveals the misdemeanours of local officials and the benign vigilance of St Cuthbert.[3] The fine for breach of the episcopal command is once given as £10 (the standard royal mulct) and commutation of court service at 1s. a year.[4] There were *wites* from emendable crimes, some of which Puiset renounced in a charter in favour of the burgesses of Norham,[5] and in addition those amercements occasionally mentioned in *acta*, resulting from legal action, or errors and ineptitudes occurring therein. In all probability there were also local equivalents to the oblations which eased the wheels of royal justice. Concords are mentioned from time to time, presumably preceded by a fee 'for licence to agree'.[6] In all £136 (2·7% of the total) was realized *de placitis et perquisitionibus* in 1195-6; the immunist's wealth was never the fruit of an especial zeal for justice and good order.

Of far greater consequence were those revenues, as yet unaffected by papal claims and the dispersal of functions, that came to the bishop from the discharge of his spiritual office—

[1] *FPD*, 218-19, 225.   [2] *FPD*, 226, 231, 236, 238, 270, 279, 288.
[3] See below, p. 217.
[4] BM, Campbell Charter, IV, 9; *Mon. Ang.* 1, 244; *BB*, 31.
[5] DC Durham, Reg. 1, sec. 11, fo. 2ᵛ, printed in *North Durham*, 257, note h.
[6] See below, p. 229, for a final concord made in the presence of Henry Puiset.

just over £844, or nearly 17 % of the total in 1196. There is good evidence that Puiset, trained in the practical competence of Henry of Winchester's administration, was a man prone to shear his flock with a keen blade. Alexander III complained of the venality of northern clerks, and twice admonished the church of Durham for the common failing of demanding tithe of exempt Orders.[1] Newburgh has a story, substantially true, that the episcopal hospital of Sherburn was a charity based on pillage and extortion.[2] The bishop's participation in the third crusade, by reason of which *non modicam a suis pecuniam extorsit*, got no further than the collection of impressive impedimenta.[3]

The same spirit moved abroad more generally. In the vast Durham peculiar in Yorkshire Puiset took the earliest opportunity to seize complete authority, entirely ignoring any claims of the archbishops, until brought up short by the kindred zeal of Roger of Bishopsbridge. Following Roger's death in 1181, however, he appears to have exercised secular and spiritual jurisdiction in both the archbishopric and the peculiar, clearly to his own profit as the complaints of Archbishop Geoffrey Plantagenet bear witness. So too the concentrated vigour of this will was in part responsible for the great disputes between Puiset and his convent. The details are of no concern here, except in so far as they illustrate the bishop's financial exactions, which ranged from filching tithes and an annual rent of £10 from the parson of Howden to sequestrating the priory revenues *c.* 1186–9. The distress caused by such a policy, and the general outlines of its enforcement, can be seen in the convent's repeated claims that the prior and chapter should have full control of the conventual church of Durham, custody and free disposition of their vacant churches, freedom from episcopal and archidiaconal exactions, and that there should be a general restitution of their alienated tithes—demands the bishop met only as he lay on his deathbed *digno dei judicio flagellat(um)*.[4]

Opposed to such buffeted windfalls were a number of

---

[1] See above, pp. 78–9, 124, and below, p. 237.   [2] See above, p. 108.

[3] *Scriptores Tres*, 13. A crusader was allowed to retain the tenth on his own tenants for his use, and such abuses were apparently common (*Gesta*, II, 31; Foreville, *L'Église et La Royauté en Angleterre*, 450).

[4] DC Durham, 4. 1. Pont. no. 1, see below, App. II, no. 9; see above, pp. 130–6.

vaguely defined rights; 'the episcopal customs' (of which the bishop was not always the sole recipient), generally expressed as *synodalia et episcopalia*, or more specifically as 'customs, aids and exactions'.[1] Only in a few cases can these terms be converted to currency. In 1193 the canons of Carlisle were prepared to pay the bishop 40 marks a year for exemption from aids and hospitality (*hospicia*).[2] In Yorkshire the priory assessed the *hospicia* of their church of Kirby Sigston at 7 marks a year, and the Chancellor's Roll of 1196 shows that the archdeacon of Northumberland might receive at least 20 marks per annum from this source.[3]

The common aid on churches, which produced just over £46 in 1195–6, was presumably levied at irregular intervals, and is occasionally mentioned in private charters. Synodals, by now something of a small customary render by such churches as had not secured exemption, were collected by, and increasingly shared with, the archdeacons. Together with *hospicia* they were the subject of sufficient litigation to suggest great value, though generally of lesser financial moment than their history proclaims. At York they produced £60 in one year.[4] No figure is available for Durham, though the bishop showed notable zeal in their exaction. In this he clashed not only with his own convent, but also with St Albans. From an agreement made *c.* 1174 it appears he had recently taken to claiming synodals from three St Albans chapelries in Northumberland, a practice which under insistent papal pressure he eventually promised to abandon. This, however, was a special concession, and in 1174, having granted that St Albans might take an increased annual pension of 30 marks from the church of Eglingham, he added *si residuum administranti honeste sufficere non possit ad synodalia solvenda et ad debita episcopalium consuetudinum onera sustinenda, abbas quod defuerit supplere debebit.*[5] There were, after all, practical limits to generosity.

Another lesser source of income lay in the pensions (worth

---

[1] DC Durham, 3. 1. Pont. no. 2 (see below, App. II, no. 8).
[2] Brand, I, 238, note t.
[3] *Chancellor's Roll 8 Richard I*, 257.   [4] PR *29 Henry II*, 59.
[5] PU, III, nos. 167 and 173; *NCH*, VIII, 64–6; see above, pp. 123–4.

just over £18 in 1195–6) and customary rents, such as church-set, which the bishop drew from the fluctuating body of churches claimed for his fee.[1] Such revenues, together with tithes and voluntary offerings, were most fully realized in the custody of vacant livings, a prerogative as yet unchecked by the threat of royal or papal provision, and consequently enforced with a tenacity reminiscent of that castigated in Rufus and the two Henries. Its value may be measured from the ferocity of the disputes in Durham and the assessments of some of the greater churches as recorded in 1196; Osmotherley £40, Norton £53, Easington £66 and Washington £33. Tithe itself must have been especially valuable at a time of rising prices and when so much new land was coming into cultivation. Renders were usually in kind, but there is already a suggestion that the sale of tithes, pillar of many a later monastic account, was not unknown. Thus in 1196 Richard Chamberlain owed £12 for the tithes of Islandshire.[2]

The details of custody in vacancies are uncertain, but we hear that after the death of William Hansard, who had held Heighington, the bishop 'had the church and enjoyed its obventions in peace, retaining its fruits in hand and leasing the altarage for 14 marks'.[3] Events were not always of this order, and the death of an incumbent was often the signal for the opening of regular military operations to gain possession of some particularly wealthy living, whose proceeds might at least take the common path of arrentation, or perhaps become the reward of a faithful clerk. In addition to the churches disputed with the priory, such as Northallerton (for which Prior Thomas was driven to seek the bleak consolation of the Farnes, *beato sicut legitur ibi fine quievit*),[4] Norham, Howden, Elvet, Aycliffe and Middleham, Puiset also set his hand to the churches of St Oswald and St Aidan in Bamburgh, belonging to the Augustinians of Nostell. These the canons hoped to appropriate after the death of the royal clerk, Hugh Murdac. The bishop,

---

[1] 'Churchset' was a yearly rent on corn.
[2] *Chancellor's Roll 8 Richard I*, 255, and cf. FPD, 228 for other examples of slightly later date.
[3] FPD, 246.   [4] *Scriptores Tres*, 8; see above, p. 133.

however, appears to have exercised unsolicited custody, and received a sharp admonitory writ from Henry II. Nevertheless, it was not until several years later that Puiset took any action, and in a grandiloquent instrument allowed the appropriation, whilst the canons, *caritatis intuitu*, agreed to admit him to the fraternity of the house.[1]

There were other lesser strokes in the same sure hand. The revenues of parochial churches might be diverted by the dedication of new cemeteries—as happened at Horton and Seaton[2]—or by the erection of chapelries within the bounds claimed by a mother church, as occurred in the monastic parish of Elvet, or was attempted in some unspecified possessions of the priory of Tynemouth.[3] Such developments were probably justified by new settlements in more distant areas, and a presumed increase in population; *propter raritatem ecclesiarum et densitatem habitantium*, as Alexander III put it.[4] But throughout Puiset's career opportunity and profit were seldom divorced.

The lord temporal was as the lord spiritual. Thus Puiset's feudal policy was of the order that supplied a ground bass to the crescendo of complaint ascending from Henry I's charter of liberties to Magna Carta. In detail he was sharp for his rights. In grants in alms he watched that the service of the lands was not impaired,[5] and on one occasion arranged for its transfer elsewhere within the donor's fee.[6] Radulf, son of Paulinus of York, paid the bishop sixty-four marks for the expenses of a case in the feudal court, and was then obliged to surrender his heritage to meet the cost of the decision which had nominally restored it.[7]

In all feudal incomes were amongst the most important sources of the episcopal wealth. In 1195–6 they provided

---

[1] *EYC*, III, nos. 1456 and 1457; BM, Cotton MS., Vesp. E xix, fo. 118ᵛ; *NCH*, I, 75 n.

[2] Above, p. 116 and cf. *PU*, III, no. 330.

[3] DC Durham, 3. 1. Pont. no. 3 (see below, App. II, no. 5); *PU*, III, no. 179 (1171).

[4] *PU*, III, no. 330.

[5] Madox, *Formulare Anglicanum*, 50, no. xcii.

[6] DC Durham, 1. 1. Finch. no. 14. Such arrangements were not uncommon (cf. Colvin, *The White Canons*, 60).

[7] See above, p. 10, n. 3.

£1583, or 31 % of the total, though the amounts must have fluctuated widely from year to year by reason of the irregularity of feudal exactions. Scutage, for example, could only be collected when the king summoned the feudal levy. Nevertheless, the bishop, as lord of a large and under-assessed barony, stood to realize just over £375 on scutages raised between 1156 and 1195. This represents the income from a surplus enfeoffment of what the Exchequer described as 'sixty knights and two-thirds of a knight and one-quarter of a knight'. The amounts varied from £60. 18s. 4d., when the royal levy was at £1 on the fee (as in 1156) to £40. 12s. 2d., when it was at a mark (as in 1168).[1] To these totals there must also have been added the proceeds of *exercitum*, or army aid, which is occasionally mentioned, and appears to have been taken from non-military tenants at a time of scutage.[2] There were, moreover, a number of *ad hoc* demands which fit somewhat uneasily within the conventional feudal framework. Unfortunately they survive only in inconclusive scraps of evidence. So, for example, we find that Adam of Stockton, a sergeant of some standing, had 'given' the bishop 15 marks to aid in the payment made for Sadberge. As is shown elsewhere Sadberge was not paid for, but whether Adam's proffer was a genuine gift, a forced loan or some part of a general aid cannot be decided.[3]

Another variable income came from wardship and marriage rights in mesne fees. This was dependent on the value of the fees and the incidence of death and minors among the honorial aristocracy. In 1195–6 the Crown drew over £326 from ten vacant baronies in the Liberty. Some of these, fitzMeldred, Hardwick, Sigston had but recently escheated, but the barony of Gilbert Hansard, which was farmed at £160 a year, in addition to profits from the sale of its produce (£16), was in the bishop's hands as early as 1185.[4] It is impossible to trace other cases in Durham, though obviously they must have occurred over half a century, but in Boldon Book there is evidence of

---

[1] PR 2 Henry II, 28; PR 14 Henry II, 89; cf. Painter, *Studies in the History of the English Feudal Barony*, 127.

[2] Cf. Pollock and Maitland, *History of English Law*, I, 267.

[3] DC Durham, Reg. I, sec. II, fo. 6.

[4] *Chancellor's Roll 8 Richard I*, 260–1; *Rotuli de Dominabus*, 5.

the exercise of the less profitable wardship of drengs. Thus at West Auckland four bovates were in the bishop's hands *donec filius Elstani sit adultus*.[1]

The scene is clearer in Northumberland, which Puiset held from 1189 to 1194. There he enjoyed £8 a year from the vacant lands of Peter Carew, £24 from those of Adam of Tynedale, £18 from those of Caugi, £58 from Umfraville, and £84 from Bertram.[2] These were not the sum profits. The widow must fine for her free marriage and the custody of the heir, which cost Helvisa of Tynedale 80 marks.[3] Equally profitable was that policy of 'waste' that forms the subject of so many complaints against the Crown, but in various forms was as familiar to the medieval as to the Elizabethan church. Thus Puiset took stock from the vacant Tynedale, Bolbec and Caugi lands,[4] and also seems to have been involved in a certain amount of forest depredation, which later cost the shire 60 marks.[5]

When the heir came of age there were further exactions. Reliefs find passing mention in charter evidence,[6] and there are suggestions that successors found it prudent to obtain from their lord a new charter restoring or confirming the ancestral fee.[7] So Richard de Umfraville fined with the bishop for his lands. The sum is unknown, except that in 1194 Richard owed the king £14 of a proffer of £100 that it might stand—no doubt in anticipation of the common request to pay twice for the same privilege.[8] Robert fitzMeldred, however, a tenant in both Northumberland and Durham, promised the bishop an entry fine of 300 marks, modest by current standards, for the Crown thought 600 more suitable—a sum which would surely have inspired comment from the author of Glanville or the *Leis Willelme*.[9] In all it is not difficult to see why Puiset was willing

---

[1] BB, 26; cf. Painter, *op. cit.* 148–51.

[2] PR 6 *Richard I*, 134; PR 28 *Henry II*, 49; PR 7 *Richard I*, 26; *Chancellor's Roll 8 Richard I*, 262.

[3] PR 6 *Richard I*, 134.   [4] PR 2 *Richard I*, 21.

[5] PR 2 *John*, 6.

[6] 'A Second Calendar of the Greenwell Deeds', 94, no. 30.

[7] Surtees, I, 181; *Priory of Finchale*, 2; *EYC*, II, no. 985; Stenton, *The First Century of English Feudalism*, 161.   [8] PR 6 *Richard I*, 134.

[9] PR 7 *Richard I*, 26; PR 8 *Richard I*, 94; Stenton, *op. cit.* 162–3; Painter, *op. cit.* 147. Such behaviour, as yet unchecked in the Liberty by any charter of rights,

to offer 2000 marks for Northumberland, or why the bidding was so brisk when Richard auctioned the assets of his kingdom.

The real foundation of the episcopal fortunes lay, however, in manorial resources, the basis of all wealth in the period. It was the possession of many fair acres in Northumberland, Durham and Yorkshire with their attendant perquisites, rather than magnificent, and in many ways inoperative, prerogatives that conferred the opulence and unique prestige of the medieval bishops and church of Durham.[1] Of a revenue of £5000 in 1196, nearly half (£2384) came from manorial profits, and since this income, with its weight of assized rents, was probably more stable than any of the sources already mentioned, its proportion of the total would be higher in a less exceptional year. The greatest part (£1388) was from rents and farms. Unfortunately the royal officers, properly more concerned with the profits of the moment than the doubts of posterity, merely record the total and not its sources. This makes it difficult to equate their return with the figures of Boldon Book, the partial and corrupt record of a survey made in 1183. In this £820 comes from rents and farms, of which some £500 represents tenurial rents and the farms of demesne manors (as opposed to those of boroughs, mills, fisheries, etc.).[2] This suggests a large discrepancy from 1196, though it must be remembered that Boldon Book excludes the rich episcopal lands in Yorkshire, and is an uncertain guide to the equally valuable Northumberland. Yet even assuming the doubtful proposition that the ratio of 1183 was maintained, the annual figure must have been at least £857. In 1196, in fact, some £957 came from tenurial rents and manorial farms *de tribus partibus anni*, which would give £1257 per annum, as was the case in 1211.[3] This emphasizes the value of lands outside Durham, but at the same time postulates an enormous increase which it is impossible to assess accurately,

or such a formal association as later resisted Antony Bek, was not, it may be suspected, without opposition. This is perhaps implied in the royal protection extended to Roger Conyers (see above, p. 192).

[1] Cf. the conclusions of Barraclough, *The Earldom of Chester*, 20.

[2] *Chancellor's Roll 8 Richard I*, 253-4, 261. For the Boldon Book figures I have used the text that appears in BM, Stowe MS. 930 (translated *VCH Durham*, 1, 327-41), not the later versions that Greenwell was obliged to employ.

[3] *Chancellor's Roll 8 Richard I*, 253 and 261; PR *13 John*, in *BB*, xiii.

though it was probably but a step in a more general process covering the whole episcopate. Puiset, like many of his illustrious contemporaries, reputedly doubled his income. He had some experience of the ways of his uncle of Winchester, who, as Gerald of Wales noted with admiration, 'was a model to all in the administration of his estates'.[1]

Of his methods we have but hints. The simplest expedient was a straight increase in the value and number of rents. So Sherburn, worth £3 a year when Puiset became bishop, was valued at £6 in 1183.[2] New rent-paying tenures came into existence by tenurial change, assart from waste and arrentation of the villeinage and demesne (the latter usually in the vicinity of episcopal residences where servants were rewarded, or in distant marginal lands, not easily accessible for exploitation). In all Puiset made about ninety-five major grants involving land; only fifteen were enfeoffments, of which only three involved the service of an integral fee, the remainder being fractional, and in practice probably rent-paying freeholds.[3] The other eighty were grants at rent, varying in size from 120 to 2 acres, and in value from £20 to 2s. In some instances it was villeins who became the new rent-paying tenants, such as that Turkill of West Sleekburn 'who was once the bishop's man'.[4] Recently Professor Postan has suggested that rent-payers, such as those at Biddick, had risen from villeinage, and somewhat earlier Lapsley had come near to this view in his comments on the communities of *firmarii*, who had probably been allowed special facilities for the composition of services to encourage them to settle in new areas.[5] In a number of other cases ancient tenures were converted to modern fee farms—though it would be equally dangerous to speak of general commutation or deliberate feudalization.[6] At Heworth, in 1183, a certain Gilbert

[1] Gerald of Wales, VII, 49. Puiset's financial skill is noticed in *Scriptores Tres*, 9, and Newburgh, II, 437. For contemporary efforts 'to augment the revenue', see S. K. Mitchell, *Taxation in Medieval England*, 267–8, 285.

[2] Surtees, I, 283–4; *BB*, 10.

[3] For similar movements elsewhere cf. E. Miller, *The Abbey and Bishopric of Ely*, 174; H. P. R. Finberg, *The Abbey of Tavistock*, 69.

[4] *BB*, 38.

[5] Postan, 'The Chronology of Labour Services', 178; *VCH Durham*, I, 281–2.

[6] As do Postan and Lapsley.

held at a rent of three marks *quietus de antiquis operationibus et servitiis, que inde...de theinagio facere solebat.*[1] Again, at Great Haughton two tenants previously holding in drengage had converted to a form of socage, and there are a further thirteen cases of this nature mentioned in Boldon Book.[2] It is important to notice, however, that this form of commutation, apparently desired by the tenant, did not universally commend itself to the lord, who could still value service as well as rent where some semi-military or administrative duty was concerned. Thus whilst Henry of Ord (senior) is said to have freed his tenure *a thenagio et fecit quod ipse et heredes tenerent illud ad feudo firmam*, Roger of Kibblesworth, holding of the priory, lost his lands at Wolviston, since *per violenciam Domini contra jus et predictorum monachorum voluntatem drengagium meum denariis adquietando tenuerim.* So also in at least two cases new episcopal tenants were required to discharge (either in person or by proxy) the old drengage duties of their new holdings.[3]

The history of the demesne is obscure, though by 1183 it showed tendencies common to the age.[4] Of 130 vills recorded in that year, only twenty-seven were either wholly or partially in the bishop's hands. On the remainder twenty-six were held in knight service or alms, and sixteen in drengage. The rest were at rent or farm, the latter rendered either in cash or the indispensable kind. This vast arrentation had, it seems, a distant ancestry, and probably sprang from the financial needs of peripatetic bishops employed in public affairs, and the inability of early administrative resource to handle such large areas directly. Puiset's policy is uncertain. It would appear that till at least 1183 he tended to concentrate the remaining demesne—perhaps for more profitable direct exploitation—in a number of definable areas.[5] These were grouped roughly in the vicinity of the chartered boroughs of Gateshead, Wearmouth, Durham

---

[1] *BB*, 16. [2] *VCH Durham*, I, 313–15.

[3] *FPD*, 224 and 141–2 n.; *BB*, App. v, printed from DC Durham, Reg. I, sec. II, fo. 6ᵛ; *EYC*, II, no. 980; *BB*, 18.

[4] Cf. Postan, *art. cit.*, and *idem*, 'The Glastonbury Estates in the Twelfth Century', 358–67.

[5] From the number of boundary disputes it would appear that similar activities were in progress on the fees of the priory and other great tenants (see above, pp. 165–6; cf. Painter, *Studies in the History of the English Feudal Barony*, 154–5).

and Norham, and the townships of Bishop Auckland and Howden.[1] All these were favourite and necessary residences, and places where some demesne had presumably always been retained. They were, moreover, the very areas where, though not without some difficulty, the bishop held the churches, in order that the tithes of the parishioners might be added to the produce of the fields.

Norham, isolated in Northumberland, was the seat of a castle and borough (both of which received Puiset's attention), and the centre of the Liberty in the north of the county. A part of the demesne was at farm, but the remainder and the borough were in hand. Horncliffe was purchased, and the priory complained of their loss of a turbary and land near Shoreswood.[2]

Further south, across the Tyne, lay another bloc roughly centred on Gateshead (where the bishop had a dwelling and his *pulchrior cascia* of Heworth), and the nascent port of Bishop Wearmouth. At Winlaton and Barlow, marsh, meadow and wood were in hand, and at Cleadon and Whitburn, the demesne pasture. At Gateshead, where a portion of the demesne was retained, there are references to assarts, and the priory was injured in its claims at Heworth.[3] The nuns of St Bartholomew's (Newcastle) were bought out from Great Usworth, and the services of that vill, once rendered at Washington, transferred to Gateshead, whilst Washington itself was exchanged for land at Hartburn.[4]

Durham and Auckland had even greater prominence. Various menial services relate to the provision of necessities and suitable amounts of food and wine. North Auckland, Escomb and Newton carted wood to either Durham or Auckland, as occasion demanded. The villeins of Stanhope brought game slaughtered in the great chase of Weardale, the essential wine being carried

[1] For Howden, see DC Durham, 4. 1. Pont. nos. 1 and 12 (see below, App. 11, nos. 9, 6); *FPD*, 254–5; DC Durham, Reg. 1, sec. 11, fo. 1.

[2] *BB*, 41–2; Dodsworth MS. xlix, fo. 7ᵛ, calendared in *Northumberland and Durham Deeds*, 100, no. 32; DC Durham, 4. 1. Pont. no. 5, printed in FPD, lxxxvi.

[3] *BB*, 35, 5 and 2; DC Durham, 3. 1. Pont. no. 19, printed in *FPD*, 108; 4. 1. Pont. no. 5, printed in *FPD*, lxxxvi.

[4] PRO, Exchequer, Augmentation Office, Ancient Deed E 326 B/11537, printed in Brand, 1, 206, note v; *BB*, 36, 3.

by the drengs of Urpeth and Hutton, the villeins of Great
Usworth and the men of Sheraton. Surrounding Durham were
the great demesne areas of Quarrington, Cornforth, Newbottle
and Witton, situated in the middle reaches of the Wear valley,
clear alike of the marginal lands of the western moors and the
withering chill of the North Sea. Of Witton and Fulforth there
is little to be discovered. Newbottle and Houghton-le-Spring
(served by Boldon, Biddick, Herrington, Warden and Murton)
attracted the attention of the priory by their encroachment on
the conventual lands at Rainton.[1] Reorganization is indicated
by the entry in Boldon Book that 'William holds Whitwell in
exchange for land Mervinus once held in Quarrington'. The
services here were drawn in from one of the local shires constituted by the Sherburns (where the bishop had assarted land
to the prejudice of the convent's holdings at Pittington),[2]
Shadforth, Cassop and Tursdale (whence Arnold the Fisher had
migrated at the price of a holding in Consett, and where, it
seems, there was an episcopal hall).[3] The next great block lay
in Middleham, Sedgefield and Cornforth, where the pattern is
repeated. There is talk of escheat and purchase at Garmondsway. Alan of Chilton was granted land at Healeyfield in
exchange for Cornforth. Another had Penshaw in return for
the surrender of Middleham, forest rights being added *quia
amicabiliter voluntati nostre concessit de predicto escambio*, whilst
Radulf the clerk received Newton-by-Durham and Roger of
Thrislington held near Grindon in exchange for holdings in
Middleham and Mainsforth.[4] The exact extent of these lands is
uncertain. It seems, however, that in one direction they were
expanding eastward to the sea, possibly to join Easington and
Thorpe, where the bishop had the demesne pasture in hand,
whilst in the south they reached to Low Hardwick (brought
under episcopal control from the convent), and so met the
demesne centred on Auckland.[5] This township, at the meeting

[1] *BB*, 24, 25, 29, 37, 36, 10 and 33; DC Durham, 4. 1. Pont. no. 5, printed in
FPD, lxxxvi.

[2] *BB*, 10; *FPD*, lxxxvi.   [3] *BB*, 9, 31 and 11.

[4] *BB*, 2, 12, 37, 7; *BF*, 1, 28; DC Durham, Reg. 1, sec. 11, fo. 6ᵛ, printed in *BB*,
App. v.

[5] *BB*, 8, 32 and App. IX.

of the Wear and Gaunless, was the natural entry to upper
Weardale, and there are mentions of elaborate provision for the
hunting season, with the attendant paraphernalia of conviviality
and piety—a hall, buttery, larder, chamber and chapel. It was
here too that those indispensable officers the cook and the
waggon-master had their sergeanties. As has already been
noted, a number of the services rendered at Durham might be
directed to Auckland, whilst in addition the men of Binchester
brought wine, and the farmers of Durham 'made four loads'.
Auckland was on the fringe of a belt of rich demesne lying to
the south-east of the body of the modern coalfield. At Coundon,
Middridge and Thickley (where the demesne was in hand) there
was a vigorous movement into the fertile lands of the Skerne
valley. Thus 'Old Thickley was made of the land of Redworth',
and had been exchanged for Redworth. Gilbert the Chamberlain was given lands at Bushblades for Bradbury, others surrendered claims on Ricknall and Ketton, and assarts were made
at Hunwick and Aycliffe, where the priory complained of the
resulting encroachment.[1] Further south there were isolated
patches of demesne at Norton, Stockton, Hartburn and Little
Haughton, where the bishop had either the pasture or meadow
in hand.[2]

The episcopal largesse was, moreover, marked by discretion.
There was no abandoned 'taking of homages and giving of
lands' in that tradition fatally essential to the baronial style.[3]
Of the ninety-five grants which Puiset made, forty were from
demesne (including sixteen in Yorkshire) and fifty-five from
escheat, waste and purchase. In sixteen cases the land came
honestly from assart, but beyond this lay a realm of dubious
transactions. The bishop's final repentance mentions certain
conventual properties which *in usus nostros converteramus*, so
explaining something of the monastic preoccupation with
'rightful boundaries'.[4] The policies which distressed the priory
in Durham raised equally bitter disputes in Yorkshire. Puiset

---

[1] *BB*, 26, 24, 37, 23, 33 and 16; *FPD*, lxxxvi.   [2] *BB*, 13, 14, n. 12.
[3] Cf. the grants made by the contemporary earls of Chester (Barraclough,
The Earldom of Chester, 13–14).
[4] DC Durham, 3. 1. Pont. no. 4, printed in *FPD*, 198.

appears to have been guilty of sharp dealing with the hospital of St Leonard's concerning land at Skelton (Howden) and in Fishergate (York).[1] The rights of St Cuthbert were infringed at the favourite episcopal manor of Howden, where Kepyer was endowed from monastic property.[2] Furthermore, the bishop had ready money he was willing to spend, and could thus exploit the feckless wants of a landed aristocracy, and incidentally create a useful fund of charity and patronage. After his death it was found that various tenants owed him some £20 for loans, and earlier Thorald of London admitted a debt of 10 marks.[3] He had the lands of Hugh Burel in mortgage by 1180. These were redeemed for 30 marks by Henry Puiset, who passed them to his pious foundation of Baxterwood, whence, after some trouble and litigation, they were secured by Durham's cell of Finchale.[4] A similar pattern occurs at Yokefleet in Yorkshire. There the tenant, Adam of Wharram, pledged his vill to Henry Puiset for 100 marks. It was then bought by the bishop (presumably at a nominal price), who passed it back to Henry to hold at an annual rent of 4 marks.[5] A more important episode reveals an adroit handling of the distress of the great northern family of Balliol. About 1190 Bernard Balliol pledged Newton and Newhouses to the bishop for 150 marks advanced to quit the royal claims arising from a debt to the ubiquitous Aaron the Jew, and to redeem the Balliol charters. Some years later Balliol died, and was succeeded by his heir, Eustace, who found the caput of the barony, Barnard Castle, also in the episcopal hands as security for a debt of unspecified size. The bishop, 'of his grace', returned the castle to Eustace, but retained Newton and Newhouses for a total debt now swollen to 400 marks (perhaps concealing some form of interest). On his death-bed Puiset made a gesture *in recompensationem gravaminum que ecclesie beati Cuthberti intulimus*; for this he

---

[1] *EYC*, II, nos. 981 and 983.
[2] See above, pp. 109, 147–8.
[3] *Chancellor's Roll 8 Richard I*, 255; DC Durham, 2. 4. Spec. no. 2, printed in Surtees, II, 393. For contemporary parallels, cf. Colvin, *The White Canons*, 122; Bongert, *Recherches sur les Cours Laïques*, 101.
[4] DC Durham, 3. 6. Spec. no. 28; *Priory of Finchale*, 5, 22–3.
[5] *EYC*, II, nos. 984, 985, 987; *Priory of Finchale*, 44–5.

found a proper and convenient offering in Balliol's vill of Newton.[1]

The overall picture is obscure. To some extent the bishop protected his demesne by confining his generosity (sergeanties excepted) to areas where his claims to ownership were at best ambiguous, or where he appears to have had little interest or prospect of profit. Thus to the west of Gateshead he gave Chopwell to the Cistercians of Newminster in exchange for Wolsingham, granted Crawcrook away and put Whickham to farm.[2] In the Tees valley grants were made from demesne at Winston and Newsham.[3] In general these were regions where, as in the episcopal lands in Northumberland or south Durham, the demesne had already largely disintegrated; the incidence of *firmarii* is, for example, particularly high in such places as Norton, Carlton and Blackwell. At the same time, in a movement recalling similar enterprise in the eighth and ninth centuries,[4] a peninsula of agriculture was being pushed westward into the sea of waste in the upper reaches of the Derwent valley, running from what is now the melancholy Consett to the perpetual bleakness of Redburn common. This area of new cultivation, where the bishop made grants at Crookhall, Rowley, Cornsay, Hedley, Ebchester, Satley, Healeyfield, Edmundbyers, Hunstanworth, Muggleswick, Rookhope and Whitelees,[5] was committed almost entirely to the efforts of pious foundations, hermits, lesser aristocrats and prosperous freemen —a pattern generally familiar in the Europe of the time.[6]

But if in some places the demesne was strengthened by the acquisition of old lands, or (more rarely) by the assarting of new, the policy was not persistent. In the closing years of the episcopate there reappears a movement of arrentation (perhaps related to the halcyon days of Puiset's ambition, when Durham

[1] DC Durham, Parv. Cart. Haliwerfolc Charter, no. 77; 3. 1. Pont. no. 8 (see below, App. II, no. 7).

[2] *Newminster Cartulary*, 45; BM, Lansdowne MS. 902, fo. 78ᵛ; BB, 34.

[3] BM, Lansdowne MS. 902, fo. 67ᵛ. [4] Symeon, I, 53.

[5] BB, 31-2; 'A Calendar of the Ravensworth Deeds', 45-6; DC Durham, Cart. Elemos. 83.

[6] An earlier instance of such expansion occurs in an agreement on tithe between Guisborough and Tynemouth, made *c*. 1142-53 (*EYC*, II, 8); for other examples, cf. Painter, *Studies in the History of the English Feudal Barony*, 162-3.

was no longer his main concern) which had already run a good course in somewhat similar circumstances before 1153. It seems to have been especially vigorous with demesne appurtenances such as boroughs, mills and fisheries, but at the same time swept away some of Puiset's earlier work, or islands of demesne hitherto untouched. Among those who profited from the change were members of a growing class of rent-paying free-men. A number now emerged, prosperous and acquisitive, opportunely buying land and accumulating holdings in areas where such tenures had formerly been rare. So, for example, William de Cumb worked at Preston, whilst William of Yarm received 120 acres at Norton and another five in Sedgefield. Some of these fortunates were possibly one-time villeins, others lesser episcopal officers, such as that Adam, son of Walter of Stockton, who secured land in Preston-on-Tees.[1] Where there was not this steady erosion of the demesne whole blocks were leased intact.[2] Whickham, which had once provided some £9 in rent, together with renders in kind and works, had but recently been put to farm at £26 in 1183.[3] At Tursdale, where the bishop had earlier consolidated his holding, the entry in Boldon Book reads *molendinum est in manu Episcopi, nondum ad firmam positum, similiter et toftum aulae et virgultum et nemus et prata.*[4] Mainsforth, where in 1183 there had been *xvii bovate de escaeta et emptione*, had gone to Dru of Middleham by 1195. At the beginning of his episcopate Puiset had shown some anxiety to secure Wolsing-ham, for which he had exchanged other property, but by 1183 his demesne there was at farm, whilst Winlaton and Witton, both in hand in 1183, had been alienated by 1195—all part of that general dissolution of the demesne to which Professor Postan has drawn attention.[5]

No single reason explains such a policy. Puiset, whose

[1] BF, 1, 29; cf. similar movements in subsequent periods in Smith, *Canterbury Cathedral Priory*, 193.

[2] It is impossible to rate the value of these alienations, though it would seem that the most substantial increase in the episcopal rental came less from this source than from the flood of minor tenurial changes and the large-scale arrenta-tion of waste.

[3] BB, 33–4.   [4] BB, 11.

[5] BB, 12; BF, 1, 29; BB, 33; BM, Lansdowne MS. 902, fo. 67ᵛ; DC Durham, Cart. Elemos. 223; Postan, 'Chronology of Labour Services', 184–5.

ambitions and personal *magnificentia* constantly demanded large sums of ready money was, as Newburgh put it, *pecuniarum sitientissimus*. The deepest well—as was almost universally recognized amongst the feudal aristocracy—was the demesne, the general remedy commutation or a lease which reflected in some profitable way the contractual nature of feudal society. Whether or not the bishop justified his reputation for financial skill by merely employing on a large scale the commonest contemporary nostrum is a matter for doubt. The element of economic realism is equally questionable. Possibly the rentability of the demesne was enhanced by a scarcity of land in relation to labour. On the other hand there is little to be said in favour of a voluntary pegging of rents in a decade of enormous price rises which clearly affected the episcopal policy.

Other manorial profits may be briefly mentioned. In 1196 demesne produce was worth nearly £400, or some 17% of the manorial total. In a normal year much of this would have been realized in kind as the bishop ate his way from manor to manor. Even so some must have been cashed,[1] for Boldon Book shows a number of gargantuan renders which would surely have defeated the energies of even Lord John Scott and his bottle companions—20,000 eggs, 2500 hens, 35 cows, 156 chalders of wheat, 456 of oats, 115 of malt, and 68 of barley, to which we must presumably add similar offerings from Yorkshire.[2] But if the Liberty was rich it was by extent rather than nature, and the figure of 1196 is low compared with similar returns from more favoured southern sees.[3] The best land was, and still is, limited to the east, and more especially the south-east, of the county. Arable farming was concentrated chiefly in south Durham.[4] Something of this relative fertility is reflected in the size of holdings, the acreage of bovates and the extent of knights' fees.

---

[1] In 1211 hens and eggs 'customarily sold' fetched £9. 18s.; corn of the same order was worth £37 (PR *13 John*, in *BB*, xiii).

[2] The renders in 1211 included 2065½ quarters of wheat and 5236 of oats in addition to what was sold (PR 13 *John*, in *BB*, xix).

[3] Sale of produce raised £715 at Winchester, £450 at Lincoln and £1500 at Canterbury, see above, p. 194, n. 4.

[4] It is interesting to notice that all the vills quit of cornage lay in the vicinity of Darlington (*VCH Durham*, 1, 271).

14-2

Thus a fee was 8 carucates at Hetton (near Sunderland) and 10 at Silksworth, as against 22 at Holmside, in the moors above Lanchester.[1] At Newbottle, Sherburn, Houghton-le-Spring and Darlington villein holdings were 12 acres, at Warden 18 and at Murton 21, as compared with 30 at Boldon and Cleadon. At Eppleton the bovate was 15 acres, 20 at Redmarshall and 24 at Castle Eden, whereas at Esh it was 45. The lands of the vale of York were therefore a necessary compensation for the bleak waste of west Durham, where mountain pasture alternated with wolf-ridden forest, so that Reginald of Durham, relating the hardships of Godric's early life, essayed the obvious alliterative etymology for Wolsingham.[2] To a southern monk, exiled at Tynemouth, the northern counties made but a poor, dark unhappy world 'where spring and summer never come', a land of dim eyes and sore throats; the end of the earth. Nor indeed did Leland find Durham any more prepossessing, though the value of the coastal plain was noticed by Camden.[3]

In all, these rigours were more suited to pastoral than arable husbandry, and, as Reginald of Durham noticed, many a local knight prospered from his flocks. In this light it is worthy of comment that in several vills (e.g. Cleadon, Whitburn, Easington, Thorpe, Little Haughton) the bishop retained the sheep and pasture in hand when the remainder of the demesne was alienated. No general estimate of the size of flocks can be given, though they were clearly large. Rievaulx surrendered pasture rights for 1000 sheep at Sheraton. There were 200 at Finchale, which like much else had found its way into the bishop's hand, and in Boldon Book 200 are mentioned at Wearmouth and Tunstall, 200 at Shotton, 100 at Little Haughton and 300 at Ryhope and Burdon.[4] From these came wool and hides,[5] and even something of a cloth industry. The sale of wool raised

[1] DC Durham, Cart. Elemos. 129–30; 3. 7. Spec. no. 18; Cart. Elemos. 137.

[2] Cf. Symeon's earlier description of Durham, *locum densissima undique silva totum occupaverat* (Symeon, I, 80).

[3] *NCH*, VIII, 72; Darby, *Historical Geography of England*, 204–6; A. L. Rowse, *The England of Elizabeth*, 70–1.

[4] DC Durham, Reg. II, fo. 323ᵛ; Surtees, I, 283–4; *Reg. Pal. Dun.* II, 1296–7; *BB*, 6, 9, 18.

[5] The burgesses of Durham owed Puiset 40s. *pro pellibus* in 1196 (*Chancellor's Roll 8 Richard I*, 255).

£216 in 1196, of which £170 came from Stockton alone. A fuller is mentioned at Durham, and dyers at Gateshead,[1] Darlington and Newcastle. For the rest there are abundant references to other livestock; horses (which were used for harrowing),[2] cows, oxen and pigs, and the sale of stock brought £100 in 1196, whilst another £10 came from cheeses and other lesser products. The staple crops seem to have been oats and barley,[3] though sufficient wheat was grown to sell for £60.[4] Barley was generally brewed—thus 115 chalders of malt were rendered in 1183 as against 68 of barley—but some ruder potion extracted from oats enjoyed much popularity,[5] except among the more fastidious, such as Bishop Insula, who, although a local man, was overcome when taking a civil draught in the wilds of Norham, *et statim a mensa surgens, evomuit*.[6] For the queasy there was the doubtful alternative of cider and perry, probably produced in some quantity, for apple and pear orchards were by no means rare. When, in 1174, the Scottish army which had invaded the northern counties was in retreat, its commanders, unable to think of any other mischief, set their men to stripping the bark off apple trees.[7] There is little trace of any specialization. Wheat was grown as far north as Horncliffe, as far south as Hartburn, on the coast at Herrington and in the western dales at Wolsingham. Its yield and quality are unknown, though it is perhaps some reflection on the climate of Weardale that the render per plough was 3 chalders at Wolsingham, only a third of the rate at Ryhope and Boldon. Barley appears as far north as Boldon and as far west as Crawcrook, but seems to have given its best yields in the south-west. Oats were universal, though it is interesting to note that in the

---

[1] *Early Newcastle Deeds*, 112.   [2] *BB*, 8.

[3] It will be recalled that St Cuthbert set his plot on Farne with oats and barley after wheat had failed (*Two Lives of St Cuthbert*, 220).

[4] Puiset had also sold £18 worth of wheat to the Northumbrian baron, Robert de Muschamps (*Chancellor's Roll 8 Richard I*, 255). The practice was widespread and extended to export, see below, p. 216. For similar activities on the priory fee, see *EYC*, ii, no. 938.

[5] Boldon Book records the render of some 300 chalders of oat malt.

[6] *Scriptores Tres*, 57.

[7] Fantosme, ll. 1683–5. For orchards, see *BB*, 24 and the introduction to *PR 31 Henry II*. The archbishop of York grew vines as far north as Askham.

vicinity of Bishop Auckland there was a concentration of vills rendering oat malt, suggesting the quality there was perhaps somewhat above the average.

The demesne tallage was an irregular levy. In 1196 it was worth £340, or 14% of the manorial total. The return, which is by no means heavy,[1] is chiefly interesting as emphasizing the bishop's position as a rentier, and revealing the economic value of such Yorkshire lands as it mentions. Thus Northallerton paid £30 against Gateshead's £10 and Stockton's £7—the highest payments by vills in Durham. The frequency and incidence of tallage are uncertain. There may well have been both annual levies on villeins and spasmodic charges on freemen, such as are mentioned in *acta*. So Puiset, in a charter for one of his sergeants, defines his 'common aid' as 2s., whilst he quits another tenant of various exactions except the *commune auxilium*. A similar state of affairs prevailed on the priory fee, where there is mention on one occasion of the *commune auxilium super liberos homines*.[2]

In addition to the vills of the demesne were the boroughs, which, as Professor Painter has shown, might constitute an important part of baronial revenue where the owner was happy enough to have mediatized a town of some commercial importance. The Liberty had no Bristol or Leicester, but by 1196 there were substantial boroughs at Gateshead ('a noble town, tho' set in a bottom'), and Durham, and more modest assemblies at Norham, Wearmouth and Darlington. Norham and Durham, and perhaps Gateshead and Wearmouth, date from the time of Flambard.[3] All, with the exception of Darlington, received charters from Puiset (for which favours he presumably took payment) in a movement fairly common at the time, by which the 'customs of Newcastle' were widely disseminated through Durham and Northumberland. Individual burgesses make fleeting appearances; from Durham there came Teroldus (*c.* 1150), Alueredus, Alan, and his brother, Tok son of Tok

---

[1] Cf. Painter, *Studies in the History of the English Feudal Barony*, 169–70.

[2] *Calendar of the Greenwell Deeds*, no. 6; DC Durham, 3. 1. Pont. no. 17; Cart. Misc. no. 875; cf. Mitchell, *Taxation in Medieval England*, 267–8.

[3] The burgesses of Durham were obliged to swear loyalty to the intruder Cumin in 1141 (Symeon, 1, 146).

(*c.* 1160–70), in addition to that prophetic figure, Peter of Claypath (*c.* 1190), who had part of the lands of Roger of Kibblesworth in mortgage.[1] The economic value of the boroughs is uncertain, but was at least sufficient to encourage the bishop to create one on monastic property at Elvet.[2] In all they produced a variety of revenues. The pleas of Durham City were worth £5 in 1130;[3] in 1196 Durham and Gateshead each paid £10 for tallage, whilst Darlington paid £8.[4] Burgage rents were apparently 1s. 7d. per house at Pipewellgate in Gateshead,[5] and for the first half of the episcopate burgesses were liable to a number of other exactions and fines—*intoll* and *utoll* on the transference of tenements, and servile dues such as merchet and heriot.[6]

There was also a developing trade to be tapped; there are hints of the sale of surplus products, some suggestions of specialization, and clear indications of the existence of a professional merchant class.[7] The contacts of the north-east were wide. Lead from the mines of Carlisle was shipped through Newcastle to Caen, La Rochelle and Rouen.[8] The hermits Bartholomew and Godric had spent some of their earlier unrepentant days in commercial pursuits in Scandinavia, and the former was visited by a Flemish female acquaintance in his retirement.[9] An early writ of Henry II mentions the episcopal interest in Tyne shipping, and the nautical miracles associated with Farne show that offshore passages were common.[10] Gateshead, whose burgesses are to be found trading under the

---

[1] DC Durham, Reg. 1, fo. 74ᵛ; 3. 6. Spec. no. 16.

[2] Above, p. 131; *Scriptores Tres*, 12; there had long been something of a commercial settlement in Elvet. Forty merchant holdings were allegedly there in the time of St Calais (*Liber Vitae*, fo. 49ᵛ).

[3] *PR 31 Henry I*, 132.

[4] *Chancellor's Roll 8 Richard I*, 256.

[5] DC Durham, 2. 3. Spec. no. 47, printed in *FPD*, 106 n., Surtees, ii, 114.

[6] The burgesses of Durham were freed from these disabilities *c.* 1175–9 (Hutchinson, ii, 13; *VCH Durham*, iii, 54–5). Wearmouth was not so favoured until *c.* 1180–3 (*BB*, App. iv).

[7] Cf. *Cambridge Economic History*, ii, 160.

[8] *PR 13 Henry II*, 73; *14 Henry II*, 109; *22 Henry II*, 137; *25 Henry II*, 27.

[9] Symeon, i, 309; ii, 202, for contact with Norway.

[10] DC Durham, Cart. iii, fo. 2ᵛ; *Scriptores Tres*, App. no. xxxv; *CChR*, iii, 393; Symeon, i, 309–10. There is mention of a merchant ship belonging to the convent of Durham in Symeon, ii, 353–4.

bishop's peace, refitted and manned the 'great ship of Durham' in 1195.[1] There was similar activity on the Wear and Tees; Hartlepool and Wearmouth had already established their sea fisheries, whilst there are references to ships and *navicule* loading and discharging at Billingham.[2] The Wearmouth charter, which is the most expansive, envisages the burgesses distraining for debt, contains a reference to the episcopal officers trading there, presupposes the burgesses travelling to other boroughs, notices the arrival and departure of ships, the trade in salt, corn and herring, and arranges for the settling of disputes between merchants.[3]

From all this the bishop had his profit. The cathedral city itself was the site of a market, with the attendant monopoly of toll.[4] Tenants of the priory wishing to trade in Durham were charged 7½d. a year in stallage.[5] Exactions elsewhere were of the same order; a ship loading at Stockton paid 6d. and at Billingham, 8d.[6] It was again the episcopal prerogative to license markets and fairs, and control the opportunities of sale for certain commodities.[7] Thus he ratified the standard of measure employed by his convent, and allowed the burgesses of Wearmouth to export wheat *sine licencia, nisi commune interdictum domini episcopi totam terram de non educendo factum fuerit*.[8] In all, the boroughs provided £103 in 1183; Durham and Gateshead were each at farm for £40, Darlington rendered £5, Wearmouth £1, and Norham some £16 'from fines, toll and stallage'.[9]

Another perquisite of lordship was the fines from the almost ubiquitous forest.[10] These were worth £47, or approximately

---

[1] *BB*, App. III; see above, p. 106.   [2] *BB*, App. IV; *FPD*, 270.

[3] *BB*, App. IV; for earlier references to shipping at Wearmouth, Symeon, II, 190.

[4] *Libellus...Godrici*, 101; Symeon, II, 336; *FPD*, 235.

[5] *FPD*, 236.   [6] *FPD*, 241, 253.

[7] Tait, *The Medieval English Borough*, 207, n. 1, and 209; Ballard, *British Borough Charters*, I, 171.

[8] *EYC*, II, no. 938; *BB*, App. IV.

[9] *BB*, 1–2, 17 n., 6, 41. The farms of Durham and Gateshead were equal to those of Bury St Edmunds, Colchester, Hereford, Orford and Yarmouth (M. D. Lobel, *Bury St Edmunds*, 62; Tait, *op. cit.* 184).

[10] The episcopal forest administration was zealously competent. The priory made considerable efforts to escape from foresty and pannage, both of which Puiset had taken on what they claimed as demesne manors (DC Durham, 4. 1. Pont. no. 5, printed in *FPD*, lxxxvi; see above, pp. 131, 163).

2% of the manorial total in 1196—a relatively small sum,[1] possibly to be explained by the disputed claims at Heworth and Howden. The revenue came from the exactions of the forest courts—like the *amerciamenta* Robert of Howden later remembered collecting, *propter incisionem bosci de Wdehalle*[2]—together with dues such as *forestagium* and pannage, numerically large renders of small amounts. Pannage was due on swine pastured in the forests, and was levied on villeins alone. In one case its rate is given as the annual payment of a pig worth 16*d.* Foresty was taken from all but magnates for the liberty of entering the episcopal forests, and, in some cases, for the right to take small wood therein.[3] The rate at Heworth for the burgesses of Gateshead was 2*d.* for a cart or a horse, and 1*d.* for a man. At Healeyfield it was 6*d.*[4]

In addition there were a number of other revenues of which little or nothing can be discovered. A mint, defunct by 1183, had once provided 10 marks.[5] Mines (lead and silver) were worth £214 in 1196, of which at least £40 came from the sale of lead. At an earlier date the bishop is said to have taken an annual render of three talents of silver from his mines. This was probably a farm, for mineral wealth, like almost everything else, was an auctionable asset. One farmer of the episcopal mines, Christian by name, has come down to posterity in an unpleasant light. Having found *quendam miserum* who knew of treasure, he had him collusively cast into prison that his secret might be extorted and a new dividend realized. The unfortunate, so it appears, was happily rescued by the timely intervention of St Cuthbert.[6]

In 1183 corn-mills, always an important source of revenue, produced £185—a figure which compares favourably with the £111 of Winchester and the smaller sums quoted by Painter. The mills were mostly farmed, usually for a cash render, though that of Carlton supplied twenty measures of wheat 'of the Yarm measure'. Common bakehouses occur in Boldon Book at Darlington, Gateshead and Durham, the last being worth £6. Fisheries yielded £16 in 1183. These were either stews, as

---

[1] The amount in 1211 was £105 (*BB*, xiii).   [2] *FPD*, 255.   [3] *FPD*, 230.
[4] *BB*, App. III; DC Durham, 4. 1. Pont. no. 13 (printed in *BB*, App. VIII).
[5] *BB*, 1–2.   [6] *Libellus...Cuthberti*, 210–12.

at Bedlington, or the exclusive right to take fish in streams and rivers, for the Tweed and Wear could then hold their own against the Wye. The two most profitable retained in the bishop's hand were at Norham and Wearmouth, later famous in the diocese for the quality of their salmon.[1]

Such were the resources at Puiset's disposal. Basically they were those of any other comparable magnate of the fifth to the sixteenth centuries, with a faint flavour of the world of Anicius and Apion, or the fourth-century aristocracy of southern France with 'their huge domains like little kingdoms'. But for a contemporary comparison, and an equivalent fusion of spiritual and secular assets, a parallel must needs be sought in France or Germany; at Metz and Bamberg, or Bayeux, Châlons and Langres.

The economy was largely self-contained, with practically all the needs of life met by local industry. Finance, however, perhaps almost as much by original render as the commutation of pre-dial duty or free service, was on a basis of currency. The bulk of this revenue, such as assized rents and ecclesiastical dues, was assured, provided (as Puiset notes on one occasion) no military or natural disaster overtook the Liberty. There was, moreover, little to debit against it apart from the whims of ambition or ostentation. It was a period when some £10–£20 a year would support a man as a knight and £4 as a scholar. £350 would provide a stone castle.[2] The king himself could live in the diocese for about £25 a week or roughly £1300 a year.[3] If, in 1196, it took £23 to repair the bishop's 'great ship' and get her to sea, the maintenance of his London palace was but 37s., whilst it cost the royal officers only £91 to harvest the episcopal crops, a further £14 for the purchase and sowing of seed, and £19 for the repair of mills.[4] Expansion in the household and the current

---

[1] BB, 2, 6, 17, 41.

[2] Painter, *Studies in the History of the English Feudal Barony*, 172–3; Poole, *From Domesday to Magna Carta*, 371. [3] BB, xvi, xvii.

[4] *Chancellor's Roll 8 Richard I*, 253. Returns from later vacancies show these figures to be fairly representative. Thus in 1211 repairs to the bishop's ship were £15, work on Durham Castle £13, and repairs of the London palace £6 (BB, xvii). Manorial expenses were, however, as high as £426 (BB, xviii). In 1213 manorial expenses, together with wages, were £132 (BB, xxi), though repairs to Bamburgh Castle cost £117.

price rise were both met by alienations of demesne; a sort of loan on posterity. The administration was largely rewarded by land grants, which were not recurring obligations, or by that eternal system of perquisites and *douceurs*, the practical operation of which led Alexander III to admonish Durham clerks for their exorbitant demands on the relatives of the dead they buried.[1] The bishop's fiscal policy was by no means unique. Its large-scale, careful application placed Puiset in an order that numbers Henry of Winchester, Beaufort and Wolsey amongst its members. His greatest political ambitions came to nothing, but his wealth endowed a legacy of buildings and manuscripts worthy of the finest tradition of the age.

Of the institutions and methods of government underlying this magnificence and opulence there is little information. The Honor had already attained some degree of political organization by 1153. Probably William of St Calais, who knew alike the ways of the Conqueror and Lanfranc, had begun the work, but the main architect was Rannulf Flambard. He came from the avaricious competence of the administration of William Rufus to exercise his powerful abilities in Durham to the accompaniment of a chorus of monastic complaint. His *acta* reveal the existence of a regular administrative staff; Papedus, sheriff of Norham, Osbert, the bishop's nephew, as sheriff of Durham, and Aelgeranus in some similar office in Allertonshire.[2] His writs and charters are precise and stereotyped in the authoritative brevity of the Anglo-Norman royal style, witnessed by a consistent body of officials, local notabilities and familiar clerks. In the normal tradition of the period, the administration was well stocked with *nepotes* and assorted relatives; Radulf, clerk, son of Bishop Rannulf, William, son of Rannulf, Robert, nephew of the bishop, Richard, nephew of the bishop, Osbert, nephew of the bishop, and Payne, son of Rannulf.[3] From these there descended at least two important families, both flourishing in Puiset's time, the one holding at

---

[1] See above, p. 124.

[2] DC Durham, 2. 1. Pont. nos. 3, 10 and 11; *EYC*, II, no. 966 and p. 306.

[3] DC Durham, 2. 1. Pont. nos. 2 and 10; 'Calendar of the Ravensworth Deeds', ed. H. E. Bell, 44; DC Durham, B IV, 24, described in Rud, *Codicum MSS. Dunelmensis Catalogus Classicus*, 215.

Houghall and Harraton, the other at Horden and Silksworth. It is typical of those energies that assisted the flagging monastic construction of the church of Durham, that the *cartae* of 1166 show the bishop with a surplus enfeoffment of sixty-eight knights, sixty-four of whom had been enfeoffed before 1135.[1]

Flambard's successor at Durham was Henry I's chancellor, Geoffrey Rufus, a less enigmatic exponent of methods similar to those of his predecessor. His administration was largely that bequeathed by Flambard, with the addition of such local families as Escolland, Conyers, Burel and Amundeville—one of whom married the bishop's daughter.[2] One important innovation appears to date from Rufus's episcopate, for in a recently discovered writ there is mention of a Durham justiciar, the earliest reference to such an officer.[3]

To all this Puiset added little. It is difficult to accept Lapsley's view that he was engaged (unsuccessfully) in 'feudalizing' the Liberty, 'normalizing' its tenures, and experimenting with legal reform.[4] The government remained rudimentary. There was a court; *curia Sancti Cuthberti, curia episcopi*, as hybrid in function as in composition, which appears elusively in charter evidence, and by the early thirteenth century has prospered and multiplied to some blurred version of the royal pattern. On occasions grants are said to have been made *consilio personarum et ecclesie nostre*, or *consilio et assensu prioris et capituli nostri necnon archidiaconorum et omnium clericorum nostrorum*. But such phrases are rare, and whatever their validity in law, the methods they presume were not in accord with the episcopal will and style. Of any comparable lay activity there is no evidence. At times there are references to *plena curia*, or some variant thereof, indicating a more formal, and more feudal, assembly than that which later met *de quindena in quindenam*. In such gatherings—held indiscriminately in the Galilee chapel, on Palace Green or *in domo Gilberti Hansard*[5]— battle was wagered, criminals condemned, fines levied, holdings

---

[1] *LR*, I, 416–18. [2] Symeon, II, 316.
[3] DC Durham, Cart. Misc. C printed below, App. II, no. 13.
[4] *VCH Durham*, I, 311–16.
[5] *FPD*, 252. Sessions in church were contrary to the canon (*Dec. Greg. IX* III, xlix, c. 5).

lost and homages taken.[1] It was in *plena curia nostra apud Dunelmum* that Geoffrey of Haswell vindicated his title to the vill of Little Haswell, before an assembly of magnates and sergeants headed by Gilbert Hansard.[2] So too the unhappy Roger of Kibblesworth surrendered his holding into the hand of the prior in the presence of the bishop *et baronum episcopatus in pleno placito*—some thirteen great feudatories of the Honor.[3] Knights and sergeants were likewise present at criminal pleas, whose history they later recounted with all the discrepancies and hesitations native to amateur justice. Indeed, it would seem that in cases of death or mutilation a distinguished layman might preside. It was Richard Punchardon, *doctus et eloquens*, who sentenced that Roger whose subsequent recovery appears among the Becket miracles.[4] For the rest there are but recorded achievements and the attestations to *acta*, suggesting an omnicompetent court, generally more lay than clerical, but which might pass with equal ease as a moribund shire court or a nascent synod.[5]

Of institutional development there is little trace. Such as there was, now appears to have been somewhat lethargic emulation of the royal exemplar. Lapsley, who unwisely viewed Puiset through legal lenses, is obliged to argue in one

[1] The bishop also exercised what might be termed appellate jurisdiction in relation to lesser courts of his Liberty. Thus the Gateshead charter contains the clause *Et si qua loquela orta fuerit inter forestarium et burgenses, terminetur in eodem Burgo, si fieri potest, sin autem in presentia nostra...* (BB, App. III).

[2] DC Durham, 2. 2. Finch, no. 3; *Priory of Finchale*, 3.

[3] DC Durham, 3. 6. Spec. no. 18, printed in *FPD*, 142 n.

[4] *Materials*, I, 420-3. The family of Punchardon, and Richard in particular, are frequent witnesses to *acta*. Apart from their Lincolnshire and Yorkshire associations their holdings are not clear (LR, 388, 429).

[5] Of Puiset's *acta* there are only nineteen charters with a purely lay address, of which only six are witnessed by laymen alone. There are likewise only six charters of purely ecclesiastical address, of which but two (inductions) are witnessed by clerks alone. The remainder address lay and religious alike and are similarly witnessed. An induction might be attested by clerks alone (3. 1. Pont. no. 12) or by clerks and laity (Reg. 1, fo. 113). A grant in favour of a knight could be witnessed by barons, knights and sergeants (4. 1. Pont. no. 13) or by clerks, knights and sergeants (*Mon. Ang.* I, 244). For a free tenant archdeacons, clerks and barons might appear (2. 2. Finch. no. 10), or clerks, knights and sergeants (2. 3. Spec. no. 47). The testing clause is, of course, by no means an infallible guide to those present on any occasion, nor did a charter necessarily pass at the time of the business it records.

place of his reforms, and at another of their absence.[1] It seems the bishop introduced the mild efficiency of the Assize of Clarendon into the Liberty's limited repertoire of criminal procedure, but thereafter legal methods are of the antique pattern. The Grand Assize was not available in 1205, whilst as late as 1211 the local knights paid John 70 marks for the right to enjoy the 'Assizes of the kingdom' in the episcopal court.[2]

Under Puiset there are references to the use of sworn inquests, concords and the primitive chance of trial by battle in land actions. Reginald of Durham often mentions preparations for such encounters (in the form of prayers to Cuthbert or Godric), which took place on the green to the north of the cathedral, much to the excitement and distraction of the monks. In 1184, Radulf, son of Paulinus of York, proved his title to a third part of the vill of Garmondsway *tanquam rectus et legitimus heres patris sui de sponsa natus*, *in curia beati Cuthberti et nostra* (i.e. the bishop's) *per finem duelli*.[3] Later, when Henry Puiset came into possession of Little Haswell, it was related that it had once belonged to a certain Geoffrey, and that Richard, son of Odo, had claimed it *et post in plena curia nostra apud Dunelmum per finem duelli...remisit*.[4] In these cases duel had been wagered, but not fought. The story might be different, and Reginald of Durham has a gruesome anecdote, illustrating Cuthbert's unbending attitude to perjury, of the slaying of a blinded and helpless man (*sub competenti moderamine*), and its wholesome influence on the spectators.[5]

If little can be said of the functions of those present on such occasions, it is at least possible to give some indication of their standing. Among the witnesses to Puiset's *acta* a group of ten names appear with marked consistency, and seem to constitute the bishop's particular council. Six are clerks (Burchard Puiset, William Puiset, William of Howden, Simon Chamber-

[1] Lapsley, *Durham*, 163–5, 169, but cf. 167.
[2] PR *13 John*, 37; Lapsley, *Durham*, 166–7.
[3] 'A Second Calendar of the Greenwell Deeds', 94, no. 30; see also above, p. 10, n. 3.
[4] Above, p. 221, n. 2.
[5] *Libellus...Cuthberti*, 115; *Libellus...Godrici*, 189–91.

lain and Master Richard of Coldingham), whose fortunes will be noted in course. Four are laymen; Henry Puiset, Gilbert Hansard, Gilbert de Laley and Jordan Escolland.

Henry Puiset was the bishop's son. His swift rise to power began in 1175 when his father bought him entry to the fitz-Herbert, and thereby family fee of Market Weighton.[1] Shortly afterwards (1182), with that felicity native to the house of Blois, he made a good marriage to the widow of Henry of Neufmarché, Denise de Tilly, a daughter of Otes de Tilly.[2] By purchase and paternal favour he steadily accumulated an extensive holding in the north, and by 1190 had land in Bishop Auckland and Durham City,[3] and at Newton,[4] Aldin Grange,[5] Nelson, Hartlepool and Wolsingham in the county of Durham.[6] Haswell he acquired from a certain Geoffrey, and Wingate from Hugh Burel.[7] In 1187 Bertram of Hetton surrendered his vill of Hetton as security for a loan.[8] Henry had a house in Newcastle,[9] whilst in Yorkshire he obtained Yokefleet at the expense of the Wharram family,[10] and received land from the episcopal waste in Deighton and Osmotherley,[11] and at Giggleswick, Settle, Stockdale, Collingham and Compton from his maternal relatives, the Percies.[12] There was a sinister facility in all this. Henry shared the paternal riches and the financial aptitude of the house. He could stand as surety for the large debts of distinguished men in Suffolk and London,[13] and was in

---

[1] *Gesta*, 1, 161; *PR 22 Henry II*, 100. Market Weighton had once belonged to Stephen fitzHerbert, half-brother of Archbishop William (*EYC*, 11, 167 and cf. *PR 5 John*, 211).

[2] *PR 28 Henry II*, 45. For the resultant acquisitions, see *EYC*, VIII, no. 105, and for Denise and her family, tenants of the Lacy fee, *ibid.* 143–7.

[3] *CChR*, 1, 432.   [4] *Chancellor's Roll 8 Richard I*, 260.

[5] DC Durham, 1. 1. Finch. no. 11; DC Durham, 3. 1. Pont. no. 9, printed in *Priory of Finchale*, 8.

[6] *Priory of Finchale*, 22–3; *PU*, 11, no. 280.

[7] DC Durham, 2. 2. Finch. no. 3, printed in *Priory of Finchale*, 3; Surtees, 1, sec. 11, 97.

[8] DC Durham, 3. 7. Spec. no. 3.

[9] *BF*, 1, 371–2; *Priory of Finchale*, 22–3.

[10] DC Durham, 3. 1. Pont. no. 23, printed in *EYC*, 11, no. 987, cf. *Priory of Finchale*, no. 50.

[11] *BF*, 1, 24.

[12] *Sallay Cartulary*, ed. McNulty, no. 422; *The Pudsay Deeds*, ed. R. P. Little-dale, 90; T. D. Whittaker, *History of Craven*, 135.

[13] *PR 9 Richard I*, 233–4, 166.

a position to emulate the episcopal policy in Durham as economic distress drove the Burel, Wharram and Hetton lands into his net. From about 1180 he was the leading baron of the see, and his name usually heads the secular witnesses to his father's *acta*. He was a frequent witness to private charters in Yorkshire and Durham, and was described as a baron at the coronation of Richard I.[1] Though his fortunes were in decline after 1195 he was a royal officer in 1196,[2] and was employed in Scotland by John in 1201.[3] He died without direct male heir before September 1212 and such of his lands as had escaped the religious were passed to Robert de Percy.[4]

Gilbert de Laley appears to have been a member of the family of Leathley,[5] neighbours and tenants of the Puiset-Percy interest at Settle,[6] and like them benefactors of the Cistercians of Sallay (Sawley)-in-Craven.[7] In 1166 he held half a fee of the new enfeoffment of St Cuthbert,[8] lying either at Crook[9] or Witton Gilbert,[10] where, through Puiset's generosity, he later acquired further property.[11] He was also an episcopal tenant at Egglestone and Kilvington in Yorkshire, held at one fee,[12] whilst in Northumberland the family held in chief at Spindleston and Budle.[13] Gilbert appears to have married into the old Durham family of Papedy, and through his wife, Matilda, acquired further interests in Northumberland at Ancroft and Ord.[14] At the same time a certain Henry de Laley (who had a brother, Lucas)[15] occurs as a clerk of the diocese.[16] Gilbert's standing in the bishop's confidence may be seen in the fact that it was he

---

[1] *Gesta*, ii, 80.   [2] *Chancellor's Roll 8 Richard I*, 173.

[3] Hoveden, iv, 163–4.

[4] *Rotuli Litterarum Clausarum*, i, 124a; BB, xx. He once appears to have had a son, John (*NCH* ix, 73 n.).

[5] He is not mentioned in W. P. Baildon, *The Family of Leathley*.

[6] *EYC*, ii, 201; *Pudsay Deeds*, nos. 2, 3, 7.

[7] *Sallay Cartulary*, no. 55.

[8] LR, 418.

[9] DC Durham, Cart. ii, fo. 104; 2. 6. Spec. nos. 54 and 61; *FPD*, 188 n.

[10] DC Durham, 2. 6. Spec. no. 68.

[11] DC Durham, Cart. Elemos. 223.

[12] *Mon. Ang.* vii, 943, no. 1; *Yorkshire Fines, John*, 4, no. 8; *EYC*, v, no. 313.

[13] BF, 1118; *NCH*, i, 177.

[14] DC Durham, Cart. iv, fo. 2; *Chancellor's Roll 8 Richard I*, 255.

[15] *Liber Vitae*, fo. 58ᵛ.

[16] *Chancellor's Roll 8 Richard I*, 256, 257.

who joined Henry Puiset as a hostage after Hugh's capitulation to Longchamp in 1190.[1]

Gilbert Hansard, who died before 1185,[2] was one of the barons of the bishopric. He came from an important family of the diocese,[3] whose lands lay at Hornby and Irby (Yorkshire)[4] and South Kelsey (Lincolnshire).[5] At some uncertain date he received Hurworth, Amerston and Washington from the bishop, and about 1160–70 property at Blacktoft and Hook (Yorkshire).[6] He married into the great Yorkshire family of Stuteville,[7] and from such slight notices of his fortunes as appear seems to have been a man of the episcopal model, ardently 'on the make'. He secured Welbury from William Ingram, and a fee at Worsall and Landmoth from William de Vesci, in addition to his holdings of Adam de Montbegon and Hugh, son of Pinceon, in Lincolnshire.[8]

Jordan Escolland was another honorial baron. He was the son of that Elias Escolland who held two fees and a fraction of the old enfeoffment in 1166,[9] the land lying in Dalton, Seaham, Seaton, Murton, Bishop Middleham and Durham City.[10] The family were also tenants of the Vescis at some uncertain place on the Durham fee.[11] The line had a long and distinguished connexion with the Liberty; Geoffrey Escolland had been one of the custodians of the vacant see after the death of Flambard, together with another honorial baron, John de Amundeville.[12] The same Geoffrey, together with Roger Conyers and Bertram Bulmer, had also been amongst the stalwarts who supported William of St Barbara against the Scottish intruder, William Cumin, in 1144.[13]

In addition to these magnates, the natural companions of the

[1] See above, p. 52. [2] *Rotuli de Dominabus*, 5.
[3] They held eight-ninths of a fee of the old enfeoffment in 1166 (LR, 416).
[4] BF, 24. [5] PR 7 *Richard I*, 33.
[6] BB, 16; *Chancellor's Roll 8 Richard I*, 261; DC Durham, 1. 3. Ebor. no. 15; EYC, II, no. 988. [7] *Liber Vitae*, fo. 23ᵛ. [8] EYC, II, 315.
[9] LR, 417; *Libellus…Godrici*, 469–70. It would seem that Elias had a wife called Christiana (DC Durham, 3. 7. Spec. no. 16).
[10] DC Durham, Cart. II, fo. 127ᵛ and 248; Surtees, III, 55; IV, 163. The family also appears to have had land in Hampshire, PR 2 *Richard I*, 136.
[11] LR, 417; *Arch. Institute Proceedings* II (1852), cxi.
[12] PR 31 *Henry I*, 130–1; Symeon, I, 141.
[13] Symeon, I, 158; above, pp. 8, 129.

bishop either by the fortunes of blood or inherited position, there were some nine other families whose names appear regularly in attestations. Their titles and the value of their fees show great diversity, but they were united in that direct contact with the lord which was the effective mark of the honorial baron. Five—Audre, Conyers, fitzRichard, Hylton and fitzThomas—held at a fee or more. The other four—Eppleton, Farlington, Layton and Thorpe—held at a fee or less.[1] They were not amongst the greatest tenants of the see, such as Vesci, who for obvious reasons make but rare appearances. Nor did they approach the national importance of those powerful Anglo-Normans, the Kymes, Wakes, Fossards and Percies, all of whom numbered St Cuthbert amongst their lords. With the exception of Farlington they owed nothing of their holdings to Puiset, and, as far as can be discovered, were not (with the same exception) employed by him in administrative office. In every case they were families long connected with the Liberty, and in particular with Durham. The name of Conyers appears frequently in the time of Flambard (by whom they were reputedly enfeoffed),[2] and thereafter under Rufus and St Barbara. FitzThomas and fitzRichard were both grandchildren of Flambard, amply endowed from monastic property. Layton and Thorpe can be traced to the time of Geoffrey Rufus, and acquitted themselves with varying success in the troubles of St Barbara's episcopate.[3] In all they constituted a local whiggery of limited territorial and political interests, interrelated by marriage and tenure; the natural repositories of tradition and the inevitable entourage of their lord. There was nothing of that general expropriation of ancient families, such as the Durham chronicle suggests[4] and as Lapsley believed. With a few great exceptions the new names introduced to the Liberty by Puiset—north Yorkshire and Northumbrian titles such as Darel, Smeaton and Skelton[5]—make but rare modest ap-

---

[1] These families will be discussed in detail elsewhere.

[2] *EYC*, ii, no. 944.   [3] Symeon, i, 150, 158–9, 166–7.

[4] *Scriptores Tres*, 8. One of the miracles of Becket concerns a Durham knight, Osbern, ejected by the bishop (*Materials*, i, 481). I cannot suggest his identity.

[5] Of these the Darels alone were of any consequence. They were tenants at Wheldrake and elsewhere of the Percy fee (*EYC*, i, no. 639; *Fountains Cartulary*,

pearances. Meanwhile the old hereditary influences rolled on, in some cases even to the fifteenth century, and Robert de Amundeville, of a family famous and active under Flambard,[1] was so burdened by cares of state as to miss certain of Godric's apposite prophecies.[2]

There were, however, inevitably some territorial readjustments in favour of the bishop's adherents, not least of whom were his own children. The same story was told in many forms. Philip, son of Hamo, sheriff of Durham from *c.* 1180 to 1195 (probably that Philip, son of Hamo de Tani, who held at Berdon (Essex) of the earls of Essex and of the Percies in Craven),[3] was present in the diocese, though without office, *c.* 1175.[4] Before 1183 Puiset granted him land at Migley,[5] and about 1189 enfeoffed him at Newton at the service of one-fifth of a fee.[6] With the bishop's favour and his own ready finance he extended his holding at the expense of his less fortunate neighbours, purchasing land at Silksworth from Walter de Insula,[7] Geoffrey fitzRichard,[8] and Roger of Eppleton.[9]

So too the bishop's engineer, Richard, bought land lying before the abbey gateway from Gerard, the episcopal marshal, for six marks (*c.* 1171–4),[10] and sold it to the convent for ten (*c.* 1175–80).[11] With the assistance of episcopal pressure he forced a grant at Wolviston from the convent[12] and was perhaps thereafter employed in ejecting some of the conventual tenants.[13] In later life (after 1180) he appears to have been concerned with

817). They likewise held of St Mary's, York, at Deighton (*EYC*, v, no. 222) and Fulford (*EYC*, I, no. 343) and had land at Hutton and Sessay (PR 28 *Henry II*, 45). They witness Percy and Puiset gifts to Sawley (*Sallay Cartulary*, nos. 2 and 422) and Fountains (*Fountains Cartulary*, 488).

[1] Symeon, I, 141.　　　　　　　　　[2] *Libellus...Godrici*, 318.
[3] PRO, Duchy of Lancaster, Ancient Deed, 27/LS. 2; *BF*, 123; *LR*, 595; Whittaker, *History of Craven*, 110.
[4] Also present were his brothers Thomas and Osmund and their sister, Maud (DC Durham, 3. 7. Spec. no. 16). Philip had a wife named Alice (*FPD*, 126 n.).
[5] *BB*, 32.　　　　　　　　　　　　[6] DC Durham, 3. 1. Pont. no. 7.
[7] DC Durham, 3. 7. Spec. no. 23, printed in *FPD*, 125 n.
[8] DC Durham, 3. 7. Spec. nos. 21, 22, 23, printed in *FPD*, 18 n., 125 n.
[9] DC Durham, 3. 7. Spec. nos. 15, 16, printed in FPD, 123 n., 124 n.
[10] DC Durham, 4. 1. Pont. no. 8, printed in *FPD*, 198 n.
[11] DC Durham, 4. 1. Pont. no. 4, printed in *FPD*, 198 n.
[12] See above, p. 154.
[13] DC Durham, 3. 1. Pont. no. 15, printed in *FPD*, 140 n.

the consolidation of a fee at Pittington,[1] and in view of such activities it is interesting to note that Richard figures among the many debtors of the usurer, Aaron of Lincoln.[2]

Similarly new families appeared, and old friends and good servants were rewarded. Puiset increasingly tended the Blois cause in place of Henry of Winchester. William of Harlsey, one of Stephen's more reputable illegitimate children, was given a small fee in West Harlsey.[3] His son, fortified by imposing patronymics—William, son of William, son of King Stephen—was enfeoffed at Little Haughton (Durham) to hold at the service of one-fifth of a knight's fee (c. 1190).[4] Arco, the steward, had land at Langley *pro servitio quod fecit Henrico bone memorie Wintoniensi episcopo . . . (et) pro eo quod fecit Domino Hugoni Dunolmensi episcopo*, and so highly were the services of this old family retainer esteemed that Puiset had bought him his land *de propria pecunia sua*.[5] During the earlier part of the episcopate the shrievalty of Durham was held by Ralph Haget, member of a Yorkshire and diocesan family closely associated with the Percies.[6] Some time before 1183 the bishop granted Richard of Ifferley 48 acres in Stanhope,[7] whilst about the same time he gave land at Hunstanworth to Robert Corbet.[8] The important

[1] DC Durham, 3. 9. Spec. no. 12, printed in *FPD*, 140 n.

[2] *PR 3 Richard I*, 23; *5 Richard I*, 68. The domestic, as opposed to the architectural, achievements of *Magister Ricardus enginur* are unknown. He seems to have had a daughter, Agnes (DC Durham, Cart. II, fo. 126) and a son and heir, Thomas (DC Durham, 3. 9. Spec. no. 12). See also above, p. 113 and below, p. 233.

[3] *BF*, I, 24.

[4] DC Durham, 3. 1. Pont. no. 21, printed in Surtees, III, 339. The mother of this obscure grandchild of Stephen was perhaps one Aubreye (*EYC*, II, 295), though William of Harlsey apparently remarried and appears with a certain Lece as his wife (DC Durham, 2. 11. Spec. no. 12; *FPD*, 181 n.).

[5] *BB*, 32.

[6] Ralph Haget held half a fee of the old enfeoffment in 1166, probably at Garmondsway (*LR*, 417; *BB*, 12). The exact relationship with the Yorkshire and Lincolnshire family of that name, tenants of the Mowbrays, Bulmers and Montbegons, is uncertain (*LR*, 419, 429). A Ralph Haget made a grant to Nostell (BM, Cotton MS. Vesp. E XIX, fo. 11ᵛ), and appears as a brother of Geoffrey Haget, founder of the priory of Helaugh Park (*Cartulary of Helaugh Park*, ed. Purvis, 7). For association with the Percies see *Sallay Cartulary*, nos. 1 and 2. Haget was related to the Durham family of Audre (DC Durham, 3. 7. Spec. no. 7; *FPD*, 136 n.).

[7] DC Durham, 3. 1. Pont, no. 17; *BB*, 29.

[8] *BB*, 32; *Mon. Ang.* VII, 733, no. ix.

Lincolnshire family of Coleville was enfeoffed in Yorkshire,[1] and Walter of Farlington, a Bulmer[2] and a man of standing in Northumberland[3] and Yorkshire, was enfeoffed at a quarter of a fee in Kirby Sigston (Yorkshire).[4] His brother, Henry, a devotee of the hunt, and later constable of Norham, received a fee at Birkby (Yorkshire).[5] Yet another brother, master Simon, eventually became archdeacon of Durham.[6] Of greater interest was the endowment of Henry Bek at Redmarshall (Stockton).[7] He was a son of Walter Bek and Agnes, daughter and heiress of that Hugh, son of Pinceon, steward of Durham, who had supported Cumin against St Barbara in 1144.[8] After 1144 Pinceon tactfully loosened his connexions with Durham. Part of his lands passed to the convent,[9] whilst of the remainder some found their way, *via* Hugh Burel, into the hands of Henry Puiset, and some part of Pinceon's great Lincoln fee went to the Beks,[10] who thus commenced what was to be a celebrated association with the see, culminating in the episcopate of Antony Bek.[11] But such vast changes were rare, and the basic feudal structure of the Liberty was left unimpaired.

The execution of the episcopal policies, and the unflagging magnificence of his style, demanded a large and efficient household and administration. Of the workings of these we have little information. In general the pattern of preceding episcopates was repeated (though Flambard's practice of employing monks had long since been abandoned), and the diocese lacked that diversity of officers which occurs in many of the great lay Honors.[12] Henry Puiset was for some time his father's justiciar, and once a final concord is said to have been made before him.[13]

[1] DC Durham, Cart. Misc. no. 486; *EYC*, VI, 168-70.

[2] *EYC*, II, 129, 367. [3] *BF*, 1116.

[4] *BF*, 24. [5] *FPD*, 235; *BF*, 24.

[6] DC Durham, Cart. Elemos. 103. [7] *BF*, 28.

[8] *Danelaw Documents*, nos. 177, 178, 529; *Feudal Docs. from the Abbey of Bury St Edmunds*, no. 215.

[9] *PU*, II, no. 82. [10] *BF*, 164, 165, 167.

[11] *Sir Christopher Hatton's Book of Seals*, ed. D. Stenton and L. C. Loyd, no. 41 and note. For suggestions as to the early history of the Pinceon fee, see Craster, 'Some Anglo-Saxon Records of the See of Durham', 189-98.

[12] Only two hereditary 'baronial' offices have been noticed, that of steward, held by Hugh, son of Pinceon, and that of constable of Durham, held by the Conyers (see above, pp. 12, 43, n. 2). [13] *NCH*, IX, 73 n.

Judicially the office was the highest in the Liberty, for it would seem that only the bishop or his justiciar were competent to rule as to whether or not there had been a denial of justice in a lower court.[1] There were sheriffs and constables at both Norham and Durham, though these officers are better known by their economic fortunes than their administrative duties.[2] The sheriff of Durham presided in what was the local shire court, controlled the gaol in Durham Castle, and was responsible for the arrest and imprisonment of criminals.[3] During the absence of the bishop secular government was vested in the sheriff, assisted by a number of *subvicarii* whose provenance is uncertain.[4] Possibly they were seneschals, of whom three are variously mentioned. As was common elsewhere they shared a large amount of routine business with the sheriffs. Robert, son of Evrard, could later recall that he had been sent by the episcopal seneschal *ad homines de Clive* (Cliffe), *ut ostenderet eis ubi deberent capere meremium*,[5] whilst the clause in Puiset's charter for Wearmouth concerning the burgesses' right to distrain debtors is conditioned by *nisi forte . . . ab episcopo vel vicecomite vel senescallo missi fuerint ad negocia ipsius episcopi facienda*.[6] The foresters were likewise men of considerable importance, and on one occasion it was a forester who was to make an act of seisin.[7] There are mentions of the chief forester, Germanus of Cowesby, *capellanus*, and his clerks, in addition to deputies at such places as Howden and Heworth.[8] It was these officers who licensed and supervised the gathering and sale of small wood,[9] and together with their sergeants pursued (and occasionally arrested) those who poached on preserves particularly dear to the episcopal heart.[10]

[1] *Mon. Ang.* VII, 732, no. II; *Memorials of St Giles's, Durham*, 195–6.

[2] The offices were usually held by relatives or close adherents of the bishop. Under Geoffrey Rufus the constable of Durham was his *nepos* (Symeon, I, 164). During Puiset's episcopate both Norham and Durham were in the hands of the Farlingtons, and the shrievalties successively committed to Haget and fitzHamo.

[3] *Libellus . . . Cuthberti*, 210; *FPD*, 214–16; Lapsley, *Durham*, 58, n. 4; 83, 84.

[4] *Libellus . . . Cuthberti*, 210.   [5] *FPD*, 259.

[6] *BB*, App. IV. For the importance of the steward, see Painter, *Studies of the History of the English Feudal Barony*, 139; Stenton, *The First Century*, 74–6; Bongert, *Recherches sur les Cours*, 66; *EYC*, IV, 105.

[7] *Mon. Ang.* VII, 732, no. II.   [8] *FPD*, 237, 247.

[9] *Reg. Pal. Dun.* II, 1296–7; *BB*, App. III.   [10] *FPD*, 279.

Germanus of Cowesby himself could well remember in later life an incident from his early career at Heworth when *semel insecutus est quemdam servientem monachorum cum equo et summagio usque ad crucem extra hostium ecclesie, quia asportaverat viride sine licencia*.[1] For such defaulters there were regional forest courts, and it may be assumed on the evidence of the Gateshead charter that presentations were common.[2] At Howden it would appear that jurisdiction was exercised by the manorial court, and Robert, son of Thomas of Howden, later recalled how foresters were appointed by the episcopal bailiffs and subsequently brought transgressors into court, and there presented them to the presiding bailiff.[3] Amongst lesser officials there were a host of tenants in Durham whose duty it was to cater for the bishop's pleasures by assisting in various small ways at the 'great chase' of Weardale. Some supplied such necessities as men, ropes and wine, others had charge of horses, dogs or falcons.[4]

On the demesne the land was either in the bishop's hand, when it was presumably cultivated under the direction of his own officers, or in the hands of a farmer who was responsible for an agreed render of produce, or cash, or both. The farmers were usually drawn from a class of small freeholders and minor administrative officers. Thus at Killerby there was Puiset's acquisitive sergeant, Simon the usher,[5] and at Ryhope and Burdon a certain Amfrid, whose own holding was two bovates and the performance of some riding service.[6] Sometimes, as at Ryton, the village itself was doing the farming,[7] in which case the system of payment varied; the villeins might individually pay so much per bovate and perform works, as at Warden and Murton,[8] or, as at South Biddick, make a joint render.[9]

All the basic needs of agricultural work, transport and communication were fulfilled by villein labour, amplified by the curious responsibilities of drengage tenants. Over the unfree were a number of minor officials, such as the son of Aldred at Great Haughton, who had 40 acres, rendered 2s., went on the bishop's messages and supervised 'the villein works'.[10] Other

---

[1] FPD, 239.   [2] BB, App. III.   [3] FPD, 255, 258.
[4] Reg. Pal. Dun. III, 268–9; CPR, 1358–61, 11.   [5] BB, 22, n. 7.
[6] BB, 6.   [7] BB, 34.   [8] BB, 7–8.
[9] BB, 6.   [10] BB, 19.

functions, as reeve, pinder and smith, were generally discharged by unfree tenants who were given small holdings free of rent and service for the duration of their activity, the equivalent of those 'manorial sergeanties' fairly common elsewhere.[1]

The episcopal household was large; fifty-three sergeants are mentioned in 1196.[2] There was a cook, 'Monk Cook', who had land at Bishop Auckland for his services.[3] There are mentions of Edmund, Henry, Richard, William, Arco and Theobald, stewards;[4] Gerard, Henry, Hugh and Alan, marshals;[5] Geoffrey and Richard, chamberlains;[6] Henry the porter;[7] Richard the hunter;[8] and William, son of John, the butler. Simon the usher[9] had 60 acres in Heighington[10] in addition to the demesne he was farming at Killerby[11] and land in Barforth, where like his lord he was an industrious assarter.[12] His colleagues included a certain Roger and Stephen.[13] Humphrey, the episcopal waggon-master, received 6 acres in Escomb for his doubtless arduous services.[14] Between 1190 and 1195 Hugh granted land at Bushblades to his sergeant, Thomas of the buttery,[15] and to Reginald of the chamber he gave the custody of the gate at Sherburn leper hospital.[16] Gilbert the chamberlain, who married into the old Durham family of Papedy,[17] held two fractional fees de novo in 1166,[18] the land lying at Bushblades, Kepyer and Durham.[19] His colleague, 'Laurence, chamberlain of the lord bishop', was a man of some consequence who paid a fine of £100 in 1196.[20] In 1189 he received the vill of Craw-

---

[1] Cf. Miller, *The Abbey and Bishopric of Ely*, 92.
[2] *Chancellor's Roll 8 Richard I*, 258-9; for other establishments cf. Cheney, *Bishops' Chanceries*, 5.
[3] DC Durham, 4. 1. Pont. no. 7; *FPD*, 177.
[4] *FPD*, 141 n.; *Chancellor's Roll 8 Richard I*, 259; *Reg. Pal. Dun.* II, 1296-7; Brand, I, 206, note v.
[5] *BB*, 32; *EYC*, II, no. 953.
[6] *Chancellor's Roll 8 Richard I*, 255; *Reg. Pal. Dun.* II, 1299-1300.
[7] *Chancellor's Roll 8 Richard I*, 259.   [8] *FPD*, 106 n.
[9] *Chancellor's Roll 8 Richard I*, 259.   [10] *BB*, 21.
[11] *BB*, 22, n. 7.   [12] DC Durham, I. 11. Spec. no. 15; *FPD*, 53 n.
[13] *Chancellor's Roll 8 Richard I*, 259.   [14] *BB*, 25.
[15] *Calendar of the Greenwell Deeds*, no. 6.
[16] *Reg. Pal. Dun.* II, 1299-1300.
[17] DC Durham, 3. 7. Spec. no. 16.   [18] *LR*, 418.
[19] *BB*, 32-3; *Mon. Ang.* VII, 734, no. XIII; DC Durham, Cart. Elemos., 104-5
[20] *Chancellor's Roll 8 Richard I*, 259.

crook from his lord with the added security of a royal confirmation,[1] and about the same time a further holding at Landieu in Weardale,[2] which he and his wife, Cecilia, eventually gave to the conventual almonry.[3]

There was even something which might be described as an incipient office of works, responsible for the bishop's buildings and, if stylistic evidence be accepted, for much else besides.[4] The engineer in chief was that Master Richard whose fortunes have already been noticed.[5] He had directed the early work at Norham and Durham, and according to Reginald his skill was celebrated throughout the diocese.[6] It is unlikely that his was the sole architectural influence, and if the 'early Gothic' at Grindon and Darlington be credited to Puiset, there is the mark of another hand, possibly that of William the architect who held in Consett, but of whom nothing else is known.[7] There are equally scant notices of those who performed, or perhaps directed, some of the manual labours of building. William the episcopal carpenter appears as a tenant in Healeyfield.[8] Lambert the marble-cutter held 30 acres in Stanhope in return for his services,[9] and at South Sherburn Christian the mason had 60 acres rent free 'so long as he is in mason work'.[10]

In addition to the laymen were the clerks of the episcopal *familia*, a number of whom Puiset had inherited from his predecessors. There was, therefore, a considerable element of continuity, both clerical and secular, in the Durham administration. Alan, the priest of Wallsend, a married man with a son,[11] witnessed deeds of William of St Barbara, Priors Laurence and Absalon (c. 1146–55), and occurs as late as 1174.[12] Ingelranus, 'the bishop's clerk', a frequent witness in the period

[1] BM, Lansdowne MS. 902, fo. 78ᵛ.
[2] DC Durham, 2. 3. Sac. no. 3.   [3] DC Durham, 2. 3. Sac. no. 4.
[4] Boase, *English Art, 1100–1216*, 150, 199.   [5] See above, p. 227.
[6] *Libellus...Cuthberti*, 96, 112; Boase, *op. cit.* 227.
[7] DC Durham, Cart. Elemos. 99.
[8] DC Durham, Cart. Elemos. 120.   [9] *BB*, 30.
[10] *BB*, 10. His alleged tombstone in Pittington church (*BB*, 10 n.) lacks creditable evidence.
[11] DC Durham, 3. 8. Spec. no. 17.
[12] DC Durham, 1. 2. Pont. no. 1; 1. 8. Spec. no. 34; Reg. 1, fo. 48; Cart. Misc. no. 490.

1156–62, attested *acta* of both Geoffrey Rufus and William of St Barbara.[1] Robert de Friebois witnessed *acta* of Geoffrey Rufus, St Barbara and prior Roger (*c.* 1133–52).[2] A Simon, canon of York, possibly to be identified with Simon, canon of Beverley,[3] not unnaturally occurs in the time of St Barbara, once dean of York, as does Master Walter, monk and chaplain.[4] The experience and vested powers of such clerks (with the tempting implication of something of an organized chancery) may have restrained Puiset in his earlier years. Their passing and replacement—perhaps hinted by the Durham chronicle—opened the chapter of the convent's woes.[5]

Their successors were largely men of more than local importance, whose fortunes speak eloquently of the episcopal confidence. John, who was archdeacon of Northumberland *c.* 1155–74,[6] lived as a secular magnate, holding the vill of Healeyfield of the bishop[7] and marrying off his *nepos*, Walter, into the local aristocracy.[8] In other details he emulated his master, and appears on one occasion accompanied by Master Thomas, his clerk, and Herbert, his chamberlain.[9] About 1174 John was succeeded by William du Puiset, who seems to have been one of the bishop's own children.[10] A little earlier (*c.* 1170) a more cherished member of the family, Burchard du Puiset, had become archdeacon of Durham. He was employed by his father in diplomatic work, and in 1172 occurs amongst the witnesses to a charter of count Henry the Liberal of Champagne given at Troyes.[11] His endowment was generous.[12] In Durham it included the conventual church of Heighington,[13] whilst in 1189 he added to his preferments his father's old position of treasurer of York,[14] and was thereafter reputedly the paternal

---

[1] DC Durham, 4. 1. Pont. nos. 18 and 19; PRO, Augmentation Office, Ancient Deed B 11535.

[2] DC Durham, 4. 1. Pont. no. 18; 1. 2. Pont. no. 1.

[3] *EYC*, IX, no. 105; Colvin, *The White Canons*, 78, 338.

[4] *EYC*, II, no. 957; DC Durham, 4. 1. Pont. nos. 18 and 19.

[5] *Scriptores Tres*, 8; above, p. 130.

[6] DC Durham, Cart. II, fo. 44ᵛ.

[7] DC Durham, 4. 1. Pont. no. 13; *BB*, App. VIII.

[8] DC Durham, 1. 1. Finch. no. 9.

[9] DC Durham, 4. 2. Spec. no. 34.

[10] See below, App. V.

[11] See above, p. 23.

[12] Newburgh, II, 441.

[13] *FPD*, 243.

[14] *Gesta*, II, 85.

candidate for the archbishopric, and then more modestly for the see of Durham.[1]

The colleagues of these ecclesiastical grandees were generally seculars, mostly *magistri*,[2] and frequently married. Simon Chamberlain, *dilectus filius et familiaris noster*, who had his own chaplains and clerks,[3] was parson of the monastic church of Billingham, where he was succeeded late in the century by his son Henry.[4] Henry, as Master Henry of Durham, himself tests a number of Puiset's *acta* and is subsequently found as official to Bishop Poitou.[5] Simon held land from the bishop at Cornsay and Hedley Hill in Durham,[6] which he duly passed to his sons or nephews, Walter of Caen and Robert, son of Roger.[7] The family appears to have prospered, for in addition to Henry's advancement, Walter is recorded to have bought land at Hartburn,[8] whilst Robert acquired an interest in Middleton and Follingsby.[9]

Master William of Blois,[10] whose name suggests some affinity with the bishop, was, in all probability, that Master William who was sub-dean (*c.* 1192-7), precentor (1197-1203) and subsequently bishop of Lincoln (1203-6).[11] He occurs alike in the *acta* of St Hugh[12] and of Puiset both as Master William and William the sub-dean,[13] and may be that Master William of Blois who tests a number of Scottish charters in this period.[14] He was of sufficient standing before his elevation to the episcopate to be commissioned in various causes by Innocent III.[15]

---

[1] See above, pp. 62, 176, 182.   [2] Cf. Cheney, *Bishops' Chanceries*, 11.
[3] DC Durham, 4. 2. Spec. no. 9.   [4] *FPD*, 249.
[5] PRO, Augmentation Office, Ancient Deed B 11538. Master Alan of Richmond, of the conventual *familia*, had a certain Master Henry as brother (DC Durham, Cart. Elemos. 136), though whether this was Henry of Durham is doubtful.
[6] *BB*, 31.   [7] *BB*, App. VII.   [8] *FPD*, 47 n.
[9] *PR 2 John*, 110; *FPD*, 113 n.
[10] According to John of Schalby, writing in the early fourteenth century, William was a graduate of Paris (Gerald of Wales, VII, 202).
[11] Diceto, II, 150; *Reg. Ant. Linc.* II, no. 637; IV, 14, 32; Gerald of Wales, VII, 124.
[12] BM, Cotton MS. Vesp. E xx, fos. 33, 34ᵛ, 35; Harley MS. 391, fo. 102.
[13] *EYC*, II, no. 983; see below, App. II, no. 9.
[14] *Liber Sancte Marie de Melrose*, ed. C. Innes, 105, 107.
[15] *Historians of the Church of York*, III, 110-12; *Chron. Abbatie Rameseiensis*, ed. W. D. Macray, 316.

William of Howden—or as he may have been, Master William of Howden[1]—was perhaps one of the episcopal justices and certainly one of the most important clerks of the diocese. He held the churches of Kirby Sigston (where he was succeeded by one of his sons, Master John of Howden),[2] Ivesley[3] and Rowley, and some title in that of Ellington.[4] He had land at Kirby Sigston[5] by grant of Bishop Hugh, and in addition purchased 100 acres in Durham from William of Butterwick.[6] On one occasion he mentions his chaplain, Peter, his brother, John, and his sons, John, William and Nicholas.[7] He had another chaplain, Adam of Barton,[8] to whom he gave 70 acres in the village of Esh, recently acquired from the unfortunate Bertram of Hetton.

Master Richard Hairon, possibly a clerk of Bishop William of Coutances,[9] was probably a member of a prospering Norman family of the diocese. In 1166 a certain Jordan Hairon held one-ninth of a fee of the old enfeoffment of St Cuthbert, the land lying in Yorkshire, to which, before 1183, Puiset added half a fee in Thimbleby[10] and a twelfth in Kepwick. Jordan, it seems, also had land at Chilton (Durham)—where he made a discreet grant to the episcopal cook[11]—in addition to a fee in chief in Northumberland.[12] His children included two sons, Radulf and Jordan,[13] whilst a certain Gilbert Hairon, whose relationship is unknown, received the vill of Holmside from the bishop c. 1175–80.[14] It is not therefore surprising to find that Master Richard granted an annual rent of 20s. to the church of Rouen for the commemoration of Puiset's death.[15]

Other clerks are more elusive. Master John de Rana, described as 'the bishop's clerk' c. 1158–62,[16] is known only by

[1] EYC, ii, no. 776; Registrum Episcopatus Glasguensis, ed. C. Innes, i, nos. 47, 48.
[2] FPD, 251.   [3] DC Durham, 2. 6. Spec. no. 13.
[4] PR 31 Henry II, 152.   [5] Cf. EYC, ii, 280.
[6] EYC, ii, no. 980.   [7] DC Durham, 2. 6. Spec. no. 13.
[8] DC Durham, 1. 3. Elemos. no. 3.   [9] Cal. Doc. France, no. 515.
[10] LR, 416; BF, 24; cf. PR 29 Henry II, 55; Records of the Templars, ed. B. A. Lees, 128.   [11] DC Durham, 2. 12. Spec. nos. 10, 13, 15; FPD, 168 n.
[12] BF, 202, 597.   [13] DC Durham, 3. 7. Spec. no. 15.
[14] Reg. Pal. Dun. iii, 268–9; CPR, 1358–61, 11.
[15] PRO, Transcripts, vol. 140 A, no. 412.
[16] DC Durham, Reg. 1, fo. 108v.

his attestations and the gift of a number of books to the conventual library.[1] It is, however, worthy of note that one Luke de Rana, who received Plawsworth from the bishop *c.* 1154–60,[2] had been enfeoffed at Burdon by the priory a little earlier.[3] The bishop's 'familiar clerk', Peter of Sedgefield,[4] who makes an entertaining appearance in Reginald as the Chaucerian lover of a daughter of the priest of Fishburn,[5] received 60 acres of waste at Rowley from his master, together with the right to erect a chapel there.[6] Master Thomas of Thixendale (fl. *c.* 1154–74)[7] was perhaps a man the bishop had known from his archidiaconal days, for the name was common in York,[8] and a Gerard de Sezevaus (Thixendale) is later found in company with Henry Puiset.[9] William, clerk of the infirmary, who tests *c.* 1180–95, received the conventual church of Castle Eden some time between 1174 and 1181.[10] There installed, and fortified by the sure support of the episcopal authority, he demanded tithes from his neighbours, the Augustinians of Guisborough. Alexander III instructed the canons to ignore the bishop's threats of excommunication, and ordered him to respect the convent's privileges.[11]

Others make even more fleeting appearance. William, son of the archbishop—a name which combined with fitzHerbert's reputation suggests a son of St William of York.[12] Radulf the clerk appears in Boldon Book as holding 24 acres at Newton-by-Durham quit of rent whilst in the bishop's service.[13] A certain Theobald is of indeterminate status. He is described on one occasion as priest, but subsequently as *clericus dispensator*.[14]

---

[1] Mynors, *Durham Cathedral Manuscripts*, nos. 143–5.

[2] *Calendar of the Greenwell Deeds*, no. 5.

[3] *Calendar of the Greenwell Deeds*, no. 3.

[4] *Chancellor's Roll 8 Richard I*, 257.

[5] *Libellus...Godrici*, 472.　　[6] DC Durham, 4. 1. Pont. no. 3.

[7] *FPD*, 10; *EYC*, II, no. 937; DC Durham, 4. 1. Pont. no. 14 (see below App. II, no. 4).

[8] *EYC*, I, no. 254; II, no. 848; V, no. 190. Robert de Sezevaus is mentioned in the *Liber Vitae*, fo. 58.

[9] *EYC*, II, no. 912.　　[10] DC Durham, Reg. 1, fo. 113.

[11] *Collectio Sangermanensis*, IV, x, 23.

[12] James Raine (in his introduction to the *Register of Walter Gray*, xxviii) makes him a son of Archbishop Roger.　　[13] *BB*, 2.

[14] DC Durham, 4. 1. Pont. no. 10; *FPD*, 10, 100; *EYC*, II, no. 952; *EYC*, IX, no. 151.

Elias the clerk makes several attestations *c*. 1158–74.[1] Reginald and Stephen fined as sergeants in 1196,[2] and Master William of Norham, who is twice mentioned, appears to have held the chuch of Norton.[3]

There were further groups whose members presumably exercised specific functions. Four frequent witnesses, Masters Robert,[4] Nicholas, Hugh,[5] and Stephen[6] were *medici*—their difficult task to administer such small professional attentions as the bishop's hardy constitution required, or his determined will and sapid palate permitted.[7] Others were *capellani*; Simon, and his brother, Richard the almoner,[8] Radulf, John,[9] Master Walter,[10] Adam, Roger, Thomas, Elias (also described as chaplain 'of the archdeacon'), and Ernaldus, who was probably related to the bishop and received land in York City from the fitzHerberts.[11] Another group comprised those who were perhaps clerical officials in the modern sense of the word, and who test low in the witness list—the traditional place for the scribe. Their number included Herbert, Patrick and Silvester,[12] and the two Master Williams, almoners, of whom the senior held land in Stanhope in 1183,[13] whilst the junior fined as a clerk in 1196.[14] Either may be that William, *clericus scriptor*, who appears on one occasion.[15] In addition there were Master Adam, clerk and chaplain,[16] and Germanus (?Puiset),[17] perhaps the son of Archdeacon Burchard.[18] A certain Richard and Germanus appear once as 'notaries of the lord bishop'.[19]

---

[1] DC Durham, Cart. Misc. no. 7126; 2. 3. Sac. no. 5.

[2] *Chancellor's Roll 8 Richard I*, 259.

[3] DC Durham, 3. 1. Pont. no. 1 (see below, App. II, no. 10); *FPD*, 250.

[4] DC Durham, 3. 1. Pont. no. 3 (see below, App. II, no. 5).

[5] DC Durham, 3. 1. Pont. no. 4; *FPD*, 198 n.

[6] DC Durham, Cart. Misc. no. 7126; 3. 1. Pont. no. 3 (see below, App. II, no. 5).   [7] Newburgh, II, 439.

[8] DC Durham, 3. 1. Pont. no. 1 (see below, App. II, nos. 9, 10); *FPD*, 198 n.

[9] DC Durham, 2. 6. Spec. no. 69.   [10] DC Durham, 4. 1. Pont. no. 12.

[11] *Guisborough Cartulary*, II, no. mcxviii, where Ernaldus refers to a brother, Master Roger.

[12] DC Durham, 3. 1. Pont. no. 3 (see below, App. II, no. 5).

[13] *BB*, 30.   [14] *Chancellor's Roll 8 Richard I*, 257.

[15] *EYC*, II, no. 952.   [16] Brand, I, 238, note t.

[17] DC Durham, 3. 1. Pont. no. 8.   [18] *FPD*, 238.

[19] DC Durham, 4. 6. Spec. no. 45*, printed in *Memorials of St Giles's*, 213–14; for the use of the word 'notary', see Cheney, *Bishops' Chanceries*, 31–2.

In all it is fairly clear that episcopal servants were well rewarded. Clerks often received churches—frequently of the priory fee—and the majority of officers, lay and clerical, had grants of land either for service or sustenance. The economic wellbeing, inseparable from such patronage, is revealed alike in the careers of Richard the Engineer, Ralph Haget and Philip fitzHamo, and the enormous fines levied on Burchard Puiset (£156) and Peter of Sedgefield (£33) in 1196.[1] More surprising are the renders of more or less undistinguished sergeants like Adam of Arden, Laurence the chamberlain and Robert of St Oswald's (each £100),[2] suggesting the near financial affinity of the *serviens* to knights and barons. It is equally worthy of comment that hereditary influence, family favour and some contemporary development could be so successfully combined. The resultant organization was doubtless rudimentary, but the achievements of some of the Durham clerks, and the sensitivity of the episcopal 'chancery' to current changes show that at least some of its officers were more than amateurs. The greatest weakness was perhaps a certain political parochialism, for Puiset was for the most part out of the general stream of royal favour. It is easy to overestimate the practical consequence of the Blois connexion and ignore that close relationship to the sees of York and Lincoln or the long years spent by the bishop in the north. In this context it is worth recalling that whilst some of his entourage (Papedy, Farlington and Coleville)[3] found employment in Scotland, few, if any—with the exception of Henry and Burchard Puiset and William of Blois—achieved any position of distinction or made their way in the English royal service. It must, however, be added that many, being contemporaries of the bishop, were too old for advancement when his death restored the see to the course of favour.

It was as lord of the Liberty of Durham that Puiset enjoyed his greatest success, though it was a success of a more modest nature than that with which he has sometimes been credited.

---

[1] *Chancellor's Roll 8 Richard I*, 257.

[2] *Chancellor's Roll 8 Richard I*, 259.

[3] *Liber Sancte Marie de Melrose*, 1, no. 76; *Cartulary of Coldstream* (ed. C. Rogers) 4, no. 4; *Liber Sancte Marie de Calchou*, 1, no. 245; *Gesta*, 1, 98; *Registrum Episcopatus Glasguensis*, 1, nos. 13 and 29.

His episcopate was not a gallant defence of the jurisdictional rights of the franchise, for there was no attack to occasion such valour—it may even be doubted whether there was a worthy cause of battle. But if Puiset was generally left to enjoy the immunist's most important possessions, he had no autarchy thereby. Immunity easily became an idle word to monarchs such as Henry II or Edward I, and the crown intervened in the Liberty in a variety of ways as occasion and necessity demanded. Nor would it be just to see Puiset's career as a conscious effort to model the administration of the franchise on that of the kingdom. The developments of the early thirteenth century lie to the credit of Bishops Poitou and Marsh. Puiset was not of the world of John Cumin or Hubert Walter, and made little or no contribution to the design and operation of the legal reforms of Henry II. His administration was, therefore, largely of a pattern inherited from his predecessors. The passage in the Durham chronicle to which Lapsley attached such importance as illustrating legal change[1] more properly refers to ecclesiastical disputes and the bishop's aggressive economics. This was the true order of his interest, for he was of a family that knew the opulence of William fitzHerbert and the Medicean competence of Henry of Winchester. His task in 1154 was not to create or define a form and area of government, but to restore order and reorganize the sources of wealth in a diocese where unruly ambitions had recently enjoyed the liberties of St Barbara's episcopate. In this he succeeded admirably, and his long tenure of office brought a peace and security only superficially disrupted by national events or his own quarrels with his convent. His economics were those of the age. His wealth was that of a rentier, augmented by the spasmodic increments of rudimentary taxation. In the contemporary setting an increase in revenue was hardly possible except by the multiplication of sources (as opposed to their more effective exploitation). Thus the vast Durham demesne—in the broadest sense of the word— was valued chiefly as a source of subsistence and a fund for arrentation, whilst windfalls such as Northumberland were

---

[1] ...*et novis institutionibus antiquas episcopatus leges et consuetudines penitus immutasse* (*Scriptores Tres*, 8).

eagerly sought, and there were unending disputes over the ownership of land, tithes and churches, or the marginal profits of judicial pleas. Puiset never slumbered where money was in question. He was one of the few English bishops to survey *omnes redditus totius episcopatus sui* in a decade when monastic surveys were common.[1] Thus by greedy care he raised the fortunes which allowed him to indulge, if not to satisfy, his political ambitions, and so found some recompense for those larger glories more generally denied him.

[1] For an episcopal survey at Worcester see *The Red Book of Worcester*, ed. M. Hollings.

CHAPTER VI

CONCLUSION

HUGH PUISET died in 1195 after one of the longest
episcopates of the century. The activity of his busy
life is now recalled only by almost chance phrases and
a skeleton of dates, and it is difficult to ensnare in words those
qualities of the man which could sustain some respect in
Henry II and Richard I, and win the ungrudging admiration
of the chronicler of Durham's oppressions.[1]

The bishop was one whose character combined the masterful
energies of his early ancestors with the charm and refinement
of the Blois princes. He was, especially if the nature of his life
be considered, clearly a man of extraordinarily hardy constitution. Nor, if Newburgh's anecdotes of the gastronomic feats
of his last days be accepted, can his longevity be attributed to
any especial concern for self-preservation. He had an ample
endowment of that health and vigour which had made his
family so formidable in various parts of the world, and almost
the first and last notices we have of him show him in active
command of an army in the field.

He was of superb presence, tall and striking, much, in fact,
like his one-time namesake whose appearance had so delighted
and troubled Emma of Jericho and Melisende of Jerusalem.[2]
A lover of pomp, he was proud and majestic on solemn
occasions with the assured dignity of stature. Yet, when he
chose, he could be genial, affable and open-handed, and had a
full measure of that amiability which all remarked in Stephen.
As an active man of affairs, more interested in the field than the
acquisition of learning, he was not well educated. Nevertheless,
like his uncle of Winchester, *Marco voce priorem*,[3] he was naturally
eloquent and persuasive, and thereby a good mediator.

[1] Puiset's character is discussed by Newburgh (ii, 437–41) and in *Scriptores
Tres* (8, 12, 13); cf. also Stubbs, 213–14.
[2] Cf. *Scriptores Tres*, 4 and William of Tyre (R.H.C. Occ. i), 628–9.
[3] Boase, *English Art, 1100–1216*, 170.

Behind this gracious façade there lay a ruthlessness which made him an unscrupulous and dangerous opponent, and the pride and arrogance of the grandee. There was about his career a superficial sense of realized ambition, and in his style such opulence and magnificence as Newburgh could only convey in the words of Ecclesiastes, 'And whatsoever mine eyes desired I kept not from them, I withheld not my heart from any joy'.[1] He travelled, hunted or sailed in regal glory. At Durham he built that he might outstrip the reputations of his predecessors, just as in the preparations for his projected crusade the aim was *ut majorum Episcoporum sive Ducum gloriam superaret*,[2] and in all his pious gestures there is a blend of natural ostentation.

He had the practical competence that could support such aspirations, and organized the finances or led the armies of his see with equal ease and success. Neither in getting nor spending was he stayed by any inhibitions. There was in his economics a single-mindedness less clearly revealed in other aspects of his career, and having decided to spend he was capable of pouring out wealth in a fashion which soon became legendary.[3] As a politician he was clearly not without astuteness. He had the elementary art of fostering faction, though, as is so often the case, his touch was somewhat heavy and his manœuvres sufficiently obvious to be remarked.[4] Nevertheless, it would be a serious underestimation of his ability to hold that the comparative ease with which he extricated himself from difficulties was due entirely to his wealth. In detail, though not in sum, his career is unimpressive. His restless energy was partnered by a will for which gold too often opened easy ways. His ambitions outstripped reality and his arrogance misjudged opponents. His behaviour in 1190 was perhaps the exhibition of the worst sort of patrician pride; a belief that one of the blood royal was immune from the ordinary workings of political chance, which delivered him directly into the hands of William de Longchamp. Determined and ruthless in his own interests he was nevertheless not free from that fatal indecision which had marred both Stephen and Henry of Winchester. He could crush a weak man like

[1] Eccles. ii. 10.
[2] *Scriptores Tres*, 13.
[3] Newburgh, II, 437.
[4] *Scriptores Tres*, 8.

Prior Thomas by a show of rage, but he was hesitant before his equals. There was a certain blustering arrogance about him, and, as his contemporaries remarked, more than a touch of the tyrant.[1]

It was Stubbs's opinion that Puiset's episcopate 'left a mark upon the north of England which is not yet effaced'.[2] This it is difficult to accept, for the nature of his rule did little to alter, except in an architectural and fiscal sense, the condition of his see. The Liberty of Durham was in organized existence by 1153. It experienced no threat of extinction, and underwent no major institutional change, before 1195. In many matters the bishop was more qualified to receive than to give. He came to a society intellectually less parochial than that which was to grace the same setting in many subsequent centuries. The church of Durham had known and felt characters as different, and talents as diverse, as those of Prior Turgot, and Bishops St Calais, Flambard and Rufus. It was already responsible for the great, and in many ways revolutionary, cathedral of St Cuthbert. Architecturally its influence had affected not only the north, but also other regions of the kingdom,[3] and in art and literature it was then at the height of its powers. There can be little doubt that had the conditions of Stephen's reign prevailed somewhat longer, Puiset would have shone more clearly in that role of defender of his church for which the Durham community had cast him, and in which, despite his manifold shortcomings and blunders, they persisted in seeing him.[4] As it was, his most important achievement hardly lies to his credit, for by his surrender of 1195 he provided the convent with what was in effect a charter of liberties which was to embitter the relations of bishop and prior for the next century and a half.

It is inevitable to compare his career with that of his uncle and one-time mentor, Henry of Winchester. In both there was the same magnificence, ambition, versatility and practical financial ability, and in both the eventual strain of inefficacy that marked the house of Blois. The differences are almost as much a measure of change as of character. Winchester, thwarted in his hopes for Canterbury, turned his will to raise his see to an

---

[1] *Scriptores Tres*, 12.
[2] Stubbs, 213.
[3] Cf. Boase, *op. cit.* 22–4.
[4] *Scriptores Tres*, 9, 12.

archbishopric,[1] yet lived to end his days in genuine piety. Puiset, ever more prince than bishop, unchanged and untaught, moved from ambition to ambition to seek his greatest secular splendour at the very end of his life. Yet the chances were unequal; Henry had already lived his greatest days through a world of political mediocrity and anarchy when the Angevin came to the throne, whereas an untimely twist of fortune deprived Puiset of that career to which his will, if not his abilities, impelled him, and only when he was too old did he see such an opportunity as that which had once made Winchester the king-maker of his age.

He died burdened, if not perhaps enriched, by an experience few can have equalled. He had touched life at most points, from the amatory adventures of youth to the dignity and responsibility of viceregal office. Like most of his contemporaries of comparable status he was affected by those great movements which determined the pattern of the age. He knew something of current theology. He hearkened, if wilfully and spasmodically, to the dictates of royal and papal policy. Yet his long life has left little mark in history. At no stage did he give a decisive twist to the course of events. He lived through one of the greatest eras of the Middle Ages, yet for many of its most important aspects he showed but small affinity. He was no canonist in the world of Alexander III. He contributed nothing to those legal and administrative reforms which made the reign of Henry II so important in the history of secular government. He saw, almost heedless, the great quarrel of Church and State which brought Becket and Henry II face to face. Beyond an undeniable competence to organize the financial basis of power and splendour, his episcopate was a succession of unrealized ambitions. He never really understood, and only impatiently tolerated, a world beyond the turbulence of his youth; 1189 was to have been as the 1140's. Though his grandeur perhaps set the style by which Durham was to be known until the Reformation, he is now best remembered in those things he would have regarded as the trappings of his glory: his buildings and his books. He was, as Stubbs justly wrote, one who had held a great position without being a great man.

[1] John of Salisbury, *Historia Pontificalis*, 80.

APPENDICES

APPENDICES

NOTE

In the following Appendices the abbreviations listed below have been used for convenience in indicating variant readings:

A	Reg. I	F	Cart. II
B	Reg. II	G	Cart. III
C	Reg. III	H	Cart. IV
D	Reg. IV	I	Parv. Cart.
E	Cart. I	J	Cart. Elemos.

Where a document has survived in its original form the spelling, grammar and punctuation have been retained in transcription.

A LETTER FROM
THE CONVENT OF DURHAM
RELATING TO THE ELECTION OF
1153

Capitulum Sancti Cuthberti Dunelmensis ecclesie uniuersum
fidelibus et Amicis suis. cunctisque paci et unitati studentibus
Seruare unitatem spiritus in uinculo pacis.[1] / Urget pondus instantis
necessitatis, nostre turbationis causam, uestrae karitatis auribus
intimare. Subito nemphe ex diutina depressione aecclesiae / nostre
quietem sperantibus. turbarum procella metum incussit, et quietis
portum prope tenentes. in ipso nos tempestatum profundo, rediuiua
procella suscepit. / Vnde cum psalmista clammare compellimur,
Saluum me fac deus quoniam intrauerunt aque usque ad animam
meam.[2] Orbati iam pridem patre nostro pie / memorie Domino
Willelmo ecclesie nostre presule, mestitia et confusione repleti
fueramus, unde et mestum factum est cor nostrum, contenebrati sunt
occuli nostri.[3] / Nos tamen gemitus gratiam respexisse supernam
credidimus quam unitatem spiritus in uinculo pacis[4] nobis contulisse
presenseramus. Siquidem muneris ipsius / esse credebamus qui
pater est misericordiarum et deus totius consolationis.[5] quod nec
clerus a monachis, nec a clero populus in episcopo eligendo dis-
sideret, set ad / exemplum primitiue illius ecclesie, multitudinis
esset cor unum et Anima una.[6] Patrum itaque uestigiis inherentes,
secundum libertatem ecclesie dei / diuinitus collatam. secundum
usum et consuetudinem in ecclesia nostra hactenus in eligendo
episcopo obseruatam, in unum conueniente totius episcopatus /
clero, presentibus religiosis quibusque totius episcopatus personis,
inuocata spiritus sancti gratia, electus est in episcopatum dunelmensis ecclesie dominus Hvgo thesaura/rius et Archidiaconus
Eboracensis ecclesiae, uir honeste uite et fame celebris. et quantum
ad humanum spectat intuitum tanto sacerdotio ido/neus, cui nec
litteratura deesse uideretur ad doctrinam. nec morum reuerentia
ad uite commendationem. Tantam denique in / electione ipsa
concordiam et uidimus et testamur ut non solum contradictorem
non habuerit. sed animis singulorum alacritatem non mediocrem

[1] Eph. iv. 3.   [2] Ps. lxix. 1.   [3] Lam. v. 17.
[4] Eph. iv. 3.   [5] II Cor. i. 3.   [6] Acts iv. 32.

ingesserit, / Aderant congrua alacritatis inditia, lacrime plurimorum quas gaudii magnitudo et pastoris recuperandi certitudo produxerat. ut etiam uocem iubilationis / communiter a cunctis celebrandam singulorum deuotio preueniret. Nec mora. singulorum in unum concordante sententia, te deum laudamus solempniter / decantatur. et res illi committur cui ab initio commissa fuerat. ut uidelicet spiritus sanctus actiones nostras et aspirando preueniret, et adiuuan/ do prosequeretur. Non multum temporis intercesserat. cum durus ad nos nuntius delabitur dominum Archiepiscopum Eboracensem maiores ecclesie nostre perso/nas de contemptu et inobedientia calumpniatos ad satisfactionem uocasse. et terminum sententiae[1] in ipsis proferende ad proximam tertiam feriam / posuisse. Quo audito continuo persone ad hoc opus idonee ad eundem diriguntur, quae et electionem nostram ipsius notitie representa/rent. et satisfactionem pro personis aecclesiae congruam offerrent. Dominus uero Archiepiscopus nec satisfactionem offerentes suscipere uoluit. nec electio/ nem auditu quidem dignam iudicauit. Insuper et post oblatam taliter satisfactionem infra terminum primitus a se constitutum, in capella sua clausis / ianuis in maiores quasdam ecclesie nostrae personas sententiam dedit. et electionem nostram taliter ut premisimus procedentem infirmauit. Super / his turbatus est pre ira occulus noster,[2] uersus est in luctum chorus noster.[3] Et qui pridem in ymnis et confessionibus dominum unanimi deuotione glorificamus,[4] nunc / in salicibus babiloniei fluminis organa nostra suspendere compellimur.[5] Secundum multitudinem igitur dolorum cordium nostrorum[6] consolationes karitatis / fraterne letificent animas nostras. attendentium illud poeticum, Et tua res agitur paries cum proximus ardet.[7] Modum nostre actionis intimauimus / Si errori deputari debet quod actum est consilium querimus necessitatis Sin rationi auxilium promotionis exposcimus. Nostre sane conscien/cie innocentia et libertate confisi libere protestamur. nos pro necessitate temporis communi non proprie utilitati quantum ad nos attinet consuluisse / aecclesiae nostre inuiolatam hactenus libertatem quesisse. et quod honestius et utilius arbitramur pro defensione ecclesie nostrae in hac electione / considerasse. Valete.

ORIGINAL: DC Durham, Loc. VI, no. 12.

SIZE: 8 × 8½ in. Written in a small charter hand on parchment. The foot of the document has been cut for the insertion of a tail.

[1] *m* erased. [2] Cf. Ps. vi. 7. [3] Lam. v. 15.
[4] II Macc. x. 38. [5] Cf. Ps. cxxxvii. 1, 2.
[6] Ps. xciii. 19. [7] Horace, *Epistles*, I, 18, 84.

SELECT DOCUMENTS

I

Archbishop Roger of York and Bishop Hugh of Durham inform Bishop Roger of Worcester of their execution of a mandate concerning Master H. of Southwell (1175–6)

R. Eboracensis archiepiscopus et H. Dunelmensis (episcopus) R. Wigorniensi episcopo.

Literas domni pape in hanc formam recepimus:

Ex constanti relatione dilecti filii nostri H. sancti Angeli diaconi cardinalis et ex literis, quas idem cardinalis nobis exhibuit, evidenter cognovimus, quod magister H. de Suellis literas tibi, frater archiepiscope, falsas exhibuit. Verum cum idem H. diceret literas illas se tibi non reddidisse, tandem sufficientia testium est probatum, quod easdem literas tibi reddiderit et cum idem cardinalis ipsum vellet sicut falsarium condempnare, idem H. ad nostram audientiam appellavit, cui appellationi idem cardinalis ita duxit, quod grave gerimus, deferendum, quod postmodum magnarum personarum supplicatione inductus eidem H. ad tempus pepercit. Quoniam igitur decet nos tam gravem excessum durius vindicare, ut alii exemplo pene illius similia attemptare formident, fraternitati vestre per apostolica scripta precipiendo mandamus, quatinus predictum H. ecclesiis de Eperest et de Salford contradictione et appellatione cessante spoliantes perpetuum ei silentium super eisdem ecclesiis imponatis et ipsum nullius contradictione vel appellatione obstante nichilominus in aliquo monasterio recludetis, ubi possit, quod tam nequiter egit, lamentis penitentie emendare.

Apostolicam itaque sententiam iuxta formam prescriptam auctoritate apostolica executioni mandantes predictum H. tanquam falsarium a domno papa condempnatum tam de ecclesia de Eper quam de ecclesia de Salfor spoliamus et eidem super ipsis repetendis perpetuum silentium imponamus, reliqua, que in misericordia domni pape continentur, ordine suo et tempore Deo annuente completuri.

TEXT: *Collectio Bridlingtoniensis*, c. 152, Oxford, Bodleian MS., 357 fo. 123ᵛ.

The churches mentioned in the text are those of Epperstone and Shelford (Notts). The document can be dated by the reference to the legate, Hugh, who was in England 1175–6 (H. Tillmann, *Die Päpstlichen Legaten in England bis zur Beendigung der Legation Gualas*, 73–7).

2

Notification of the settlement of a dispute between Nicholas, prior of Lancaster, and Norman the clerk, concerning the church of Melling and the chapel of Gressingham (Lancashire) (1154–95)

Hugo dei gratia Dunelmensis episcopus, Universis sancte dei ecclesie, salutem. Noverit universitas vestra controversiam que inter Nicholaum priorem de Lancastre et Normannum clericum super ecclesia de Mellingues et capella de Wersingueham vertebatur, ita in presentia nostra, transactione inveniente, sopitam esse, quod prefatus prior concessit eidem Normanno ecclesiam predictam, cum prefata capella, tenendam in vita sua de ecclesia beate Marie de Lancastre per annuam pensionem xx solidorum, reddendo x ad Pentecosten et x ad festum sancti Martini. Hanc autem transactionem fidei interpositione factam auctoritate nobis a domino Pape commissa confirmavimus, et hac charta nostra confirmamus.

TEXT: P.R.O. Transcripts (31/8/140), *Cartulaire de la Basse Normandie*, vol. III, 187, no. 15, from the *Livre Blanc de l'abbaye de S Martin de Séez*.

CALENDARED: *Cal. Doc. France*, no. 671.

3

Notification of a mediation by Hugh, bishop of Durham, Clement, abbot of St Mary's, York, and Silvanus, abbot of Rievaulx, in a dispute between the convent of Bury St Edmunds and the nuns of Stixwould over the church of Wainfleet (Lincolnshire) (1183)

[Hugo] dei gratia Dunelmensis Episcopus et C[lemens] sancte marie Eboracensis et S[ilvanus] Riauallensis eadem gratia abbates. omnibus ad quos etc. salutem. Vniversitati uestre notum esse [quod] controuersiam que uertebatur, in presentia nostra, ex mandato

APPENDIX II

domini lucii pape .III. inter abbatem Samsonem et monachos sancti aedmundi et Robertum clericum de Scresdefeld, super ecclesia sancte marie de Waynflet et eius capella hoc fine quieuisse. scilicet quod moniales de stikeswald quarum nomine idem Robertus ecclesiam ipsam tenebat eam in perpetuum tenebunt et reddent ecclesie sancti aedmundi de eadem ecclesia nomine transactionis singulis annis quadraginta sextaria salis, in festo sancti petri ad uincula apud Waineflet. Capella autem de Waineflet libera remanebit ecclesie sancti aedmundi et monachis eiusdem loci. ita quod per monachos occasione illius capelle in nullo leditur ius matricis ecclesie. et precipue ut monachus uel monachi qui ibidem manserint uel illuc uenerint, extra antiqua septa illius capelle nullum ius parochiale exerceant neque in terra neque mari. nec in eadem capella aliquis secularis presbiter nomine monachorum ministrabit, nisi de consensu matricis ecclesie. Convenit etiam quod nullam nisi religiosam personam ad uiaticum uel penitenciam suscipiendam, monachi ibidem admittant. nisi fuerit pro penuria sacerdotis matricis ecclesie et immineat egrotanti mortis articulus. Prefatus autem R[obertus] toto tempore uite sue ecclesiam ipsam de monialibus tenebit. reddendo eis singulis annis .xx. sextaria salis nomine pensionis. Abbas uero de Bardeneia, qui in uita p[redicti] R[oberti] bizantium unum a prefatis monialibus recipit et post eius decessum .ii. marcas de ecclesia ipsa ab eisdem est recepturus, litteris suis nobis signicavit, quod composicionem que de auctoritate nostra et uoluntate et assensu parcium fieret, ratam haberet et firmiter obseruaret. Adiectum est etiam et fidei religione utriusque firmatum quod per hanc transactionem remisse sunt undique omnes controuersie et omnes inurie a quacumque persona circumque parte ab alterutra parte illate. promiserunt etiam unanimiter quod nullus eorum quos contingebat negocium istud alii super iamdictam ecclesiam uel eius aliqua porcione in posterum mouebit questionem. aut motam aut summissam aut summittendam personam suscitabit. Hanc autem transactionem se firmiter observaturos abbas sancti aedmundi et frater hugo canonicus procurator monialium litteris ex inde rati habicionis exibitis ex parte monialium et antedictus Robertus fide interposita promiserunt. et nos eandem sigillorum nostrorum appositione communiamus, et auctoritate apostolica confirmamus. Acta sunt hec, anno ab incarnacione domini M. Centisimo. Lxxxiii.

TEXT: P.R.O. Duchy of Lancaster, D.L. 42, Miscellaneous Books, no. 5, *Cartulary of Bury St Edmunds*, fo. 52.

4

Bishop Hugh grants to his convent the same liberty it had when
he acceded to the see (1154-7)

H[ugo] dei gratia Dun[elmensis] Episcopus. Omnibus suis successoribus et parrochianis Sancti Cuthberti. tam presentibus quam
successuris salutem et bene/dictionem. Sciatis uos qui presentes
estis. Sciant et posteri nostri, quod ego hvgo episcopus eandem
libertatem ecclesie sancte Marie / et Sancti cuthberti. et monachis in
eadem ecclesia deo seruientibus do. / et concedo quam eadem
ecclesia et fratres in eadem comorantes ha/buerunt ea die qua ad
episcopatum dunelmensem dei gratia non meis meritis consecratus
sum. tam in ecclesiis quam in uillis et in / terris. et in siluis et in
aquis. et in omnibus aliis rebus quibus predicti fratres eadem die
saisiti et inuestiti erant. Concessi etiam / priori et eis ut ad dispositionem omnium rerum suarum liberam in omnibus habeant
facultatem. Et nullus eis super hoc queso / sit molestus. sed in his
et in omnibus aliis que teste deo concessi. plenam ex integro habeant
potestatem. salua in / omnibus mea episcopali autoritate. His
test[ibus]. Cuthberto priore de Giseburna, Johanne archidiacono,
Hugone de fuddebi / Johanne de Rana. Sim[one] camerario,
Thoma de Sedecim vallibus.

ORIGINAL: DC Durham, 4. 1. Pont. no. 14.

SIZE: 7 × 2½ in., written in a small cursive hand on a sheet of
unruled parchment. There is a double tail at the foot of the document, but no seal.

ENDORSED: *Hugonis epi de libertatibus nostris. Secundam tertie, non
registratur* (thirteenth century).

A date of 1154-7 is suggested by a reference to what is probably
this charter in the bull *Religiosis desideriis* of Adrian IV (3 February
1157; *PU*, II, no. 94). The text of the charter, which, it will be
noticed, is free from the language of the forgeries, is almost identical
with that issued by the repentant Flambard (DC Durham 2. 1. Pont.
no. 2, printed in *Scriptores Tres*, App. no. xx).

5

Licence to the convent of Durham to appropriate the church
of Elvet after the death of the incumbent, Master Richard of
Coldingham. The monastery is also to have control of institution to the chapels of Witton and Croxdale (1189-95)

H[ugo] d[e]i gr[ati]a Dunelmen[sis] Ep[is]c[opus] Omnib[us]
S[an]c[t]e matris Eccl[es]ie filiis ad quos litt[er]e p[re]sentes
per/uenerint, sal[u]t[em] in domino. Sciat vniuersitas u[est]ra
q[uo]d nos paci filiorum nostrorum et quieti. monachorum / scilicet
in Eccl[es]ia Dunelmen[si] deo seruientium parit[er] et vtilitati
pat[er]na sollicitudine p[ro]uidere uolen/tes in posterum, Eccl[es]iam
de Alueta¹ cu[m] Capellis et om[n]ib[us] reb[us] ad eam pertinenti-
b[us] eis Ep[iscop]ali au/toritate et presentis scripti munimine confirmamus (*sic*) Statuentes ut post decessum Mag[ist]ri Ric[ardi] / De
Coldingha[m] cui prefatam Eccl[es]iam sub annua pensione quam
disposuerunt tenendam et ha/bendam in uita sua contulerunt, eam
omnino lib[er]am in manu sua sine alterius persone / p[re]sentatione
uel institutione retineant, eoru[m] usib[us] et hospitu[m] omnimodis
in perpetuum profu/turam. Ita dum taxat q[uo]d in ipsa Eccl[es]ia
et in Capella de Wittona. quam loci necessitate remotiori[em] / con-
struxim[us] et Cimit[er]ium dedicauimus. Et in Capella de Crocke-
steil² idoneos³ sacerdotes ad libitum / suum remouendos instituent
qui tam matrici Eccl[esi]e quam Capellis deseruient. Prior uero /
Dunelm[ensis] tanquam persona Synodalia et Ep[iscop]alia soluet.
sicut alie persone Ep[iscop]atus facere / solent. Siquis aut[em] huic
nostre constitutioni sciens contraire temptau[er]it, iram et In-
dignati/onem dei omnipotentis et Inp[re]catione[m] beatissimi⁴
Cuthb[er]ti nisi resipuerit, incurrat. Qui/cunque uero seruauerint,
Eiusdem pat[ri]s p[re]cibus et m[er]itis deo largiente felicitatis
et[er]ne / p[re]mia consequantur.⁵ Hiis testib[us]. Will[el]mo
archid[iacono] Sim[one] Cam[erario]. Mag[ist]ro Ric[ardo] de
Coldingham. / Mag[istro] Will[el]mo blesens[i]. Mag[istro]
steph[ano] lincoln[iensi]. Will[el]mo filio archiepiscopi. Will[el]mo
de houed' / henrico de augo. Arnaldo et Sim[one] Capellanis
Ep[iscop]i. Mag[ist]ro Joh[ann]e de houed'. Will[el]mo Ele/mosi-
nario. Rad[ulfo] dapif[er]o. Mag[ist]ro Steph[ano] medico.
Mag[ist]ro Ric[ardo] de lindes[eia].⁶ Mag[ist]ro Walt[ero] / de
adi[n]gtona. Rob[erto] de adi[n]gtona. helia Capellano archi-
d[iaconi]. Will[elm]o de Infirm[ario]. Walt[ero] / p[re]sb[ite]ro filio
dolfini. Mag[ist]ro ham[one]. Mag[ist]ro Ang[er]io. Rob[erto]
medico. Walt[ero] / de kettona. / Pat[ri]cio cl[er]i[c]o. Silu[est]re
cl[er]ico et Aliis multis.

ORIGINAL: DC Durham, 3. 1. Pont. no. 3.
ENDORSED: 1. *C' hug' epi' de eccl'ia de Elued* (early thirteenth
century). 2. *Eluet.* 3 *prime pont. C.* 1. (fifteenth century). 3. *Prime* 8
...(fifteenth century). 4. 3 16 *sp'alium. B.* 1 (sixteenth century).

¹ *elueta* I and F.   ² *crokestail* I and F.   ³ *ydoneos* I.
⁴ *beati* I.   ⁵ I finishes.   ⁶ *lyndesey* F.

SIZE: 9½ × 8½ in. The writing of the charter does not follow as closely as its phraseology the style of the papal chancery. It is a large bold hand, set out irregularly on a sheet of unruled parchment. Margins have been left on all sides of the text, including one of some two inches at the foot of the document, where the scribe appears to have made a vain attempt to use his liberal allowance of parchment by opening the spacing of his lines. There is a good seal in green wax (varnished) hanging *sur double queue*, though it is not possible to observe those minute details noted by Greenwell and Blair (*Durham Seals*, II , 443, n. 28).

COPIES: DC Durham, Parv. Cart. (Pont.), fo. 16ᵛ; Cart II, fo. 272ᵛ.

6

Restoration to Roger, the parson of Howden, of tithes the bishop had granted to the hospital of St Giles (*c.* 1180–5)

H[ugo] d[e]i gr[ati]a Dunelm[ensis] ep[is]c[opus] Priori.[1] archidiaconis. et om[n]ib[us] cl[er]icis et laicis toti[us] ep[isco]patus sui. francis et angl[icis], sal[u]t[em]. Sciatis nos reddidisse. et conces/sisse. et p[re]senti carta confirmasse. Rog[ero] de Houedena et eccl[esi]e S[an]cti Petri de Houed[ena] in p[er]petuum omnes decimas et obuent[i]o[n]es tam in frugib[us] quam / in aliis rebus de quibus decime dari debent. de sartis. paludibus. et mareschis[2] quocunque m[odo] p[ro]uen[er]int. et de om[n]ib[us] t[er]ris q[ue] m[odo] culte s[un]t. uel in post[er]um colen/tur infra t[er]minos parrochie eccl[esi]e de Houed[ena] a quocunque culte fu[er]int. Et quia decimas de t[er]ris q[ua]s de paludib[us] et frutectis et mareschis[2] arab[i]les fecimus / Hospitali S[an]cti Egidii de Dunelmo ded[er]am[us]. et cartis d[omi]ni p[a]p[e] et d[omi]ni Reg[is] confirmari fec[er]amus, assensu et concessione Ade de Karrum qui t[un]c t[em]p[or]is p[ro]/curator erat eiusdem hospital[is] p[re]dictam donat[i]o[n]em reuocauimus. et cartam nostram quam p[re]dicto hospitali de sup[ra]dictis decimis ded[er]amus, in p[re]sentia nostra et / multorum aliorum frangi fecimus. cartis d[omi]ni p[a]pe et d[omi]ni Reg[is] quantum ad illas decimas adu[er]sus eccl[esi]am de Houed[ena] null[um] unquam robur habentib[us] uel habi/turis. Nos au[tem] inde[m]pnitati eccl[esi]e de Houed[ena] in post[er]um p[re]cauentes. sepe dicto Hospitali S[an]c[t]i[3] Egidii de nostro satisfecimus et ne aliquo t[em]p[or]e quicquam sibi de / decimis infra parrochiam eccl[esi]e de houed[ena] uendicare possit, da[m]pnum

---

[1] G adds *et*.   [2] *mariscis* I and G.   [3] *scilicet* G.

q[uo]d de reuocat[i]one decimar[um] illar[um] sustinuit, ei reco[m]-
pensauim[us]. Volumus etiam q[uo]d / eccl[esi]a de Houed[ena]
omnes rectitudines et decimat[i]o[n]es tam de t[er]ris illis q[ue]
t[em]p[or]e illo q[uo] hanc cartam fecimus culte fuerunt quam
de illis[1] q[ue] in post[er]um erant colende. et de / omnibus aliis
reb[us] infra parrochiam suam de quibus decime dari debe[n]t
sic[ut] de cet[er]is t[er]ris cultis dari sole[n]t, libere et s[i]n[e] ulla
diminut[i]o[n]e p[er]cipiat. Et quicunque hanc / n[ost]re confirma-
tionis paginam infirmare uel infringere temptau[er]it, indigna-
t[i]o[n]em dei om[n]ipot[e]ntis. et beatorum apostolorum[2] Petri et
Pauli. et beati Cuthb[er]ti et nostram, / se nou[er]it incursurum.[3]
Testibus Germano priore Dunelmensi. Will[el]mo archidiacono et
Hug[one] de Puteaco fratre suo. Sim[one] cam[er]ario. Mag[ist]ro
Ric[ardo] de Cholding[ham] / Mag[ist]ro Will[el]mo Blesen[si].
Will[el]mo de Houed[ena]. Will[el]mo filio archiep[isco]pi.
Mag[ist]ro Walt[er]o et Thoma et Ernaldo capellanis. Mag[ist]ro
Hamo[n]e. Rad[ulfo] de Cestria. Will[elm]o / elemosin[ario].
Ric[ardo] cl[er]ico. Henr[ico] de Puteaco. Gilleb[erto] hausard.
Mich[aele] filio Brienni. Ric[ardo] de parca. Regin[aldo] de
Anesleia. Will[elm]o pulano. Ric[ardo] de Wa/rewic. Ric[ardo]
filio Hawise. Jacobo de Selebi. Rob[erto] filio Grai. et multis aliis.

ORIGINAL: DC Durham, 4. 1. Pont. no. 12.
ENDORSED: 1. *C hug' epi' de decimis ecclie' de houedene de t'ris cultis
et incultis* (thirteenth century). *s. d'micis suis ecclie' de houeden i'tegre
soluend'* (fourteenth century). 2. 4ᵃ 9ᵐᵉ *D. houden'* (fifteenth century).
3. 4ᵃ *prime pont. M.2.* (fifteenth century).
SIZE: 9½ × 6 in. The charter is written in a neat, close, spiky hand
on a sheet of unlined parchment without margins. The writing is
characterized by the long tails attached to initial capitals and final
consonants, especially 'r' and 's'. There is a good seal in white wax
(varnished) attached to a tapering double tail some 9 in. in length.
COPIES: DC Durham, Parv. Cart. (Pont.) fo. 17ᵛ; Cart. III, fo. 10ᵛ.

This document must have been issued before the end of 1189,
since it is witnessed by Prior Germanus. Gilbert Hansard, who tests
high among the laymen, is presumably that Gilbert who died before
1185 (see above, p. 225), for his son was not of age till the end of
Puiset's episcopate. The charter was confirmed by Celestine III on
27 March 1192 (*PU*, II, no. 269).

[1] *tempore illo...quam de illis* omitted in I.
[2] *Petri et Pauli apostolorum* I and G.
[3] I and G end.

HUGH DU PUISET

7

Grant by Puiset to the convent of Durham, as compensation
for former oppressions, of the vill of Newton, acquired from
Eustace Balliol (March 1195)

H[ugo] d[e]i gr[ati]a dunelm[ensis] ep[is]c[opus] Om[n]ibus
S[an]cte matris eccl[esi]e filiis sal[u]t[em]. Sciatis nos in reco[m]-
pe[n]/satione[m] grauaminvm q[ue] eccl[esi]e b[eat]i Cuthb[er]ti
intulimus concessisse. dedisse. et hac p[re]senti carta n[ost]ra / confirmasse deo et b[eat]o Cuthb[er]to. et priori dunelm[en]si et
conuentui eiusdem loci.¹ villam nostram de / de (sic) Neutona cum
o[mn]ibus ad eam pertinentibus. quam h[ab]uimus in excambium
pro Westwic.²/et pro cccc. marcis sterlingorum quas inde Eustatio
de Baillol³ dedim[us]. In puram et p[er]petv/am elemosinam.
lib[er]am. et quietam ab om[n]i seculari s[er]uicio. et exactione.
Quare uolumus quod ide[m] prior et conuent[us] eiusdem loci.
teneant. habeant. et possidea[n]t, / p[re]dictam villam de Neuton.
Cum om[n]ibus ad eam p[er]tine[n]tibus. lib[er]am. et quietam./In
Bosco et plano. In p[ra]tis et pascuis. In uiis et semitis. In aquis.
moris. mari/cis.⁴ molendinis et stagnis.⁵ et⁶ omnibus aliis reb[us] ad
p[re]dictam villam de Nevtona / p[er]tinentibus. Hiis T[estibus].⁷
Arnulfo abbate de Rievall. Will[elmo] abb[at]e de Ruhford.
Burc/cardo Thesaur[ario] Ebor[acensi]. Will[elmo] Archid[iacono]
dunelmensi. Mag[ist]ro Will[elm]o de Bleis. Mag[ist]ro / Ric[ardo]
de Coldigh[am]. Rog[er]o p[er]sona de Hoved[ena]. Philippo
canon[ico] de Bev[er]l[eia]. Hug[one] / de feritate. Will[elmo]
fil[io] archiep[iscop]i. steph[an]o de heinden[a]. Germano cl[er]ico. /
Ric[ardo] Heiron. Michaele fil[io] Will[elmi]. Nichol[ao] medico.
Et multis aliis. /

ORIGINAL: DC Durham, 3. 1. Pont. no. 8.

ENDORSED: 1. *Carta hug' epi' de Neutona* (thirteenth century) *dat'
priori et monach' dun'* (fourteenth century). 2. *Neuton'* (fifteenth
century). 3. *3ᵃ prime pont H.I.* (fifteenth century). 4. On the back
of the seal tail the letter 'C', either fourteenth or fifteenth century.

SIZE: 6 × 5½ in. The charter is written in a neat, small, spiky hand,
with occasional tendencies to elongate the ascenders and tails of
such letters as s, p, and r, and to decorate certain capitals such as the
initial H of Hugo, and some subsequent E's and Q's. The parchment
has been ruled in crayon, and margins left on all sides of the text.

¹ I omits *eiusdem loci.*   ² *Westwich* I, *Westwyk* F.   ³ *balleolo* I.
⁴ I adds *in.*   ⁵ *stangnis* I.   ⁶ I adds *in.*   ⁷ F ends.

258

There is a fractured seal in white wax (varnished) hanging *sur double queue*.

COPIES: DC Durham, Parv. Cart. fo. 15ᵛ; Cart. II, fo. 119.

This charter was almost certainly issued at Howden in March, 1195, as Puiset lay in his final illness, surrounded by three Cistercian abbots, his own children and an impressive array of doctors (cf. nos. 8, 9, 10.). In *c.* 1218 one Richard Brown, *laicus et libere conditionis*, testified that he was present when Puiset restored to the convent of Durham their wood of Heworth *apud Houedene, tercio die antequam obiit, per cartam suam. (FPD,* 263.) The document recording this restoration *(FPD,* 108) is witnessed by an almost identical assembly to that which appears in the present charter. The Durham chronicler also states that whilst at Howden Puiset returned a number of properties, together with Newton, *quam propriis sumptibus emerat (Scriptores Tres,* 15).

8

Grant to the convent of Durham of free control of its churches, with quittance therein from episcopal and archidiaconal aids and exactions (March 1195)

Hugo d[e]i gr[ati]a Dunelm[ensis] Ep[is]c[opus] Om[n]ib[us] s[an]cte Matris eccl[es]ie filiis ad quos presens carta peruenerit. sal[ute]m. Sciatis nos concessisse et presenti carta confirmasse deo / et beato Cuthb[er]to et B[ertramo] priori et conuentui Dunelm[ensis] eccl[es]ie inperpetuum liberam disposicionem. et institucionem. et personatum Omnium eccl[es]iarum suarum. et capellarum / ad eas pertinencium. et uolumus ut uacantibus ecclesiis suis in proprios usus et in propria manu sua eas retineant. inperpetuum. et Capellanos pro uoluntate sua ineis con/stituant. qui eccl[es]iis et Capellis honeste deseruiant. et ep[iscop]alia persoluant. Concedimus etiam ut in ipsis eccl[es]iis suis quieti sint et liberi inperpetuum ab omnibus con/suetudinibus. auxiliis. et hospiciis. et exactionibus omnium successorum nostrorum episcoporum et archidiacon[orum]. et omnium officialium. Quare uolumus et districte p[re]cipimus / quatinus predicti prior et conuentus habeant et teneant inperpetuum supradictas lib[er]tates et iura. lib[er]e et quiete. et honorifice. sicut predictum est. Si quis uero huic / nostre concessioni. et confirmacioni. contraire presumpserit, indignationem dei o[mn]ipotentis et beati Cuthb[er]ti et n[ost]ram maledictionem nisi resipuerit incurrat. / Testibus his. Burcardo et Will[elm]o archidiaconis. Mag[ist]ro Will[elm]o blesensi. Mag[ist]ro

Ricardo de Coldingam. Mag[ist]ro Rob[er]to de Edingtun. Rog[er]o persona de houed[ena] / Hugone de feritate. Mag[ist]ro henrico de Dunelmo. Walt[er]o de Pitingdun.¹ Radulfo hareng. Ricardo persona de Winestun.² Henrico de puteaco. Jordano Escolund./ Will[elm]o filio thome. Galfrido filio Ric[ardi]. Rog[er]o de Coingn[er]es.³ Osb[er]to de laton. Rob[er]to filio Meldredi. Thoma de amundeuill[a]. Rog[er]o de Epplinden[a].⁴ Rogero Pun/chard. Rogero Burdun[a]. Simone de hautorn[a]. Waltero Capellano de houed[ena]. Roberto et Galfrido Cl[er]icis de houed[ena]. ada de keuill[a] et multis aliis.

ORIGINAL: DC Durham, 3. 1. Pont. no. 2.

ENDORSED: 1. *Carta hug' epi de libera disposicione et institucione et personatu omnium ecclesiarum* (early thirteenth century). 2. *B. 1. 3ᵃ prime pon* (fifteenth century).

SIZE: 9½ × 6 in. The hand in which this charter is written, that of one of the scribes of the Durham forgeries, is discussed below, pp. 301, 304–6. There is a fractured seal in white wax glued back to front on to a double tail. This damage and repair are not noted in *Durham Seals* (443).

COPIES: DC Durham, Parv. Cart. fo. 14ᵛ; Cart. 1, fo. 72; BM, Cotton MS., Claud. D IV, fo. 86.

For the date, cf. above, no. 7.

9

Quittance of Roger, parson of Howden, from an annual payment of ten pounds sterling (March 1195)

Hugo dei gr[ati]a Dunelm[ensis] Episcopus. Om[n]ibus s[an]cte matris eccl[es]ie filiis ad quos p[re]sentes litt[er]e p[er]uenerint, Sal[u]t[e]m. Sciatis nos digno dei / iudicio flagellatos, quietum clamasse Rog[er]um p[er]sonam eccl[es]ie de houedena et eius successores, de decem libris Esterlinggorum / quas ab eo sing[u]lis annis contra conscienciam nostram iniuste cepimus. Statuentes quod quicumque illas decem libras uel causa il/larum aliquid ab eo uel ab eccl[es]ia sua uel a successoribus suis de cetero exigerit, uel ad soluendum cogerit, indignationem dei / omnipotentis et beati confessoris sui Cuthberti et nostram incurrat maledictionem. Testibus hiis. Ernaldo abb[at]e Rieuall'. Will[elm]o / abb[at]e de Rucford. Will[elm]o abb[at]e de Nouo monasterio. Bertramno priore

---

¹ *Pitingdun* I, *pittington* E.   ² *Winston* E.
³ *Coinners* I.   ⁴ *Epplingd'* I.

Dunelm[ensi]. Burcardo thesaurario Eboraci. Will[elm]o subde-
cano / lincoln[iensi]. Will[elm]o archidiacono northimbrie. Mag-
[ist]ro Ric[ardo] de Collingha[m]. Henrico de puteaco. Walt[er]o
capp[e]ll[an]o eccl[es]ie de houed[ena]. Symone. / et arnaldo. et
Ricardo Elemosinario. et Rog[er]o capp[e]ll[an]is Domini Hugonis
Dunelm[ensis] Ep[iscop]i. et ALIIS MVLTIS.

ORIGINAL: DC Durham, 4. 1. Pont. no. 1.

ENDORSED: 1. *Quieta clam' hug' epi' de x li quas iniuste se fatetur
recepisse de rectore eccli'e de houeden* (fourteenth century). 2. *4ª. prime
pont. A. 2. houden'* (fifteenth century).

SIZE: 9½ × 5 in. The parchment has been carefully ruled in ink
and trimmed to shape after lining. Ample margins have been left at
the head and foot of the document, but reduced to the minimum on
either side of the text. The writing is in a careful and regular cursive
hand, with a tendency to enlarge the ascenders and tails of initial and
final consonants. The remains of a seal in white wax are attached to
a double tail some 10 in. long.

COPIES: DC Durham, Cart. III, fo. 42 (new fol.).

For the date, cf. above, no. 7.

10

Grant of certain liberties to the convent of Durham, namely
free election of the prior, who should be the second dignitary
of the church; free control of all their churches and lands;
liberty to hold their court as freely as the episcopal court;
exemption from aids and other episcopal and archidiaconal
exactions, and freedom from tithe on their demesne and newly
cultivated lands (March 1195)

Hugo d[e]i gr[ati]a Dunelm[en]sis Ep[is]c[opus] Om[n]ibus s[an]cte
matris Eccl[es]ie filiis ad quos litt[er]e presentes peruenerint,
sal[u]t[e]m. Nou[er]it uniu[er]sitas u[est]ra / nos concessisse et
p[re]senti Carta co[n]firmasse quatin[us] ta[m] temp[or]ibus
n[ost]ris quam om[n]iu[m] successoru[m] n[ost]roru[m]. monachi
dunelm[en]ses / lib[er]am semp[er] Electione[m] Prioris habea[n]t.
et quicunque de suo Conuentu co[m]muni monachoru[m] co[n]silio
et eoru[m] p[ropri]a uoluntate. Prior / electus fu[er]it, sit s[e]c[un]-
dus ab Episcopo in omni dignitate et honore abbatis nomine prioris
infra Eccl[es]iam Dunelm[en]sem et extra. et ut ha/beat stallum in
sinistra p[ar]te chori sicut abbas. et dext[er]am Ep[iscop]i. et
facultatem plenariam cum co[n]silio cap[itu]li sui ordinandi /

domu[m] suam in int[er]ioribus et ext[er]ioribus agendis suis ta[m] in Eccl[es]iis qua[m] in t[er]ris et cet[er]is possessionibus suis. Concedimus etiam predicto priori / et monachis lib[er]am disposicione[m] om[n]iu[m] Eccl[es]iaru[m] suaru[m]. et om[n]iu[m] reru[m] ad eas p[er]tinentiu[m]. et ut habeant omnes t[er]ras suas / cum omnibus ad eas p[er]tinentibus et cum om[n]ibus diuisis lib[er]e. et quiete. et honorifice. sicut unqua[m] aliquo te[m]p[or]e. lib[er]ius. quietius. et melius. / habuerunt. Curiam etiam sua[m] lib[er]e et honorifice sicut habem[us] n[ost]ram eis concedimus et co[n]firmam[us] cum omnibus lib[er]tatibus et / co[n]suetudinib[us] que ad curiam p[er]tinent. Si u[ero] alique decime te[m]p[or]ibus an[te]cessorum nostrorum uel nostro. ab Eccl[es]iis eorum aliena/te fu[er]int, eis plenarie restituimus. Volumus etiam quod p[re]dicti Prior et monachi quieti sint ab hospiciis. et auxiliis. et omnibus / grauaminibus episcoporum. archidiaconorum. et omnium officialium. tam in eccl[es]iis suis quam in t[er]ris. et ut de illis supra eos nullus / se intromittat. nec ab eis decimas de dominiis suis aut nutrimentis uel noualibus in Ep[iscop]atu nostro exigat. Quicu[n]que igitur huic / nostre confirmationi in aliquo contraire p[re]su[m]pserit, indignatione[m] dei om[n]ipot[e]ntis et beati Cuthb[er]ti reuerendi confessoris. et / n[ost]ram malediction[e]m se nou[er]it incursurum. Hiis Test[ibus]. Ernaldo abb[at]e Rieuall'. Will[elm]o abb[at]e noui monasterii. Will[elm]o abb[at]e / de Ruhford.[1] Burchardo et Will[elm]o archidiacon[is]. Mag[ist]ro Will[elm]o Blesensi. Mag[ist]ro Ric[ardo] de Coldigh[am]. Rog[er]o p[er]sona de houede[na]. Hug[one] / de feritate. mag[ist]ro Rob[er]to de Edintona.[2] Nicholao medico. Sim[one]. Ernaldo. Ric[ardo]. cap[e]ll[anis]. Will[elm]o fil[io] archiepiscopi. Rob[er]to de Elle/wic. Ric[ardo] heirun. Will[elm]o de Norh[am]. Rad[ulfo] de tornoure. Rob[er]to de houed[ena]. Henrico de puteaco. Jordano escoll[and]. Gauf[rido] fil[io] Ric[ardi] / Will[elm]o fil[io] thome. Osb[er]to de lat[una]. Rob[er]to fil[io] meldredi. Rog[er]o de audre. Rog[er]o burd[una]. Gileb[er]to[3] cam[erario]. alano de lund'. Rob[er]to scotto. / Gileb[er]to de feschau[m]p. Besing. Rog[er]o de kaiuill'. ada de keiuill. Ric[ardo] de au[er]enches hugo[n]e hauet. et multis aliis.

ORIGINAL: DC Durham, 3. 1. Pont. no. 1.

ENDORSED: 1. *confirmacio hug' epi' De libertatibus scdm' Cartam Willelmi epi' primi* (early thirteenth century). 2. *3ª. prime. pont. A. 1.* (fifteenth century). 3. *N[ot]a pro decimis n[on] dand' infra dioc' Dunelm'* (thirteenth century).

---

[1] *ruford* I.   [2] *hadingtona* I.
[3] I omits from *Gaufrido filio Ricardi* to *Gileberto*.

SIZE: 10½ × 9 in. The charter is boldly written in a large, round hand. No margins have been left around the text, but the parchment has been carefully ruled in graphite, and the spacing of the lines is more regular than usual. There is a fractured seal in white wax (varnished) repaired in recent times with liberal quantities of glue (*Durham Seals*, II, 443).

COPIES: DC Durham, Parv. Cart. fo. 14; Cart. I. fo. 72; BM, Cotton MS, Claud. D IV, fo. 85ᵛ.

For the date, cf. above, no. 7. The contents of this charter, the reference to Bishop William in a related document (*FPD*, 108), and a comparison of hands, suggest the conventual forgeries were submitted to Puiset for his confirmation at Howden in 1195.

11

A notification by Bishop Hugh that he was present at Pacy when King Henry II issued a charter in favour of Bishop Hilary of Chichester (1169–95)

Hugo dei gratia Dunolmensis episcopus, Omnibus sancte matris ecclesie filiis ad quos littere presentes pervenerint, Salutem. Noverit universitas vestra nos interfuisse donationi illi et concessioni quam dominus noster Rex Anglorum Henricus, Matilde imperatricis filius, fecit ecclesie Cyc' et bone memorie Hyl[ario], eiusdem ecclesie episcopo et successoribus eius, apud Pasceum, de capellaria de Pevenesel, cum omnibus pertinenciis et libertatibus suis, in liberam et perpetuam elemosinam, de qua eundem episcopum annulo nostro quem ad hoc faciendum ei tradidimus et donavimus, investivit et carta sua confirmavit quam nos vidimus, et in qua testes scripti sumus. Valete.

TEXT: DC Chichester, Liber Y, fo. 158ᵛ.

CALENDARED: *Cartulary of the High Church of Chichester*, no. 114, where it is dated 1169–97.

The document dates after the death of Bishop Hilary (1169) and before that of Puiset. The style of the royal title, and the nature of the reference to Henry II, may suggest a date before 1189.

12

An indulgence by Puiset of ten days to all those visiting the abbey of Reading in the right dispositions (19 April 1164)

Hugo dei gratia Dunelmensis episcopus omnibus sancte matris ecclesie fidelibus salutem et benedictionem. Loca sancta et religiosorum ac Deo servientium virorum habitacula a fidelibus populis eo devotius visitanda et veneranda sunt quod in eis sanctorum celebres existunt memorie, et eorum relique venerabiles noscuntur esse recondite. Ea propter, de Dei confidentes misericordia, concedimus omnibus qui ecclesiam beate Marie apud Rading positam, in festo beati Jacobi apostoli, cuius reliquie in ea creduntur esse reposite, vel in octo diebus sequentibus, pia devotione et impendende sanctissimis gloriosi apostoli reliquiis venerationis gratia adierint, visitaverint, et ad honorem Dei et apostoli sui reverentiam, beneficium aliquod contulerint, decem dierum remissionem de iniuncta sibi penitencia concedimus, et orationum ac beneficiorum Dunelmensis ecclesie participes esse statuimus. Valete.

TEXT: BM, Egerton MS. 3031, fo. 59.

A number of similar documents were issued by other members of the episcopate at the same date (cf. Morey, *Bartholomew of Exeter*, 146, no. 25).

13

A writ of Bishop Geoffrey Rufus granting Garmondsway to Paulinus, son of Ralph, bishop of the Orkneys, and his brothers

(1133–40)

G[alfridus] dei Gra[tia] Dunelm[en]sis ep[iscopu]s. Omnibus Justic' et Ministris et fidelibus suis. et / Osberto nepoti ep[iscop]i. et hominibus de Middelham'. Sal[utem]. Sciatis quod uolo et c[on]cedo et / firmiter p[re]cipio quod Paulinus filius Rad[ulfi] Orcadensis ep[iscop]i. et fratres eius in pace / et quiete et honorifice teneant t[er]ram de Garmundeswege. amodo et inper/petuum sine omni disturbatione. Valete.

ORIGINAL: DC Durham, Cart. Misc. Unsorted, [c].
ENDORSED: 1. *Carta de Garmundesway* (thirteenth century).
2. *A precept from ye Bish of Durham to ye men of Middleham touching Garmondswey* (seventeenth century).
SIZE: 5½ × 2½ in. Written regularly on unruled parchment. The document is provided with the normal writ style seal and tying tags, though the seal is lost.

This document is attributed to Bishop Rufus rather than to William of St Barbara largely on diplomatic grounds, since it reflects, like other of his *acta*, the models of the royal chancery which he directed. It is assumed to be a grant, though its language might be construed as a confirmation, but it seems improbable that the sons of Bishop Ralph would have been of an age to receive property before 1133. Osbert, *nepos* of Bishop Flambard, who is named in the writ, was sheriff of Durham during the episcopates of Flambard, Rufus and St Barbara. He received the vill of Middleham from Flambard, and was still in possession in 1146 (DC Durham, 3. 12. Spec. nos. 1, 2; Surtees, III, 385; *VCH Durham*, III, 205).

14

An alleged privilege of Archbishop Roger of York for the convent of Durham

Rogerius dei Gratia eboreacensis Archiep[iscopus] Capitulo aecclesiae Sancti Petri Eboreacensis et omnibus Sancte matris aecclesiae filiis tam presentibus quam futuris. Salutem et bene-dictionem. Quia deo auctore in facie p[ro]lati sumus aecclesiae, iura ipsius magis / tueri debemus quam prohibendo diminuere. pluris hec augendo fouere, quam aliquatenus circumuolando pre-pedire. Anime nimirum ille quae in ecclesia deseruiunt, proculdubio Christi matris uiscera sunt. Ea propter / uniuersati uestrae notum esse uolumus quod ego Rogerius dei gratia eboreacensis archiepis-copus zelo fidei et amore dei et Sancti Cvthberti succensus do et concedo deo et sancto Cuthberto et priori et monachis ei in dunel-mo / seruientibus omnes libertates antiquas et dignitates quascunque aliquo tempore predecessorum meorum in archiepiscopatu ebora-censi meliores habuerunt. tam in omnibus aecclesiis suis quam capellis et terris et ceteris cunctis suis perti/nentibus. liberas et quietas a me et meis omnibus successoribus. Preterea constituo et archiepiscopali auctoritate decerno. quatinus priori et monachis sancti Cutberti (*sic*) liceat omnes ecclesias suas et capellas secundum morem antiquum in manu sua habere. et ad profec/tum ecclesiae suae secundum quod utilius sibi uiderint esse disponere. Vicarios etiam suos quos in ipsis aecclesiis posuerint nemo ad synodum uel capitulum uenire compellat. neque archidiaconus siue decanus aliquod eis grauamen inferat. uel auxilium siue hospicium / ab eis exigere presumat. nisi forte hoc ipsi gratis facere uoluerint. Si autem ipsi eorum capellani in aliquo reprehensibiles reperiantur, delata prius priori et fratribus querela ad curiam Sancti Cuthberti sum-moneantur, et excessus eorum ibi / Canonice emendentur. Sin autem talia fuerint de quibus accusantur. ut nisi nostro auxilio cor-rigi non potuerint. Prior uel fratres illos in nostra presentia ad-ductos statuant, ut litis accusationem equo iudicio terminando decidant. Has libertates / et omnes antiquas Sancti Cuthberti consuetudines meo priuilegio renouo et confirmo. et quascunque alias unquam plures uel quietiores per archiepiscopatum Sanctus Cvthbertus uel sui habuerunt, libere, honorifice, et quiete. ei et suis in perpetuam elemosinam concedo. / pro animae meae redemptione. et omnium successorum meorum salute. Valete. Testibus. Roberto episcopo lincolniensi. Atheldredo abbate de Rievall'. Rodberto decano. Thoma de sotewania. Acardo et Willelmo canonicis et Simundo del seil. / Roberto sacrista beuerl'. Gwidone dapifero.

ORIGINAL: DC Durham, 1. 1. Archiep. no. 4.

ENDORSED: 1. *Carta Rogeri archiepiscopi de libertatibus Ecclesiarum in Euerwykshire* (thirteenth century). 2. D 1, *prima prime archiepiscopalium* (fifteenth century).

Size: 14 × 4½ in. Ruled in graphite. Cut at foot from right to left to provide sealing and tying tags. The seal has been opened, and is now sideways across the tail. Though accepted without any comment by Greenwell and Blair (*Durham Seals*, 11, no. 3220) the seal shows clear signs of interference, and, presumably as the result of re-setting, is markedly thicker than any of the authentic seals of Archbishop Roger which I have been able to examine. For comments on the writing and contents of the privilege, see above, pp. 174–5, and below, Appendix iv. The witnesses are derived from a document dating 1154–66, limits being fixed by the accession of Roger to York and the death of Robert of Lincoln.

AN ITINERARY OF HUGH DU PUISET
1154–95[1]

1154

2 May. DURHAM (*Scriptores Tres*, 6.)

June. YORK (Hoveden, I, 213.)

July. DRAX (Henry of Huntingdon, 291; Newburgh, I, 94; Hoveden, *loc. cit.*)

A charter of Stephen in favour of the monks of Selby. Witnessed by: Hugh, bishop of Durham; Robert, bishop of Lincoln; Richard de Luci; Richard de Camville. At Drax, 'in the siege'. (*Selby Coucher Book*, I, 6; *EYC*, I, no. 480.)

A writ of Stephen in favour of Robert, bishop of Lincoln. Witnessed by: Hugh, bishop of Durham; Richard de Luci; Richard de Camville. At Drax. (*CChR*, IV, 139; *Reg. Ant. Linc.* I, 63, no. 103.)

August. YORK (Newburgh, *loc. cit.*)

A charter of Stephen in favour of the abbey of Sawley. Witnessed by: Hugh, bishop of Durham; Richard de Luci; Hugh de Essartis. At York. (*CChR*, II, 163; *Sallay Cartulary*, I, 35; *Mon. Ang.* v, 515.)

A charter of Stephen in favour of St Peter's, York. Witnessed by: Theobald, archbishop of Canterbury; Hugh, bishop of Durham, Richard de Luci; Richard de Camville; Eustace fitzJohn. At York. (*CChR*, II, 438; *EYC*, I, no. 202.)

A charter of Stephen in favour of the church of St John of Pontefract. Witnessed by: Robert, bishop of Lincoln; Hugh, bishop of Durham; Eustace fitzJohn; Henry de Laci; Richard de Luci; Richard de Camville. At York. (*EYC*, III, no. 1448.)

October. LINCOLN

A charter of Stephen in favour of the church of Lincoln. Witnessed by: Hugh, bishop of Durham; Robert de Gant, chancellor; Baldric de Sigillo; Richard de Luci; Richard de Camville. At Lincoln. (*CChR*, IV, 382; *Reg. Ant. Linc.* I, 58, no. 186, where it is dated 1148–54.)

---

[1] This does not purport to be a comprehensive collection of royal charters witnessed by Hugh Puiset, but merely records those which may be dated within reasonably narrow margins to provide an itinerary. In the nature of the evidence the dating of the bishop's movements can be no more than approximate.

?WORKSOP

A charter of Stephen in favour of the monks of Rufford. Witnessed by: ?, bishop of Durham; Richard de Luci; Richard de Camville. At Worksop. (BM, Harley MS. 1063, fo. 1.)

LONDON (Newburgh, I, 95)

A charter of William, son of Stephen, in favour of Richard de Luci, at London, in the presence of Stephen. Witnessed by: Henry, bishop of Winchester; Hugh, bishop of Durham; William, prior of St Pancras; Reginald de Warenne; Hugh de Pet'Pont; Richard de Hanesti; Osbert Martel; Turold de Borram; Robert de Ruilli; Philip de Querceto; Simon de Gerartmoli'. (*Cart. Ant.* II, 10; J. H. Round, 'The Honour of Ongar', 144; *EYC*, VIII, 47.)

(?) ? A charter of Stephen in favour of the canons of Welbeck. Witnessed by: Hugh, bishop of Durham. (Colvin, *The White Canons*, 66.)

1155

? January. DURHAM

A mediation by Hugh, bishop of Durham, between the convent of Durham and Elias Escolland concerning land at Dalton, Seaham, and Seaton. (DC Durham, I. 8. Spec. no. 34, printed in *FPD*, 121 n.)

January. LINCOLN (Eyton, *Henry II*, 4.)

A writ of Henry II in favour of the monks of Revesby. Witnessed by: Theobald, archbishop of Canterbury; Hugh, bishop of Durham; Philip, bishop of Bayeux; Arnulf, bishop of Lisieux; Thomas the chancellor; Reginald, earl of Cornwall. At Lincoln. (*DB*, no. XLIV)

February. YORK (Gervase of Canterbury, I, 161; Eyton, *Henry II*, 5.)

A writ of Henry II in favour of the abbey of Fountains. At York. (*EYC*, I, no. 74.)

A charter of Henry in favour of the abbey of *Newbottle*. (*CPR, 1281-92*, 501.)

These two documents were witnessed by Theobald, archbishop of Canterbury; Hugh, bishop of Durham; Robert, bishop of Lincoln; Philip, bishop of Bayeux; Arnulf, bishop of Lisieux; Thomas the chancellor; Earl Reginald.

A charter of Henry in favour of the abbey of Selby. Witnessed by: Theobald, archbishop of Canterbury; Robert, bishop of Lincoln; Hugh, bishop of Durham; Adalwold, bishop of Carlisle; Thomas the chancellor; Reginald, earl of Cornwall; Richard de Humez;

Richard de Luci; Henry de Essex; William, earl of Aumâle. (Eyton, *Henry II*, 5.)

A charter of Henry in favour of the canons of Nostell. Witnessed by: Theobald, archbishop of Canterbury; Roger, archbishop of York; Robert, bishop of Lincoln; Hugh, bishop of Durham; Thomas the chancellor; Reginald, earl of Cornwall; William, earl of Aumâle; Robert, earl of Leicester; Earl Hugh; Henry de Essex; Henry d'Oilli; William de Percy; Eustace fitzJohn. At York. (BM, Cotton MS., Vesp. E xix, fo. 4; *Mon. Ang.* vi, 93; *EYC*, iii, p. 135; Eyton, *Henry II*, 5.)

Three charters of Henry in favour of the monks of Louth Park. Witnessed by: Theobald, archbishop of Canterbury; Robert, bishop of Lincoln; Hugh, bishop of Durham; Philip, bishop of Bayeux; Arnulf, bishop of Lisieux; Thomas the chancellor; Reginald, earl of Cornwall. At York. (*CChR*, iii, 247–8, 268; *DB*, no. lxxvii; *The Chronicle of Louth Park*, ed. E. Venables, 52.)

A writ of Henry in favour of the monks of Woburn. Witnessed by: Theobald, archbishop of Canterbury; Hugh, bishop of Durham; Philip, bishop of Bayeux; Arnulf, bishop of Lisieux; Thomas the chancellor; Reginald, earl of Cornwall. At York. (*CChR*, iii, 286; *DB*, no. lxxvi.)

A writ of Henry in favour of Robert, bishop of Lincoln. Witnessed by: Roger, archbishop of York; Hugh, bishop of Durham; Richard de Luci. At York. (*CChR*, iv, 110; *Reg. Ant. Linc.* i, 108, no. 170.)

A writ of Henry in favour of the abbey of Meaux. Witnessed by: Theobald, archbishop of Canterbury; Hugh, bishop of Durham; Robert, bishop of Lincoln. (*EYC*, iii, no. 1389.)

1156

28 October. ST NEOT'S (*Gesta Abbatum Monasterii Sancti Albani*, i, 131; Eyton, *Henry II*, 20.)

1157

? July. NORTHAMPTON

A charter of Henry II in favour of the monks of Pontefract. Witnessed by: Thomas the chancellor; Henry, bishop of Winchester; Robert, earl of Leicester; Earl Hugh of Norwich; Hugh, bishop of Durham; Richard de Humez; Richard de Luci; Henry de Essex; Henry de Laci. At Northampton. (*EYC*, iii, no. 1451.) This charter, which must date before 24 May 1162, since it is witnessed by Becket as chancellor, may have passed in either July 1157 or August 1158. The presence of Henry of Winchester, who was reconciled with the king between Michaelmas 1157 and Michaelmas 1158 (Eyton, *Henry II*, 14 n.) suggests August 1158.

? *September.* WOODSTOCK

A charter of Henry in favour of the abbey of Furness. Witnessed by: Robert, bishop of Lincoln; Hugh, bishop of Durham; Robert, earl of Leicester; Richard de Luci; William de Vesci; Geoffrey de Valoniis; William de Aegremont; Aubri Gresli; John Constable; Richard Pincerna; Henry fitzSwain; Gospatric fitzOrm; Richard fitzIvo, by the hand of Stephen chaplain. At Woodstock. (*Coucher Book of Furness*, ed. J. C. Atkinson, II, 343; Eyton, *Henry II*, 30.) A date after July 1157 is suggested by the presence of William de Vesci, who succeeded Eustace fitzJohn at that time (cf. Eyton, *op. cit.* 30 n.). An alternative date would be the summer of 1158.

A charter of Henry in favour of the Templars. Witnessed by: Roger, archbishop of York; Robert, bishop of Lincoln; Hugh, bishop of Durham; Richard de Luci; Reginald de St Valery. At Woodstock. (*Records of the Templars*, 204.)

1158

January. NEWCASTLE UPON TYNE (Eyton, *Henry II*, 33.)

A charter of Henry in favour of Hubert de Vaux. Witnessed by: Roger, archbishop of York; Robert, bishop of Lincoln; Hugh, bishop of Durham; Hugh, earl of Norfolk; Earl Aubri; Earl Geoffrey; Richard de Luci; Manasser Bisset; Henry de Essex; Hugh de Morville; Robert de Dunstanville; William fitzJohn; Simon fitzPeter; Nigel de Broc; William Malet; Roger fitzRichard; Robert de Stuteville; Turgisius de Russedal. (*Register of Wetherhal*, App. XXII; Eyton, *Henry II*, 33.) A charter of Hubert de Vaux, with these witnesses, was given at Newcastle (Cart. Ant. DD, I).

c. *January.* DURHAM

A charter of Henry in favour of the monks of Tynemouth. Witnessed by: Roger, archbishop of York; Robert, bishop of Lincoln; Hugh, bishop of Durham; R(ichard), prior of Hexham; Earl Hugh of Norfolk; Richard de Luci; William fitzJohn; William de Vesci; Hubert de Vaux; Manasser Bisset; Henry fitzGerald. At Durham. (*CChR*, II, 170–1; Gibson, *Tynemouth*, II, App. 34; *NCH*, VIII, 62 n.)

January. YORK

Two charters of Henry in favour of Robert, bishop of Lincoln. Witnessed by: Roger, archbishop of York; Hugh, bishop of Durham; Richard de Luci; Manasser Bisset. At York. (*Reg. Ant. Linc.* I, nos. 155, 170.)

A charter of Henry in favour of the citizens of Scarborough. Witnessed by: Roger, archbishop of York; Robert, bishop of Lincoln; Hugh, bishop of Durham; Richard de Luci; Robert de Dunstanville; Roger fitzRichard; Robert de Stuteville; Robert de Ros; Bertram de Bulmer. At York. (*CChR*, I, 417; *EYC*, I, no. 364.) For the king's contact with the citizens of Scarborough at this date see *Materials*, III, 44–5.

A charter of Henry in favour of Moxby. Witnessed by: Roger, archbishop of York; Robert, bishop of Lincoln; Hugh, bishop of Durham; Hugh, earl of Norfolk; Richard de Luci; Richard de Camville; William fitzJohn; Simon fitzPeter; Nigel de Broc. At York. (*Mon. Ang.* VI, 198, no. 1; *EYC*, I, no. 419.)

?c. *August.* NORTHAMPTON. (See above, *sub* July 1157.)

?c. *August.* WOODSTOCK (See above, *sub* September 1157.)

1159

There is no evidence for the bishop's movements in this year.

1160

22 May. ROUEN

An agreement between Louis VII of France and Henry II of England concerning the Vexin. Witnessed by: Peter, bishop of Paris; Hugh, bishop of Soissons; Rotrou, bishop of Evreux; Arnulf, bishop of Lisieux; Philip, bishop of Bayeux; Froger, bishop of Séez; Hugh, bishop of Durham; Thomas the chancellor; Count Theodore of Flanders; Count Henry of Troyes; the count of Soissons; the count of Beaumont; Earl Waleran of Mellent; William Pavet, master of the Temple; Brothers Otto de S. Audimerio, Gilbert de Lacy, Richard de Hastings, Peter Bishop, Robert de Piro; William, brother of the king; Richard de Humez; Jordan Taxo. (*DB*, no. CXLI; Eyton, *Henry II*, 49.)

c. *May.* ROUEN

A notification by Hugh, archbishop of Rouen, that the dispute between the church of Avranches and the monastery of St Michael, over the churches of Pontorson, was settled in the presence of: King Henry II; Philip, bishop of Bayeux; Rotrou, bishop of Evreux; Herbert, bishop of Avranches; Hugh, bishop of Durham; Thomas the chancellor; Richard de Humez; William fitzHamo. At Rouen, 1160. (*Cal. Doc. France*, no. 743; *DB*, no. CXXXVIII; Eyton, *Henry II*, 50.)

A charter of Henry in favour of the canons of St Denis of Southampton. Witnessed by: Arnulf, bishop of Lisieux; Philip, bishop of Bayeux; Hugh, bishop of Durham; Richard de Humez; Manasser Bisset; William fitzHamo. At Rouen. (*CChR*, III, 337; *DB*, no. CCXV.)

A charter of Henry in favour of the abbey of Foucarmont. Witnessed by: Hugh, bishop of Durham; Thomas the chancellor; Ralph, abbot of Billewas; Geoffrey, chaplain of the king; Gerard, sheriff of Pinchonio; Richard the writer, by the hand of Stephen de Fougères, writer. At Rouen. (*Cal. Doc. France*, no. 186; *DB*, no. CLXXVI.)

1161

There is no evidence for the bishop's movements in this year.

1162

April. ROUEN

A writ of Henry in favour of the church of St Mary of Lincoln. Witnessed by: Roger, archbishop of York; Hilary, bishop of Chichester; Hugh, bishop of Durham; Thomas the chancellor. At Rouen. (*CChR*, IV, 108; *Reg. Ant. Linc.* I, 85, no. 136; *DB*, no. CLXXXIX.)

A writ of Henry in favour of the church of Lincoln. Witnessed by: Hilary, bishop of Chichester; Hugh, bishop of Durham; Thomas the chancellor. At Rouen. (*Reg. Ant. Linc.* I, 87, no. 138; *DB*, no. CLXXVII.)

A writ of Henry in favour of the church of Lincoln. Witnessed by: Roger, archbishop of York; Hilary, bishop of Chichester; Hugh, bishop of Durham; Thomas the chancellor. At Rouen. (*Reg. Ant. Linc.* I, 90, no. 142; *DB*, no. CLXXXVII.)

April–May. ROUEN–PACY

A charter of Henry in favour of the church of Chichester. Witnessed by: Roger, archbishop of York; Rotrou, bishop of Evreux; Arnulf, bishop of Lisieux; Robert, bishop of Lincoln; Hugh, bishop of Durham; Thomas the chancellor; Manasser Bisset; Robert de Dunstanville; Richard de Camville; Ralph fitzStephen. At Pacy. (See above, App. ii, no. 11; *CChR*, i, 31; *DB*, no. clxvi.)

ROUEN–FALAISE

A confirmation by the legate, Cardinal Henry of Pisa. Those present: Roger, archbishop of York; Robert, bishop of Lincoln; Hugh, bishop of Durham; Froger, bishop of Séez. (*PU*, ii, no. 106; Eyton, *Henry II*, 56, n. 4.)

1163

8 March. WESTMINSTER (Eyton, *Henry II*, 59.)

Notification by Henry II that the dispute between the bishop of Lincoln and the abbot of St Albans, touching the subjection of the abbot and the monastery, has been ended in his presence. Witnessed by: Thomas, archbishop of Canterbury; Roger, archbishop of York; Henry, bishop of Winchester; Nigel, bishop of Ely; William, bishop of Norwich; Hilary, bishop of Chichester; Jocelin, bishop of Salisbury; Walter, bishop of Rochester; Hugh, bishop of Durham; Gilbert, bishop of Hereford; Bartholomew, bishop of Exeter; Richard, bishop of Coventry; Godfrey, bishop of St Asaph; Laurence, abbot of Westminster; William, abbot of Ramsey; Gregory, abbot of Malmesbury; Reginald, abbot of Pershore; Clement, abbot of York; Ailred, abbot of Rievaulx; Geoffrey, archdeacon of Canterbury; Richard, archdeacon of Poitiers; Robert, earl of Leicester; Earl Hugh Bigod; Earl William of Arundel; Richard de Luci; Richard de Humez; Henry fitzGerald. At Westminster. (*Reg. Ant. Linc.* i, 64–6; *CChR*, iv, 141–2; *Mon. Ang.* viii, 1276; Eyton, *Henry II*, 59–60.)

19–21 May. TOURS (Diceto, i, 310.)

? October. WESTMINSTER

A charter of Henry in favour of the abbey of St Valery. Witnessed by: Richard de Luci; Thomas, archbishop of Canterbury; Gilbert, bishop of London; Hugh, bishop of Durham; Bartholomew, bishop of Exeter. At Westminster. (*DB*, no. ccxxxiii; *Early Oxford Charters*, ed. H. E. Salter, no. 30.) The charter must date after 19 March, when Alexander III licensed Foliot's translation from Hereford to London.

? October. NOTTINGHAM

A charter of Henry in favour of Rievaulx. Witnessed by: Roger, archbishop of York; Robert, bishop of Lincoln; Hugh, bishop of

Durham; Richard, bishop of Chester; Robert, earl of Leicester; Earl Geoffrey; Richard de Luci. At Nottingham. (*EYC*, IX, no. 156.) This charter must date after the accession of Richard Peche to Coventry-Chester in April 1161, and before the death of Geoffrey of Essex in October 1166.

1164

19 April. READING (*Materials*, VII, 97; *Mon. Ang.* IV, 31.)

An indulgence by Hugh, bishop of Durham, for the abbey church of Reading. (See above, App. II, no. 12.)

1165

? November–December. WESTMINSTER

A charter of Henry in favour of the canons of Sempringham. Witnessed by: Roger, archbishop of York; Hugh, bishop of Durham; Hilary, bishop of Chichester; Reginald, earl of Cornwall; Roger de Mowbray; Reginald de Courtenay. At Westminster. (*CChR*, IV, 52; *Reg. Ant. Linc.* I, 120–1.)

A charter of Henry in favour of Lenton. Witnessed by: Roger, archbishop of York; Gilbert, bishop of London; William, bishop of Norwich; Hugh, bishop of Durham; Earl Robert of Leicester; Earl Hugh Bigod; Roger de Cornerio; Roger de Mowbray; Reginald de Courtenay. At Westminster. (*CChR*, I, 446.) This charter must date between the accession of Foliot to London in April 1163 and the death of Robert of Leicester in April 1168. Other reasons for assuming the king's presence at Westminster at this date are given by Eyton, *Henry II*, 87 n.)

1166

There is no evidence for the bishop's movements in this year.

1167

There is no evidence for the bishop's movements in this year.

1168

There is no evidence for the bishop's movements in this year.

1169

May. LONDON (*Materials*, VII, 57.)

1170

14 June. WESTMINSTER

Puiset was present at the coronation of the young King Henry. (*Gesta*, I, 5–6; Hoveden, II, 5; Eyton, *Henry II*, 138.)

1171

18 October. ? DURHAM

An agreement made in the presence of Bishop Puiset between the convent of Durham and the abbey of Kelso. (DC Durham, Cart. Misc. no. 1354; *North Durham*, DCXLIII.)

1172

11 November. DURHAM

Bishop Hugh mediates between the convent of Durham and Alexander of Hylton on the rights of the mother church of Wearmouth. (DC Durham, Cart. II, fo. 82.)

1173

There is no evidence for the movements of the bishop during this year.

1174

31 July. NORTHAMPTON (*Gesta*, I, 73; Hoveden, II, 64–5; Eyton, *Henry II*, 182.)

A charter of Henry in favour of Walter Bloet. Witnessed by: Hugh, bishop of Durham; G[eoffrey], elect of Ely; Earl Reginald of Cornwall; William de Albini; Hugh de Cressi; Thomas Bardolf. At Northampton. (*CPR, 1399–1401*, 181.)

1175

1–8 July. WOODSTOCK (*Gesta*, I, 93; Hoveden, II, 79; Eyton, *Henry II*, 192.)

A charter of Henry in favour of the citizens of Cologne. Witnessed by: R[ichard], bishop of Winchester; Hugh, bishop of Durham; John, dean of Salisbury; William fitzAudelin. At Woodstock. (*DB*, no. ccccxcv.) This charter dates after the consecration of Richard of Winchester (6 October 1174) and before the election of the dean of Salisbury to the see of Norwich (14 December 1175).

? July. WALLINGFORD

A charter of Henry in favour of Holy Trinity, York. Witnessed by: Hugh, bishop of Durham; Reginald, bishop of Bath; Stephen de Tours; Robert, earl of Leicester; William Marshal; William de St John. At Wallingford. (*EYC*, vi, no. 6.)

1 August. NOTTINGHAM (*Gesta*, i, 94; Eyton, *Henry II*, 193.)

Two charters of Henry in favour of the canons of Welbeck. Witnessed by: Roger, archbishop of York; Hugh, bishop of Durham; G[eoffrey], elect of Lincoln; William fitzAudelin; Reginald de Courtenay; Henry de Laci; William de Lanvalei; Thomas Basset; Hugh de Cressi; Rannulf de Glanville; Walter de Dunstanville; William Basset; William fitzRadulf. At Nottingham. (*CChR*, iv, 69–70.) For the date, see A. Hamilton Thompson, *The Premonstratensian Abbey of Welbeck*, 15–16.

A charter of Henry in favour of Stixwould. Witnessed by: Roger, archbishop of York; Hugh, bishop of Durham; William fitzAudelin; Reginald de Courtenay; William de Lanvalei; Thomas Basset; Hugh de Cressi; Rannulf de Glanville; Walter de Dunstanville; William Basset; William fitzRadulf. At Nottingham. (*CPR, 1405–8*, 218.)

A charter of Henry in favour of the leper house of Lincoln. Witnessed by: Roger, archbishop of York; Hugh, bishop of Durham; William fitzAudelin; Reginald de Courtenay; Fulk Paynel; William de Lanvalei; Thomas Basset; Walter de Dunstanville; William fitzRadulf. At Nottingham. (*CPR, 1405–8*, 271.)

A charter of Henry in favour of the church of Carlisle. Witnessed by: Henry, the king, my son; Hugh, bishop of Durham; John, dean of Salisbury; Geoffrey, Nicholas, Roger, chaplains; William fitzAudelin; Rannulf de Glanville; Hugh de Cressi; Reginald de Luci; William Malovicino; Thomas Bardolf; Gerard de Camville. At Nottingham. (*CChR*, iii, 82.)

10 August. YORK (*Gesta*, i, 94–5; Torigni, 267–8; *Melrose Chronicle*, *sub anno*; Eyton, *Henry II*, 193; *EYC*, vi, no. 106.)

A charter of Henry in favour of the priory of Gokewell. Witnessed by: Roger, archbishop of York; Geoffrey, bishop of Ely; Hugh, bishop of Durham; John, dean of Salisbury; William fitzAudelin; Reginald de Courtenay; William de Lanvalei; Thomas Basset; John de Solineio; Gerard de Camville; William fitzRadulf; William Basset. At York. (*EYC*, vi, no. 106.)

A charter of Henry in favour of the nuns of St Clement's, York. Witnessed by: Geoffrey, bishop of Ely; Hugh, bishop of Durham; John, dean of Salisbury; Earl William de Mandeville; Richard de Luci; Richard de Humez; William fitzAudelin; Rannulf de Glanville; Reginald de Courtenay; William de Lanvalei; Thomas Basset; Hugh de Cressi; Thomas Bardolf. At York. (Eyton, *Henry II*, 193–4; *EYC*, I, no. 359.)

A charter of Henry in favour of the abbey of Fountains. Witnessed by: Hugh, bishop of Durham; John, dean of Salisbury; Richard, abbot of Mortimer; William fitzAudelin; Rannulf de Glanville; Reginald de Courtenay; Hugh de Cressi; Thomas Bardolf. At York. (*EYC*, I, no. 78.)

A charter of Henry in favour of the monks of Whitby. Witnessed by: Hugh, bishop of Durham; Geoffrey, bishop of Ely; Richard de Luci; William, earl of Aumâle. At York. (*EYC*, II, no. 869.)

1176

January. ? NOTTINGHAM (Hoveden, II, 87.)

25 January. NORTHAMPTON (*Gesta*, I, 107; Eyton, *Henry II*, 198–9.)

A charter of Henry in favour of the abbey of Cluny. Witnessed by: R[ichard], bishop of Winchester; G[eoffrey], bishop of Ely; John, bishop of Norwich; Hugh, bishop of Durham; William, earl of Arundel; Earl William de Mandeville; Richard de Luci; Richard de Camville; Rannulf de Glanville; Hugh de Cressi; Thomas Bardolf; Bertram de Verdun; William fitzRadulf; Radulf Brito. At Northampton. (*Cal. Doc. France*, no. 1400; *DB*, no. DII.)

14 March. WESTMINSTER (*Gesta*, I, 112; Hoveden, II, 92; Eyton, *Henry II*, 200.)

A charter of Henry in favour of Richard, bishop of Winchester. Witnessed by: the lord Hugh Pier Leoni, legate; Richard, archbishop of Canterbury; Rotrou, archbishop [of Rouen]; Gilbert, bishop of London; Geoffrey, bishop of Ely; Roger, bishop of Worcester; Bartholomew, bishop of Exeter; Reginald, bishop of Bath; John, bishop of Norwich; John, bishop of Chichester; Robert, bishop of Hereford; Hugh, bishop of Durham; Herbert, archdeacon of Canterbury; Walter de Coutances, archdeacon of Oxford; Roger and Nicholas, chaplains of the king; Richard de Luci; Earl William de Mandeville; Earl Simon; Earl William of Warwick; William fitzAudelin; Ralph fitzStephen. At Westminster. (*CChR*, III, 350.)

A charter of Henry in favour of Rievaulx. Witnessed by: Roger, archbishop of York; Richard, bishop of Winchester; Roger, bishop of Worcester; Hugh, bishop of Durham; Robert, earl of Leicester; Hamelin, earl of Warenne; Earl Simon; Richard de Luci; Reginald de Courtenay; William fitzAudelin. At Westminster. (Eyton, *Henry II*, 200; *EYC*, I, no. 406.) The charter must date before the death of Roger of Worcester in August 1179. It may have passed in March or May 1176, or in March 1177.

1177

13 March. WESTMINSTER

Henry II arbitrates in a dispute between the kings of Castile and Navarre. (*Gesta*, I, 145; Hoveden, II, 121; Diceto, I, 418–20; *DB*, no. DV; Eyton, *Henry II*, 211–12.)

May. ? WINDSOR (*Gesta*, I, 160–1.)

II June. WALTHAM (*Gesta*, I, 173; Eyton, *Henry II*, 216.)

I July. WINCHESTER (*Gesta*, I, 177.)

1178

25 December. WINCHESTER

A charter of Henry in favour of the canons of Waltham. (*Mon. Ang.* VI, 63, dated Eyton, *Henry II*, 224 n.)

A charter of Henry in favour of the nuns of Godstow. (Eyton, *Henry II*, 225.)

1179

March. ROME

Bishop Hugh of Durham was present at the third Lateran Council. (Hoveden, II, 171; Mansi, XXII, c. 217.)

1180

3 March. DURHAM

Roger of Kibblesworth surrenders his vill of Wolviston in the presence of Bishop Puiset. At Durham. (DC Durham, 3. 6. Spec. no. 18, mistranscribed in *FPD*, 142 n.)

1181

26 May. BERMONDSEY

Bishop Hugh of Durham and Simon, abbot of St Albans, sat as

judges delegate in the dispute between the archbishop of Canterbury and the convent of St Augustine's. (*PU*, I, no. 202.)

August. NOTTINGHAM (*Gesta*, I, 280: Eyton, *Henry II*, 241.)

YORK

A charter of Henry in favour of the church of Kirkham. Witnessed by: Roger, archbishop of York; Hugh, bishop of Durham; Hugh Murdac; Rannulf de Glanville; Reginald de Courtenay; William de Lanvalei; Thomas Basset; Michael Belet; William de Bending. At York. (*CChR*, IV, 361-2; Eyton, *Henry II*, 242.)

KNARESBOROUGH

A charter of Henry in favour of the priory of Finchale. Witnessed by: Hugh, bishop of Durham; John Cumin; Hugh Murdac; Rannulf de Glanville; Michael Belet; William de Bending. At Knaresborough. (Eyton, *Henry II*, 242.)

November. YORK (*Gesta*, I, 283.)

1182

22 October. WESTMINSTER

A final concord made before: R[ichard], archbishop of Canterbury; R[ichard], bishop of Winchester; G[eoffrey], bishop of Ely; H[ugh], bishop of Durham; J[ohn], bishop of Norwich; B[aldwin], bishop of Worcester; R[eginald], bishop of Bath; P[eter], bishop of St David's; R[annulf] de Glanville, justiciar. (BM, Harley MS. 742, 200.)

1183

22 October. DURHAM (DC Durham, Cart. Misc. unsorted.)

1184

26 March. DURHAM

Bishop Hugh mediates between the convent of Durham and Ralph of Fishburn concerning the chantry of Hardwick. (DC Durham, I. 8. Spec. no. 41; Surtees, I, 282.)

18 June. DURHAM (DC Durham, Cart. Misc. unsorted.)

August. WOODSTOCK (Eyton, *Henry II*, 257.)

November. WESTMINSTER (*Gesta*, I, 319; Eyton, *Henry II*, 258.)

25 December. WINDSOR (*Gesta*, I, 333–4; Eyton, *Henry II*, 259.)

31 December. GUILDFORD (*Gesta, loc. cit.*)

1185

? January. MARLBOROUGH

A charter of Henry in favour of the abbey of Foucarmont. Witnessed by: Hugh, bishop of Durham; Rannulf de Glanville; Bertram de Verdun; Hugh de Morwick; Rannulf de Gedding. At Marlborough. (*Cal. Doc. France*, no. 191.)

February. CLIPSTONE

Two charters of Henry in favour of the abbey of Thurgarton. (*Mon. Ang.* VI, 192.)

A charter of Henry in favour of the abbey of Barlings. (*Mon. Ang.* VII, 916.)

These two charters were witnessed by: Hugh, bishop of Durham; William, earl of Arundel; Rannulf de Glanville; Bernard de St Valery; Roger de Stuteville; William de Stuteville; Hugh Bardolf. (Eyton, *Henry II*, 261.)

?17 March. READING

18 March. CLERKENWELL (Diceto, II, 33.)

WESTMINSTER

A charter of Henry in favour of the canons of Butley. (Eyton, *Henry II*, 262.)

A charter of Henry in favour of the convent of Leiston. (*CChR*, III, 199.)

These two charters were witnessed by: Baldwin, elect of Canterbury; John, bishop of Norwich; Geoffrey, bishop of Ely; Hugh, bishop of Durham; Reginald, bishop of Bath; Seffrid, bishop of Chichester; Herbert, archdeacon of Canterbury; Godfrey de Luci, archdeacon of Richmond; Hubert Walter; Hamelin, earl of Warenne; William, earl of Sussex; Earl Aubri; Richard, earl of Clare; Bernard de St Valery; Walter fitzRobert.

16 April. Hugh leaves England in company with the king. (*Gesta*, I, 337; Diceto, II, 34; Eyton, *Henry II*, 263.)

21 April. ROUEN (Diceto, *loc. cit.*)

A charter of Henry in favour of the monks of Reading. Witnessed by: Hugh, bishop of Durham; John, bishop of Evreux; William fitzRadulf, seneschal of Normandy; Seher de Quinci; Hugh de

Cressi; Thomas Bardolf; Aluered de St Martin. (BM, Egerton MS. 3031, fo. 23ᵛ.) This charter must date after 1181, being witnessed by John of Evreux. 1185 seems the most probable date, though January 1188 is possible.

A confirmation by Henry of the agreement between Walter, archbishop of Rouen, and Henry, abbot of Fécamp. Witnessed by: Hugh, bishop of Durham; Robert, son of William, archdeacon of Nottingham; William, clerk of the chamber; Earl William de Mandeville; William fitzRadulf, seneschal of Normandy; Seher de Quinci; Hugh de Cressi. At Rouen. (*Cal. Doc. France*, no. 43; *DB*, no. DCCLXIII.)

April. S. PIERRE-SUR-DIVES

A charter of Henry confirming the union of the abbeys of St Hélier of Jersey and Notre Dame of Cherbourg. Witnessed by: Walter, archbishop of Rouen; Hugh, bishop of Durham; John, bishop of Evreux; Martin, abbot of Cerisy; Robert, archdeacon of Nottingham; William, clerk of the chamber; William fitzRadulf; Roger fitzReinfred; Gilbert fitzReinfred; Robert Poherius. At St Pierre-sur-Dives. (*Cal. Doc. France*, no. 952; *DB*, no. DCLII.)

? *May.* IVRY

A charter of Henry in favour of Marmoutier. Witnessed by: Hugh, bishop of Durham; John, bishop of Evreux; William de Mandeville; Robert, earl of Leicester; William, earl of Salisbury; William de Humez; William fitzRadulf; Seher de Quinci; Hugh de Cressi. At Ivry. (*DB*, no. DCLIII.)

ALENÇON

A charter of Henry in favour of the abbey of Fontevrault. Witnessed by: Hugh, bishop of Durham; Geoffrey, my son, chancellor; William de Humez; William fitzRadulf; Stephen de Tours; Maurice de Creon; Peter fitzGuy; Hugh de Cressi; Aluered de St Martin; William de Ostilli. At Alençon. (*Cal. Doc. France*, no. 1082; *DB*, no. DCLV.)

1186

11 March. GISORS (*Gesta*, I, 343.)

A charter of Margaret, queen of England, widow of Henry the Younger. Witnessed by: William, archbishop of Rheims; Nivelon, bishop of Soissons; Philip, bishop of Beauvais; Henry, elect of Orleans; Philip, count of Flanders; Count Theobald; Count Stephen; the count of Clermont; Earl Robert; Walter, chamberlain;

Gerard, reeve of Poissy; Haico, chancellor of the countess of Champagne; Robert de Milliaco; Artaudus, chamberlain; Hugh, bishop of Durham; John, bishop of Evreux; Hugh, elect of Chester; Earl William de Mandeville; Bernard de St Valery; William de Humez; William fitzRadulf; Hugh de Cressi; Aluered de St Martin; William de Mara. (*Cal. Doc. France*, no. 1084; *DB*, no. DCLX.)

DOVER (*Gesta*, I, 345.)

Before 6 April. DURHAM (*Gesta, loc. cit.*; Eyton, *Henry II*, 267.)

July. CARLISLE (*Gesta*, I, 348–9; Eyton, *Henry II*, 269.)

A charter of Henry in favour of the abbey of Furness. Witnessed by: Hugh, bishop of Durham; Jocelin, archdeacon of Chichester. At Carlisle. (*Furness Coucher Book*, I, no. 70.)

July. SCOTLAND–CARLISLE (*Gesta, loc. cit.*)

14 September. MARLBOROUGH (*Gesta*, I, 352; Eyton, *Henry II*, 271.)

A charter of Henry in favour of the priory of Witham. Witnessed by: Hugh, bishop of Durham; Geoffrey, bishop of Ely; John, bishop of Norwich; Reginald, bishop of Bath; John, my son; Earl William of Sussex; Rannulf de Glanville; Walter fitzRobert; Reginald de Courtenay; Hugh Bardolf; Hugh de Morwick; Ralph fitzStephen; Gilbert fitzReinfred; Geoffrey fitzPeter; Robert de Whitfield; Michael Belet. At Marlborough. (*Mon. Ang.* VI, 2; Eyton, *Henry II*, 271–2.)

? September. LUDGERSHALL

A charter of Henry in favour of the church of St Mary, Sibton. Witnessed by: Hugh, bishop of Durham; Henry, bishop of Bayeux; Geoffrey, bishop of Ely; Rannulf de Glanville; Hugh de Morwick; Hugh Bardolf. At Ludgershall. (*CChR*, II, 95–6.) The charter must date after the consecration of Geoffrey of Ely in October 1174. Alternative dates would be October 1175, or January 1182.

30 September. WOODSTOCK

A charter of Henry in favour of the abbey of St Mary, York. Witnessed by: Geoffrey, bishop of Ely; Hugh, bishop of Durham; William, earl of Essex; Rannulf de Glanville; Hugh Bardolf. At Woodstock. (*Wetherhal Register*, no. 13; Eyton, *Henry II*, 273.)

c. 2 October. WINCHESTER

A charter of Henry in favour of St Peter's, York. Witnessed by: Hugh, bishop of Durham; John, bishop of Norwich; William, bishop of Worcester; H[ubert], dean of York; Rannulf de Glanville;

Hugh de Morwick; Hugh Bardolf; Robert de Whitfield; Michael Belet. At Winchester. (*Mon. Ang.* VI, 612; *CChR*, II, 439–40; Eyton, *Henry II*, 274.)

1187

11 February. CANTERBURY (Gervase of Canterbury, I, 353; Eyton, *Henry II*, 276.)

February. CLARENDON

A charter of Henry in favour of the priory of Wombridge. Witnessed by: Hugh, bishop of Durham; Peter, bishop of St David's; H[ubert], dean of York; Rannulf de Glanville; Roger Almoner; Hugh de Morwick; Hugh Bardolf. At Clarendon. (Eyton, *Henry II*, 277.)

17 February. Bishop Hugh crossed from Dover to Wissant in company with the king. (*Gesta*, II, 4; Diceto, II, 47; Eyton, *Henry II*, 277.)

November. BUR-LE-ROI

A charter of Henry in favour of the canons of Havering. Witnessed by: Hugh, bishop of Durham; Henry, bishop of Bayeux; John de Coutances, archdeacon of Oxford; Robert, son of William fitzRadulf, archdeacon of Nottingham; William de Humez; William fitzRadulf; Gilbert fitzReinfred. At Bur-le-Roi. (*DB*, no. DCCLV; *Early Oxford Charters*, no. 40.)

c. 30 December. CAEN

Three charters of Henry in favour of the abbey of Préaux. Witnessed by: Walter, archbishop of Rouen; Hugh, bishop of Durham; Henry, bishop of Bayeux; Hugh, elect of Coventry; Robert, archdeacon of Nottingham; Earl William de Mandeville; Earl William of Salisbury; William de Humez; William fitzRadulf; Aluered de St Martin; William de Mara; Gilbert fitzReinfred. At Caen. (*DB*, nos. DCLXXV, DCLXXVI, DCLXXVII; *Cal. Doc. France*, nos. 352, 353; Eyton, *Henry II*, 282.)

1188

11 February. GEDDINGTON (*Gesta*, II, 33; Newburgh, I, 275; Eyton, *Henry II*, 285.)

A confirmation by Henry of the agreement between the abbey of St Wandrille and Jeremiah, clerk of Ecclesfield. Witnessed by: Hugh, bishop of Durham; John, bishop of Norwich; William, earl of

Sussex; Rannulf de Glanville; William de Humez; Walter fitz-Robert; Seher de Quinci; William Marshal; Geoffrey fitzPeter; Richard de Camville. At Geddington. (*DB*, no. DCLXXII; *EYC*, III, no. 1278; *Cal. Doc. France*, no. 178.)

A charter of Henry in favour of the church of Bungay. Witnessed by: Hugh, bishop of Durham; John, bishop of Norwich; Earl William of Sussex; Earl David, brother of the King of Scots; Rannulf de Glanville; William de Humez; Walter fitzRobert; Seher de Quinci; William Marshal; Geoffrey fitzPeter; Richard de Camville; Stephen de Turnham. At Geddington. (*CChR*, IV, 225–6; Eyton, *Henry II*, 285.)

February–March. WARK (*Gesta*, II, 44–5; Hoveden, II, 339.)

? March. KEMPSEY

A charter of Henry relating to a dispute between the bishops of Hereford and Worcester. Witnessed by: Baldwin, archbishop of Canterbury; Hugh, bishop of Durham; Hugh, bishop of Coventry; Peter, bishop of St David's; Rannulf de Glanville; Rannulf, earl of Chester; Earl Robert of Leicester; William, earl of Arundel; Waleran, earl of Warwick; Robert Marmion; William Marshal; Richard de Camville; Gilbert fitzReinfred. At Kempsey. (*CChR*, IV, 337.)

14 June. GEDDINGTON

A final concord taken before: the king; Hugh, bishop of Durham; John, bishop of Norwich; Godfrey de Luci; Rannulf de Glanville; William de Humez; Bertram de Verdun; Geoffrey fitzPeter; Hugh Pantulf. (Eyton, *Henry II*, 287.)

October. Bishop Hugh was a justice in eyre in the counties of Yorkshire, Northumberland and Cumberland. (*PR 1 Richard I*, 84, 139, 243.)

9 October. YORK

A fine was taken before Bishop Hugh as justice. (*Fountains Cartulary*, II, 490, no. 20.)

1189

1 February. YORK

A fine was taken before the bishop as justice. *Guisborough Cartulary*, I, no. 326, and cf. *EYC*, II, no. 701.)

26 July. DURHAM

Bishop Hugh mediates in a dispute between the convent of

Durham and the hospital of St Giles of Durham. (DC Durham, 4. 16. Spec. no. 45.)

August. SALISBURY (*Gesta*, II, 76)

3 September. WESTMINSTER
Bishop Hugh was present at the coronation of King Richard I. (*Gesta*, II, 79.)

5 September. WESTMINSTER
A charter of Richard in favour of the abbey of Bec. (*Cart. Ant.* XXXI, 11; L. Landon, *Richard I, sub anno.*)
A charter of Richard in favour of the abbey of Waverley. (*Cart. Ant.* XVIII, 20; Landon, *Richard I, sub anno.*)
A charter of Richard in favour of the abbey of Rievaulx. (*CChR*, I, 398; Landon, *Richard I, sub anno.*)

6 September. WESTMINSTER
A charter of Richard in favour of the abbey of Malmesbury. (*Cart. Ant.* XXI, 1; XVI, 4; Landon, *Richard I, sub anno.*)
A charter of Richard in favour of the abbey of Rievaulx. (*CChR*, I, 399; Landon, *Richard I, sub anno.*)

11 September. GEDDINGTON
A charter of Richard in favour of the church of Worcester. (*Cart. Ant.* XIX, 40; Landon, *Richard I, sub anno.*)

13 September. GEDDINGTON
A charter of Richard in favour of the nuns of Sempringham. (Landon, *Richard I, sub anno.*)
A charter of Richard in favour of the abbey of Bordesley. (*CChR*, II, 65–6.)

15 September. GEDDINGTON
A charter of Richard in favour of the church of Worcester. (*CChR*, IV, 338; Landon, *Richard I, sub anno.*)
A charter of Richard in favour of the abbey of Wardon. (*CChR*, II, 335; Landon, *Richard I, sub anno.*)
A charter of Richard in favour of the monks of Bruern. (*Cart. Ant.* XVII, 1; *CChR*, V, 221; Landon, *Richard I, sub anno.*)
A charter of Richard in favour of the abbey of Stratford. (*CChR*, II, 313; Landon, *Richard I, sub anno.*)
A charter of Richard in favour of the abbey of Rievaulx. (*Rievaulx Cartulary*, 129; Landon, *Richard I, sub anno.*)
PIPEWELL (*Gesta*, II, 85; Hoveden, III, 15.)

16 September. GEDDINGTON

A charter of Richard in favour of the abbey of Ford. (*Cart. Ant.* XVIII, 21; Landon, *Richard I, sub anno.*)

A charter of Richard in favour of the abbey of Ramsey. (*Cart. Ant.* XLII, 3; Landon, *Richard I, sub anno.*)

Two charters of Richard in favour of the nuns of Holy Trinity, Caen. (*CChR*, v, 161; *Cart. Ant.* xv, 16; Landon, *Richard I, sub anno.*)

PIPEWELL (*Gesta*, II, 87; Hoveden, III, 16.)

GEDDINGTON

A charter of Richard in favour of the Hospitallers. (BM, Harley Charter, 43, C 28; Landon, *Richard I, sub anno.*)

17 September. GEDDINGTON

A charter of Richard in favour of the abbey of St Albans. (*CChR*, III, 20; Landon, *Richard I, sub anno.*)

Two charters of Richard in favour of the priory of Christchurch, Canterbury. (DC Canterbury, C 28; F 93.)

A charter of Richard in favour of the abbey of Kirkstall. (*CChR*, IV, 46; Landon, *Richard I, sub anno.*)

A charter of Richard in favour of Hugh, bishop of Coventry. (Gervase of Canterbury, I, 461; Landon, *Richard I, sub anno.*)

A writ of Richard to the citizens and priory of Coventry. (*HMC, Report* XIV, App. 8, 220; Landon, *Richard I, sub anno.*)

A charter of Richard in favour of the priory of Wymondham. (BM, Cotton MS. Tit. C VIII, fo. 16^v; Landon, *Richard I, sub anno.*)

A charter of Richard in favour of the abbey of Rievaulx. (*CChR*, I, 395; *Rievaulx Cartulary*, 124; Landon, *Richard I, sub anno.*)

A charter of Richard in favour of the abbey of St Mary, York. (*CChR*, III, 112; Landon, *Richard I, sub anno.*)

22 September. FECKENHAM

A charter of Richard in favour of the abbey of Cîteaux. (Cartellieri, *Philip August*, II, no. 15; Landon, *Richard I, sub anno.*)

23 September. FECKENHAM

A charter of Richard in favour of the abbey of Merevale. (*CChR*, III, 485; Landon, *Richard I, sub anno.*)

27 September. ? BREWD

A charter of Richard in favour of Robert, son of Maurice de Berkeley. (*CChR*, IV, 178; Landon, *Richard I, sub anno.*)

28 September. WARWICK

A charter of Richard in favour of the citizens of Southampton. (*CChR*, III, 340; Landon, *Richard I, sub anno.*)

30 September. WOODSTOCK

Three charters of Richard in favour of the lepers of St Laurence of Jerusalem. (*Cart. Ant.* XXXIV, 20, 21, 22.)

6 October. WESTMINSTER

A charter of Richard in favour of the Templars. (*Cart. Ant.* XIX, 17; Landon, *Richard I, sub anno.*)

A charter of Richard in favour of the nuns of Stratford. (*CChR*, I, 323; Landon, *Richard I, sub anno.*)

A charter of Richard in favour of the abbey of Ramsey. (BM, Add. Charter, 33649; Landon, *Richard I, sub anno.*)

A charter of Richard in favour of the abbey of Westminster. (BM, Cotton MS. Faust. A III, fo. 80; Landon, *Richard I, sub anno.*)

7 October. WESTMINSTER

Two charters of Richard in favour of the abbey of St Benet of Holme. (*CChR*, II, 327; Landon, *Richard I, sub anno.*)

A charter of Richard in favour of the abbey of Boscherville. (*Cal. Doc. France*, no. 213; Landon, *Richard I, sub anno.*)

A charter of Richard in favour of the nuns of Haliwell. (*Cart. Ant.* XXI, 8; Landon, *Richard I, sub anno.*)

A charter of Richard in favour of the abbey of Westminster. (BM, Cotton MS., Faust. A III, fo. 81ᵛ; Landon, *Richard I, sub anno.*)

8 October. WESTMINSTER

A charter of Richard in favour of Thomas fitzRalf. (*CChR*, I, 27; Landon, *Richard I, sub anno.*)

A charter of Richard in favour of the men of Cookham. (*CChR*, II, 176; Landon, *Richard I, sub anno.*)

A charter of Richard in favour of the priory of Christchurch. (*CChR*, III, 234; Landon, *Richard I, sub anno.*)

A charter of Richard in favour of Twineham. (BM, Cotton MS., Tib. D VI, fo. 18ᵛ.)

9 October. WESTMINSTER

A charter of Richard in favour of Walter de St Valery. (*Cal. Doc. France*, no. 45; Landon, *Richard I, sub anno.*)

A charter of Richard in favour of the abbey of St Mary, York. (*Cart. Ant.* XVII, 5; Landon, *Richard I, sub anno.*)

A charter of Richard in favour of the Templars. (*Cart. Ant.* xix, 18; Landon, *Richard I, sub anno.*)

A charter of Richard in favour of Waltham Abbey. (BM, Harley MS. 391, fo. 44ᵛ; Landon, *Richard I, sub anno.*)

A charter of Richard in favour of the citizens of Hereford. (*CChR*, iii, 240; Landon, *Richard I, sub anno.*)

A charter of Richard in favour of the nuns of Stratford. (*CChR*, v, 194; Landon, *Richard I, sub anno.*)

10 October. WESTMINSTER

A final concord taken before: H[ugh], bishop of Durham; R[ichard], elect of London; William de St John; Hugh Bardolf; Geoffrey fitzPeter; R[obert] de Whitfield; W[illiam] de Longchamp. (PRO List, 16/103 A, 29.)

A charter of Richard in favour of the abbey of Ely. (*CChR*, i, 183; Landon, *Richard I, sub anno.*)

A charter of Richard in favour of the hospital of St Lazar of Jerusalem. (*Cart. Ant.* iii, 6; Landon, *Richard I, sub anno.*)

A charter of Richard in favour of the monks of Bruern. (*CChR*, iii, 270; Landon, *Richard I, sub anno.*)

A confirmation by Richard for the abbey of Ely. (*Cart. Ant.* xxxiii, 43; Landon, *Richard I, sub anno.*)

A charter of Richard in favour of the abbey of Newhouse. (*CChR*, iii, 385; Landon, *Richard I, sub anno.*)

11 October. WESTMINSTER

A writ of Richard in favour of Henry of Cornhill. (BM, Harley Charter, 43, C 29.)

12 October. GUILDFORD

Two charters of Richard in favour of the abbey of St Augustine, Canterbury. (*CChR*, v, 434; Landon, *Richard I, sub anno.*)

14 October. ARUNDEL

A charter of Richard in favour of the nuns of Amesbury. (*CChR*, iii, 55; Landon, *Richard I, sub anno.*)

15 October. ARUNDEL

A charter of Richard in favour of the abbey of Fontevrault. (*Cal. Doc. France*, no. 1085; Landon, *Richard I, sub anno.*)

17 October. WINCHESTER

A charter of Richard in favour of the nuns of Godstow. (PRO, Exchequer, KR, Misc. Book, xx, fo. 165ᵛ; Landon, *Richard I, sub anno.*)

20 October. WINCHESTER

A writ of Richard in favour of the abbey of Waltham. (BM, Harley MS. 391, fo. 48ᵛ; Landon, *Richard I, sub anno.*)

A charter of Richard in favour of Merton Priory. (*CPR, 1422–9,* 288; Landon, *Richard I, sub anno.*)

A charter of Richard in favour of the nuns of Holy Trinity, Caen. (*CChR,* v, 161; Landon, *Richard I, sub anno.*)

21 October. WINCHESTER

A charter of Richard in favour of the abbey of Buildwas. (BM, Harley Charter, 43, C 30; Landon, *Richard I, sub anno.*)

A charter of Richard in favour of Savigny. (Cartellieri, *Philip August,* II, no. 26; Landon, *Richard I, sub anno.*)

These two charters were witnessed by Hugh, bishop of Durham, alone.

22 October. WINCHESTER

A charter of Richard in favour of the abbey of Evreux. (*Cal. Doc. France,* no. 307; Landon, *Richard I, sub anno.*)

23 October. WINCHESTER

A charter of Richard in favour of the abbey of Sawley. (*CChR,* II, 163; Landon, *Richard I, sub anno.*)

A charter of Richard in favour of the nuns of Holy Trinity, Caen. (*CChR,* v, 161; Landon, *Richard I, sub anno.*)

26 October. WINCHESTER

A charter of Richard in favour of the abbey of St Mary du Pin. (Landon, *Richard I,* no. 107.)

7 November. WESTMINSTER

A charter of Richard in favour of the abbey of Waltham, witnessed by Hugh, bishop of Durham, alone. (BM, Harley MS. 391, fo. 50; Landon, *Richard I, sub anno.*)

8 November. WESTMINSTER

Two charters of Richard in favour of the Knights Templars. (*Cart. Ant.* XIX, 19, 20; Landon, *Richard I, sub anno.*)

A charter of Richard in favour of the canons of St Mary de Pré. (*Cart. Ant.* XXII, 20; Landon, *Richard I, sub anno.*)

9 November. WESTMINSTER (Gervase of Canterbury, I, 469.)

10 November. WESTMINSTER

A charter of Richard in favour of Alexander Barentin. (Madox, *Formulare,* 51; Landon, *Richard I, sub anno.*)

A charter of Richard in favour of the Templars. (*Cal. Doc. France*, no. 271; Landon, *Richard I, sub anno*.)

11 November. WESTMINSTER

A charter of Richard in favour of the citizens of Shrewsbury. (*HMC Report* xv, App. x, 2; Landon, *Richard I, sub anno*.)

Two charters of Richard in favour of John, his Marshal. (*Cart. Ant.* XXI, 9, 10; Landon, *Richard I, sub anno*.)

12 November. WESTMINSTER

A charter of Richard in favour of the church of Rouen. (*Cal. Doc. France*, no. 53; Landon, *Richard I, sub anno*.)

A charter of Richard in favour of the citizens of Bedford. (*CChR*, v, 356; Landon, *Richard I, sub anno*.)

A charter of Richard in favour of the canons of Cirencester. (*CChR*, v, 212; Landon, *Richard I, sub anno*.)

A charter of Richard in favour of the abbey of Bury. (BM, Add. MS. 14847, fo. 40ᵛ; Landon, *Richard I, sub anno*.)

A charter of Richard in favour of the citizens of Worcester. (Landon, *Richard I*, no. 128.)

13 November. WESTMINSTER

A charter of Richard in favour of the priory of St Swithun, Winchester. (*CChR*, III, 356; Landon, *Richard I, sub anno*.)

A charter of Richard in favour of the priory of Spalding. (*CChR*, IV, 164; Landon, *Richard I, sub anno*.)

A charter of Richard in favour of the abbey of Cirencester, witnessed by Hugh, bishop of Durham, alone. (*CChR*, v, 451; Landon, *Richard I, sub anno*.)

14 November. WESTMINSTER

A charter of Richard in favour of the abbey of Stanlaw. (*CChR*, I, 38; Landon, *Richard I, sub anno*.)

Two charters of Richard in favour of the abbey of Grestain. (*Mon. Ang.* VI, 1090; Landon, *Richard I, sub anno*.)

15 November. WESTMINSTER

A charter of Richard in favour of the abbey of Bordesley. (*CChR*, II, 65; Landon, *Richard I, sub anno*.)

17 November. WESTMINSTER

A charter of Richard in favour of the abbey of Rievaulx. (*Cart. Ant.* XIX, 7; Landon, *Richard I, sub anno*.)

18 November. BURY ST EDMUNDS

A charter of Richard in favour of Royston Priory. (*CPR, 1400*, 198; Landon, *Richard I, sub anno*.)

A charter of Richard in favour of the abbey of Bury. (BM, Add. MS. 14847, fo. 41; Landon, *Richard I, sub anno.*)

A charter of Richard in favour of the abbey of Buckfastleigh. (*Cart. Ant.* XVIII, 19; Landon, *Richard I, sub anno.*)

A charter of Richard in favour of the citizens of Northampton. (Landon, *Richard I, sub anno.*)

21 November. BURY ST EDMUNDS

A charter of Richard in favour of the abbey of Bury. (*CChR*, III, 273; Landon, *Richard I, sub anno.*)

A charter of Richard in favour of the abbey of St Mary du Pin, witnessed by Hugh, bishop of Durham, alone. (Landon, *Richard I,* no. 144.)

25 November. WESTMINSTER

A charter of Richard in favour of Roger Bigod. (*Cart. Ant.* XVIII, 14; Landon, *Richard I, sub anno.*)

25 November. CANTERBURY

A charter of Richard in favour of the abbey of Colchester. (*CChR*, I, 423; Landon, *Richard I, sub anno.*)

26 November. CANTERBURY

A charter of Richard in favour of the church of Wells. (*HMC, Wells*, I, 308; Landon, *Richard I, sub anno.*)

A charter of Richard in favour of Reginald, bishop of Bath. (*CChR*, III, 474; Landon, *Richard I, sub anno.*)

Three charters of Richard in favour of the church of Bath. (*CChR*, I, 7; III, 470; Landon, *Richard I, sub anno.*)

27 November. CANTERBURY

A charter of Richard in favour of Reginald, bishop of Bath. (*CChR*, V, 180; Landon, *Richard I, sub anno.*)

A charter of Richard in favour of the citizens of York. (*EYC*, I, no. 204; Landon, *Richard I, sub anno.*)

28 November. CANTERBURY

A charter of Richard in favour of the nuns of Wix. (*CPR, 1436–41*, 263; Landon, *Richard I, sub anno.*)

Two charters of Richard in favour of the church of Ely. (*Cart. Ant.* II, 30; Landon, *Richard I, sub anno.*)

A charter of Richard in favour of William de Derneford. (Landon, *Richard I,* no. 158.)

A charter of Richard in favour of Robert de Warneford. (*Cart. Ant.* X, 29; Landon, *Richard I, sub anno.*)

29 November. CANTERBURY

A charter of Richard in favour of the nuns of Amesbury. (*Cart. Ant.* VI, 1; Landon, *Richard I, sub anno.*)

30 November. CANTERBURY

A charter of Richard in favour of Hugh, bishop of Coventry. (*CChR*, I, 118; Landon, *Richard I, sub anno.*)

A charter of Richard in favour of Richard, son of Ancherus. (BM, Add. MS. 37665, fo. 26ᵛ.)

A charter of Richard in favour of Laurence, chamberlain of the bishop of Durham. (BM, Lansdowne MS. 902, fo. 78ᵛ.)

A charter of Richard in favour of Osbert de Longchamp. (*Cart. Ant.* XVII, 9; Landon, *Richard I, sub anno.*)

A charter of Richard in favour of Aluered de St Martin. (BM, Egerton Charter, 372; Landon, *Richard I, sub anno.*)

1 December. CANTERBURY

A charter of Richard in favour of Christchurch, Canterbury. (DC Canterbury, Register A, fo. 93.)

A charter of Richard in favour of the archbishop of Canterbury. (*CChR*, V, 126; Landon, *Richard I, sub anno.*)

A charter of Richard in favour of Waltham Abbey. (*Mon. Ang.* VI, 66; Landon, *Richard I, sub anno.*)

A charter of Richard in favour of Ralph fitzRalph. (*CPR, 1391–6*, 190; Landon, *Richard I, sub anno.*)

2 December. CANTERBURY

A charter of Richard in favour of William fitzPeter. (*Cart. Ant.* XIX, 42; Landon, *Richard I, sub anno.*)

A charter of Richard in favour of Hugh Bardolf. (*Cart. Ant.* XXIX, 10; Landon, *Richard I, sub anno.*)

A charter of Richard in favour of the monks of Thame. (*Cart. Ant.* XV, 31; Landon, *Richard I, sub anno.*)

A charter of Richard in favour of Hugh de Neville (*HMC Report* IV, App. 228; Landon, *Richard I, sub anno.*)

3 December. CANTERBURY

A charter of Richard in favour of the monks of Holme Cultram. (*CChR*, III, 79; Landon, *Richard I, sub anno.*)

Two charters of Richard in favour of the abbey of St Augustine, Canterbury. (BM, Cotton MS., Jul D. 11, fos. 94, 97ᵛ; Landon, *Richard I, sub anno.*)

A charter of Richard in favour of the abbey of St Augustine, Canterbury. (BM, Cotton MS., Claud. D 10, fo. 257ᵛ.)

4 December. CANTERBURY

A charter of Richard in favour of the abbey of St Augustine, Canterbury. (BM, Cotton MS., Jul. D 11, fo. 88ᵛ; Landon, *Richard I, sub anno.*)

A charter of Richard in favour of the church of Coventry. (*CChR,* II, 347; Landon, *Richard I, sub anno.*)

A charter of Richard in favour of Henry of Cornhill. (*CChR,* II, 138; Landon, *Richard I, sub anno.*)

A charter of Richard in favour of Alan de Valognes. (*Cart. Ant.* XXII, 27; Landon, *Richard I, sub anno.*)

A charter of Richard in favour of Geoffrey fitzPeter. (*Cart. Ant.* XXI, 17; Landon, *Richard I, sub anno.*)

A charter of Richard in favour of the abbey of St Botolph, Colchester. (*CPR, 1399–1401,* 374; Landon, *Richard I, sub anno.*)

A charter of Richard in favour of the monks of Biddlesden. (BM, Harley MS. 4714, fo. 98ᵛ.)

5 December. CANTERBURY

A charter of Richard in favour of the abbey of Selby. (*Cart. Ant.* XV, 15; Landon, *Richard I, sub anno.*)

A charter of Richard in favour of the men of Surfleet, Gosberton, Quadring and Donington. (*Cart. Ant.* XXI, 3; Landon, *Richard I, sub anno.*)

A charter of Richard in favour of the abbey of Peterborough. (*CChR,* IV, 274; Landon, *Richard I, sub anno.*)

6 December. DOVER

A charter of Richard in favour of the abbey of Peterborough. (*Cart. Ant.* XXIX, 21; Landon, *Richard I, sub anno.*)

A charter of Richard in favour of Wigan de Cherbourg. (Landon, *Richard I,* no. 188.)

A charter of Richard in favour of John de Palerna. (*Cart. Ant.* XV, 27; Landon, *Richard I, sub anno.*)

A charter of Richard in favour of Philip fitzHelget. (*Cart. Ant.* XVII, 8; Landon, *Richard I, sub anno.*)

A charter of Richard in favour of Walter fitzThurstan. (*Cart. Ant.* XXVIII, 10; Landon, *Richard I, sub anno.*)

A charter of Richard in favour of Henry of Cornhill. (PRO, Duchy of Lancaster Charter DL 10/42; Landon, *Richard I, sub anno.*)

A charter of Richard in favour of Vassal, the king's singer. (Landon, *Richard I, sub anno.*)

A charter of Richard in favour of the citizens of Colchester. (*CChR,* I, 410; Landon, *Richard I, sub anno.*)

7 December. DOVER

A charter of Richard in favour of William de S. Mère Église. (*Cart. Ant.* XXXI, 15; Landon, *Richard I, sub anno.*)

A charter of Richard in favour of the abbey of Stratford. (*CChR*, II, 311; Landon, *Richard I, sub anno.*)

A charter of Richard in favour of the abbey of Boxley. (*CChR*, II, 354; Landon, *Richard I, sub anno.*)

A charter of Richard in favour of the bishop of Coventry. (*Cart. Ant.* XV, 24; Landon, *Richard I, sub anno.*)

A charter of Richard in favour of the abbey of Beeleigh. (*CChR*, V, 186; Landon, *Richard I, sub anno.*)

A charter of Richard in favour of the Hospital of St John of Jerusalem. (BM, Cotton MS., Nero, C IX, fo. 29^v; Landon, *Richard I, sub anno.*)

A charter of Richard in favour of the merchant guild of Bath. (*CChR*, I, 311; Landon, *Richard I, sub anno.*)

8 December. DOVER

A charter of Richard in favour of the lepers of St Mary Magdalene, Colchester. (*Mon. Ang.* VI, 631; Landon, *Richard I, sub anno.*)

A charter of Richard in favour of the nuns of Shaftesbury. (BM, Harley MS. 61, fo. 25^v; Landon, *Richard I, sub anno.*)

The charters of 16 December–20 February were granted in Richard's name by the chancellor in England after the king's departure, and witnessed by Hugh du Puiset

16 December. WESTMINSTER

A charter of Richard in favour of the abbey of Westminster, witnessed by: Hugh, bishop of Durham, etc. (BM, Cotton MS., Faust. A III, fo. 132.)

28 December. CANTERBURY

A charter of Richard in favour of the priory of Tynemouth. Witnessed by: Baldwin, archbishop of Canterbury; Geoffrey, elect of York; Hugh, bishop of Durham; William Marshal. (*Cart. Ant.* XXVI, 18; *CChR*, II, 173.)

1190

23 January. WESTMINSTER

A charter of Richard in favour of the men of Ainsty. Witnessed by: H[ugh], bishop of Durham; G[odfrey], bishop of Winchester;

R[ichard], bishop of London; H[ugh], bishop of Coventry; William (*sic*), earl of Clare; William Marshal; Hugh Bardolf; Geoffrey fitz-Peter; Bertram de Verdun. (*Historians of the Church of York*, III, 87.)

24 January. WESTMINSTER

A charter of Richard in favour of the abbey of Ramsey. Witnessed by: H[ugh], bishop of Durham; J[ohn], bishop of Norwich; H[ugh], bishop of Coventry; Bertram de Verdun, Gilbert Pipard, Geoffrey fitzPeter. (*Cart. Ant.* III, 13.)

A charter of Richard in favour of Robert Corbet. Witnessed by: H[ugh], bishop of Durham; R[ichard], bishop of London; H[ugh], bishop of Coventry; Herbert, archdeacon of Canterbury; J[ocelin], archdeacon of Chichester; William fitzAudelin; Bertram de Verdun; William Pipard; R[obert] de Whitfield; Michael Belet; William fitzAlan; Hugh Pantulf; John de Strange; Vivian de Roshall; Helias de Etingeham. (Eyton, *Antiquities of Shropshire*, VII, 12.)

A final concord made before: H[ugh], bishop of Durham; W[illiam], bishop of Ely; H[ugh], bishop of Coventry; Jocelin, archdeacon of Chichester; Roger fitzReinfred; Master Thomas de Husseburn; Michael Belet; Simon de Patteshall. (BM, Egerton MS. 3031, fo. 43.)

25 January. WESTMINSTER

A final concord made before: William, bishop of Ely; Hugh, bishop of Durham; and Hugh, bishop of Coventry. (*Cal. Doc. France*, nos. 442, 443.)

A charter of Richard in favour of the church of Lincoln. Witnessed by: H[ugh], bishop of Durham; R[ichard], bishop of London; G[odfrey], bishop of Winchester; Earl William of Salisbury; William Marshal; Geoffrey fitzPeter; Hugh Bardolf. (*Reg. Ant. Linc.* I, 124, no. 199.)

20 February. WESTMINSTER

A writ of Richard in favour of the canons of Lincoln. Witnessed by Hugh, bishop of Durham. (*Reg. Ant. Linc.* I, 122; no. 196.)

12 March. Bishop Hugh joins the king at Bonsmoulins. (*Gesta*, II, 105; Hoveden, III, 32.)

14 March. NONANCOURT

A charter of Richard in favour of the citizens of Winchester. (*Cart. Ant.* XVII, 30; Landon, *Richard I, sub anno.*)

A charter of Richard in favour of the abbey of Waltham. (*CChR*, IV, 264; Landon, *Richard I, sub anno.*)

18 March. ROUEN

A charter of Richard for the house of La Chartreuse. (*Cart. Ant.* XIX, 16; Landon, *Richard I, sub anno.*)

20 March. ROUEN

A charter of Richard in favour of the archbishop of Canterbury. (*Cart. Ant.* XV, 18; Landon, *Richard I, sub anno.*)
A charter of Richard in favour of the nuns of Clerkenwell. (BM, Cotton MS., Faust. B II, fo. 8; Landon, *Richard I, sub anno.*)
A charter of Richard in favour of the abbey 'de Voto' of Cherbourg. (*Mon. Ang.* VI, 1111; Landon, *Richard I, sub anno.*)

21 March. ROUEN

Four charters of Richard in favour of the abbey of Peterborough. (*Cart. Ant.* XXII, 3; Landon, *Richard I, sub anno.*)

22 March. ROUEN

A charter of Richard in favour of the hospital of St Bartholomew, London. (*Cart. Ant.* XI, 9; Landon, *Richard I, sub anno.*)
Three charters of Richard in favour of the abbey of Peterborough. (*CChR,* IV, 278; Landon, *Richard I, sub anno.*)
A charter of Richard in favour of Isaac, son of Rabbi Joce. (*Cart. Ant.* XXI, 11; Landon, *Richard I, sub anno.*)

23 March. ROUEN

A charter of Richard in favour of Roger de St Mannes. (*CChR,* III, 432; Landon, *Richard I, sub anno.*)

24 March. ROUEN

Eight charters of Richard in favour of the abbey of Peterborough. (*Cart. Ant.* XXII, 2; Landon, *Richard I, sub anno.*)
A charter of Richard in favour of the hospital of St Bartholomew, London. (*CPR, 1416–22,* 243–5; Landon, *Richard I, sub anno.*)

27 March. LYONS-LA-FORÊT

A charter of Richard in favour of Richard Ruffus. (*Cart. Ant.* III, 8; Landon, *Richard I, sub anno.*)

29 March. GISORS

A charter of Richard in favour of the abbey of Abingdon. (*Chronicle of Abingdon,* II, 245; Landon, *Richard I, sub anno.*)

31 March. GOURNAY

A charter of Richard for Franco de Bohun. (*CPR, 1381–5,* 512; Landon, *Richard I, sub anno.*)

6 April. ARGENTAN

A charter of Richard in favour of the abbey of Gouffern. (*Cal. Doc. France*, no. 603; Landon, *Richard I, sub anno.*)

11 April. MORTAIN

A charter of Richard in favour of Walkelin de Ferrers. (*Cart. Ant.* XIII, 37; Landon, *Richard I, sub anno.*)

12 April. GORRON

A charter of Richard in favour of the priory of Nostell. (BM, Cotton MS., Vesp. E XIX, fo. 4; Landon, *Richard I, sub anno.*)

?12 April. At about this date Bishop Hugh returned to England.

April. WESTMINSTER

c. *May.* BLYTH

TICKHILL [? SOUTHWELL]

c. *June.* LONDON

HOWDEN (Devizes, 391; *Gesta*, II, 109; Hoveden, III, 35.)

1191

July. WINCHESTER (Hoveden, III, 134; *Gesta*, II, 208; Devizes, 407.)

8–10 October. LONDON (*Gesta*, II, 218; Hoveden, III, 145.)

25 December. HOWDEN (Hoveden, III, 169; *Gesta*, II, 235–6.)

1192

c. *15 March.* WESTMINSTER (*Gesta*, II, 238.)

31 March. WESTMINSTER

A final concord taken before: W[alter], archbishop of Rouen; H[ugh], bishop of Durham; [Richard], bishop of London; William Marshal; Geoffrey fitzPeter; William Brewer; Roger fitzReinfred; R[obert] de Wite[feld]; Osbert fitzHervey; Master Thomas de Husse[burna]—the king's justices. (DC Canterbury, Register B, fo. 315.)

c. *April.* NORTHAMPTON (Hoveden, III, 172.)

c. *July*. DOVER

WISSANT

PARIS

VÉZELAY (*Gesta*, II, 247–50; Hoveden, III, 193–4.)

October. NORTHAMPTON (Hoveden, III, 172; Gervase of Canterbury, I, 513.)

1193

c. *20 March*. TICKHILL (Hoveden, III, 206–8.)

16 October. WESTMINSTER

A final concord taken in the Exchequer before: W[alter], archbishop of Rouen; R[ichard], bishop of London; H[ugh], bishop of Durham; G[odfrey], bishop of Winchester, and others. (BM, Cotton MS., Vesp. E II, fo. 50ᵛ.)

1194

21 February. DURHAM

A charter of Hugh in favour of the canons of Carlisle. (DC Durham, Cart. Misc. no. 6548.)

February. TICKHILL (Hoveden, III, 237.)

c. *20 March*. SOUTHWELL

c. *25 March*. TICKHILL (Hoveden, III, 238.)

27 March. NOTTINGHAM (Hoveden, III, 239.)

28 March. NOTTINGHAM

A charter of Richard in favour of the bishop of Norwich. (Landon, *Richard I, sub anno*.)

30 March. NOTTINGHAM (Hoveden, III, 240.)

April. BRACKLEY (Hoveden, III, 245.)

16 April. WINCHESTER

A charter of Richard for Robert fitzRoger. (*Cart. Ant.* XXIX, 6; Landon, *Richard I, sub anno*.)

17 April. WINCHESTER (Hoveden, III, 247–8.)

A charter of Richard in favour of William, king of Scotland. (See above, p. 186, n. 6; Landon, *Richard I, sub anno*.)

20 April. WINCHESTER

A charter of Richard in favour of the church of St Mary, Strood. (*Cart. Ant.* VI, 15; Landon, *Richard I, sub anno.*)

A charter of Richard for Simon, the butler. (*Cart. Ant.* XVIII, 26; Landon, *Richard I, sub anno.*)

21 April. WINCHESTER

A confirmation of Richard for the abbey of Furness. (*CChR,* V, 444; Landon, *Richard I, sub anno.*)

22 April. WINCHESTER

A charter of Richard for Theobald Walter. (*Cart. Ant.* XVII, 24; Landon, *Richard I, sub anno.*)

A charter of Richard in favour of the canons of Drax. (Landon, *Richard I,* no. 411.)

23 April. BISHOPS WALTHAM

A charter of Richard in favour of William, son of Robert, son of Martin. (Landon, *Richard I, sub anno.*)

24 April. PORTSMOUTH

A charter of Richard in favour of Henry fitzCount. (*Ancient Charters,* no. 62; Landon, *Richard I, sub anno.*)

25 April. PORTSMOUTH

A charter of Richard in favour of the abbey of Haughmond. (BM, Harley MS. 2188, fo. 123; Landon, *Richard I, sub anno.*)

A charter of Richard for Noel, his servant. (*CChR,* II, 100; Landon, *Richard I, sub anno.*)

A charter of Richard for Thomas Basset. (*HMC Report* IX, App. 2, 404; Landon, *Richard I, sub anno.*)

28 April. PORTSMOUTH

A charter of Richard in favour of Alard, the Fleming. (*CChR,* I, 355; Landon, *Richard I, sub anno.*)

A charter of Richard in favour of Earl William de Vernon. (*HMC Report* IX, App. 2, 405; Landon, *Richard I, sub anno.*)

September. YORK (Hoveden, III, 273.)

1195

c. *January.* DURHAM

February. YORK (Hoveden, III, 284.)

        CRAYKE

        DONCASTER

3 March. HOWDEN. The death of Hugh du Puiset. (*Scriptores Tres,* 15; Hoveden, III, 285.)

A NOTE ON THE FORGERIES
RELATING TO THE RIGHTS CLAIMED
BY THE CONVENT OF DURHAM

The main body of the Durham forgeries is printed in the introduction to the *Feodarium Prioratus Dunelmensis*.[1] Some of these reputed charters of the Conqueror, Archbishops Lanfranc and Thomas of York and Bishop William of St Calais, together with the bull attributed to Gregory VII, were proved to be forgeries by William Greenwell in 1872, and his conclusions have since remained unquestioned.[2] His list, however, is incomplete,[3] and his suggested date of *c.* 1147 for their fabrication unacceptable.

The hands in which the charters are written are those of the late twelfth century[4] and some may be identified with those of the latter half of Puiset's episcopate.[5] Dating by regnal years, more usually associated with the period after 1189, is common.[6] Some of the charters are sealed on cord, improbable early in the twelfth century and unusual at the end, though the practice was not unknown at Durham, and a late authentic deed of Puiset, unconnected with this dispute, is so sealed.[7] One charter has the great seal of Henry II attached,[8] another a seal which Greenwell was able to identify as that of Prior Bertram (1189–1212).[9] Farrer noted that the witnesses to the charter of Thomas I include the York dignitaries Fulk, Serlo, Tosti and Hugh Sottovagina, who were all alive *c.* 1130–40.[10] Where care has generally been taken to attach venerable subscriptions it seems improbable that a forger would include his own contem-

---

[1] *FPD*, xxxviii–lxxxi.

[2] Cf. Knowles, *Monastic Order*, 626, n. 1; Barlow, *Durham Jurisdictional Peculiars*, 12–14.

[3] There are in fact forty-five drafts and documents of the period *c.* 1160–1230 surviving in the Durham archives. I hope to discuss the making of these forgeries more fully elsewhere.

[4] This view is corroborated, for such material as he inspected, by Mr Neil Ker.

[5] DC Durham, 3. 1. Pont. nos. 2, 13, 14.

[6] DC Durham, 1. 1. Reg. no. 18 (supposedly William I); 1. 1. Reg. no. 1 (supposedly Henry I).

[7] *FPD*, lxxi–lxxii; DC Durham, 4. 2. Ebor. no. 16.

[8] DC Durham, 1. 1. Reg. no. 2B; *FPD, loc. cit.*

[9] DC Durham, 1. 1. Reg. no. 2A; *FPD*, lxxii–lxxiii.   [10] *EYC*, II, 265.

poraries, whereas such names might later have seemed of sufficient obscurity to pass unmarked. Some of the phraseology of the deeds is of late origin; the royal style of *Rex Anglie*, not authentically employed till 1189;[1] the distinction of *beneficia* from *cura animarum*;[2] the mention of 'deans, archdeacons, deacons and other vicars and ministers'.[3] Moreover, it is highly improbable that, had the charter of Archbishop Thomas I been in existence in 1166–72, the miraculous cure of the archbishop there recorded[4] would have been omitted from the catalogue of Cuthbert's achievements which Reginald of Durham was then compiling.[5] Finally, other deeds claiming a later origin than those noticed by Greenwell are undoubted forgeries: a charter of Henry II, purporting to grant 'regalian' rights, and a privilege of Archbishop Roger of York (d. 1181), probably based on an earlier original, but of the general format of the recognized forgeries, written in a characteristic hand on the same vellum.[6]

The dating of the forgeries is difficult. Greenwell accepted two dated charters of William of St Barbara (1147) as being in the hands of the spurious deeds.[7] This does not appear to be the case. There is, moreover, no evidence that the forgeries were employed by the convent before 1185, though in the circumstances of Puiset's episcopate their use might have been opportune. In 1165 Alexander III confirmed the liberties granted by Bishop William of St Calais, without, however, specifying them;[8] and in 1182–3 Lucius III confirmed to the convent the privileges granted by Archbishops Thomas and Thurstan, without further amplification.[9] The spurious charter of Thomas, in its earlier version, was copied for transmission to Rome in 1185–7.[10] Thereafter, the whole series underlay Puiset's

---

[1] DC Durham, 1. 1. Reg. no. 11, printed in *FPD*, lxix–lxxi (supposedly William I); 2. 1. Reg. nos. 4A, 4B (allegedly Henry I); 3. 1. Reg. no. 25 (allegedly Henry II).

[2] DC Durham, 1. 1. Pont. nos. 4A, 4B, printed in *FPD*, l–li (supposedly William of St Calais); DC Durham, 1. 1. Archiep. nos. 1, 2, printed in *FPD*, lxxvi–lxxix (supposedly Archbishop Thomas I).

[3] Cf. *FPD*, lxxvii.

[4] *FPD*, lxxvi–lxxvii.

[5] Mynors, *Durham Cathedral Manuscripts*, no. 123.

[6] DC Durham, 3. 1. Reg. no. 25; 1. 1. Archiep. no. 4 (see above, App. II, no. 14).

[7] *FPD*, lx. I hope to demonstrate this more fully elsewhere with the aid of photographic reproductions.

[8] *PU*, II, no. 120.   [9] *PU*, II, no. 223.

[10] DC Durham, 1. 1. Archiep. no. 8, cf. *EYC*, II, 265. The transcript is dated by reference to Urban III. Thomas's charter is copied from the version of DC Durham, 1. 1. Archiep. no. 1 (printed in *FPD*, lxxvi–lxxix). The existence of another version is not noticed by Greenwell.

surrender in March 1195,[1] and the bull of Gregory VII was confirmed verbatim by Celestine III in 1196.[2] Phrases from the spurious *Venerabilibus patribus* occur for the first time in a charter of Richard I in favour of the convent, given at Chinon on 4 February 1195; for example, *occidentalem partem ville de Halieland*; *terram ex occidentali parte Dunelmi ultra aquam de Wer usque ad aquam de Brun*; *in Werhale totam terram in bosco et plano juxta tynam ex orientali parte de mareburne usque ad mare.*[3]

This burgeoning of original documents at the same time as the increasing trials of the convent suggests that evidence not previously available was being used in the later part of Puiset's episcopate. This view may be substantiated on palaeographical grounds. The spurious deeds were not apparently produced in one short orgy of fabrication, but were in course of construction and revision from about the time of the deposition of Prior Thomas to the end of the century (*c.* 1162–1200). The earliest hand is that responsible for one version of St Calais's alleged privilege *Ego Willelmus.*[4] This charter is nearest in content to that which is contained in the *Liber Vitae*, which in turn, as Greenwell suggests, has the greatest claim to represent what may have been a genuine diploma.[5] The scribe of the forgery, whose work is not unlike that of parts of the Puiset Bible,[6] was at some pains to produce an initial capital E similar to that of the *Liber Vitae* text, presumably his exemplar. It is possible that it was the *Ego Willelmus* that was mentioned by Alexander III in 1165.[7] The same hand is also responsible for the alleged charter of Lanfranc,[8] and for one version of that of Thomas I—the copy known to exist before 1187.[9] In each case the writing is small, in an ink which has now tinted brown, and the words are formed well clear of the ruled lines. The charters have cut seal tags with slender tying tags above. That of Lanfranc has been endorsed by the hand of the scribe of *In nomine Patris.*[10] In Thomas's charter there has been an erasure at the phrase *quiete eas possideant* where a correction has been made by the hand of *In nomine Patris.*[11] It may be suggested that this group, one of whose members was in existence by 1187, formed the nucleus

[1] See above, pp. 135, 259, 263.　　　　　　[2] *PU*, ii, no. 278.
[3] DC Durham, 1. 1. Pont. no. 1, printed in *FPD*, lii–lvi; DC Durham, Cart. 1, fo. 51; *CChR*, iv, 323–5.
[4] DC Durham, 1. 1. Pont. no. 2B, noticed by Greenwell, *FPD*, xxxvii.
[5] *Liber Vitae*, fo. 49; *FPD*, xxxvii.
[6] DC Durham, A II, 1 (2), fo. 223.　　　　　[7] *PU*, ii, no. 120.
[8] DC Durham, 1. 1. Archiep. no. 3, printed in *FPD*, lxxv–lxxvi.
[9] DC Durham, 1. 1. Archiep. no. 1, printed in *FPD*, lxxvi–lxxix.
[10] DC Durham, 1. 1. Pont. nos. 3A, 3B, printed in *FPD*, xlvii–xlix.
[11] *FPD*, lxxvii, at the sentence commencing *Quare volo et* . . .

of the later large collection of forgeries. The fact that one has been revised by a later hand is perhaps evidence of some preparatory editing.

The next group contains two versions of *In nomine Patris*,[1] the variant copy of *Ego Willelmus*,[2] a supposed grant of William I relating to liberties in Yorkshire,[3] and a charter of Archbishop Roger of York.[4] Since it seems unlikely that this latter privilege would have been constructed before the archbishop's death in 1181, and since a scribe of this group has retouched a charter of the preceding group, the date of their production must be placed well within the last decade of Puiset's episcopate. In each case the parchment has been ruled in graphite, the spacing of the lines varying from 10 to 15 mm. With the exception of Roger's charter the documents have multi-strand seal tails inserted at the foot, and in two cases the incision has been strengthened with an additional square of parchment. Of the two versions of *In nomine Patris* it appears that A is a more mature version of B. In the fold at the foot of B the word IN has been written three times, as though the scribe indulged in some practice before embarking on his text. In A the Latin has been improved in some small points, and a clause relating to Tynemouth added, but the general effect is spoiled by the difficulty the writer experienced in getting all his witnesses on to the parchment. The first two columns are cautiously crushed together and the last two placed wide apart. There seems to have been the same revision and amplification of the text in the case of *Ego Willelmus*, as represented in 1. 1. Pont. 2 A. An important clause stating that the prior should have archidiaconal rights in the conventual churches in the bishopric has been added,[5] as also a sentence adding the church of Tynemouth,[6] and a phrase embracing the churches of Jarrow and Wearmouth.[7]

Two other related documents probably belong to this group, an alleged privilege of William I and a shortened version of *In nomine Patris*.[8] They are both ruled in graphite at an average spacing of 7–10 mm., though the hand of the first is larger than that of the second. Both are provided with multi-strand seal tails each of which ends with a V cut. Both these documents are more concise recensions

---

[1] DC Durham, 1. 1. Pont. nos. 3 A, 3 B, printed in *FPD*, xlvii–xlix.
[2] DC Durham, 1. 1. Pont. no. 2 A, printed in *FPD*, xxxviii–xliii.
[3] DC Durham, 1. 1. Reg. no. 9, printed in *EYC*, 11, no. 990.
[4] DC Durham, 1. 1. Archiep. no. 4, see above, App. 11, no. 14.
[5] Cf. *FPD*, xl, n. 1.   [6] Cf. *FPD*, xxxix, n. 4.
[7] Cf. *FPD*, xli, n. 4.
[8] DC Durham, 1. 1. Reg. no. 1, printed in *FPD*, lxvii–lxix; 1. 1. Pont. no. 4 B, printed in *FPD*, l–li.

of earlier material. Neither contains a list of property or churches and they have an abrupt air which suggests compilation. It is worth noting in this connexion that both are marred by mistakes, erasures and corrections. The use of the style *Rex Anglorum* is possibly evidence of composition before 1189.[1]

Of the remaining documents, one of the most important and comprehensive is the alleged bull of Gregory VII. Possibly some version of this document underlay the earliest forgeries, but it seems on the whole more probable that it was not produced until *c.* 1190, for its drafting and precision are of a higher order than most of the documents so far mentioned. Unfortunately it exists only in copies, the earliest of which is entered in a Durham manuscript, where it was discovered by the late Professor W. Levison.[2] The hand is of the late twelfth century, but disguised by remarkable attempts to copy the Northumbrian script of the manuscript itself, combined with occasional emulation of what must have been the writing of an early papal privilege, probably that of Calixtus II or Honorius II.

A related charter of the same date is a revised version of the alleged confirmation of Archbishop Thomas I.[3] It is written in a small cursive hand and improves on the text of 1187 in a number of points. The word 'precept' is used to describe William I's instructions to Thomas;[4] the phrase *tam presentes omnes quam futuri* has been rendered more regular by the omission of *omnes*;[5] *meis successoribus* has been correctly reversed;[6] and the document is made to end with *Valete in domino*, without the addition of witnesses.[7] A *notitia* of the Thomas charter is contained in the same codex as contains the bull of Gregory VII.[8]

Two later charters are attributed to William I and Henry I.[9] Both are ruled in graphite at an average spacing of 8–10 mm., and written throughout in a bold charter hand well clear of the lines. In each case the document is on a wide sheet of parchment of no great length (40 × 11 cm.). Both have been cut for sealing tags from right to left at the foot. In both the king is styled *Rex Anglie*. The scribe of this group has endorsed the record of the arbitration between the prior and archdeacon in 1147.[10]

---

[1] Cf. *FPD*, lxvii.

[2] DC Durham, A II, 16, fo. 101ᵛ. I owe this reference to the kindness of Mrs Levison, who has allowed me to consult her husband's notes. The bull is printed from a later source in *PU*, II, no. 2; cf. Mynors, *Durham Cathedral Manuscripts*, no. 7.

[3] DC Durham, I. I. Archiep. no. 2.   [4] Cf. *FPD*, lxxvii.   [5] *FPD, loc. cit.*

[6] *FPD, loc. cit.*   [7] *FPD*, lxxix.   [8] DC Durham, A II, 16, fo. 60ᵛ.

[9] DC Durham, I. I. Reg. no. 11, printed in *FPD*, lxix–lxxi; 2. I. Reg. no. 4A.

[10] DC Durham, I. I. Archid. no. 2, printed in *FPD*, lxii–lxiii.

Another charter of William I exists in two copies which are both of the last decade of the twelfth century.[1] The earlier version, B, has the great seal of Henry II attached; the later, A, that of Prior Bertram (1189–1212). Their differences in content are negligible and both show the same characteristics as have been noticed in other late groups. The writing is comparatively concise and there is a concentration on the enumeration of essential privileges and not properties. A in copying from B has misread the witnesses by reading across their columns instead of down them, and has thus produced the hybrid *Ursonis capellani* in place of *Willelmi capellani* and *Ursonis (Abetot')*.

A further late group, written *c.* 1200, possibly in preparation for the submission of conventual liberties for royal confirmation, consists of a copy of Richard I's charter granting Puiset the earldom of Northumberland (endorsed in a contemporary hand),[2] and two extracts in the same hand from William I's alleged privilege, 1. 1. Reg. no. 2 B, and Henry I's charter, 2. 1. Reg. 4 B.[3] Of similar date are two extracts from two alleged charters of Henry II, the first of which refers to regalian rights.[4]

A late origin for the forgeries is also suggested by certain elements in their phraseology. It is worthy of note that when, in 1157, Adrian IV confirmed the prior in his position of second dignitary of the church of Durham he used a simile *(dexteram episcopi . . . sustentare)*[5] which had been employed by the mediators of 1147 *(dexteram Episcopi . . . sustentasse)*.[6] It is fairly clear that a copy or abstract of the 1147 settlement had been forwarded for papal confirmation. If it be admitted that at this date no other conventual titles existed, then the mild nature of Adrian's privilege presents no difficulty: the prior was confirmed in a position to which he had written right. If on the other hand it be assumed the body of forgeries was already in existence it is difficult to see why only one comparatively small and general point was submitted for confirmation in 1157 and 1162. On the whole the priory was quick to seek papal record of any privileges secured in the early part of Puiset's episcopate.[7]

Again, scattered through the papal documents in favour of the convent of Durham in the later twelfth century are a number of phrases which may be found in the forgeries. The most important are those dealing with the appropriation of churches, and the convent's control over its property. Thus in 1162 Alexander III con-

---

[1] DC Durham, 1. 1. Reg. nos. 2 A, 2 B, printed in *FPD*, lxxii–lxxiii.
[2] DC Durham, 3. 13. Pont. no. 3.   [3] DC Durham, 1. 1. Reg. no. 19.
[4] DC Durham, 3. 1. Reg. no. 25.   [5] *PU*, II, no. 94.
[6] DC Durham, 1. 1. Archid. no. 2, printed in *FPD*, lxii–lxiii.
[7] See above, p. 133.

firmed that the convent should have *de omnibus rebus vestris disponendi facultatem liberam*.[1] This, which may be traced, *via* a charter of Puiset, to one of Flambard,[2] appears in one spurious deed as *liberam dispositionem in omnibus tam ecclesiis*, etc.[3] Here it seem shighly probable that the language of the forgery is derived from the papal privilege. The evidence is more conclusive in another instance. Some time between 1160 and 1176 Alexander III wrote of the Durham churches *liceat vobis clericos absque impedimento aliquo eligere, et diocesanis episcopis presentare, quibus, si idonei fuerint, episcopi curam animarum committant, ut illis de spiritualibus vobis de temporalibus respondeant*.[4] This appears in various fashions in the forgeries; thus St Calais is alleged to grant *ut vicarios suos semper in eis statuant, qui de beneficiis earum illis respondeant, nobis vero...de cura animarum intendant*;[5] William I supposedly writes of vicars *qui episcopis de cura animarum respondeant*; *de redditibus vero...Prioribus...existant*.[6] It can scarcely be argued that an important aspect of papal policy and a standard phrase of papal diplomatic in the later twelfth century was drawn from these clumsy sentences. The forger could find no early warrant for his distinctions in the products of the papal chancery, and was thus obliged to incorporate formulae not current till after *c.* 1160.

Something of this same borrowing from genuine documents of the pontificates of Alexander III and Urban III can be seen in other matters. The phrase of the forgeries *omnes dignitates, honores et potestates abbatis*[7] or *omnes libertates, dignitates et honores abbatis*[8] bears a strong resemblance to that used by Alexander III in 1162, of which it is presumably an expansion: *Omnes quoque dignitates quas predecessores eius habuisse*, etc.[9] Nor can the predilection of the forger for that favoured verb of Alexander III's chancery, *optineat, optineant*, be merely a coincidence.[10]

It is difficult to avoid the suspicion that the Durham forgeries were an elaborate pastiche from late twelfth-century sources. The clauses relating to the free election of the prior seem but an adaptation of papal formulae for episcopal elections. Thus in 1186, and in no previous instance, the pope ruled that a bishop be elected by the common consent of the monks (*fratres communi consensu...*).[11] In the clauses relating to the prior in the spurious deeds (there is no warrant in papal privileges for the election of a prior before that of

---

[1] *PU*, II, no. 107.   [2] See above, pp. 133, 254.
[3] DC Durham, I. I. Pont. no. 4A.
[4] *PU*, II, no. 149.   [5] *FPD*, li.   [6] *FPD*, lxx.
[7] DC Durham, I. I. Reg. no. 18.
[8] DC Durham, I. I. Pont. nos. 3A, 3B, printed in *FPD*, xlvii–xlix; I. I. Pont. nos. 4A, 4B, printed in *FPD*, l–li.   [9] *PU*, II, no. 107.
[10] Cf. *FPD*, lxvii, lxix.   [11] *Scriptores Tres*, App. no. xxxix.

Celestine III based on the forgeries) the process is to be *communi fratrum consilio*,[1] or *communi fratrum assensu*.[2] Again, the words of the papal chancery *Obeunte vero Dunelmensis ecclesie antiste*, used in 1157 and 1162, seem to have inspired the *decedente vero priore*...of the forgeries.[3] Another feature of a number of the spurious deeds is the provision that the prior, once elected, should not be removed from office except he be proved unworthy, or for some reasonable cause.[4] This was no doubt devised to avoid a repetition of the events of 1162, when Puiset deposed Prior Thomas.[5] The language of the charters is again significant; according to that attributed to Lanfranc the priors were to remain in office, *nisi rationabili causa exigente*..., a phrase which recurs in the alleged privilege of Thomas I.[6] The wording is almost that of a papal ruling which, based on a Lateran decree, came into circulation during the pontificate of Urban III. Thus, in 1187, the pope granted the monks of Canterbury that none should depose their prior, *sine manifesta causa et rationabili*.[7]

In sum, the palaeography and other aspects of the conventual charters point to a date in the second half of the twelfth century for their manufacture. The general elaboration of the priory's claims postulates a high degree of prosperity and organization in the diocese, which made it desirable to share those episcopal regalian rights, not authentically formulated before Richard I's charters of 1189, granting Puiset Sadberge and the earldom of Northumberland. The nature of the remaining claims, the concern with the independence of the prior and his obedientiaries and with the integrity of monastic property, suggest a dispute of considerable violence between bishop and prior, a far greater issue than any such quarrel of prior and archdeacon for precedence as may have taken place in 1147. The nature of Puiset's episcopate suggests a reason for the manufacture of the charters, and the form of his surrender indicates their existence in 1195. It would be remarkable if, as Professor Barlow has written, the documents were forged *c.* 1150, not as occasion demanded, but with wise foresight of impending trouble,[8] and it is hard to believe their existence could have been ignored during years of obvious distress. It would seem the first forgeries were produced *c.* 1165, followed by more elaborate groups *c.* 1185–9 and at the end of the century.

[1] DC Durham, 1. 1. Pont. no. 1, printed in *FPD*, lii–lvi.

[2] DC Durham, 1. 1. Archiep. no. 2. DC Durham, 1. 1. Reg. no. 11, printed in *FPD*, lxix–lxxi, compromises with *communi fratrum consensu*.

[3] DC Durham, 2. 1. Reg. no. 1; cf. *FPD*, xlix, l. The papal formulae are in *PU*, II, nos. 94, 107.   [4] Cf. *FPD*, lxxvi, lxxviii.   [5] *Scriptores Tres*, 8.

[6] DC Durham, 1. 1. Archiep. no. 3, printed in *FPD*, lxxv–lxxvi; 1. 1. Archiep. no. 1, printed in *FPD*, lxxvi–lxxix.

[7] *PU*, II, no. 250.   [8] Barlow, *Durham Jurisdictional Peculiars*, 17.

THE FAMILY OF DU PUISET

HARDUIN. Occ. 985.[1]

GILDUIN (*c.* 1019–1048).

Appears to have been a son of Harduin. His wife was Emmaline.[2] His children included Ebrard or Evrard,[3] Harduin,[4] Hugh, Waleran, Gilduin and Adelaide.[5] He is described as *vicomte* of Chartres in 1028[6] and again in 1035.[7] He became a monk in 1048 and appears to have died *c.* 1050.[8]

HARDUIN (*c.* 1048–*c.* 1050).

Son of Gilduin. His wife was Elizabeth.[9] He is described as *vicomte* of Chartres.[10]

EVRARD I (*c.* 1050–70).

Another son of Gilduin. His children included Waleran, Evrard, Robert, Adelaide and Hugh.

EVRARD II (*c.* 1070–5).

Occ. as *vicomte* of Chartres in 1073. He surrendered his office, his *honorem* and all his domains to his brother Hugh, and departed to the Holy Land. On his return he became a monk at Marmoutier, despite the opposition of his wife, Hunberga.[11] He occurs as late as 1095.[12]

HUGH I (*c.* 1075–94).

Son of Evrard I, succeeded his brother Evrard II as *vicomte* of Chartres. In his own right he was styled lord of Le Puiset. His movements are well attested for the years 1070, 1075, 1077, 1094.[13]

[1] *Un Manuscrit Chartrain*, 115; *Obituaires de Sens*, II, 18.
[2] *Cart. S. Père de Chartres*, I, 161.
[3] *Cart. Notre Dame de Chartres*, I, no. xiv.
[4] *Cart. S. Père de Chartres*, loc. cit.
[5] Cf. the table in La Monte, 'The Lords of Le Puiset on the Crusades'.
[6] *Cart. S. Jean en Vallée de Chartres*, no. 1; *Cart. Marmoutier* (ed. Mabille), no. xcix.
[7] *Cart. Marmoutier*, no. cix; Prou, *Philippe I*[er], no. lxxv.
[8] *Un Manuscrit Chartrain*, 115, 163.
[9] *Cart. S. Père de Chartres*, loc. cit.; *Cart. Marmoutier*, no. cxvii.
[10] *Un Manuscrit Chartrain*, 166.
[11] *Cart. S. Père de Chartres*, I, 159; *Cart. Tiron*, I, 33, n. 3.
[12] *Cart. Marmoutier*, nos. xli, cxlviii and Introduction, xiii.
[13] *Cart. Notre Dame de Paris*, I, no. 50; Prou, *Philippe I*[er], nos. lxxvi, lxxxvii, lxxxix; *Cart. S. Père de Chartres*, I, 240.

He was at war with Philip I in 1079 and was responsible for the imprisonment of Ivo of Chartres in 1092.[1] His wife was Alice de Rochefort, daughter of Guy of Montlhéry and sister of that Elizabeth who married into the famous crusading family of Courtenay.[2] His children included Hugh, Evrard, Guy, Rodulf,[3] Gilduin,[4] and Waleran.[5] His sister Adelaide married Roger of Montgomery, whose son Ebrard became bishop of Norwich.[6]

EVRARD III (c. 1094–7).

Succeeded his father, Hugh I, at Chartres and Le Puiset.[7] He married Alice, daughter of Burchard of Corbeil and Alice of Crécy, by whom he had a son Hugh.[8] He died 21 August? 1099.[9]

HUGH II (1097–1106).

Son of Hugh I and brother of Evrard III; was lord of Le Puiset and *vicomte* of Chartres as regent for his nephew, Hugh. He subsequently became count of Jaffa, and died in the East after 1110.[10]

GUY DE MÉRÉVILLE (1106–8).

Son of Hugh I, brother of Evrard III, and Hugh II, whom he succeeded as guardian of the young Hugh III.[11] He was originally a canon of Chartres,[12] but after 1101 married Lettice, daughter of the *vicomte* of Etampes, by whom he had children Hugh, Evrard and Galeran.[13]

HUGH III (1108–28).

Son of Evrard III, was a minor until c. 1108, before which date he appears in the company of his tutor (*magister*).[14] At his accession he became lord of Le Puiset, *vicomte* of Chartres and count of Corbeil. He held of the king,[15] the bishop of Paris, the counts of Mellent and

---

[1] Suger, *Vie de Louis VI*, 132, 134.

[2] *Cart. Tiron*, I, 33, n. 3; *Recueil S. Martin des Champs*, I, no. 95; La Monte, *art. cit.*

[3] *Recueil S. Martin des Champs*, I, no. 95.

[4] *Ibid.* no. 123.

[5] *Cart. Notre Dame de Chartres*, I, no. 24.

[6] Ordericus Vitalis, II, 412.   [7] *Ibid.* III, 481.

[8] Bouquet, XV, 96, 104; *Cart. S. Père de Chartres*, II, 452.

[9] *Cart. Tiron*, I, 33; *Un Manuscrit Chartrain*, 173.

[10] *Recueil S. Martin des Champs*, I, no. 95.

[11] *Recueil S. Martin des Champs*, I, nos. 114, 123.

[12] As such he witnesses a charter of Stephen Henry of Blois, together with his brother Waleran, *Cart. Notre Dame de Chartres*, I, no. 24. Waleran was lord of Villepreux and later of Bira, *Recueil S. Martin des Champs*, no. 123.

[13] Bouquet, XII, 71; XV, 136; *Cart. Josaphat*, no. ix.

[14] *Recueil S. Martin des Champs*, nos. 123, 129.

[15] Bouquet, XII, 795.

Blois.[1] Practically his whole life was spent in war, and his charters, like those of his uncle, Hugh II, have a constant military concern. Thus a grant in favour of St Martin's is prefaced by the proviso *ut per hoc servicium suum et stationem castelli sui non amittat*.[2] He was married to Agnes of Blois, sister of Theobald IV and the future Stephen of England,[3] by whom he had three sons, Evrard, Burchard[4] and Hugh.[5] He appears to have gone to the Holy Land *c.* 1129 and died in 1141.[6]

EVRARD IV (*c.* 1129–90).

Succeeded his father Hugh III as lord of Le Puiset and *vicomte* of Chartres. He continued the traditional violences of his house against neighbouring religious.[7] Like his father he was a frequent associate of the counts of Blois. He witnessed charters of Theobald V in 1158,[8] 1168,[9] 1176,[10] 1183.[11] He appears to have married more than once, his first wife being Mary,[12] his second Helvisa.[13] By the latter he had sons Hugh and Waleran,[14] and probably also Henry.[15]

HUGH IV (fl. *c.* 1148–89).

The eldest son of Evrard IV. It is doubtful whether he ever held the lordship of Le Puiset or the other family offices. He married Petronilla of Bar-sur-Seine in 1168, by whom he had a son Milo.[16] As count of Bar he led an army to England in 1174; he is mentioned in the *Gesta* in 1181 and appears to have died at what may be identified as (Bishop) Auckland in 1189.[17] He was succeeded as count of Bar by his son Milo, who also took the titles of Le Puiset and Chartres.[18] It is worthy of note that the family of Bar were tenants of

---

[1] *Recueil S. Martin des Champs*, nos. 124, 128.

[2] *Recueil S. Martin des Champs*, no. 129.

[3] *Cart. Tiron*, I, 127–8. For attestations in the presence of Theobald IV and Stephen, *Cart. Notre Dame de Chartres*, I, 108; *Cart. Tiron*, I, no. 4.

[4] *Cart. Tiron*, I, 127–8.　　　　[5] *Cart. Josaphat*, no. xxx.

[6] *Cart. S. Jean-en-Vallée*, no. 14; *Cart. Marmoutier*, no. clx; *Cart. Tiron*, I, 127–8.

[7] Luchaire, *Louis VII*, nos. 73, 115, 116; Bouquet, XVI, 8; *Archives de la Maison Dieu de Châteaudun*, no. xvii.

[8] *Cart. du Grand Beaulieu*, no. 44.

[9] *Ibid.* no. 73.　　　　[10] *Ibid.* no. 102; *Cart. Josaphat*, no. 6..

[11] *Archives de la Maison Dieu de Châteaudun*, no. xxv.

[12] *Ibid.* no. xxxiv.

[13] *Cart. Notre Dame de Chartres*, I, nos. xciii, xciv.

[14] *Recueil S. Martin des Champs*, II, no. 314; *Cart. du Grand Beaulieu*, no. 97.

[15] *Cart. Marmoutier*, no. clxxxv.

[16] *Recueil S. Martin des Champs*, no. 314; *Trésor des Chartes*, v, no. 118.

[17] By his marriage with Petronilla Hugh became count of Bar, and as such a tenant of Champagne, as he appears in 1172; Longnon, *Documents Relatifs*, I, 3. For his appearance in England, *Gesta*, II, 92; Hoveden, III, 19.

[18] *Archives de la Maison Dieu de Châteaudun*, no. XLVI.

the counts of Champagne. Milo II was one of the *barones* of Count Hugh.[1] A Milo of Bar was also a canon of Troyes (fl. *c.* 1180).[2]

HENRY PUISET (fl. 1158–90).

The son of Evrard IV, and not to be confused with his namesake and contemporary, the son of Hugh of Durham. He occurs at Chartres in 1159, when he is described as son of Evrard the *vicomte*.[3] He witnessed a charter of Hugh of Châteaudun, who may have been a brother, in 1175–84.[4] He was at Chartres in 1181,[5] and again in 1187 when he witnessed a charter of Bishop Reginald.[6] He witnessed charters of Theobald of Blois in favour of Grand Beaulieu in 1189 and 1190, and for La Madelaine in 1190.[7]

HUGH PUISET, bishop of Durham.

The youngest son of Hugh III.[8] His only liaison for which there is charter evidence is with Alice de Percy.[9] She was of a moderately distinguished Anglo-Norman family who had land at Morières in Normandy,[10] and in Hampshire, Lincolnshire and Yorkshire (including four fees of the bishopric of Durham).[11] Her father was William de Percy (1136–75), which gave her Alan de Percy as a brother and Matilda and Agnes as sisters. Agnes was married to Jocelin of Louvain, a well-known figure of the century, brother of Adelaide, Henry I's queen.[12] Matilda was married to William, earl of Warwick.[13] The names are all of good pedigree, but none of their holders, with the exception of Jocelin, was of any consequence. It is worth noting that Henry Puiset, Hugh's son by Alice,[14] was well favoured by his aunts Agnes and Matilda,[15] and was much in company with Agnes's eldest son, Henry.[16] Alice herself later married Richard

---

[1] *Cart. S. Pierre de Troyes*, no. 4.   [2] *Ibid.* nos. 36, 44.
[3] *Cart. du Grand Beaulieu*, no. 48.   [4] *Cart. Marmoutier*, no. clxxxv.
[5] *Cart. Notre Dame de Chartres*, I, 206.
[6] *Cart. du Grand Beaulieu*, no. 130.
[7] *Cart. du Grand Beaulieu*, nos. 136, 145; *Cart. de la Madelaine de Châteaudun*, no. xxxvi.
[8] *Cart. Josaphat*, no. xxx.
[9] G. E. C. *Complete Peerage*, x, 442, note c.
[10] *Ibid.* 435, note b.   [11] LR, 416.   [12] *Mon. Ang.* v, 512, no. v.
[13] *Sallay Cartulary*, II, no. 615.
[14] *Priory of Finchale*, no. 51; *Sallay Cartulary*, II, nos. 420–2; *Mon. Ang.* VII, 977, no. v.
[15] Whitaker, *History of Craven*, 135, for grants at Settle and Giggleswick.
[16] *Fountains Cartulary*, 320; BM, Egerton MS. 3031, fo. 37ᵛ (Reading Cart.); *Sallay Cartulary*, II, no. 422; and cf. *Pudsay Deeds*, no. 6. It was through the Percies that Puiset was related to the family of Malebisse; Richard Malebisse was the nephew of Matilda (*Fountains Cartulary*, 817).

de Morville, by whom she had a son Alan, who refers to Henry Puiset as his brother.[1]

According to William of Newburgh, Hugh Puiset had three children by various noble matrons before he reached the decorum of the episcopal dignity.[2] These were a knight (Henry), an archdeacon (?Burchard), and a son who became chancellor of France (Hugh).[3] But Howden, who had no reason to be squeamish in such matters, refers to Hugh and Henry alone as the bishop's sons, and Archdeacon Burchard as his nephew.[4] By a fortunate clerical slip in the draft of a charter, we know that Archdeacon William of Northumberland was also a Puiset.[5] He may be the archdeacon behind Newburgh's story, and since he has the good Percy name of William, he may be assumed to be the bishop's son. On two occasions he refers to a certain Hugh Puiset as his brother.[6] In all probability this is Hugh, the chancellor, who came to Canterbury with Louis VII in 1179, for the name stands high in the witness list.[7] It may, however, be Hugh, count of Bar, who was the son of Evrard IV, and who is described by Howden as the bishop's nephew and the brother of Archdeacon Burchard. He was in England in 1174 and appears to have died at Bishop Auckland in 1189.[8] It may also be that elusive Hugh du Puiset who held a fee of the Honor of Tickhill,[9] and who occurs in York (c. 1185–1205), where he had a holding in Walmgate in which he was succeeded by his daughter Margaret.[10] This Hugh was clearly not the chancellor, who died prematurely c. 1180.[11] He may be another of Puiset's children by an unknown mother, or he may be the son of that unidentified Evrard Puiset who twice witnesses acta of the bishop of Durham.[12]

The evidence, though inconclusive, suggests that at least Henry, Hugh and William were the bishop's sons. For Henry and Hugh there is good testimony. William is more uncertain, though he may

---

[1] *Complete Peerage*, x, 442, note c. Henry Puiset came into possession of land in Yorkshire at Collingham and Compton which had once belonged to Richard de Morville, PR *13 Henry II*, 94; *29 Henry II*, 48; *2 Richard I*, 67.

[2] Newburgh, II, 440–1. [3] See above, p. 25.

[4] Hoveden, II, 193; III, 16; *Gesta*, II, 85; and see above, pp. 25, 223.

[5] DC Durham, 4. 9. Spec. no. 30.

[6] *EYC*, IX, no. 121; DC Durham, 4. 1. Pont. no. 12 (see above, App. II, no. 6).

[7] *Gesta*, I, 241; Hoveden, II, 193; DC Canterbury, Cart. Ant. F 90, F 92; Gervase of Canterbury, I, 293; Diceto, I, 433.

[8] Hoveden, III, 19; *Gesta*, II, 92.

[9] PR *9 Richard I*, 155. For a Hugh Puiset holding in Lincolnshire in the early thirteenth century, see *Reg. Ant. Linc.* IV, 38, 41.

[10] PR *2 Richard I*, 73; *EYC*, I, nos. 208, 246, 321; II, nos. 852, 853; PR *3 Richard I*, 70.

[11] See above, p. 25. [12] *EYC*, II, nos. 953, 971.

fit the facts of Newburgh's story, and his Christian name was a distinguished Percy name. Howden's evidence on the parentage of Archdeacon Burchard is weakened by his failure to notice William, and the fact that no charter source supplies Evrard IV with a son Burchard. Again, if William Puiset were the bishop's own son it seems curious that so much preferment should have been bestowed on Burchard, assuming he was a nephew. In all it is difficult to avoid the suspicion that both Burchard and William were as much the bishop's sons as Henry or Hugh.[1]

[1] The above note does not purport to be a complete genealogy of the family of Puiset. No details have been given of their relatives among the lesser French aristocracy, or of the position they occupied in the Holy Land. Tables explaining a large part of these matters are available in La Monte, 'The Lords of Le Puiset on the Crusades', and in Runciman, *The Kingdom of Jerusalem and the Frankish East*.

BIBLIOGRAPHY

I. MANUSCRIPT AND RECORD SOURCES

THE BRITISH MUSEUM

(a) Cotton manuscripts

Claudius D IV (fifteenth-century compilation, containing the *De exordio et statu ecclesie cathedralis...Dunelmensis*).
Claudius D x (Register of St Augustine's, Canterbury).
Claudius D XIII (Register of Binham).
Faustina A III (Register of Westminster).
Faustina B II (Register of Clerkenwell).
Julius D II (Cartulary of St Augustine's, Canterbury).
Nero C IX (Register of the Hospital of St John of Jerusalem).
Nero D VII (Register of St Albans).
Otto D III (Cartulary of St Albans).
Tiberius C IX (Register of Waltham).
Tiberius D VI (Register of Twineham).
Tiberius E VI (Cartulary of St Albans).
Vespasian E II (Register of Ramsey).
Vespasian E XIX (Register of Nostell).
Vespasian E XX (Register of Bardney).
Vitellius A XIII (Cartulary of Chertsey).

(b) Other collections

Additional 14847 (Register of Bury).
Additional 37665 (Cartulary of Waltham).
Additional 46353 (Cartulary of Dereham).
Egerton 2819 (*Collectio Cheltenhamensis*).
Egerton 3031 (Cartulary of Reading).
Harley 61 (Register of Shaftesbury).
Harley 391 (Register of Waltham).
Harley 742 (Cartulary of Spalding).
Harley 1063 (Transcripts relating to Rufford, etc.).
Harley 1708 (Register of Reading).
Harley 2188 (Transcripts relating to Haughmond).
Harley 3739 (Register of Waltham).
Harley 4714 (Register of Biddlesden).
Lansdowne 902 (Transcripts relating to Durham).
Stowe 925 (Register of Bradenstoke).
Stowe 930 (Durham charters and letters).

(c) Cotton charters and rolls

Cotton Rolls II, nos. 19, 21.
Cotton Roll IV, no. 57.
Cotton Charter II, 1.
Cotton Charter IV, 36.

(d) Other charters

Additional 33649.
Campbell IV, 9; XII, 1; XII, 3; XII, 4.
Egerton 372.
Harley 43 c; 28, 29, 30.
Wolley 1, 46.

THE PUBLIC RECORD OFFICE

Chancery, Cartae Antiquae (C. 52), rolls and membranes as cited.
Exchequer, Augmentation Office, Ancient Deeds B, 11535; B, 11537;
    B, 11538.
—— King's Remembrancer, Misc. Book XX (A register of Godstow).
—— Treasury of Receipt, Ancient Deed E 40/A 6112.
Palatinates, Durham Cursitor Roll 43.
—— Duchy of Lancaster, Great Coucher.
—— Duchy of Lancaster, Misc. Book no. 5 (Cartulary of Bury)
—— Duchy of Lancaster Charters and Ancient Deeds, DL 10/42;
    27/LS/2.
PRO Transcripts, 8 vols. 140 A and B.
—— List 16/103 A.

MUNIMENTS OF DEANS AND CHAPTERS

(a) DC Canterbury

Cartae Antiquae, nos. C 28; C 1208; F 90; F 92; F 93.
Prior's Register A.
Prior's Register B.

(b) DC Chichester

Liber Y.

(c) DC York

Register of the Abbey of St Mary, York.

(d) DC Durham

(i) Charters, rolls and other documents from the following classes:
    Archidiaconalia (Archidiac.).
    Archiepiscopalia (Archiepisc.).
    Eboracensia (Ebor.).
    Elemosinaria (Elemos.).
    Finchale (Finch.).

Locelli (Loc.).
Miscellaneous Charters (Cart. Misc.).
Papalia (Pap.).
Pontificalia (Pont.).
Regalia (Reg.).
Sacrist (Sac.).
Specialia (Spec.).

The medieval classifications are still in use. The classes are divided into first, second, third, etc., and then again into first of the first, second of the first, etc., with the document then numbered, e.g. 3. 1. Pont. no. 1.

(ii) Records in book form:
Cartuarium Primum (Cart. I).
Cartuarium Secundum (Cart. II).
Cartuarium Tertium de munimentis specialibus et generalibus in diocesibus Eboracensi et Lincolniensi (Cart. III).
Cartuarium Quartum (Cart. IV).
Cartuarium Vetus (Parv. Cart.).
Cartuarium Elemosinarie Dunelmensis (Cart. Elemos.).
Liber Sacristarie Dunelmensis (Lib. Sac.).
Registrum Primum (Reg. I).
Registrum Secundum (Reg. II).
Registrum Tertium (Reg. III).

These volumes are described in the introduction to vol. II of *PU*, and also by J. Conway Davies, 'The muniments of the Dean and Chapter of Durham', in *Durham University Journal*, XIII (3) (1952), 77–87.

(iii) Manuscripts of the Dean and Chapter of Durham (the majority of these volumes are described in Mynors, *Durham Cathedral Manuscripts*, to which the numbers in brackets refer):
A II, 1, four-volume Pudsey Bible (no. 146).
A II, 2, two-volume Pudsey Bible (no. 147).
A II, 19, Pauline Epistles (no. 149).
A II, 21, *Eulogium ad A III, Papam*.
A III, 6, A book of Master John de Rana (no. 144).
A III, 7, glossed Psalter (no. 148).
A III, 23, A book of Master John de Rana (no. 145).
A IV, 1, Leviticus glossed (no. 152).
A IV, 10, Matthew glossed (no. 151).
B II, 35, twelfth-century genealogies and other works (no. 47).
B III, 13, *Gregorianum* (no. 150).

B IV, 24, calendar, martyrology (no. 51).

C II, 1, Decretals (no. 134).

C III, 1, Decretals.

C IV, 1, Decretals (no. 104).

C IV, 5, Cicero, *De Inventione* etc. (no. 154).

Randall 354 (Transcripts made in the eighteenth century from deeds in the episcopal chancery, etc.).

OTHER MUNIMENTS

Merton College, Oxford, Deed no. 578.

Oxford, Bodleian MS. 357 (*Collectio Bridlingtoniensis*).

Jesus College, Cambridge, MS. 50 (Isaiah glossed).

Trinity College, Cambridge, MS. o. 3. 32 (Mynors, *op. cit.* no. 155).

University of Durham, Cosins Library, MS. v. ii. 1 (Numbers glossed; Mynors, *op. cit.* no. 153).

II. PRINTED SOURCES

Ancient Charters prior to 1200, ed. J. H. Round (Pipe Roll Soc. x; London, 1888).

Bath, Two Chartularies of the Priory of St Peter at, ed. W. Hunt (Somerset Record Society, vol. 7; London, 1893).

Bede, The Venerable, *Opera Historica*, ed. C. Plummer (2 vols.; Oxford, 1896).

Boldon Buke, ed. W. Greenwell (SS, 8, 1852).

Bouquet, M., *Rerum Gallicarum et Francicarum Scriptores*, re-ed. L. Delisle, vols. I–XIX (1868–80).

Bridlington Priory, An Abstract of Charters and other Documents contained in the Chartulary of, ed. W. T. Lancaster (Leeds, 1912).

Brinkburn, The Cartulary of, ed. W. Page (SS, 90, 1892).

British Borough Charters, 1042–1216, ed. A. Ballard (Cambridge, 1913).

Bury St Edmunds, Feudal Documents from the Abbey of, ed. D. C. Douglas (*Records of the Social and Economic History of England and Wales*, VIII; London, 1932).

Calendar of Charter Rolls.

Calendar of Close Rolls.

Calendar of Patent Rolls.

Canterbury, Gervase of, *Opera*, ed. W. Stubbs (RS, 73, 2 vols., 1879–80).

Cantuarienses, Epistolae, ed. W. Stubbs, in vol. II of *Chronicles and Memorials of the reign of Richard I* (RS, 38, 2 vols., 1864–5).

Champagne et Brie, Documents relatifs au comté de, 1172–1361, ed. A. Longnon (3 vols.; Paris, 1901–14).

Champagne et Brie, Le Trésor des pièces rares et curieuses de la, ed. J. Carnandet (2 vols.; Chaumont, 1863–6).

Chartres, Cartulaire de l'abbaye de S. Jean-en-Vallée de, ed. R. Merlet (Chartres, 1906).

Chartres, Cartulaire de Notre Dame de, ed. E. de Lépinois and L. Merlet (3 vols.; Chartres, 1862–5).

Chartres, Cartulaire de l'abbaye de S. Père de, ed. M. Guérard (2 vols.; Paris, 1840).

Châteaudun, Archives de la Maison Dieu de, ed. L. Merlet and A. de Belfort (Paris, 1881).

Châteaudun, Cartulaire de l'abbaye de la Madelaine de, ed. L. Merlet (Châteaudun, 1896).

Cheshire, The Domesday Survey of, ed. J. Tait (Chetham Soc. 75, 1916).

Chichester, The Cartulary of the High Church of, ed. W. D. Peckham (Sussex Record Society, 46; Hove, 1946).

Chronicles of the Reigns of Stephen, Henry II and Richard I, ed. R. Howlett (RS, 82, 4 vols., 1884–9).

Coggeshall, Ralph of, *Chronicon Anglicanum,* ed. J. Stevenson (RS, 1875).

Coldstream, The Cartulary of, ed. C. Rogers (London, 1879).

Collectio Sangermanensis, ed. H. Singer, 'Neue Beiträge über die Dekretalensammlungen vor und nach Bernard von Pavia', in *Sitzungsberichte der Wiener Akademie (Phil.-Hist. Kl.* 171, 1 (1913)).

Colne Priory, The Cartulary of, ed. J. L. Fisher (Essex Arch. Soc. Occasional Publications, no. 1; Colchester, 1946).

Corpus Juris Canonici, ed. E. Friedberg (2 vols.; Leipzig, 1879–81).

Cuthbert, St, Two Lives of, ed. B. Colgrave (Cambridge, 1940).

Danelaw, Documents illustrative of the Social and Economic History of the, ed. F. M. Stenton (*Records of the Social and Economic History of England and Wales,* v, 1920).

Devizes, Richard of, *De Rebus Gestis Ricardi Primi,* ed. R. Howlett (*Chronicles,* III).

Dialogi Laurentii Dunelmensis Monachi ac Prioris, ed. J. Raine (SS, 70, 1880).

Diceto, Ralph of, *Opera Historica,* ed. W. Stubbs (RS, 68, 2 vols., 1876).

Domerham, Adam of, *Historia de Rebus Gestis Glastoniensibus,* ed. T. Hearne (2 vols.; London, 1727).

Domesday Book, The, 4 vols. (London, 1783–1816).

Dunelmensis, Catalogi Veteres Librorum, ed. B. Botfield (SS, VII, 1838).

Dunelmensis, Feodarium Prioratus, ed. W. Greenwell (SS, 58, 1871).

Dunelmensis, Historiae, Scriptores Tres, ed. J. Raine (SS, IX, 1839).

Dunelmensis, Liber Vitae, ed. A. Hamilton Thompson (SS, 136, 1923).

Dunelmense, Registrum Palatinum, ed. T. D. Hardy (RS, 62, 4 vols., 1873–8).

Durham, Memorials of St Giles's, ed. J. Barmby (SS, 95, 1895).

Durham Seals, ed. W. Greenwell and C. H. Blair (2 vols.; Newcastle, 1911–21).

Durham, Symeon of, *Opera*, ed. T. Arnold (RS, 75, 2 vols., 1882–5).

Edwinesburg, Liber Cartarum Sancte Crucis de, ed. C. Innes (Bannatyne Club, Edinburgh, 1840).

Elmham, Thomas of, *Historia Monasterii Sancti Augustini Cantuariensis*, ed. C. Hardwick (RS, 8, 1858).

Evesham, Chronicon Abbatie de, ed. W. D. Macray (RS, 29, 1863).

Eynsham, Cartulary of, ed. H. E. Salter (2 vols.; Oxford Historical Society, 49, 51, 1907–8).

Fantosme, Jordan, *Chronique de la guerre entre les Anglois et les Ecossois* (ed. R. Howlett in *Chronicles*, III).

Fees, The Book of, 1198–1293 (3 vols.; London, 1920–31).

Finchale, The Charters of Endowment, Inventories and Account Rolls of the Priory of, ed. J. Raine (SS, 11, 1837).

Flete, John, *The History of Westminster Abbey*, ed. J. A. Robinson (Notes and Documents relating to Westminster Abbey, II, 1909).

Fountains, An Abstract of Charters and other Documents contained in the Cartulary of, ed. W. T. Lancaster (2 vols., Leeds, 1915).

Fountains, Memorials of the Abbey of St Mary of, ed. J. S. Walbran (SS, 42, vol. I, 1862).

France, A Calendar of Documents preserved in, 918–1206, ed. J. H. Round (London, 1899).

Friedberg, E. (ed.), *Quinque Compilationes Antiquae* (Leipzig, 1882).

Furness, The Coucher Book of, ed. J. C. Atkinson (Chetham Soc., NS IX, XI, XIV, 3 vols.; Manchester, 1886–8).

Gesta Henrici Secundi and *Gesta Ricardi*, ed. W. Stubbs as the work of Benedict of Peterborough (RS, 49, 2 vols., 1867).

Glasguensis, Registrum Episcopatus, ed. C. Innes (Bannatyne Club, 2 vols.; Edinburgh, 1843).

Grand Beaulieu, Cartulaire de la Léproserie du, ed. R. Merlet and M. Jusselin (Chartres, 1909).

Gray, Walter, Archbishop of York, The Register of, ed. J. Raine (SS, 56, 1870).

Greenfield, William, Archbishop of York, The Register of, V, ed. A. Hamilton Thompson (SS, 153, 1938).

Greenwell Deeds, A Calendar of the, ed. J. Walton (Newcastle, 1927).

'Greenwell Deeds, A Second Calendar of', ed. J. Walton, in *Arch. Ael.* 4 (7), 1930, 81–114.

Guisborough Cartulary, ed. W. Brown (SS, 86, 89, 1891).

HADDAN, A. W. and STUBBS, W. *Councils and Ecclesiastical Documents relating to Great Britain and Ireland*, vols. II and III (Oxford, 1873, 1878).

Hatton's, Sir Christopher, Book of Seals, ed. D. Stenton and L. C. Loyd (Northants. Rec. Soc. XV, 1950).

Helaugh Park, The Cartulary of, ed. J. S. Purvis (Yorks. Rec. Soc., 92, 1936).

Historical Manuscripts Commission, Reports VI, IX, XV.

Holm Cultram, The Register and Records of, ed. F. Grainger and W. G. Collingwood (Cumberland and West. Arch. Soc. Record Series, VII, 1929).

Holme, The Register of the Abbey of St Benet of, ed. J. R. West (Norfolk Rec. Soc., 2 vols., 1932).

HOLTZMANN, W. *Papsturkunden in England* (3 vols.; Berlin, 1932–52).

Holyrood, A Scottish Chronicle known as the Chronicle of, ed. A. O. and M. O. Anderson (Scot. Hist. Soc. 30, 1938).

Hoveden, Roger of, *Chronica*, ed. W. Stubbs (RS, 51, 4 vols., 1868–71).

JAFFÉ, PH. *Regesta Pontificum Romanorum*, ed. W. Wattenbach, S. Loewenfeld, F. Kaltenbrunner and P. Ewald (2 vols.; Leipzig, 1885–8).

Jocelin of Brakelond, *Chronicle concerning the acts of Samson, Abbot of the Monastery of Bury*, ed. H. E. Butler (London, 1949).

Josaphat, Cartulaire de Notre Dame de, ed. Charles Métais (Chartres, 1898).

Kelso (Calchou), Liber S. Marie de, 1113–1567, ed. C. Innes (Bannatyne Club, 2 vols.; Edinburgh, 1846).

Kuttner, S. (ed.), *Repertorium der Kanonistik, 1140–1234* (Vatican, 1937).

Lanercost, A Breviate of the Cartulary of, ed. M. E. C. Walcott (Trans. Royal Society of Literature, 2nd ser., VIII, 1866).

Le Romeyn, John, Archbishop of York, The Register of, ed. J. M. Marshal (SS, 123, 128, 1913–16).

Libellus de admirandis Beati Cuthberti Virtutibus, Reginaldi monachi Dunelmensis, ed. J. Raine (SS, 1; 1835).

Libellus de Vita et Miraculis Sancti Godrici, ed. J. Stevenson (SS, 20, 1845).

Liber Rubeus de Scaccario, ed. H. Hall (RS, 99, 3 vols., 1896).

Lincolnshire Domesday, ed. C. W. Foster (Lincs. Rec. Soc. 19, 1924).

Lincoln, The Registrum Antiquissimum of, ed. C. W. Foster and K. Major (Lincs. Rec. Soc., in progress).

Louis VI le Gros, Annales de sa Vie et de son Règne, ed. A. Luchaire (Paris, 1890).

Louth Park, The Chronicle of, ed. E. Venables (Lincs. Rec. Soc. I, 1891).

LÖWENFELD, S. (ed.). *Epistolae Pontificum Romanorum Ineditae.* (Leipzig, 1885).

MADOX, T. *Formulare Anglicanum* (London, 1702).

MANSI, J. D. *Sacrorum Conciliorum nova et amplissima collectio* (Florence and Venice, 1759–98).

Marmoutier, Cartulaire de, pour le Dunois, ed. E. Mabille (Châteaudun, 1874).

Materials for the History of Thomas Becket, ed. J. C. Robertson and J. B. Sheppard (RS, 67, 7 vols., 1875–85).

Melrose, The Chronicle of, ed. A. O. and M. O. Anderson (London School of Economics, Studies in Economics and Political Science, no. 100, 1936).

Melrose, Liber Sancte Marie de, ed. C. Innes (Bannatyne Club, 2 vols., 1837).

Memoranda Roll, I John, ed. H. G. Richardson (Pipe Roll Society, XXI, 1943).

Migne, J. P. ed., *Patrologiae Cursus Completus, Series Latina* (Paris, 1844–64).

Monasticon Anglicanum, re-ed. J. Caley, H. Ellis and B. Bandinel, 6 vols. in 8 (London, 1817–30).

Newburgh, William of, *Historia Rerum Anglicarum* (ed. R. Howlett in *Chronicles*, I, II).

Newcastle, Early Deeds, ed. A. M. Oliver (SS, 137, 1924).

Newminster Cartulary, The, ed. J. T. Fowler (SS, 66, 1876).

Northumberland and Durham Deeds from the Dodsworth MSS. in Bodley's Library, Oxford (Newcastle upon Tyne, Records Committee, VII; Newcastle, 1929).

Norwich, The Registrum Primum of, ed. H. W. Saunders (Norfolk Rec. Soc. XI, 1939).

Ordericus Vitalis, *Ecclesiastica Historia*, ed. A. le Prévost (Société de l'Histoire de France, 5 vols.; Paris, 1838–55).

Oxford Muniment Rooms, Fascimiles of Early Charters in, ed. H. E. Salter (Oxford, 1929).

Paris, Cartulaire de l'Église de Notre Dame de, ed. M. Guérard (4 vols.; Paris, 1850).

Petri Blesensis Opera, ed. J. A. Giles (4 vols.; Oxford, 1846–7).

Pipe, Great Roll of the, ed. Pipe Roll Society.

Pudsay Deeds, The, ed. R. P. Littledale (Yorks. Arch. Soc. Record Series, 56, 1916).

Rameseiensis, Chronicon Abbatie, ed. W. D. Macray (RS, 83, 1886).

'Ravensworth Deeds, A Calendar of', ed. H. E. Bell in *Arch. Ael.* IV (XVI), 1939, 43–70.

Recueil des Actes de Henri II Roi d'Angleterre et Duc de Normandie Concernant les Provinces Françaises et les Affaires de France, ed. L. Delisle and E. Berger (4 vols.; Paris, 1909–27).

Recueil des Actes de Philippe Auguste, ed. H. F. Delaborde, E. Berger, Ch. Petit-Dutaillis, C. Brunel, J. Monicat (2 vols.; Paris, 1916–43).

Recueil des Actes de Philippe Auguste, ed. L. Delisle (Paris, 1856).

Recueil des Actes de Philippe Ier, Roi de France, 1059–1108, ed. M. Prou (Paris, 1908).

Rievaulx, The Cartulary of (Cartularium Rievallense), ed. J. C. Atkinson (SS, 83; 1887).

Rotuli Chartarum, ed. T. D. Hardy (Record Commission, London, 1837).

Rotuli de Dominabus, ed. J. H. Round (Pipe Roll Soc. 35, 1913).

Rotuli Litterarum Clausarum, ed. T. D. Hardy (Record Commission; London, 1833)

Rud, T. ed. *Codicum MSS Ecclesie Cathedralis Dunelmensis Catalogus Classicus* (Durham, 1825).

S. Benoît-sur-Loire, Recueil des chartes de l'abbaye de, ed. M. Prou (Documents publiés par la société historique et archéologique du Gatinais, v, 1907).

S. Martin-des-Champs, Recueil de chartes et de documents de, ed. J. Depoin (Archives de la France Monastique, XIII–XX; Paris, 1912–21).

St Osmund, Salisbury, The Register of, ed. W. Rich-Jones (RS, 78, 2 vols., 1883–4).

St Paul, London, Early Charters of the Cathedral Church of, ed. M. Gibbs (Camden Soc., 3rd ser. 58, 1939).

Salisbury, John of, *Historia Pontificalis*, ed. R. L. Poole (Oxford 1927).

—— *Opera*, ed. J. A. Giles (5 vols.; Oxford, 1848).

Sallay in Craven, The Cartulary of, ed. J. McNulty (Yorks. Arch. Soc., vols. 87, 90, 1933–4).

Sancti Albani, Gesta Abbatum Monasterii, in vol. III of *Chronica Monasterii Sancti Albani*, ed. H. T. Riley (RS, 28, 12 vols., 1863–76).

Scottish History, Early Sources of, A.D. 500–1286, ed. A. O. Anderson (2 vols.; Edinburgh, 1922).

Selby Abbey, The Coucher Book of, ed. J. T. Fowler (Yorks. Arch. and Top. Association, Rec. Series, 10, 13, 2 vols., 1891–3).

Sens, Obituaires de la Province de, ed. A. Longnon, M. A. Molinier, A. Vidier and L. Mirot (3 vols.; Paris, 1902–9).

Suger of St Denis, *Vie de Louis VI le Gros*, ed. H. Waquet (Paris, 1929).

Templars, Records of the, in England; the Inquest of 1185, ed. B. A. Lees (Oxford, 1935).

Tiron, Cartulaire de l'abbaye de la Sainte Trinité de, ed. L. Merlet (2 vols.; Chartres, 1883).

Torigni, Robert of, *Chronica*, ed. R. Howlett (*Chronicles*, IV).

Trésor des Chartes, Layettes du, ed. A. Teulet, J. de Laborde and E. Berger (5 vols.; Paris, 1863–1909).

Troyes, Collection des Principaux Cartulaires du Diocèse de, ed. C. Lalore (7 vols.; Paris–Troyes, 1875–90).

Tyre, William of, *Historia Rerum in Partibus Transmarinis Gestarum* in *Recueil des Historiens des Croisades (Occidentaux)*, I.

Un Manuscrit Chartrain du XIᵉ siècle, ed. R. Merlet and J. A. Clerval (Chartres, 1893).

Vendôme, Cartulaire de l'abbaye Cardinale de la Trinité de, ed. C. Métais (6 vols.; Paris, 1893–1904).

Vita Sancti Roberti Novi Monasterii, ed. P. Grosjean, S.J., in *Analecta Bollandiana*, LVI (1938), 343–60.

Vita Sancti Waltheni, auct. Jocelino Furnesiensi, in *Acta Sanctorum*, August, I, 248 *seqq.*

Wales, Gerald of, *Opera*, ed. J. S. Brewer, J. F. Dimock and G. F. Warner (RS, 21, 8 vols.; 1861–91).

Wendover, Roger of, *Chronica*, ed. H. G. Hewlett (RS, 84, 3 vols., 1886–9).

Wetherhal, The Register of, ed. J. E. Prescott (London, 1897).

Wickwane, William, Archbishop of York, The Register of, ed. W. Brown (SS, 114, 1907).

Wills and Inventories illustrative of the History, Manners, Language, etc. of the Northern Counties of England, ed. J. Raine (SS, 2, 1835).

Winchester Cathedral Cartulary, ed. A. W. Goodman (Winchester, 1927).

Winchester, The Pipe Roll of the Bishopric of, 1207–8, ed. H. Hall (London, 1903).

Worcester, John of, *Chronica*, ed. J. R. H. Weaver (Oxford, 1908).

York, Historians of the Church of, ed. J. Raine (RS, 71, 3 vols., 1879–94).

Yorkshire Charters, Early, 9 vols., 1914–52, ed. W. Farrer (vols. I–III) and C. T. Clay (vols. IV–IX).

Yorkshire Fines, John, ed. W. Brown (SS, 94, 1894).

III. MODERN WORKS

BARLOW, F. *Durham Jurisdictional Peculiars* (Oxford, 1950).

—— 'The English, Norman and French Councils called to deal with the Papal Schism of 1159', in *EHR*, LI (1936), 264–8.

—— 'Roger of Howden', in *EHR*, LXV (1950), 352–60.

BARRACLOUGH, G. *The Earldom and County Palatine of Chester* (Oxford, 1953).

BARROW, G. W. S. 'The Cathedral Chapter of St Andrews and the Culdees in the Twelfth and Thirteenth Centuries', in *The Journal of Ecclesiastical History*, 3 (1), 1952, 23–39.

BILSON, J. 'Weaverthorpe Church and its Builder', in *Archaeologia*, LXXII (1922), 51–70.

BISHOP, E. *Liturgica Historica* (Oxford, 1918).

BLOCH, M. *La Société Féodale, Les Classes et le Gouvernement des Hommes* (Paris, 1940).

BOASE, T. S. R. *English Art, 1100–1216* (Oxford, 1953).

BONGERT, Y. *Recherches sur les Cours Laïques du Xe–XIIIe siècle* (Paris, 1949).

BOURNE, H. *The History of Newcastle upon Tyne* (Newcastle, 1736).

BRAND, J. *The History and Antiquities of Newcastle upon Tyne* (2 vols.; London, 1789).

BROOKE, C. N. L. and MOREY, A. 'The Cerne Letters of Gilbert Foliot and the Legation of Imar of Tusculum', in *EHR*, LXIII (1948), 523–7.

BROOKE, Z. N. *The English Church and the Papacy* (Cambridge, 1931).

Cambridge Economic History, The (in progress), vol. I, ed. J. H. Clapham and E. Power (1941); vol. II, ed. M. M. Postan and E. E. Rich (1952).

CARTELLIERI, A. *Philipp II August, König von Frankreich* (4 vols.; Leipzig, 1899–1921).

CHENEY, C. R. *English Bishops' Chanceries, 1100–1250* (Manchester, 1950).

CHENEY, M. 'The Compromise of Avranches of 1172, and the spread of Canon Law in England', in *EHR*, LVI (1941), 177–97.

CHEW, H. M. *Ecclesiastical Tenants-in-chief and Knight-service, The English* (Oxford, 1932).

CLAPHAM, A. W. *English Romanesque Architecture after the Conquest* (Oxford, 1934).

CLAY, C. T. 'Early Treasurers of York', in *YAJ*, XXXV (1943), 7–34.

COLVIN, H. M. *The White Canons in England* (Oxford, 1951).

COULTON, G. G. *The Medieval Village* (Cambridge, 1925).

CRASTER, H. E. E. 'Some Anglo-Saxon Records of the See of Durham', in *Arch. Ael.* IV, 1 (1925), 189–98.

CRASTER, H. E. E. 'A Contemporary Record of the Pontificate of Rannulf Flambard', in *Arch. Ael.* IV, 7 (1930), 33–56.

CUISSARD, C. 'Les Seigneurs du Puiset', in *Bulletins de la Société Dunoise*, III (1875–80), 313–98.

DARBY, H. C. *Historical Geography of England* (Cambridge, 1936).

DAVIES, J. C. *Episcopal Acts Relating to Welsh Dioceses* (2 vols.; Cardiff, 1946–8).

DE GHELLINCK, J. *L'Essor de la Littérature Latine au XIIe Siècle* (2 vols.; Brussels, 1946).

DICKINSON, J. C. *The Origins of the Austin Canons* (London, 1950).

DION, A. DE. 'Le Puiset aux XIe et XIIe siècles', in *Mémoires de la Société archéologique d'Eure et Loir*, I, 1889, 1–34, 71–85.

DOWDEN, J. *The Medieval Church in Scotland* (Glasgow, 1910).

—— *The Bishops of Scotland* (Glasgow, 1912).

EDWARDS, K. *English Secular Cathedrals* (Manchester, 1949).

EYTON, R. W. *The Court, Household and Itinerary of King Henry II* (London, 1878).

FINBERG, H. P. R. *The Abbey of Tavistock* (Cambridge, 1951).

FLICHE, A. *Le Règne de Philippe Ier, Roi de France* (Paris, 1912).

—— *L'Europe Occidentale de 888–1125* (Paris, 1930).

FLOWER, C. T. *An Introduction to the Curia Regis Rolls, 1199–1230* (Selden Soc. 62; London, 1944).

FOREVILLE, R. *L'Église et la Royauté en Angleterre sous Henri II Plantagenet, 1154–89* (Paris, 1942).

GIBBS, M. and LANG, J. *Bishops and Reform, 1215–1272* (Oxford, 1934).

GIBBS, V., DOUBLEDAY, H. A., WHITE, G. H. (re-ed.). *The Complete Peerage* by G. E. C. (13 vols.; London, 1910–40).

GIBSON, W. S. *A History of the Monastery of Tynemouth* (2 vols.; London, 1846).

GLEASON, S. E. *An Ecclesiastical Barony of the Middle Ages, the Bishopric of Bayeux, 1066–1204* (Harvard, 1936).

GLUNZ, H. H. *History of the Vulgate in England* (Cambridge, 1933).

GROUSSET, R. *Histoire des Croisades* (3 vols.; Paris, 1934–6).

HILL, J. W. F. *Medieval Lincoln* (Cambridge, 1948).

HODGSON, J. F. 'The Churches of Darlington and Hartlepool', in *Arch. Ael.* XVII (1895), 145–243.

HURNARD, N. D. 'The Jury of Presentment and the Assize of Clarendon', in *EHR*, LVI (1941), 374–410.

HUTCHINSON, W. *The History and Antiquities of the County Palatine of Durham* (3 vols.; Newcastle, 1785–94).

IMBERT, J. *Les Hôpitaux en Droit Canonique* (Paris, 1947).

JAMES, M. R. *The Ancient Libraries of Canterbury and Dover* (Cambridge, 1903).

JUBAINVILLE, H. D'ARBOIS DE. *Histoire des Ducs et des Comtes de Champagne* (7 vols.; Paris–Troyes, 1859–69).

KER, N. *Medieval Libraries of Great Britain* (London, 1941).

KNOWLES, D. *The Episcopal Colleagues of Archbishop Thomas Becket* (Cambridge, 1951).

—— 'Case of St William of York, The', in *Cambridge Historical Journal*, V, 2 (1936), 162–77, 212–14.

KNOWLES, D. 'Growth of Exemption, The', in *Downside Review*, L (1932), 201–31, 396–436.

—— *Monastic Order in England, The* (Cambridge, 1941).

—— 'Revolt of the Lay Brothers of Sempringham, The', in *EHR*, L (1935), 465–87.

KUTTNER, S. 'Notes on a Projected Corpus of Twelfth-Century Decretal Letters', in *Traditio*, VI (1948), 345–51.

KUTTNER, S. and RATHBONE, E. 'Anglo-Norman Canonists of the Twelfth Century', in *Traditio*, VII (1949–51), 279–358.

LA MONTE, J. L. 'The Lords of Le Puiset on the Crusades', in *Speculum*, XVII (1942), 100–18.

LANDON, L. *The Itinerary of King Richard I* (Pipe Roll Soc., n.s. 13, 1935).

LAPSLEY, G. *The County Palatine of Durham* (London, 1900).

LOBEL, M. D. *Bury St Edmunds* (Oxford, 1935).

LUCHAIRE, A. *Études sur les actes de Louis VII* (Paris, 1885).

MAHN, J.-B. *L'Ordre Cistercien et son Gouvernement, 1098–1265* (Paris, 1945).

MALDEN, H. E. 'The possession of Cardigan Priory by Chertsey Abbey', in *TRHS*, 3, V (1911), 141–55.

MATHOREZ, J. *Guillaume aux Blanches Mains, Évêque de Chartres* (Chartres, 1911).

MILLAR, E. G. *English Illuminated Manuscripts from the Tenth to the Thirteenth Century* (Paris and Brussels, 1926).

MILLER, E. *The Abbey and Bishopric of Ely* (Cambridge, 1951).

MITCHELL, S. K. *Taxation in Medieval England* (Newhaven, 1951).

MOREY, A. *Bartholomew of Exeter* (Cambridge, 1937).

MORGAN, M. 'The Organization of the Scottish Church in the Twelfth Century', in *TRHS*, 4, XXIX (1947), 135–49.

MORTET, V. *Maurice de Sully* (Paris, Soc. de l'Histoire de Paris, 1890).

MYNORS, R. A. B. *Durham Cathedral Manuscripts to the end of the Twelfth Century* (Oxford, 1939).

NEWMAN, W. M. *Le Domaine Royal sous les premiers Capétiens* (Paris, 1937).

Northumberland, A History of, ed. Northumberland County History Committee (15 vols.; Newcastle, 1893–1940).

PAINTER, S. *Studies in the History of the English Feudal Barony* (Baltimore, 1943).

PETIT-DUTAILLIS, C. *L'Essor des États d'Occident* (vol. IV, 2 of *L'Histoire du Moyen Âge*, ed. G. Glotz (Paris, 1944)).

—— *La Monarchie Féodale en France et en Angleterre du Xe au XIIIe siècle* (Paris, 1933).

PFISTER, C. *Études sur le Règne de Robert le Pieux, 996–1031* (Paris, 1885).

POLLOCK, F. and MAITLAND, F. W. *History of English Law* (2nd ed.; Cambridge, 1898).

POOLE, A. L. *From Domesday Book to Magna Carta* (Oxford, 1951).

POOLE, R. L. 'The Appointment and Deprivation of St William of York', in *EHR*, XLV (1930), 273–81.

—— *Studies in Chronology and History*, ed. A. L. Poole (Oxford, 1934).

POSTAN, M. M. 'The Chronology of Labour Services', in *TRHS*, IV, XX (1937), 169–93.

—— 'Glastonbury Estates in the Twelfth Century', in *Econ. Hist. Rev.* V, 3 (1953), 358–67.

POWICKE, F. M. 'The Reigns of Philip Augustus and Louis VIII of France', in *Cambridge Medieval History*, VI (1929).

—— Maurice of Rievaulx, in *EHR*, XXXVI (1921), 17–29.

RABY, F. J. E. *The History of Christian Latin Poetry* (Oxford, 1927).

RAINE, J. *The History and Antiquities of North Durham* (London, 1852).

RATHBONE, E. 'John of Cornwall, a brief biography', in *Recherches de Théologie Ancienne et Médiévale*, XVII (1950), 46–60.

RICHARDSON, R. K. 'The Bishopric of Durham under Anthony Bek, 1283–1311', in *Arch. Ael.* 3, IX (1903), 89–229.

ROBINSON, J. A. 'Lanfranc's Monastic Constitutions', in *JTS*, X, (1908–9) 375–88.

ROTH, C. *A History of the Jews in England* (Oxford, 1941).

—— 'The Jews in the Middle Ages', in *Cambridge Medieval History*, VII (Cambridge, 1932).

ROUND, J. H. *The Commune of London* (London, 1899).

—— *Feudal England* (London, 1895).

—— *Geoffrey de Mandeville* (London, 1892).

—— 'The Honor of Ongar', in *Essex Arch. Soc. Trans.*, n.s. VII (1900), 142 *seqq.*

ROWSE, A. L. *The England of Elizabeth* (London, 1950).

RUNCIMAN, S. *The Kingdom of Jerusalem and the Frankish East, 1100–87* (Cambridge, 1952).

SANDYS, J. E. (ed.). *A Companion to Latin Studies* (Cambridge, 1910).

SINGER, C. *A Short History of Medicine* (Oxford, 1928).

SMITH, R. A. L. *Canterbury Cathedral Priory* (Cambridge, 1943).

SOUTHERN, R. W. 'Ranulf Flambard and early Anglo-Norman Administration', in *TRHS*, 4, XVI (1933), 95–128.

STENTON, D. M. 'England, Henry II', in *Cambridge Medieval History*, V (Cambridge, 1926).

STENTON, F. M. *The First Century of English Feudalism* (Oxford, 1932).

STUBBS, W. *Constitutional History of England* (3 vols.; Oxford, 1875–8).

STUBBS, W. *Historical Introductions to the Rolls Series*, ed. A. Hassall (London, 1902).

SURTEES, R. *The History and Antiquities of the County Palatine of Durham* (4 vols.; London, 1816–40).

TAIT, J. *Medieval Manchester and the Beginnings of Lancashire* (Manchester, 1904).

—— *The Medieval English Borough* (Manchester, 1936).

THOMPSON, A. HAMILTON. *The Premonstratensian Abbey of Welbeck* (London, 1938).

TILLMANN, H. *Die Päpstlichen Legaten in England bis zur Beendigung der Legation Gualas* (Bonn, 1926).

TURNER, C. H. 'The Earliest List of Durham Manuscripts', in *JTS*, XIX (1917–18), 121–32.

ULLMANN, W. 'A Scottish Charter and its Place in Medieval Canon Law', in *Juridical Review*, 61 (1949), 225 *seqq.*

—— 'A Forgotten Dispute at Bridlington Priory', in *YAJ*, 37 (1948–51), 456–73.

Victoria County History, Durham (3 vols., 1905–28).

—— *Northamptonshire* (4 vols., 1902–37).

—— *Shropshire* (vol. I, 1908).

—— *Yorkshire* (3 vols., 1907–13).

VOSS, L. *Heinrich von Blois* (Berlin, 1932).

WADDELL, H. *The Wandering Scholars* (London, 1927).

WHITE, G. H. 'Stephen's Earldoms', in *TRHS*, 4, XIII (1930), 51–82.

WHITTAKER, T. D. *History of Craven in the County of York* (2nd ed.; London, 1812).

WILKINSON, B. *The Government of England during the absence of Richard I on the Third Crusade* (Manchester, 1944).

WILLIAMS, J. R. 'William of the White Hands and Men of Letters', in *Haskins Anniversary Essays in Medieval History*, ed. C. H. Taylor and J. L. La Monte (Boston, Mass., 1929).

Since this volume was completed Mr K. R. Potter has published a new text of the *Gesta Stephani* (London 1955). This supplies details hitherto lacking concerning Puiset's activities as Henry of Winchester's lieutenant in 1149–50. It now appears that his military actions, which are alluded to in general terms by other chroniclers (cf. above, p. 11), consisted of recovering for Winchester the castle of Downton which had been seized by the followers of Earl Patrick of Salisbury (Potter, *Gesta Stephani*, 141–2).

INDEX

Durham, episcopal Liberty of (*cont.*)
 sheriffs of, 151, 230 *and* n. 2; *see also*
 FitzHamo, Philip; Haget, Ralph;
 Osbert
 stewards of, 230 *and* n. 6; *see also*
 Hugh, son of Pinceon
 wardship and marriage in, 200-1

Earlston (Berwickshire), church of,
 98, 144, 145
 disputed between Durham and
 Kelso, 119, 159
Easington (Co. Durham), 206, 212
 church of, 99, 198
Ebchester (Co. Durham), 95, 209
Ebrard, bp. of Norwich, 7 n. 4; 309
Ecgred, bp. of Lindisfarne, 145, 169
Edingtun, see Haddington
Edintona, see Haddington
Edlingham (Northumberland), church
 of, 111
Edmund the steward, 232
Edmundbyers (Co. Durham), 209
Ednam (Roxburghshire), church of,
 98, 101, 144, 145
Edrom (Berwickshire), 159
Edward I, k. of England, 193, 240
Egglestone (Co. Durham), 224
Eleanor of Aquitaine, w. of Henry II
 of England, 55, 179, 180
 supports rebellion of 1173, 35
 and government of England in
 absence of Richard I, 53-5
Elias the chaplain, 238, 255
Elias the clerk, 238
Elizabeth, w. of Harduin *vicomte* of
 Chartres, 308
Ellingham (Northumberland), church
 of, 98, 101, 117, 126, 145
Ellington (Northumberland), church
 of, 236
Elvet (Co. Durham), 96, 101, 152, 153,
 165
 borough at, 131, 154 *and* n. 4; 215
 bridge at, 111
 church of, 97, 119, 120-1, 134, 135,
  144, 146, 163, 198, 254-5
 fair at, 192
Elwick (Northumberland), 153
Ely, bps. of, *see* Longchamp, William
 de; Nigel; Ridel, Geoffrey
 cathedral priory of, 288
 church and diocese of, 6, 291

Elyas, sacrist of Durham, 94
Emmaline, w. of Gilduin, *vicomte* of
 Chartres, 308
Empingham (Rutland), 150
Engaine, Race, 107 n. 2; 108
Eperest, see Epperstone
Epperstone (Notts), church of, 73, 251
Eppleton (Co. Durham), 212
 family of, 226
 Roger of, 227, 260
Epplindena, see Eppleton
Ernaldus (Arnulfus), abbot of Rie-
 vaulx, 258, 260, 262
Ernaldus the chaplain, 238, 255, 257,
 261, 262
Escolland, family of, 220
 Elias, 165, 225, 268
 Geoffrey, 151, 225
 Jordan, 223, 225, 260, 262
Escomb (Co. Durham), 205, 232
Esh (Co. Durham), 212, 236
Essartis, Hugh de, 267
Essex, earls of, *see* Mandeville,
 Geoffrey de; Mandeville, William
 de
 Henry de, 269, 270
Eston (Yorks, NR), church of, 84
Eugenius III, Pope, 11, 14, 16, 18,
 20 *and* n. 3
Eustace, son of K. Stephen, 12, 25
 supports Hugh du Puiset, 15
Evesham, abbey of, 81, 136, 139, 142
Evreux, abbey, 289
 bps. of, *see* John; Rotrou
Exeter, bps. of, *see* Bartholomew;
 Robert
 church and diocese of, 46
Eye, Honor of, 5; *see also* Blois,
 Stephen of
Eynsham, visionary monk of, 183

Falaise, 273
 convention of, 95
Familia of Hugh du Puiset, 233-8
Fantosme, Jordan, 25
Farlington, family of, 226
 Henry of, 61, 188, 190, 229, 239
 Simon of, 229
 Walter of, 229
Farne Island (Northumberland), 95,
 153, 213 n. 3; 215
 church and cell of cathedral priory
  of Durham, 195

338

Henry (*cont.*)
II of Champagne, K. of Jerusalem
50 n. 4
son of K. Henry II (the Young
King), 276; coronation of, 31;
marries Margaret of France, 28,
30; rebellion of, 35–42; death of,
46
Heraclius, patriarch of Jerusalem, 45
Herbert, archdeacon of Canterbury,
280, 295
Herbert, bp. of Avranches, 272
Herbert, Master, *medicus*, 70
prior of Coldingham, 95
the chamberlain of Archdeacon
John, 234
the clerk, 238
Hereditary benefices, 98–9, 100–1, 145,
147, 235, 236
Hereford, bps. of, *see* Foliot, Gilbert;
Foliot, Robert; Melun, Robert of
borough of, 216 n. 9
church of, 19
Herrington (Co. Durham), 206, 213
church of, 93
Hetton-le-Hole (Co. Durham), 110,
212, 223
Bertram of, 110, 223, 236
Heworth (Co. Durham), 131, 153, 203,
259
forest and chase at, 164 *and* n. 6, 188,
205, 217, 230–1
Hexham, church of, 8, 97
as peculiar of see of York, 96, 102
relations of with church of Durham,
115, 126, 169, 170
Hilary, Master, clerk of Henry bp. of
Winchester, bp. of Chichester,
6, 26, 86, 263; as witness, 272–4,
passim; candidate for see of York,
11; dean of Twineham, 6; mediation by, 26; position in Becket
dispute, 34
monk of Durham, 92
Holme, abbey of St Benet at, 6, 287
Holme Cultram (Cumberland), abbey
of, 95
monks of, 292
Holmside (Co. Durham), 212, 236
Holtby (Yorks, NR), 169
church of, 172
Holy Island, or Lindisfarne (Northumberland), 102, 153, 158 n. 2

church and cell of priory of Durham
on, 94–5, 97, 144
Hook (Yorks, WR), 225
Horden (Co. Durham), 220
Hornby (Yorks, NR), 225
Horncliffe (Northumberland), 205, 213
Horton (Northumberland), 116, 199
Hospital of St John of Jerusalem,
Knights of, 96, 286, 294
Hospitals, 95, 107–9
Houedena, Houedene, see Howden
Houghall (Co. Durham), 165, 220
Houghton-le-Spring (Co. Durham),
131, 154, 206, 212
Household of Hugh du Puiset, 232–3
Howden (Yorks, ER), 55, 60, 165,
169, 205, 208, 259, 297, 299;
fair at, 192; forest of, 149, 163,
217, 230; Hugh du Puiset im-
prisoned at, 52, 54
church of, 9, 97, 109, 131, 134, 145,
163, 172, 198; Hugh du Puiset
and, 147–8, 256, 260; *see also*
Howden, Master Roger of
Geoffrey, clerk of, 260
John of, 236
Master John of, 236, 255
Master Roger of, 146–8, 256, 258,
260, 262
Nicholas son of William of, 236
Robert of, 217, 231, 260, 262
Robert of, monk of Durham, 94
Robert, parson of, 147, 174
Walter, chaplain of, 260, 261
William of, 84, 222, 236, 255, 257;
see also Barton, Adam of
William, son of William of, 236
Hubert, dean of York, *see* Walter,
Hubert
Hubreville, Robert de, 154
Hugh, abbot of Bury St Edmunds, 82,
157
abbot of Lagny, formerly abbot of
Chertsey, 6 *and* n. 2
abp. of Rouen, 271
bp. of Coventry, *see* Nunant, Hugh
de
bp. of Lincoln, *see* Avalon, Hugh of
bp. of Soissons, 271
chaplain of K. William the Lion of
Scotland; disputed election of to
St Andrews, 80–1
II, earl of Chester, 36, 37

Hugh (*cont.*)
  earl of Norfolk, 269, 270, 271
  Master, *medicus*, 238
  Pierleone, cardinal and papal legate,
    72–3, 251, 277
  son of Pinceon, 225, 229
  the cellarer of Durham, 94
  the marshal, 232
Huguccio, 69
Humez, Richard de, as witness, 268–9,
    272–3, 277
  William de, as witness, 281–4 *passim*
Humphrey the waggon-master, 232
Hunberga, w. of Evrard II du Puiset,
    308
Hunstanworth (Co. Durham), 209, 228
Hunwick (Co. Durham), 207
Hurworth (Co. Durham), 225
Husseburn, Master Thomas de, 295,
    297
Hutton Henry (Co. Durham), 206
Hutton Sessay (Yorks, NR), 226 n. 5
Hylton (Co. Durham), chapel at, 97,
    119–20
  family of, 186, 226
  Alexander of, 119–20, 275

Ifferley, Richard of, 228
Ilchester, Richard of, bp. of Win-
    chester, 43, 279
  as witness, 275–7, *passim*
Ingelranus the clerk, 233–4
Ingram, William, 225
Innocent III, Pope, 67, 235
Insula, Alan de, 103
  John de, 94
  Walter de, 227
Irby (Yorks, NR), 225
Ivesley (Co. Durham), 236
Ivo, bp. of Chartres, canonical collec-
    tions of, 68, 104
  imprisoned by Hugh I du Puiset, 2,
    309
Ivry, 281

Jaffa, ct. of, *see* Du Puiset, Hugh II
James, St, of Compostella, 159
Jarrow (Co. Durham), church of, 97,
    153, 158, 164, 303
Jerusalem, Frankish kingdom of, 5, 45
  kings of, *see* Baldwin IV; Henry II of
    Champagne
  queens of, *see* Melisende

Jews, in eastern counties, 194
  massacre of at York, 51–2, 65
  papal rulings on relations of Chris-
    tians with, 124–5
Jocelin, archdeacon of Chichester,
    282, 295
  bp. of Glasgow, 168
  of Louvain (Jocelin the Castellan),
    26, 311
John, archdeacon of Northumberland,
    115, 234, 254
  bp. of Evreux, 280, 281, 282
  bp. of Norwich, *see* Oxford, John of
  son of Henry II, ct. of Mortain,
    subsequently k. of England, 61,
    182, 282; and episcopal Liberty of
    Durham, 191–2; position under
    Richard I, 53–5, 56–8; rebellion
    of, 57–8; relations with Hugh du
    Puiset, 55; relations with Philip
    Augustus, 54, 57; and William de
    Longchamp, 53–5; revenues of
    palatinate of, 194 n. 4
  dean of Rouen, 56
  Faventius, 69
  hermit of Yearhaugh, 110
  the chaplain, 238
  the clerk, nephew of the prior, 93
  the hermit, 106
  the Scot, disputed election of to
    St Andrews, 80–1
Jordan, cardinal priest of S. Puden-
    tiana, papal legate in Normandy,
    55–6
Justiciar, office of, 50–1, 62–5, 178;
  see also Coutances, Walter de;
  Glanville, Rannulf de; Longchamp, William de; Luci, Richard
  de; Mandeville, William de;
  Walter, Hubert

Kaivill, Kevill, Keivill, see Cavil
Karrum, Adam de, proctor of Kepyer
    hospital, 256
Kelloe (Co. Durham), church of, 108
Kelso, abbey of, 119, 159, 275
Kempsey, 284
Kepwick (Yorks, NR), 236
Kepyer (Co. Durham), 232
  Hospital of St Giles at, founded by
    Rannulf Flambard, 108 *and* n. 5
  refounded by Hugh du Puiset, 107–
    9, 113, 114